SAGA OF THE SWAMP THING BOOK ONE

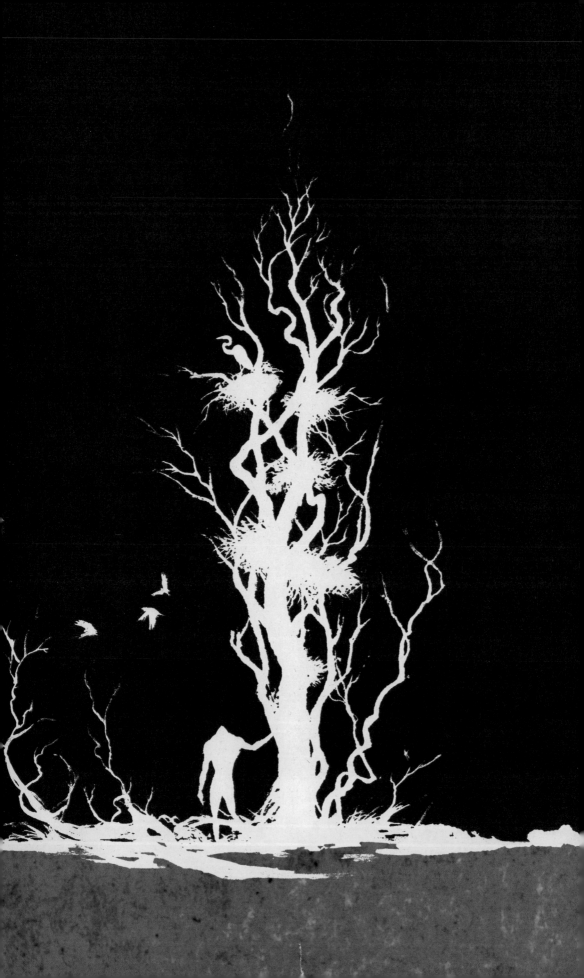

Written by **Alan Moore**

Art by Stephen Bissette John Totleben Dan Day Rick Veitch

Colored by Tatjana Wood

Lettered by John Costanza Todd Klein

Original Series Cover Art by **Tom Yeates** Stephen Bissette John Totleben

Original Series Cover Color by Tatjana Wood

Swamp Thing created by **Len Wein** and Bernie Wrightson

SAGA OF THE
SWAMP THING
BOOK ONE

Karen Berger Len Wein Editors – Original Series
Scott Nybakken Editor
Robbin Brosterman Design Director – Books
Louis Prandi Publication Design

Karen Berger Senior VP – Executive Editor, Vertigo
Bob Harras VP – Editor-in-Chief

Diane Nelson President
Dan DiDio and **Jim Lee** Co-Publishers
Geoff Johns Chief Creative Officer
John Rood Executive VP – Sales, Marketing and Business Development
Amy Genkins Senior VP – Business and Legal Affairs
Nairi Gardiner Senior VP – Finance
Jeff Boison VP – Publishing Operations
Mark Chiarello VP – Art Direction and Design
John Cunningham VP – Marketing
Terri Cunningham VP – Talent Relations and Services
Alison Gill Senior VP – Manufacturing and Operations
David Hyde VP – Publicity
Hank Kanalz Senior VP – Digital
Jay Kogan VP – Business and Legal Affairs, Publishing
Jack Mahan VP – Business Affairs, Talent
Nick Napolitano VP – Manufacturing Administration
Sue Pohja VP – Book Sales
Courtney Simmons Senior VP – Publicity
Bob Wayne Senior VP – Sales

SAGA OF THE SWAMP THING BOOK ONE
Published by DC Comics.

DC Comics
1700 Broadway
New York, NY 10019.
A Warner Bros. Entertainment Company.
Printed in the USA.
First Printing.
ISBN: 978-1-4012-2083-9

SUSTAINABLE FORESTRY INITIATIVE Certified Sourcing
www.sfiprogram.org
SFI-01042
APPLIES TO TEXT STOCK ONLY

Cover pencils by Stephen Bissette.
Cover inks by John Totleben.
Cover color by Lee Loughridge.

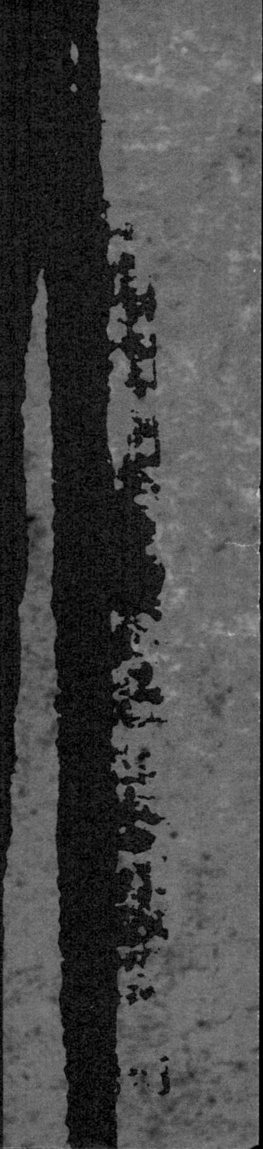

Home Again, Home Again
An Introduction of Sorts

The acclaimed American author and playwright Thomas Wolfe once famously wrote, "You can't go home again." I'm going to let you in on a little secret. Mister Wolfe was, quite frankly, full of bullpucky.

In "The Death of the Hired Man," legendary Pulitzer Prize-winning poet Robert Frost wrote, "Home is the place where, when you go there, they have to take you in." Trust me when I tell you that's a whole lot closer to the truth. But permit me to explain.

In the autumn of 1970, I was living in Levittown, New York, and writing short mystery stories for the always-amiable Joe Orlando, editor of such spine-chilling titles as *The House of Mystery* and *The House of Secrets*. I was on the subway, heading for one of my then-weekly meetings with Joe, when I realized I had nothing to pitch him. No story ideas. Nothing.

Desperate professional that I was, by the time I reached the office I had concocted a little period piece, a tale of a scientist murdered by his jealous best friend, then resurrected by the swamp his body was left to rot in so he could seek his revenge. To this day, if my life depended on my telling you where the idea came from on such short notice, you'd have no choice but to put me up against a wall and hand me a blindfold. Still, Joe eagerly bought the idea and I quickly went to work. I kept referring to the story as "that swamp thing I'm working on," and when the time came to find a title the name just stuck. Swamp Thing it was.

At a party that month, I asked my old buddy (and budding young superstar artist) Bernie Wrightson if he'd be willing to draw the story, and was gratified when he said he was in. We were off and running.

When *The House of Secrets* #92 hit the newsstands in April of 1971, it was the best-selling DC comic of the month, outgrossing even such stalwarts as *Superman, Batman* and *Wonder Woman.* Being an astute businessman, DC's then-publisher, the great artist Carmine Infantino, quickly asked Bernie and myself to turn our short story into an ongoing series. But being young, extremely foolish and rather full of ourselves at the time, Bernie and I said no. That particular short story had grown to have deep personal meaning to the two of us and we did not want to diminish that by commercializing the story. (I know. I know. Look, I just told you we were young and foolish.) Fortunately, a year later I suddenly realized we didn't have to continue our original story, but could start anew, and that's precisely what Bernie, Joe and I did.

Swamp Thing #1, which hit the stands in August of 1972, was an immediate success, and for the next few years Bernie and I had a blast. We populated Alec Holland's world with such sterling supporting characters as the ultimate mad scientist Anton Arcane, his beautiful niece Abigail, hard-bitten Federal agent Matt Cable, and an assortment of the most gruesome, grotesque, and simply wonderful monsters you could possibly imagine.

After ten spectacular issues, Bernie decided to leave the book.

I soldiered on for three more issues, working with the extraordinary Filipino artist Nestor Redondo, until I realized I just wasn't having as much fun without Bernie, and left the title myself. The good folks at DC attempted to keep the book going, first with writer David Michelinie, then with my old apartment-mate and friend Gerry Conway, but the law of diminishing returns held sway and, after another dozen issues or so, *Swamp Thing* was, mercifully, sent to that great back-issue box in the sky.

And there it might have remained, had not writer/director Wes Craven — of *The Last House on the Left* and *A Nightmare on Elm Street* fame — decided to turn *Swamp Thing* into a feature film.

It was now 1982, and after a several-year sojourn across town at our Marvelous competition (where I had created, among other things, a certain adamantium-clawed Canadian mutant), I was back at DC, writing several titles and serving as the editor for a number of others. When I heard about Wes's plans, I went to see Jenette Kahn, DC's then-publisher, to suggest that if there was going to be a *Swamp Thing* movie, there should probably be a *Swamp Thing* comic again to support it. Jenette agreed, despite the fact that I was unwilling to write this new incarnation myself, and I set out to find a new creative team for the book.

For the writer's slot I tapped my good friend Martin Pasko (who would later return the favor by dragging me kicking and screaming into the field of animation writing by assigning me my first episode of the Emmy-winning *Batman: The Animated Series*). For the book's artist, I chose one of the foremost graduates of the Joe Kubert School of Cartoon and Graphic Art, the talented Tom Yeates. With the team now in place, we were ready, as they say, to rock and roll.

For nineteen issues under Marty and Tom's skilled guidance (less a two-issue fill-in by writer Dan Mishkin), *The Saga of the Swamp Thing* took Swampy through a whole new set of adventures, introducing new supporting players such as Dennis Barclay and Liz Tremayne, and new foes for the character, not the least of whom was one General Avery Carlton Sunderland, whose efforts to uncover the secrets of the Swamp Thing would eventually lead to a whole new rebirth of everybody's favorite muck-encrusted mockery of a man.

When Marty chose to leave the book after issue #19, I was in a quandary, struggling to find a writer of equal caliber to replace him. Having exhausted all of the available choices (of which there were, frankly, darn few) on this side of the Atlantic, I looked across the pond to Great Britain, where I had been following the work of one particular young writer whose efforts in such British weeklies as *2000 AD* and *Warrior* seemed to stand head and shoulders above the rest. The guy's name was Alan Moore.

I no longer recall how I got hold of Alan's phone number, but I rang him up (as they say over there) and introduced myself. Alan promptly hung up on me. I called him back and spent several exasperating minutes convincing him that I was indeed who I said I was and not one of his mates playing some cruel prank on him. When Alan finally accepted me at face value, I offered him *Swamp Thing*. He told me he'd think about it and get back to me.

Several days later, Alan called back and told me what he'd been thinking. He asked if it was all right with me, as both the editor and the creator of the character, if he might make a few changes in ol' Swampy along the way. When I heard what he had planned, I eagerly agreed, and you, lucky reader, will get to see the first flowering fruits of the seeds Alan planted in the pages ahead.

By this time, it should also be noted, the talented Tom Yeates had given way to his two artistic assistants on the book, Steve Bissette and John Totleben. When Tom decided that the pressures of a monthly book were too much for him, Steve and John arrived at my door, samples in hand, pleading for the opportunity to replace Tom. Once I saw what they had to offer, their pleas did not fall on deaf ears. They brought an enthusiasm and an intricacy to the art that perfectly complemented Alan's elaborate scripts.

One last observation and I'll leave you to the wonderment ahead. This volume collects, for the first time, issue #20 of *The Saga of the Swamp Thing*, Alan's first issue. Appropriately entitled "Loose Ends," the issue brings closure to most of Marty's dangling plotlines while at the same time setting up the remarkable storylines to come. Its absence from the series' existing collected editions has caused it to be unfairly overlooked — a situation that, hopefully, will now be remedied. As you'll see, it certainly deserves permanent preservation in a package such as this.

Okay, I guess that's everything you really need to know at this point. When I began this little stroll down memory lane, I told you that Wolfe was wrong and Frost was right, that if you have the need and the means and the fortitude, you can indeed go home again, as I did when we revived the Swamp Thing.

What I neglected to tell you was what a weird and wonderful place home can be. Come on in, set yourself down in that moldering old easy chair, and get comfortable. In this case, home is where the horror is.

— **Len Wein**
October 31, 2008

Veteran comics writer and editor Len Wein is the creator of such memorable characters as Wolverine, the New X-Men and the Human Target, as well as the co-creator (with Bernie Wrightson) of the Swamp Thing. In his long and prolific career he has written for hundreds of titles, encompassing nearly every significant character in the medium. He has also built a successful career in TV animation, scripting such hit series as X-Men, Spider-Man and Batman: The Animated Series.

Foreword

"It's raining in Washington tonight. Plump, warm summer rain that covers the sidewalks with leopard spots. Downtown, elderly ladies carry their houseplants out to set them on the fire escapes, as if they were infirm relatives or boy kings."

I didn't write that, but I would be happy to have done so. These are the opening lines of Alan Moore's *Swamp Thing #21*, and I think they demonstrate that Moore needs no special pleading at all. Let me explain what I mean. Back in the late sixties a change overtook many of the comic books on the shelves; even familiar series became harsher, more cutting, more willing to take on reality in ways that, when the Comics Code was at its most suffocating, would have been unthinkable. Some of the loudest applause was mine. Still, when I look back now at some of the comics I praised, it seems to me that for all their seriousness about issues such as heroin addiction and racial intolerance, they weren't necessarily very well-written: too shrilly and melodramatic, perhaps, or too given to dull Hollywoodish preaching in the dialogue; characters intoning lines that would be groaned off the screen in a movie. It's possible, as with the rock music of those years that used classical themes or was played from scores, that some of us — especially those like myself who hadn't previously been drawn to the field — tended to overrate what we found unexpected. But then again, without the progress made in those years, we might not have comics written by Alan Moore, in which case we would be a good deal poorer.

In some ways, his merits are those of the finest tradition of comics: his ear for dialogue, his talent for concise, clear story-telling, his unerring sense of pace and timing. In other ways, he and his collaborators, Stephen Bissette and John Totleben, pretty well lead the field, especially in building a sense of terror. You'll find a hint of this on the first page of "The Anatomy Lesson," a promise gruesomely kept by the finale of the story. But it's the uncompromising radicalism of "The Anatomy Lesson" that announces most clearly this team is a force to be respected. There surely can't be many writers who, having taken over an established character, would begin by demonstrating (in the autopsy scene) that the character has never made sense as he was presented and is in fact something far less human than even he himself believed. Moore, Bissette, and Totleben take Swamp Thing apart in order to rebuild him.

It's a moving and disturbing process, illuminated by the resurrection of a minor DC villain, the Floronic Man, to represent the dark side of identification with the vegetable kingdom, Swamp Thing's darker self. Jason Woodrue is all the more disconcerting for expressing genuine ecological concerns; he's more articulate than monsters usually are — since Frankenstein's, anyway (though comic books are more prepared than most fiction to let their monsters have their say). He is given some of the best and most unsettling lines, and a poignant farewell. "If there's one thing I despise, it's the sound of steak sobbing," he muses, and later sums up humanity as "screaming meat," a phrase one could use to summarize splatter movies: maybe they are the revenge of vegetables, and Woodrue seems to acknowledge this by wielding a chainsaw.

Meanwhile we're taken on a hallucinatory journey by Swamp Thing's changing consciousness, introduced by the extraordinary image of Swamp Thing's face filling up with rain. (Here I restrain myself from raving on about the visual inventiveness of the comic, preferring to let you discover that pleasure for yourself in your own time, but let me take the opportunity to celebrate Tatjana Wood's coloring, especially effective in the mental landscapes.) Here as elsewhere, Moore's language and imagery is simultaneously comic and horrifying, as is the way with horror fiction. Horror fiction at its best is in the business of pushing back the barriers, of risking the absurd in order to reach the sublime, just as Jason Woodrue does by eating a tuber of Swamp Thing's. By this stage no reader can doubt that here is a story prepared to go to the end of itself, whatever it may find there or on the way.

One troubling character it finds is Abby Arcane, still understandably suffering from all she went through, and not only in previous issues: one nightmarish childhood memory, powerfully depicted, seems to have no immediate narrative significance. Perhaps it stands for the horror that underlies the world of these stories and can break through at any time without warning: a world where one may buy a panel from a Francis Bacon crucifixion study as a poster, or be the life of the party by turning one's friends into zombies, or where all the pupils at a school for autistic children may suddenly draw the same monster. But perhaps it also means that Abby has suffered enough to be able to reach the children. We can only hope.

Having passed through the vegetable consciousness, with his own skull playing Yorick to his Hamlet and getting the best lines, Swamp Thing is resurrected in an awesome full-page panel. From here on the comic becomes what I would call a poetic reinvention of the super-hero, not only Swamp Thing but the Justice League (one of whom is brilliantly epitomized as "a man who moves so fast that his life is an endless gallery of statues") and later, Jack Kirby's Demon. It seems to me that this creates a real problem in sustaining a tale of terror: after all, if the terror only needs a handy super-hero to thump it into submission, we might as well not lose any sleep about it. But Alan Moore's terrors are too profound to be gotten rid of so easily. They are rooted deeper in the characters than a super-hero can reach.

Len Wein and Bernie Wrightson's *Swamp Thing* was a remarkable fusion of the super-hero comic and the horror story, but I should like to claim even more for the new *Swamp Thing*. "All I knew were the suburbs of fear... and now here I am, in the big city." Indeed. The notion of the horror that can take the form of the victim's deepest fear is hardly new, but I have never seen a more terrifying image of it than the one that visits Jessica in "...A Time of Running..." One test of art is that it is deeply felt, and can anyone doubt that this is? I believe that at its best, the new *Swamp Thing* can stand beside the finest works of contemporary horror fiction. I believe horror fiction is capable of encompassing a great range of human experience — comedy, tragedy, terror, and awe — and now it is beginning to do so. It is all the richer for Messrs. Moore, Bissette, and Totleben. Long may they continue to light up our darkest dreams.

— **Ramsey Campbell**

A winner of numerous awards for his horror fiction, Ramsey Campbell has received the British Fantasy Award for his novels The Parasite, Incarnate, The Hungry Moon, The Influence *and* Midnight Sun, *as well as the World Fantasy Award for his short story* "The Chimney." *Campbell is also an accomplished editor whose anthologies include* Uncanny Banquet *(featuring literature out of print since 1914) and* Gathering the Bones.

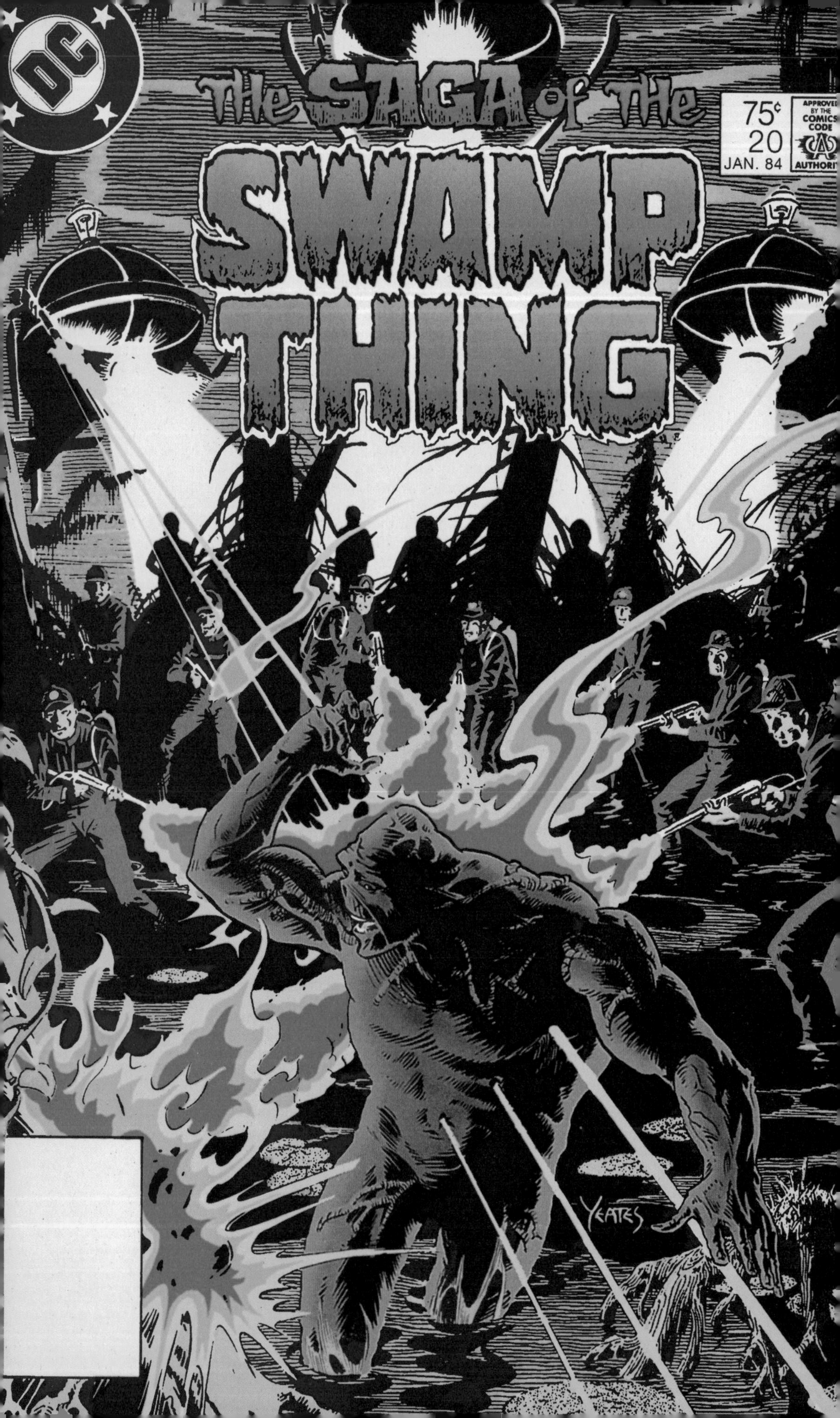
DC
The SAGA of the
SWAMP THING
75¢
20
JAN. 84
APPROVED BY THE COMICS CODE AUTHORITY
YEATES

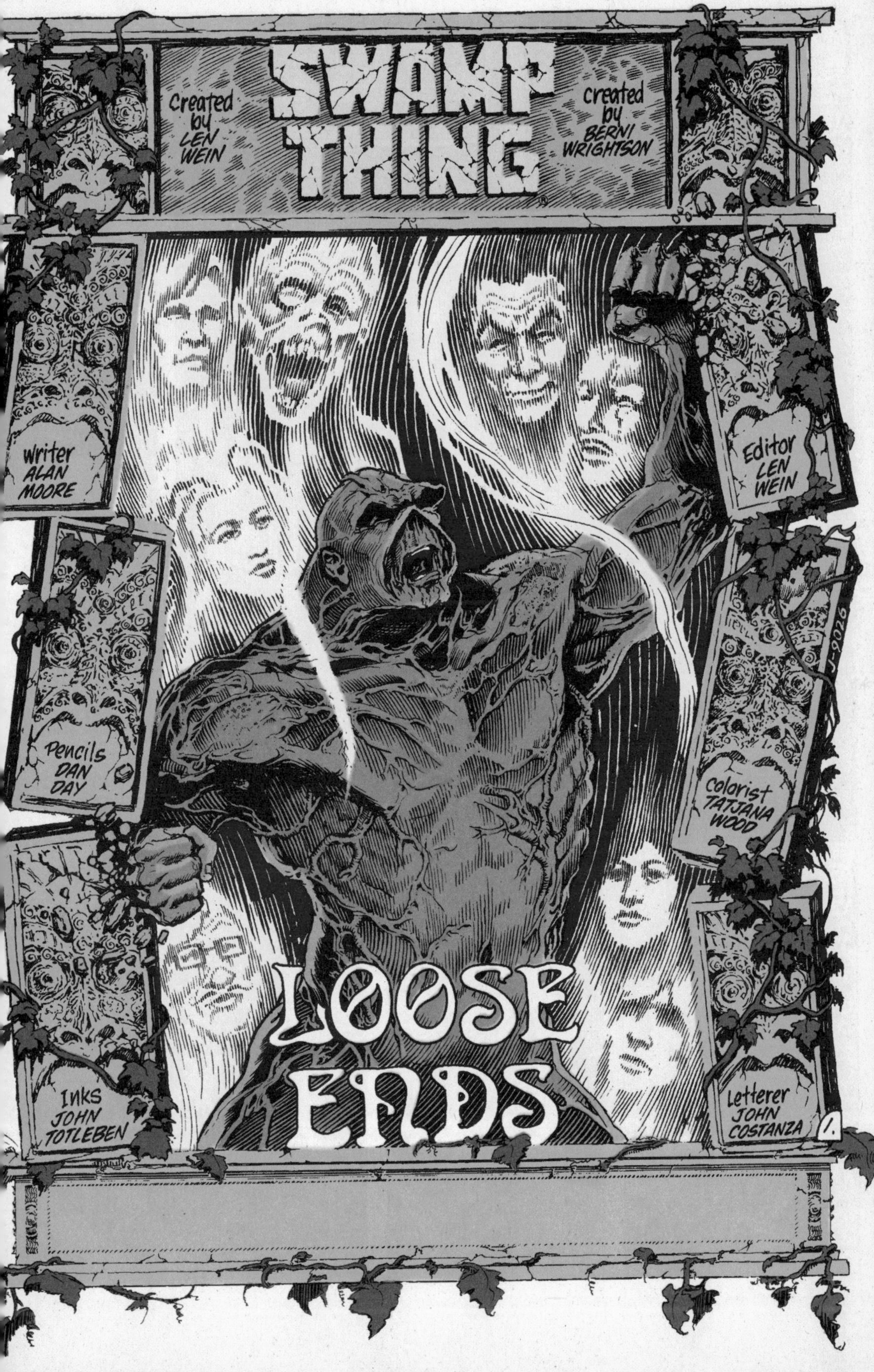
SWAMP THING
Created by LEN WEIN
created by BERNI WRIGHTSON
Writer ALAN MOORE
Editor LEN WEIN
Pencils DAN DAY
Colorist TATJANA WOOD
Inks JOHN TOTLEBEN
Letterer JOHN COSTANZA
LOOSE ENDS
J-9026
1.

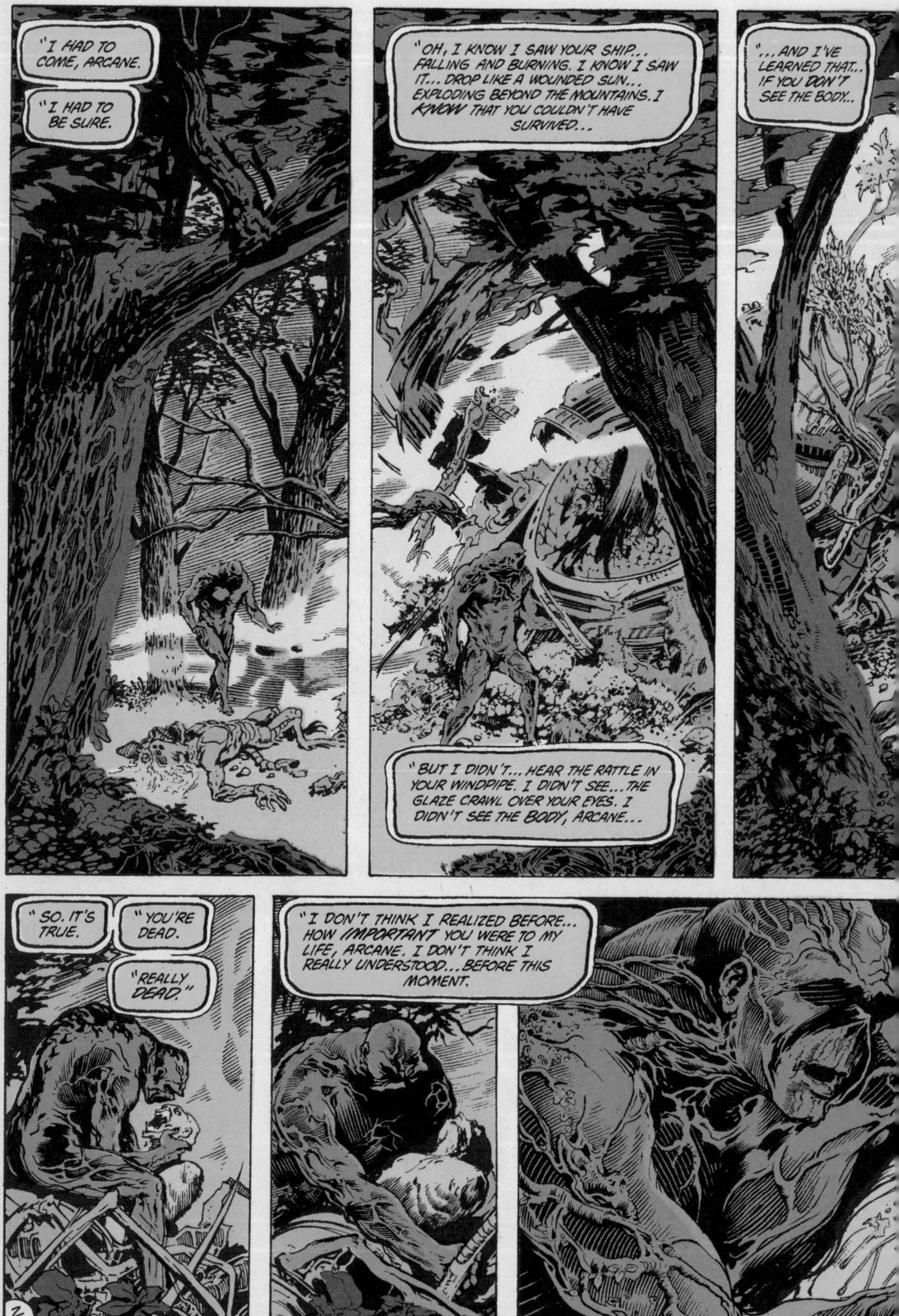
"I HAD TO COME, ARCANE.
"I HAD TO BE SURE.
"OH, I KNOW I SAW YOUR SHIP... FALLING AND BURNING. I KNOW I SAW IT... DROP LIKE A WOUNDED SUN... EXPLODING BEYOND THE MOUNTAINS. I KNOW THAT YOU COULDN'T HAVE SURVIVED...
"BUT I DIDN'T... HEAR THE RATTLE IN YOUR WINDPIPE. I DIDN'T SEE... THE GLAZE CRAWL OVER YOUR EYES. I DIDN'T SEE THE BODY, ARCANE...
"... AND I'VE LEARNED THAT... IF YOU DON'T SEE THE BODY...
"SO. IT'S TRUE.
"YOU'RE DEAD.
"REALLY DEAD."
"I DON'T THINK I REALIZED BEFORE... HOW IMPORTANT YOU WERE TO MY LIFE, ARCANE. I DON'T THINK I REALLY UNDERSTOOD... BEFORE THIS MOMENT.

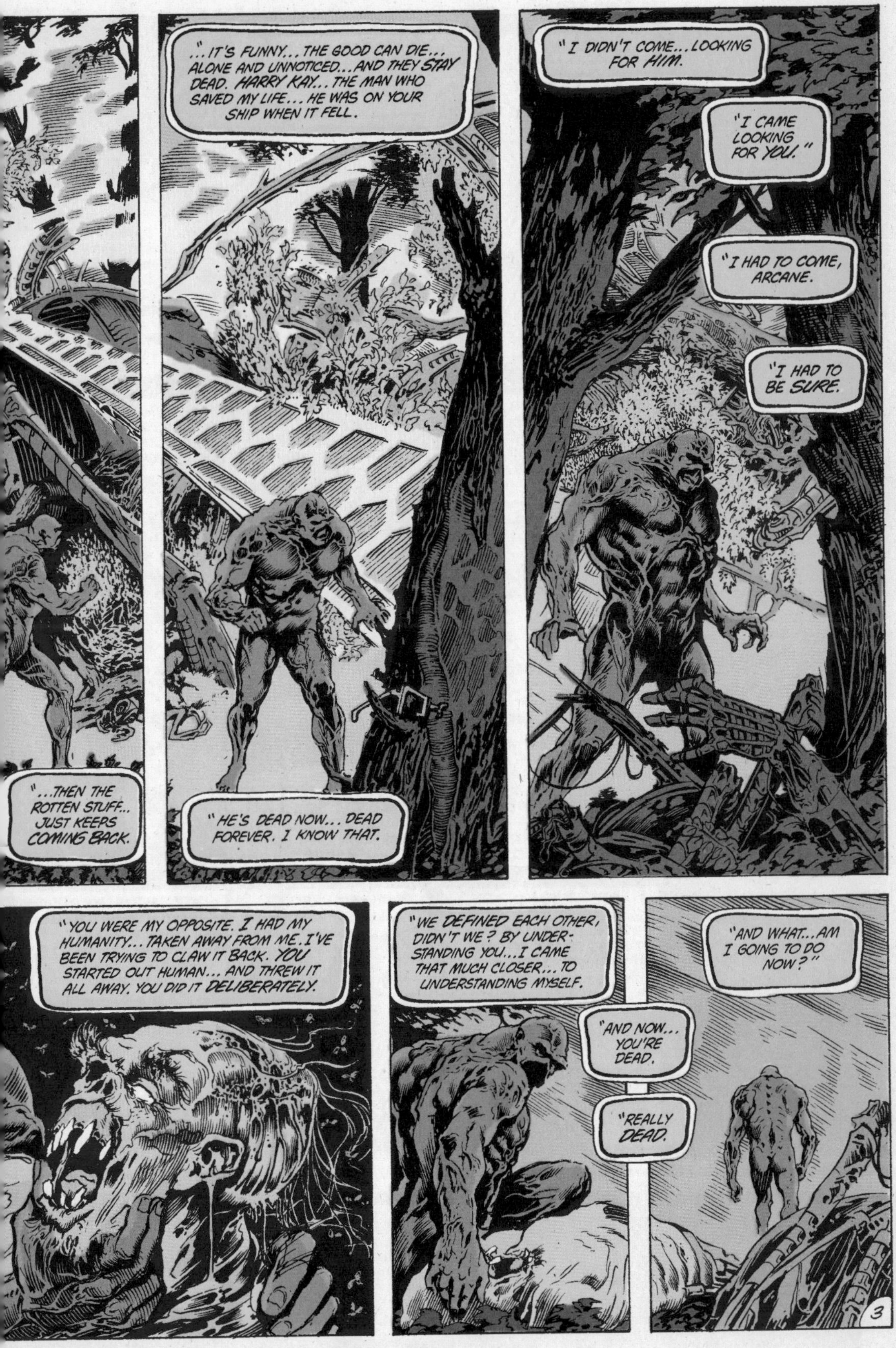
"...THEN THE ROTTEN STUFF... JUST KEEPS COMING BACK.
"...IT'S FUNNY...THE GOOD CAN DIE... ALONE AND UNNOTICED...AND THEY STAY DEAD. HARRY KAY...THE MAN WHO SAVED MY LIFE... HE WAS ON YOUR SHIP WHEN IT FELL.
"HE'S DEAD NOW... DEAD FOREVER. I KNOW THAT.
"I DIDN'T COME...LOOKING FOR HIM.
"I CAME LOOKING FOR YOU."
"I HAD TO COME, ARCANE.
"I HAD TO BE SURE.
"YOU WERE MY OPPOSITE. I HAD MY HUMANITY...TAKEN AWAY FROM ME. I'VE BEEN TRYING TO CLAW IT BACK. YOU STARTED OUT HUMAN... AND THREW IT ALL AWAY. YOU DID IT DELIBERATELY.
"WE DEFINED EACH OTHER, DIDN'T WE? BY UNDER-STANDING YOU...I CAME THAT MUCH CLOSER...TO UNDERSTANDING MYSELF.
"AND NOW... YOU'RE DEAD.
"REALLY DEAD.
"AND WHAT...AM I GOING TO DO NOW?"
3

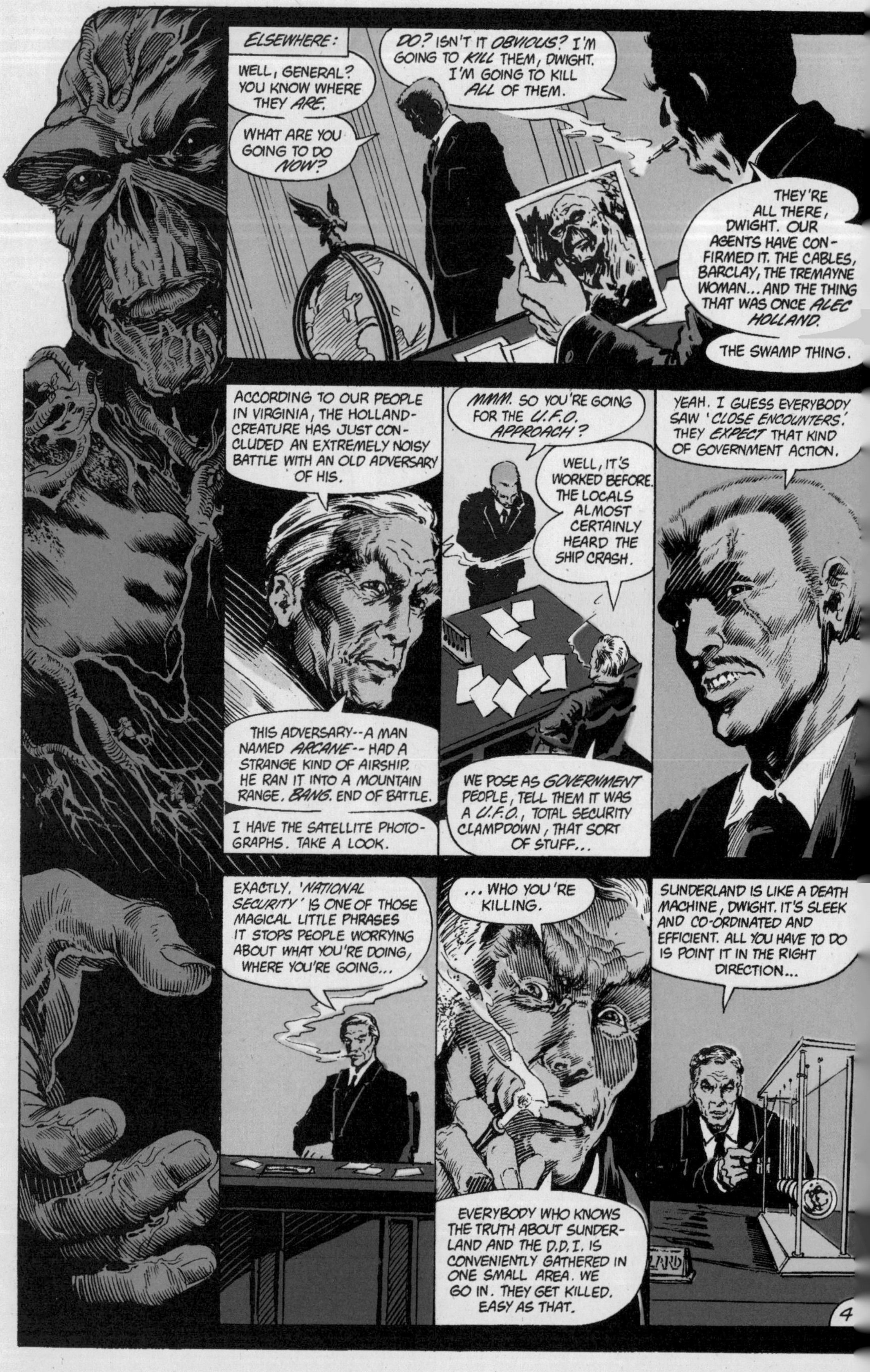
ELSEWHERE:
WELL, GENERAL? YOU KNOW WHERE THEY ARE.
WHAT ARE YOU GOING TO DO NOW?
DO? ISN'T IT OBVIOUS? I'M GOING TO KILL THEM, DWIGHT. I'M GOING TO KILL ALL OF THEM.
THEY'RE ALL THERE, DWIGHT. OUR AGENTS HAVE CONFIRMED IT. THE CABLES, BARCLAY, THE TREMAYNE WOMAN... AND THE THING THAT WAS ONCE ALEC HOLLAND.
THE SWAMP THING.
ACCORDING TO OUR PEOPLE IN VIRGINIA, THE HOLLAND-CREATURE HAS JUST CONCLUDED AN EXTREMELY NOISY BATTLE WITH AN OLD ADVERSARY OF HIS.
THIS ADVERSARY--A MAN NAMED ARCANE--HAD A STRANGE KIND OF AIRSHIP. HE RAN IT INTO A MOUNTAIN RANGE. BANG. END OF BATTLE.
I HAVE THE SATELLITE PHOTOGRAPHS. TAKE A LOOK.
MMM. SO YOU'RE GOING FOR THE U.F.O. APPROACH?
WELL, IT'S WORKED BEFORE. THE LOCALS ALMOST CERTAINLY HEARD THE SHIP CRASH.
WE POSE AS GOVERNMENT PEOPLE, TELL THEM IT WAS A U.F.O., TOTAL SECURITY CLAMPDOWN, THAT SORT OF STUFF...
YEAH. I GUESS EVERYBODY SAW 'CLOSE ENCOUNTERS.' THEY EXPECT THAT KIND OF GOVERNMENT ACTION.
EXACTLY. 'NATIONAL SECURITY' IS ONE OF THOSE MAGICAL LITTLE PHRASES IT STOPS PEOPLE WORRYING ABOUT WHAT YOU'RE DOING, WHERE YOU'RE GOING...
... WHO YOU'RE KILLING.
EVERYBODY WHO KNOWS THE TRUTH ABOUT SUNDERLAND AND THE D.D.I. IS CONVENIENTLY GATHERED IN ONE SMALL AREA. WE GO IN. THEY GET KILLED. EASY AS THAT.
SUNDERLAND IS LIKE A DEATH MACHINE, DWIGHT. IT'S SLEEK AND CO-ORDINATED AND EFFICIENT. ALL YOU HAVE TO DO IS POINT IT IN THE RIGHT DIRECTION...
4

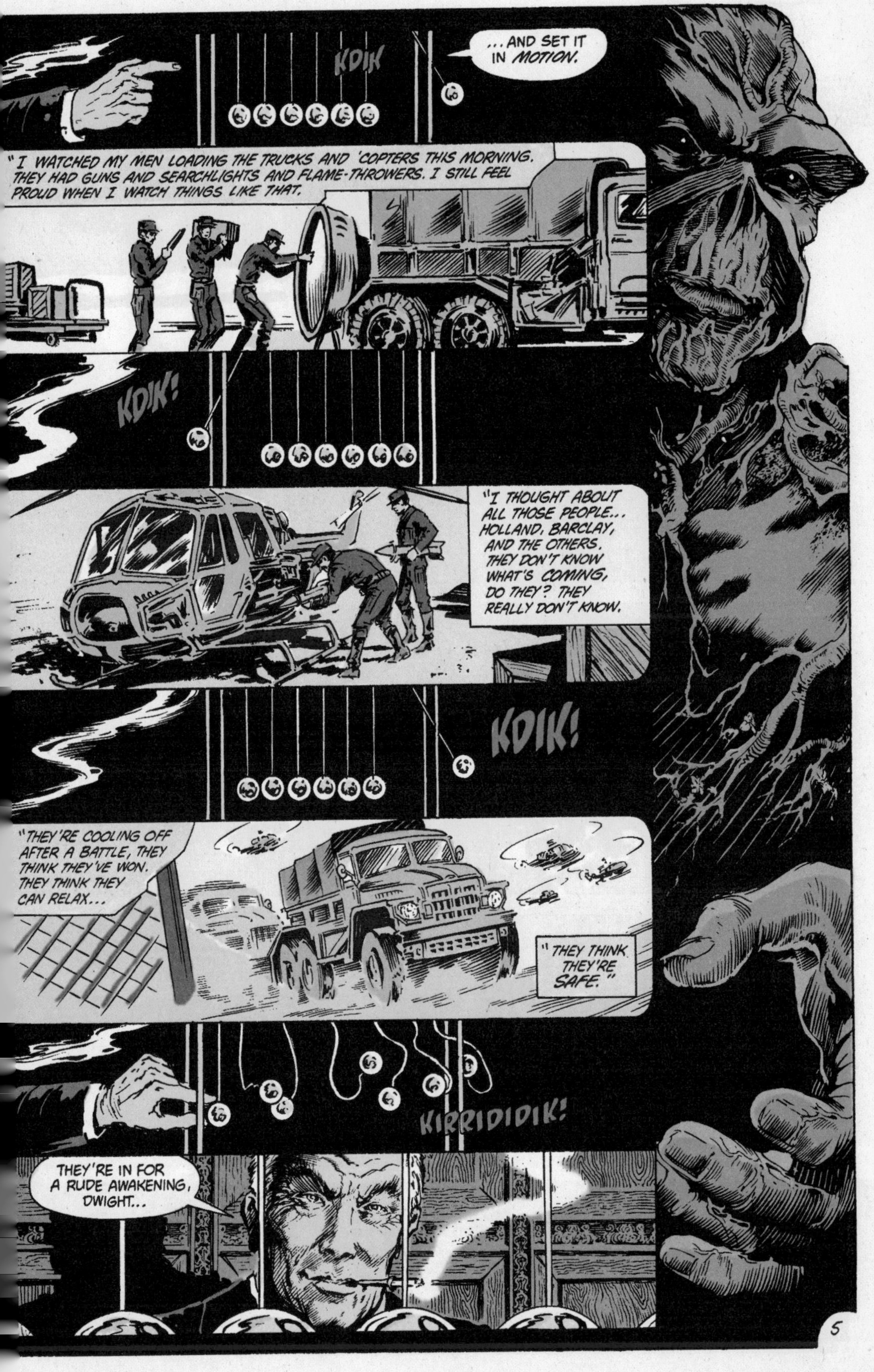
KDIK
...AND SET IT IN MOTION.
"I WATCHED MY MEN LOADING THE TRUCKS AND 'COPTERS THIS MORNING. THEY HAD GUNS AND SEARCHLIGHTS AND FLAME-THROWERS. I STILL FEEL PROUD WHEN I WATCH THINGS LIKE THAT.
KDIK!
"I THOUGHT ABOUT ALL THOSE PEOPLE... HOLLAND, BARCLAY, AND THE OTHERS. THEY DON'T KNOW WHAT'S COMING, DO THEY? THEY REALLY DON'T KNOW.
KDIK!
"THEY'RE COOLING OFF AFTER A BATTLE, THEY THINK THEY'VE WON. THEY THINK THEY CAN RELAX...
"THEY THINK THEY'RE SAFE."
KIRRIDIDIK!
THEY'RE IN FOR A RUDE AWAKENING, DWIGHT...
5

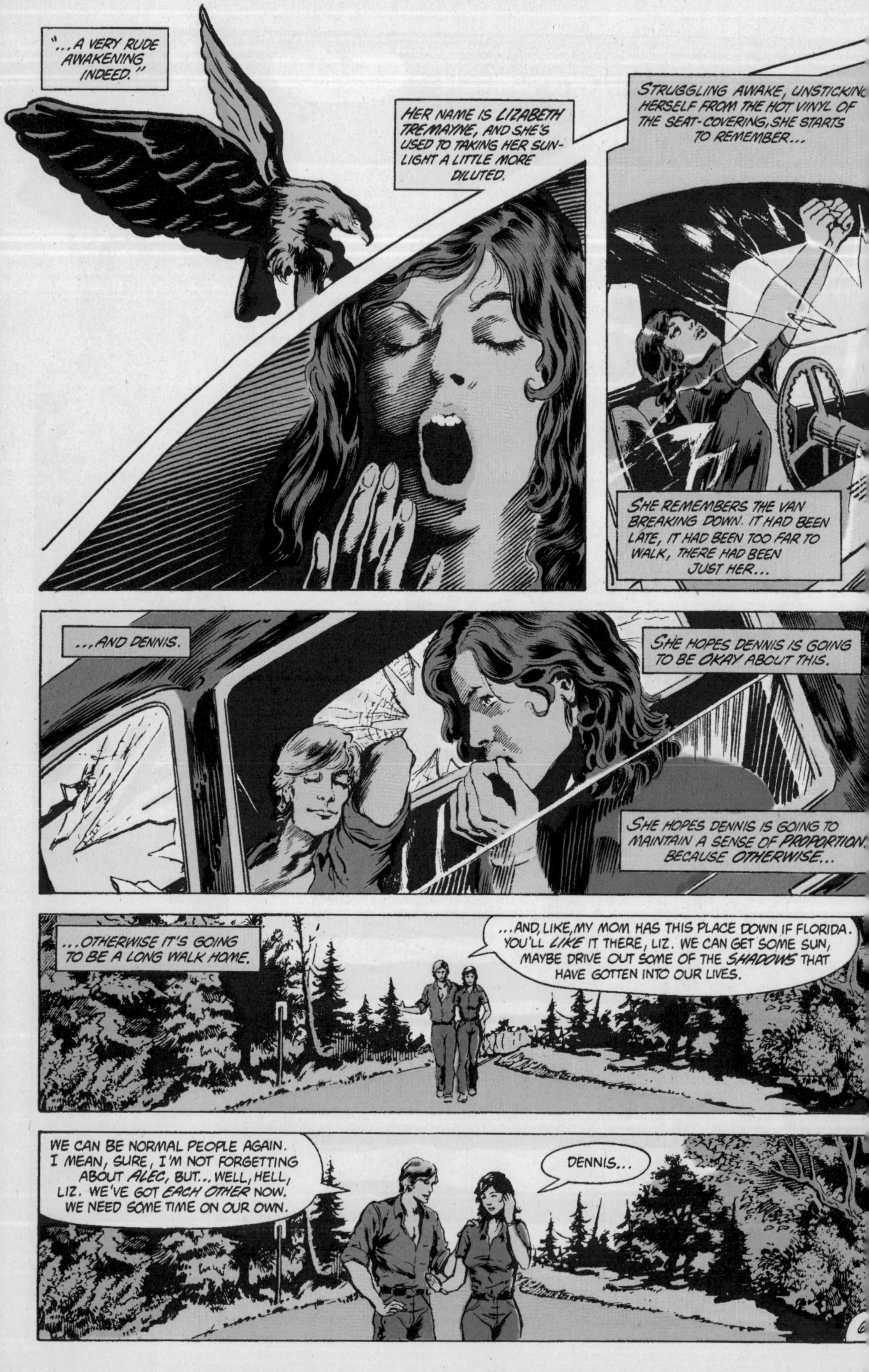
"...A VERY RUDE AWAKENING INDEED."
HER NAME IS LIZABETH TREMAYNE, AND SHE'S USED TO TAKING HER SUNLIGHT A LITTLE MORE DILUTED.
STRUGGLING AWAKE, UNSTICKING HERSELF FROM THE HOT VINYL OF THE SEAT-COVERING, SHE STARTS TO REMEMBER...
SHE REMEMBERS THE VAN BREAKING DOWN. IT HAD BEEN LATE, IT HAD BEEN TOO FAR TO WALK, THERE HAD BEEN JUST HER...
...AND DENNIS.
SHE HOPES DENNIS IS GOING TO BE OKAY ABOUT THIS.
SHE HOPES DENNIS IS GOING TO MAINTAIN A SENSE OF PROPORTION. BECAUSE OTHERWISE...
...OTHERWISE IT'S GOING TO BE A LONG WALK HOME.
...AND, LIKE, MY MOM HAS THIS PLACE DOWN IF FLORIDA. YOU'LL LIKE IT THERE, LIZ. WE CAN GET SOME SUN, MAYBE DRIVE OUT SOME OF THE SHADOWS THAT HAVE GOTTEN INTO OUR LIVES.
WE CAN BE NORMAL PEOPLE AGAIN. I MEAN, SURE, I'M NOT FORGETTING ABOUT ALEC, BUT... WELL, HELL, LIZ. WE'VE GOT EACH OTHER NOW. WE NEED SOME TIME ON OUR OWN.
DENNIS...

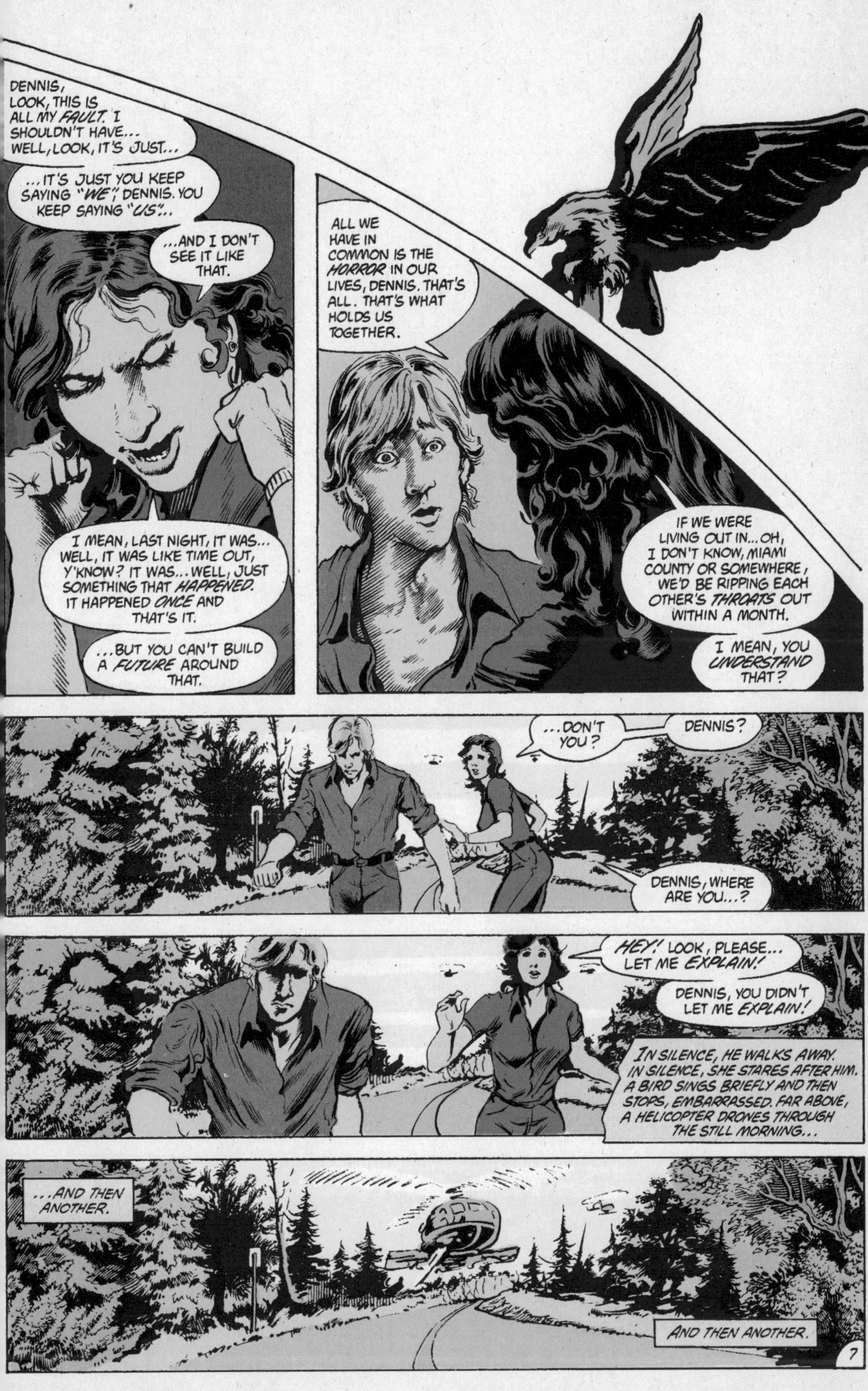
DENNIS, LOOK, THIS IS ALL MY FAULT. I SHOULDN'T HAVE... WELL, LOOK, IT'S JUST...
...IT'S JUST YOU KEEP SAYING "WE," DENNIS. YOU KEEP SAYING "US"...
...AND I DON'T SEE IT LIKE THAT.
I MEAN, LAST NIGHT, IT WAS... WELL, IT WAS LIKE TIME OUT, Y'KNOW? IT WAS... WELL, JUST SOMETHING THAT HAPPENED. IT HAPPENED ONCE AND THAT'S IT.
...BUT YOU CAN'T BUILD A FUTURE AROUND THAT.
ALL WE HAVE IN COMMON IS THE HORROR IN OUR LIVES, DENNIS. THAT'S ALL. THAT'S WHAT HOLDS US TOGETHER.
IF WE WERE LIVING OUT IN... OH, I DON'T KNOW, MIAMI COUNTY OR SOMEWHERE, WE'D BE RIPPING EACH OTHER'S THROATS OUT WITHIN A MONTH.
I MEAN, YOU UNDERSTAND THAT?
...DON'T YOU?
DENNIS?
DENNIS, WHERE ARE YOU...?
HEY! LOOK, PLEASE... LET ME EXPLAIN!
DENNIS, YOU DIDN'T LET ME EXPLAIN!
IN SILENCE, HE WALKS AWAY. IN SILENCE, SHE STARES AFTER HIM. A BIRD SINGS BRIEFLY AND THEN STOPS, EMBARRASSED. FAR ABOVE, A HELICOPTER DRONES THROUGH THE STILL MORNING...
...AND THEN ANOTHER.
AND THEN ANOTHER.
7

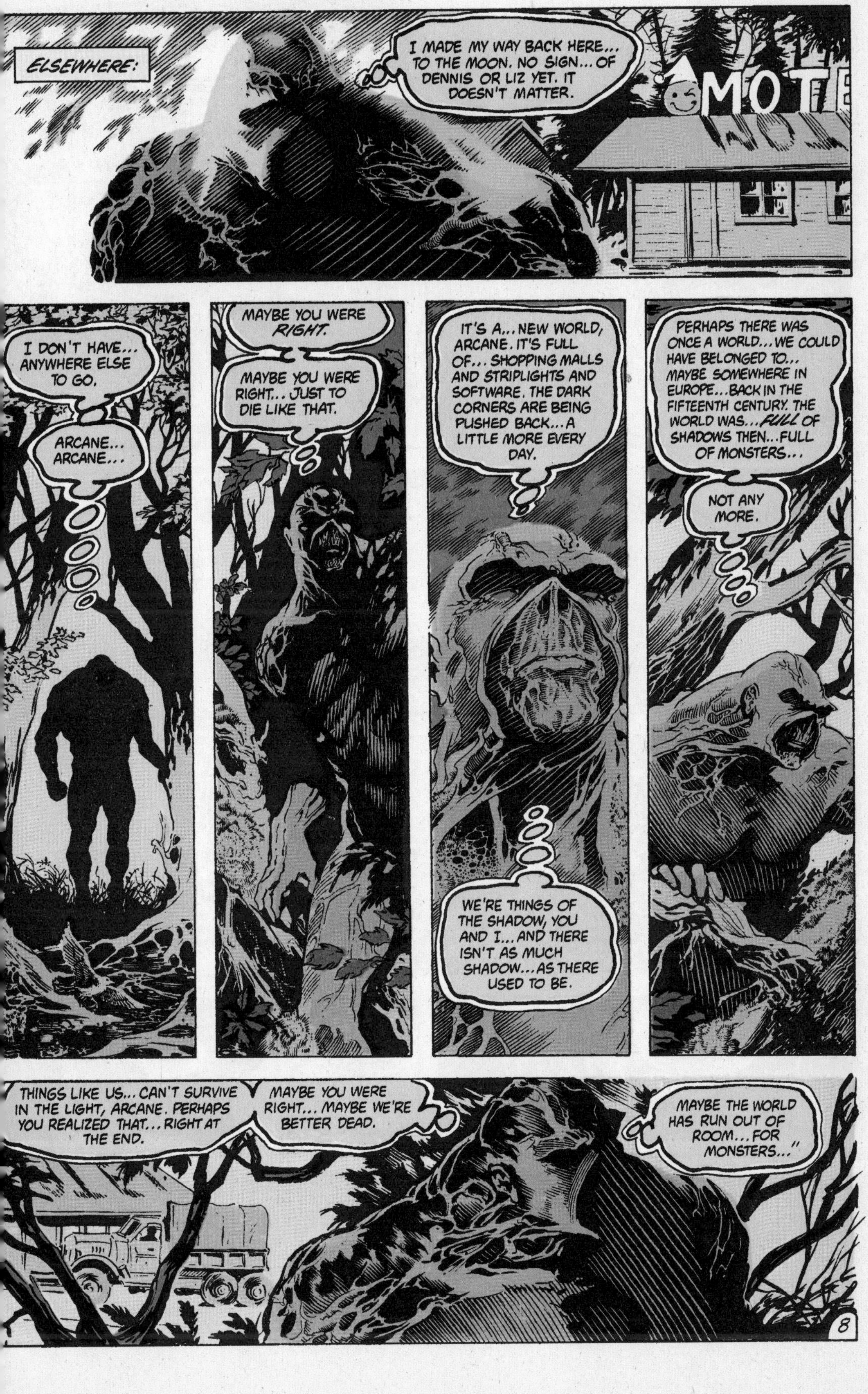
ELSEWHERE:
I MADE MY WAY BACK HERE... TO THE MOON. NO SIGN... OF DENNIS OR LIZ YET. IT DOESN'T MATTER.
MOTE
I DON'T HAVE... ANYWHERE ELSE TO GO.
ARCANE... ARCANE...
MAYBE YOU WERE RIGHT.
MAYBE YOU WERE RIGHT... JUST TO DIE LIKE THAT.
IT'S A... NEW WORLD, ARCANE. IT'S FULL OF... SHOPPING MALLS AND STRIPLIGHTS AND SOFTWARE. THE DARK CORNERS ARE BEING PUSHED BACK... A LITTLE MORE EVERY DAY.
WE'RE THINGS OF THE SHADOW, YOU AND I... AND THERE ISN'T AS MUCH SHADOW... AS THERE USED TO BE.
PERHAPS THERE WAS ONCE A WORLD... WE COULD HAVE BELONGED TO... MAYBE SOMEWHERE IN EUROPE... BACK IN THE FIFTEENTH CENTURY. THE WORLD WAS... FULL OF SHADOWS THEN... FULL OF MONSTERS...
NOT ANY MORE.
THINGS LIKE US... CAN'T SURVIVE IN THE LIGHT, ARCANE. PERHAPS YOU REALIZED THAT... RIGHT AT THE END.
MAYBE YOU WERE RIGHT... MAYBE WE'RE BETTER DEAD.
MAYBE THE WORLD HAS RUN OUT OF ROOM... FOR MONSTERS..."
8

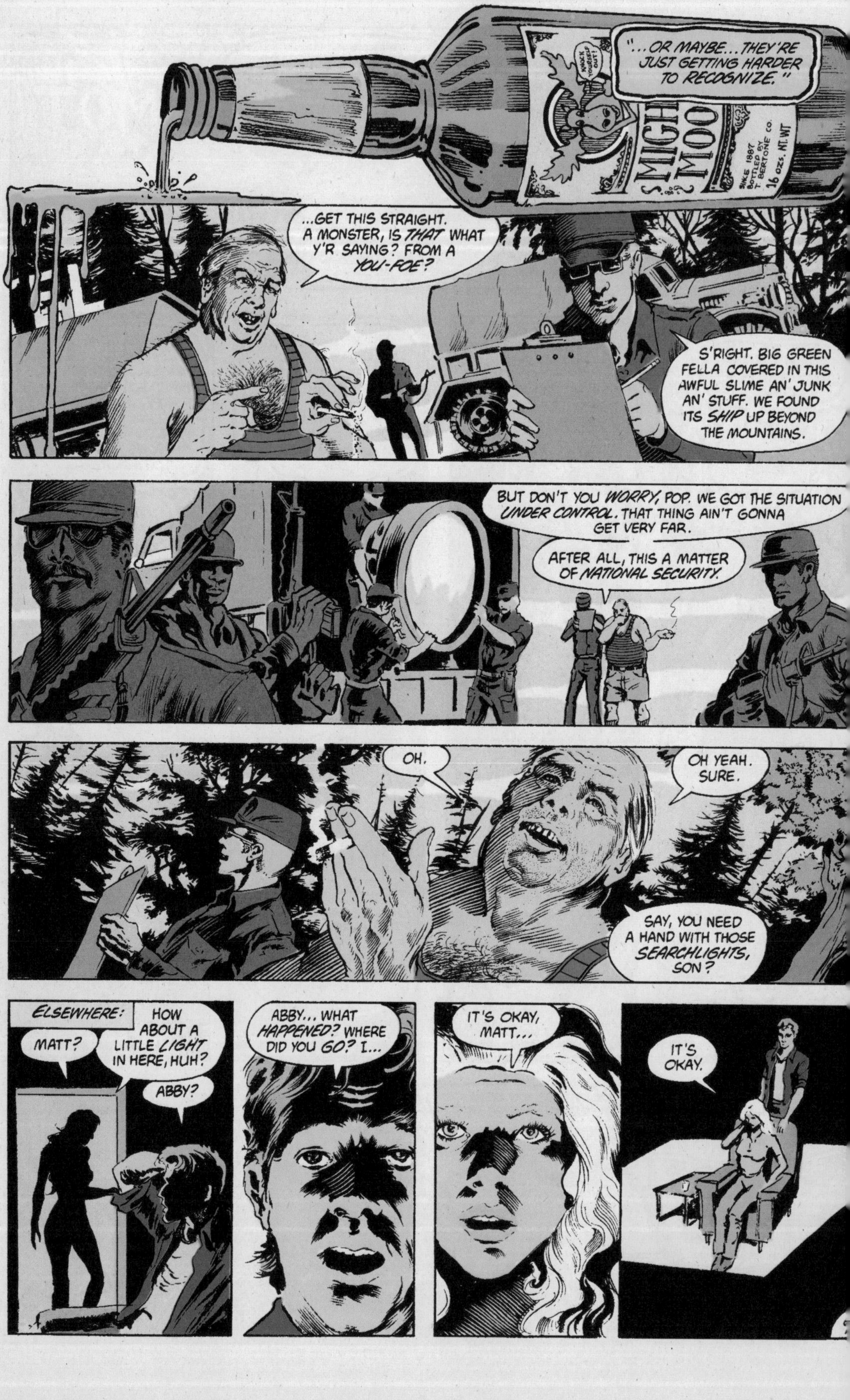
"...OR MAYBE...THEY'RE JUST GETTING HARDER TO RECOGNIZE."
...GET THIS STRAIGHT. A MONSTER, IS THAT WHAT Y'R SAYING? FROM A YOU-FOE?
S'RIGHT. BIG GREEN FELLA COVERED IN THIS AWFUL SLIME AN' JUNK AN' STUFF. WE FOUND ITS SHIP UP BEYOND THE MOUNTAINS.
BUT DON'T YOU WORRY, POP. WE GOT THE SITUATION UNDER CONTROL. THAT THING AIN'T GONNA GET VERY FAR.
AFTER ALL, THIS A MATTER OF NATIONAL SECURITY.
OH.
OH YEAH. SURE.
SAY, YOU NEED A HAND WITH THOSE SEARCHLIGHTS, SON?
ELSEWHERE:
MATT?
HOW ABOUT A LITTLE LIGHT IN HERE, HUH?
ABBY?
ABBY... WHAT HAPPENED? WHERE DID YOU GO? I...
IT'S OKAY, MATT...
IT'S OKAY.

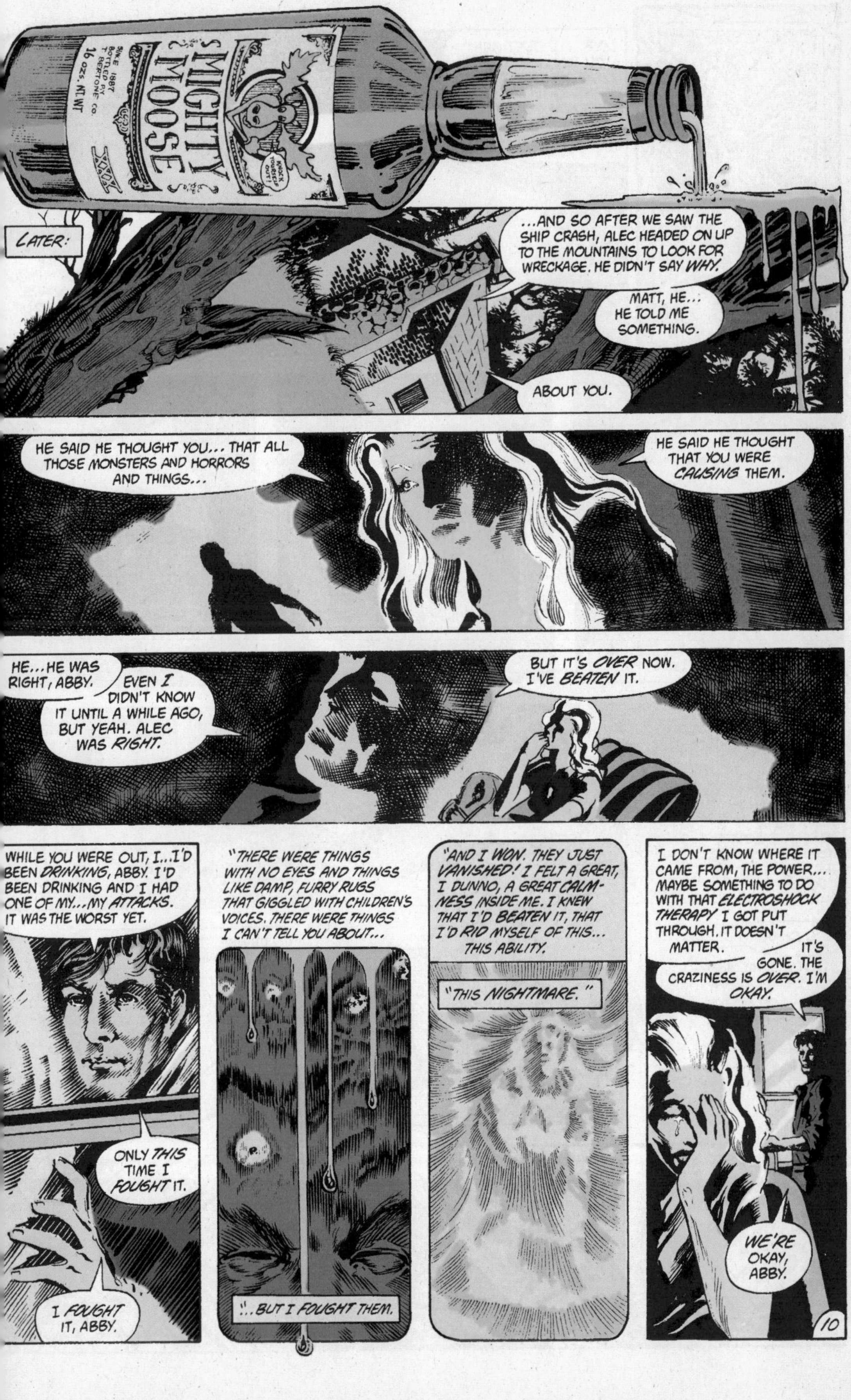
MIGHTY MOOSE
SINCE 1887 BOTTLED BY T. BERTONE CO. 16 OZS. NT. WT.
KNOCK YOURSELF OUT!
LATER:
...AND SO AFTER WE SAW THE SHIP CRASH, ALEC HEADED ON UP TO THE MOUNTAINS TO LOOK FOR WRECKAGE. HE DIDN'T SAY WHY.
MATT, HE... HE TOLD ME SOMETHING.
ABOUT YOU.
HE SAID HE THOUGHT YOU... THAT ALL THOSE MONSTERS AND HORRORS AND THINGS...
HE SAID HE THOUGHT THAT YOU WERE CAUSING THEM.
HE... HE WAS RIGHT, ABBY.
EVEN I DIDN'T KNOW IT UNTIL A WHILE AGO, BUT YEAH. ALEC WAS RIGHT.
BUT IT'S OVER NOW. I'VE BEATEN IT.
WHILE YOU WERE OUT, I...I'D BEEN DRINKING, ABBY. I'D BEEN DRINKING AND I HAD ONE OF MY... MY ATTACKS. IT WAS THE WORST YET.
ONLY THIS TIME I FOUGHT IT.
I FOUGHT IT, ABBY.
"THERE WERE THINGS WITH NO EYES AND THINGS LIKE DAMP, FURRY RUGS THAT GIGGLED WITH CHILDREN'S VOICES. THERE WERE THINGS I CAN'T TELL YOU ABOUT...
"...BUT I FOUGHT THEM.
"AND I WON. THEY JUST VANISHED! I FELT A GREAT, I DUNNO, A GREAT CALMNESS INSIDE ME. I KNEW THAT I'D BEATEN IT, THAT I'D RID MYSELF OF THIS... THIS ABILITY.
"THIS NIGHTMARE."
I DON'T KNOW WHERE IT CAME FROM, THE POWER... MAYBE SOMETHING TO DO WITH THAT ELECTROSHOCK THERAPY I GOT PUT THROUGH. IT DOESN'T MATTER.
IT'S GONE. THE CRAZINESS IS OVER. I'M OKAY.
WE'RE OKAY, ABBY.
10

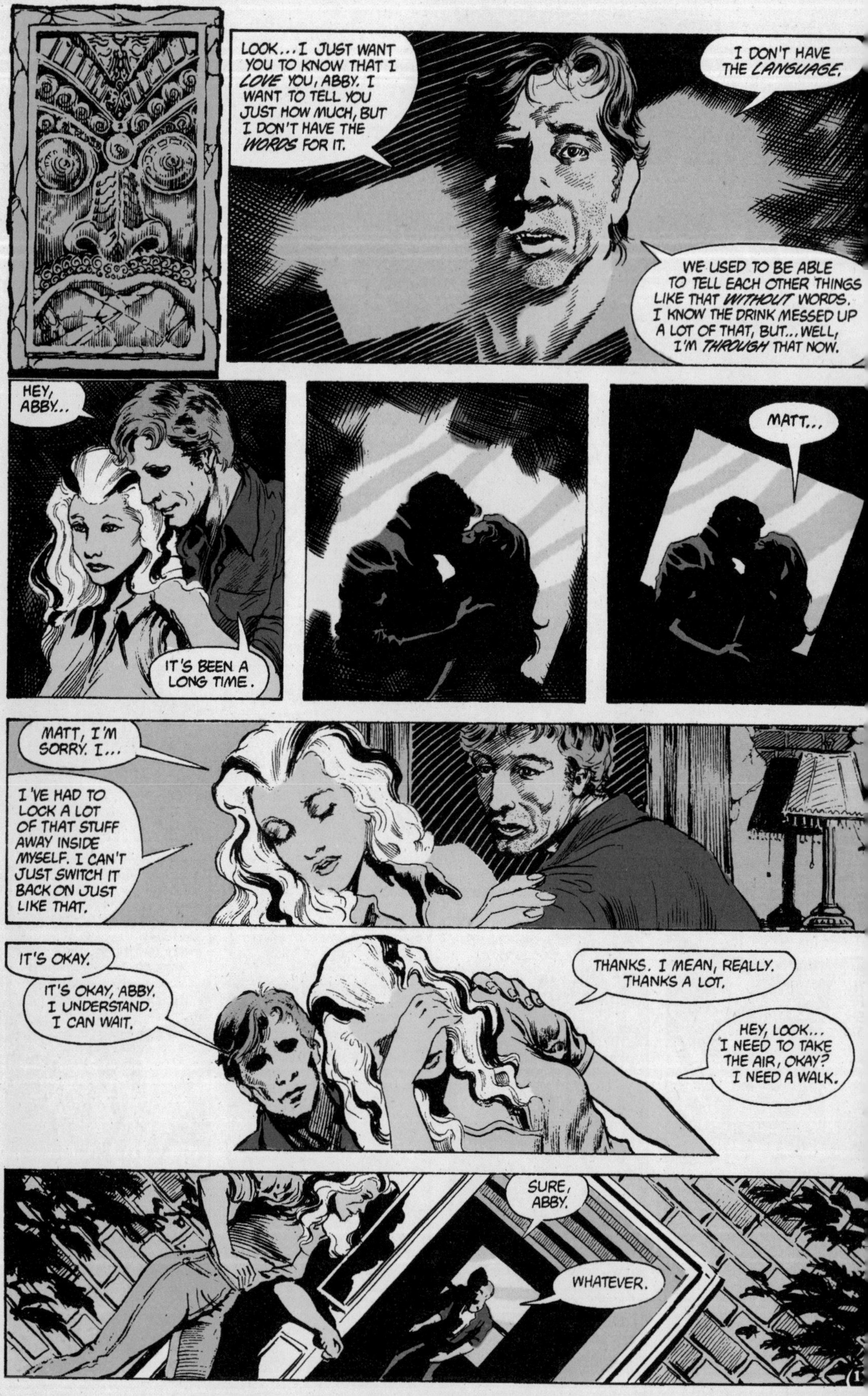
LOOK... I JUST WANT YOU TO KNOW THAT I LOVE YOU, ABBY. I WANT TO TELL YOU JUST HOW MUCH, BUT I DON'T HAVE THE WORDS FOR IT.
I DON'T HAVE THE LANGUAGE.
WE USED TO BE ABLE TO TELL EACH OTHER THINGS LIKE THAT WITHOUT WORDS. I KNOW THE DRINK MESSED UP A LOT OF THAT, BUT... WELL, I'M THROUGH THAT NOW.
HEY, ABBY...
IT'S BEEN A LONG TIME.
MATT...
MATT, I'M SORRY. I...
I'VE HAD TO LOCK A LOT OF THAT STUFF AWAY INSIDE MYSELF. I CAN'T JUST SWITCH IT BACK ON JUST LIKE THAT.
IT'S OKAY.
IT'S OKAY, ABBY. I UNDERSTAND. I CAN WAIT.
THANKS. I MEAN, REALLY. THANKS A LOT.
HEY, LOOK... I NEED TO TAKE THE AIR, OKAY? I NEED A WALK.
SURE, ABBY.
WHATEVER.

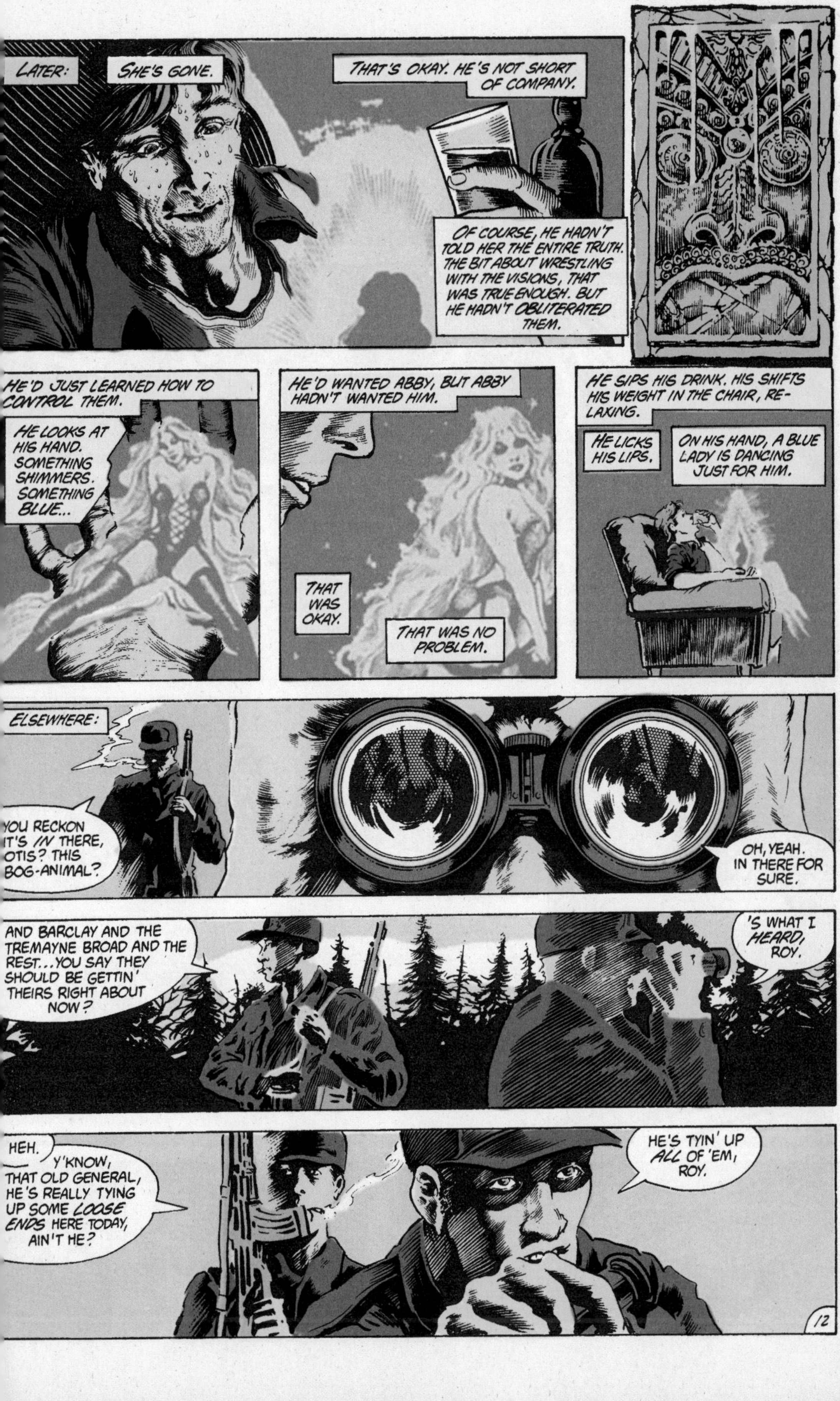
LATER:
SHE'S GONE.
THAT'S OKAY. HE'S NOT SHORT OF COMPANY.
OF COURSE, HE HADN'T TOLD HER THE ENTIRE TRUTH. THE BIT ABOUT WRESTLING WITH THE VISIONS, THAT WAS TRUE ENOUGH. BUT HE HADN'T OBLITERATED THEM.
HE'D JUST LEARNED HOW TO CONTROL THEM.
HE LOOKS AT HIS HAND. SOMETHING SHIMMERS. SOMETHING BLUE...
HE'D WANTED ABBY, BUT ABBY HADN'T WANTED HIM.
THAT WAS OKAY.
THAT WAS NO PROBLEM.
HE SIPS HIS DRINK. HIS SHIFTS HIS WEIGHT IN THE CHAIR, RE-LAXING.
HE LICKS HIS LIPS.
ON HIS HAND, A BLUE LADY IS DANCING JUST FOR HIM.
ELSEWHERE:
YOU RECKON IT'S IN THERE, OTIS? THIS BOG-ANIMAL?
OH, YEAH. IN THERE FOR SURE.
AND BARCLAY AND THE TREMAYNE BROAD AND THE REST... YOU SAY THEY SHOULD BE GETTIN' THEIRS RIGHT ABOUT NOW?
'S WHAT I HEARD, ROY.
HEH.
Y'KNOW, THAT OLD GENERAL, HE'S REALLY TYING UP SOME LOOSE ENDS HERE TODAY, AIN'T HE?
HE'S TYIN' UP ALL OF 'EM, ROY.
12

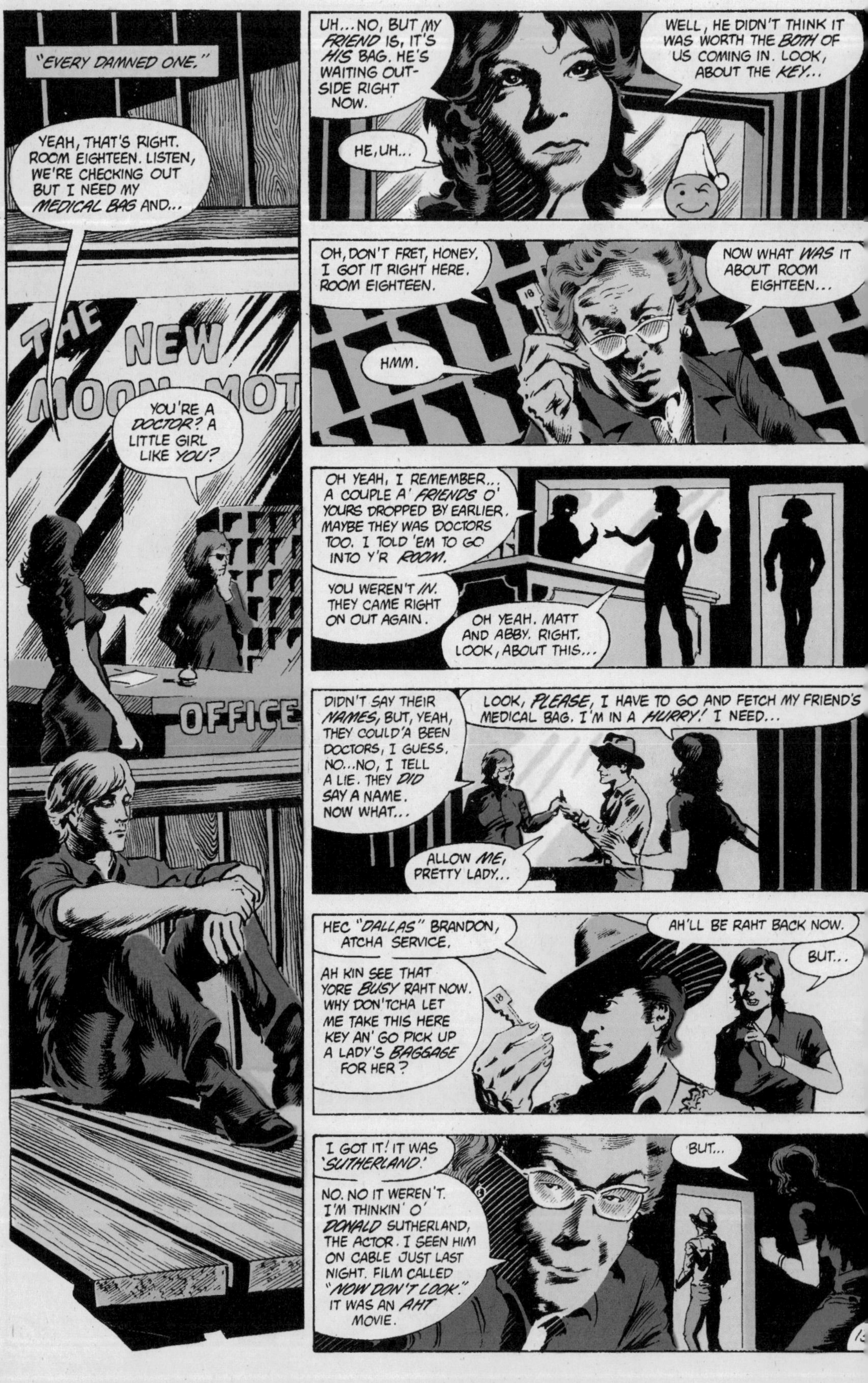
"EVERY DAMNED ONE."
YEAH, THAT'S RIGHT. ROOM EIGHTEEN. LISTEN, WE'RE CHECKING OUT BUT I NEED MY MEDICAL BAG AND...
THE NEW MOON MOT
YOU'RE A DOCTOR? A LITTLE GIRL LIKE YOU?
OFFICE
UH... NO, BUT MY FRIEND IS, IT'S HIS BAG. HE'S WAITING OUT-SIDE RIGHT NOW.
HE, UH...
WELL, HE DIDN'T THINK IT WAS WORTH THE BOTH OF US COMING IN. LOOK, ABOUT THE KEY...
OH, DON'T FRET, HONEY. I GOT IT RIGHT HERE. ROOM EIGHTEEN.
HMM.
NOW WHAT WAS IT ABOUT ROOM EIGHTEEN...
OH YEAH, I REMEMBER... A COUPLE A' FRIENDS O' YOURS DROPPED BY EARLIER. MAYBE THEY WAS DOCTORS TOO. I TOLD 'EM TO GO INTO Y'R ROOM.
YOU WEREN'T IN. THEY CAME RIGHT ON OUT AGAIN.
OH YEAH. MATT AND ABBY. RIGHT. LOOK, ABOUT THIS...
DIDN'T SAY THEIR NAMES, BUT, YEAH, THEY COULD'A BEEN DOCTORS, I GUESS. NO... NO, I TELL A LIE. THEY DID SAY A NAME. NOW WHAT...
LOOK, PLEASE, I HAVE TO GO AND FETCH MY FRIEND'S MEDICAL BAG. I'M IN A HURRY! I NEED...
ALLOW ME, PRETTY LADY...
HEC "DALLAS" BRANDON, ATCHA SERVICE.
AH KIN SEE THAT YORE BUSY RAHT NOW. WHY DON'TCHA LET ME TAKE THIS HERE KEY AN' GO PICK UP A LADY'S BAGGAGE FOR HER?
AH'LL BE RAHT BACK NOW.
BUT...
I GOT IT! IT WAS 'SUTHERLAND.'
NO. NO IT WEREN'T. I'M THINKIN' O' DONALD SUTHERLAND, THE ACTOR. I SEEN HIM ON CABLE JUST LAST NIGHT. FILM CALLED "NOW DON'T LOOK." IT WAS AN AHT MOVIE.
BUT...

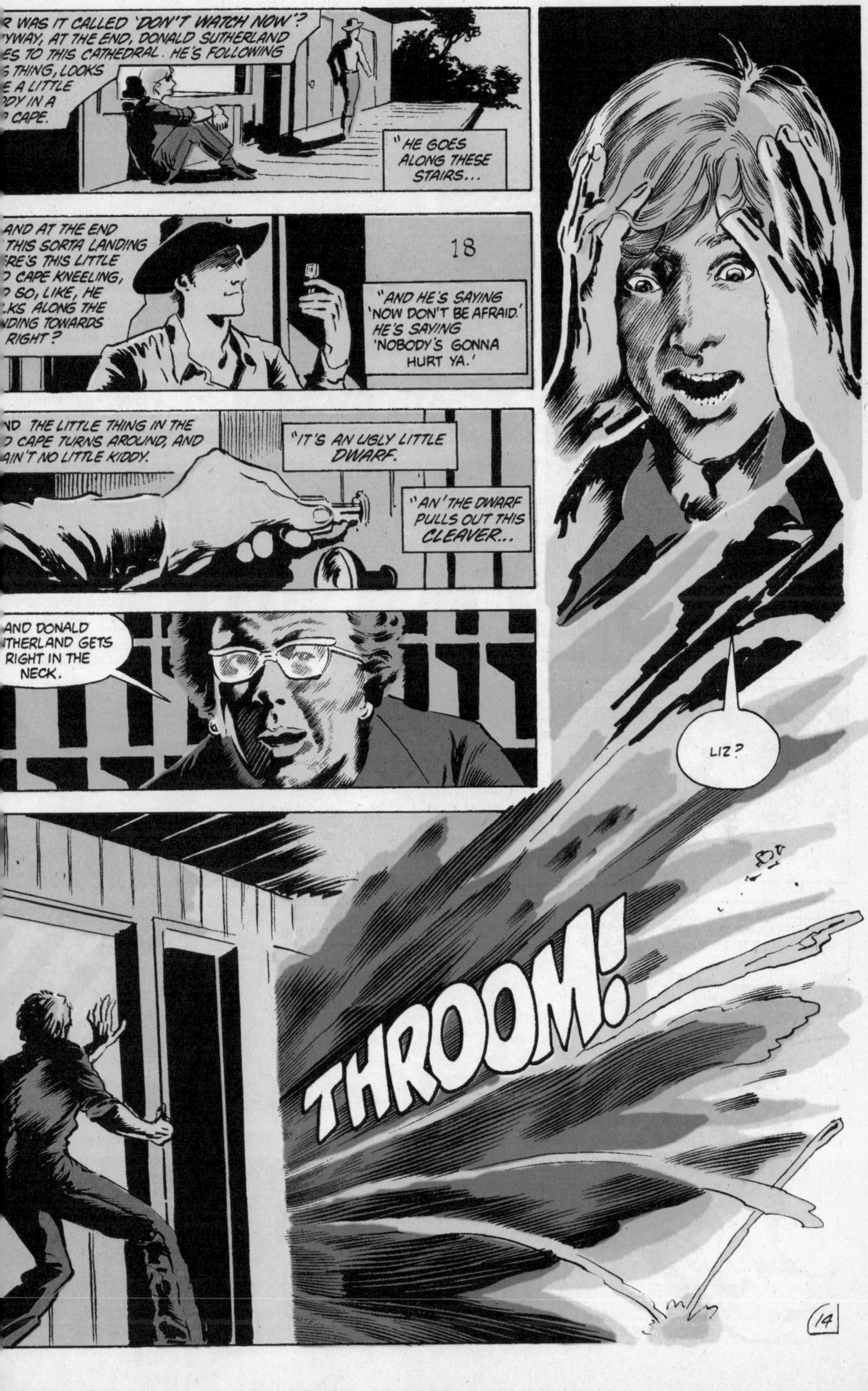
R WAS IT CALLED 'DON'T WATCH NOW'? YWAY, AT THE END, DONALD SUTHERLAND ES TO THIS CATHEDRAL. HE'S FOLLOWING S THING, LOOKS E A LITTLE DDY IN A D CAPE.
"HE GOES ALONG THESE STAIRS...
AND AT THE END THIS SORTA LANDING RE'S THIS LITTLE D CAPE KNEELING, D SO, LIKE, HE KS ALONG THE NDING TOWARDS RIGHT?
18
"AND HE'S SAYING 'NOW DON'T BE AFRAID.' HE'S SAYING 'NOBODY'S GONNA HURT YA.'
ND THE LITTLE THING IN THE D CAPE TURNS AROUND, AND AIN'T NO LITTLE KIDDY.
"IT'S AN UGLY LITTLE DWARF.
"AN' THE DWARF PULLS OUT THIS CLEAVER...
AND DONALD THERLAND GETS RIGHT IN THE NECK.
LIZ?
THROOM!
14

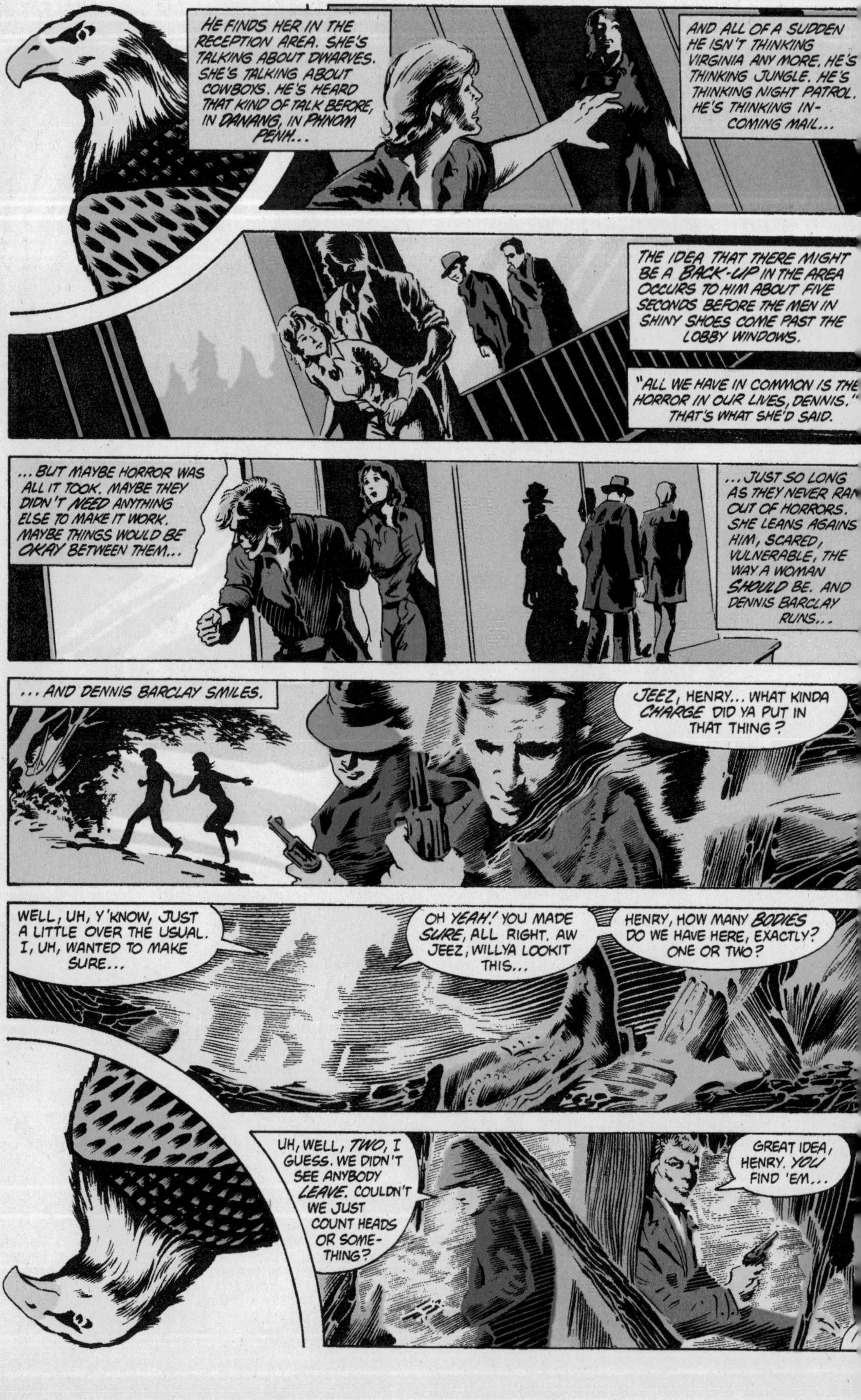
HE FINDS HER IN THE RECEPTION AREA. SHE'S TALKING ABOUT DWARVES. SHE'S TALKING ABOUT COWBOYS. HE'S HEARD THAT KIND OF TALK BEFORE, IN DANANG, IN PHNOM PENH...
AND ALL OF A SUDDEN HE ISN'T THINKING VIRGINIA ANY MORE. HE'S THINKING JUNGLE. HE'S THINKING NIGHT PATROL. HE'S THINKING IN-COMING MAIL...
THE IDEA THAT THERE MIGHT BE A BACK-UP IN THE AREA OCCURS TO HIM ABOUT FIVE SECONDS BEFORE THE MEN IN SHINY SHOES COME PAST THE LOBBY WINDOWS.
"ALL WE HAVE IN COMMON IS THE HORROR IN OUR LIVES, DENNIS." THAT'S WHAT SHE'D SAID.
...BUT MAYBE HORROR WAS ALL IT TOOK. MAYBE THEY DIDN'T NEED ANYTHING ELSE TO MAKE IT WORK. MAYBE THINGS WOULD BE OKAY BETWEEN THEM...
...JUST SO LONG AS THEY NEVER RAN OUT OF HORRORS. SHE LEANS AGAINST HIM, SCARED, VULNERABLE, THE WAY A WOMAN SHOULD BE. AND DENNIS BARCLAY RUNS...
...AND DENNIS BARCLAY SMILES.
JEEZ, HENRY... WHAT KINDA CHARGE DID YA PUT IN THAT THING?
WELL, UH, Y'KNOW, JUST A LITTLE OVER THE USUAL. I, UH, WANTED TO MAKE SURE...
OH YEAH! YOU MADE SURE, ALL RIGHT. AW JEEZ, WILLYA LOOKIT THIS...
HENRY, HOW MANY BODIES DO WE HAVE HERE, EXACTLY? ONE OR TWO?
UH, WELL, TWO, I GUESS. WE DIDN'T SEE ANYBODY LEAVE. COULDN'T WE JUST COUNT HEADS OR SOME-THING?
GREAT IDEA, HENRY. YOU FIND 'EM...

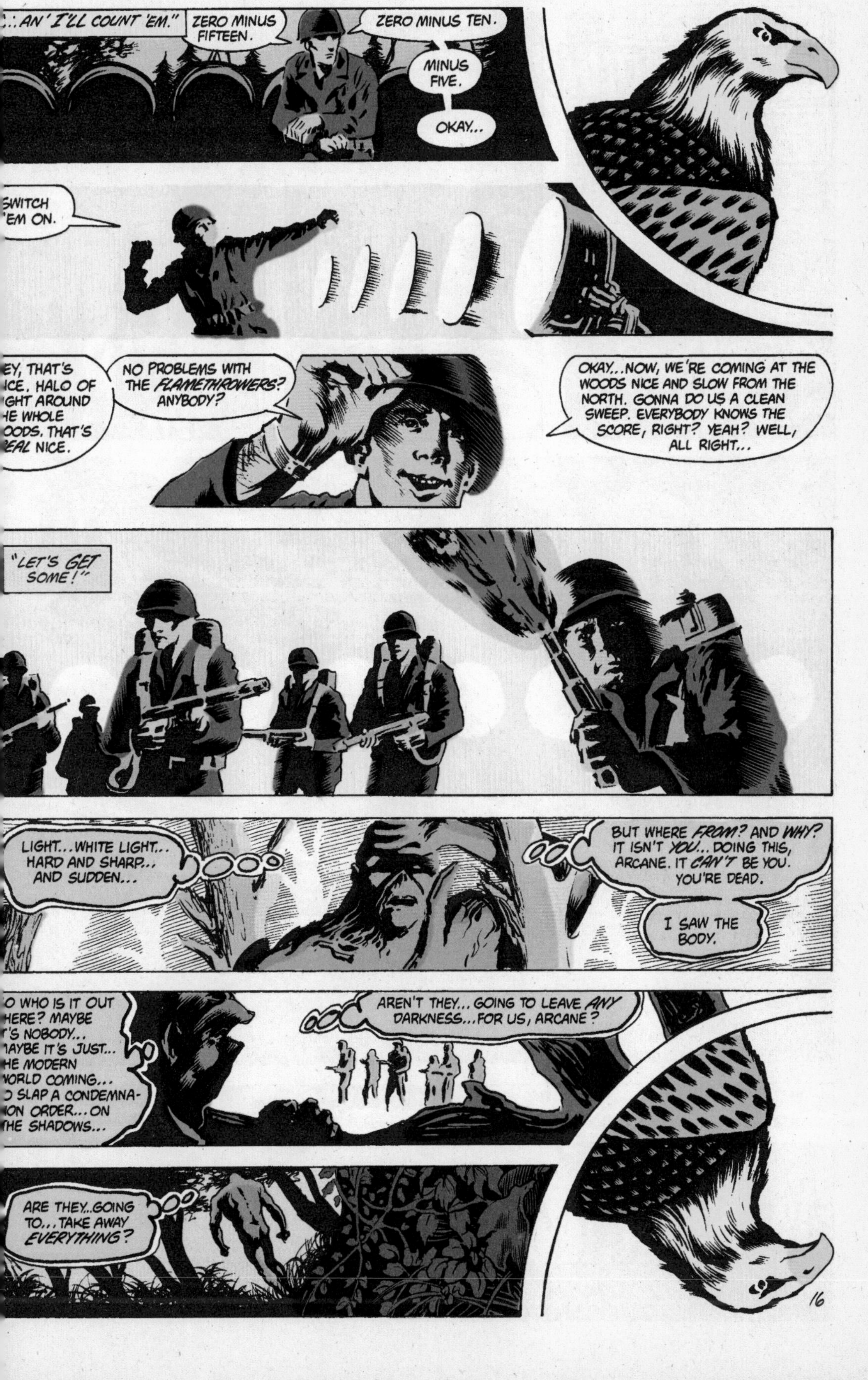
"...AN' I'LL COUNT 'EM."
ZERO MINUS FIFTEEN.
ZERO MINUS TEN.
MINUS FIVE.
OKAY...
SWITCH 'EM ON.
EY, THAT'S ICE. HALO OF GHT AROUND HE WHOLE OODS. THAT'S EAL NICE.
NO PROBLEMS WITH THE FLAMETHROWERS? ANYBODY?
OKAY...NOW, WE'RE COMING AT THE WOODS NICE AND SLOW FROM THE NORTH. GONNA DO US A CLEAN SWEEP. EVERYBODY KNOWS THE SCORE, RIGHT? YEAH? WELL, ALL RIGHT...
"LET'S GET SOME!"
LIGHT...WHITE LIGHT... HARD AND SHARP... AND SUDDEN...
BUT WHERE FROM? AND WHY? IT ISN'T YOU... DOING THIS, ARCANE. IT CAN'T BE YOU. YOU'RE DEAD.
I SAW THE BODY.
O WHO IS IT OUT HERE? MAYBE T'S NOBODY... MAYBE IT'S JUST... HE MODERN WORLD COMING... O SLAP A CONDEMNA- ION ORDER...ON HE SHADOWS...
AREN'T THEY... GOING TO LEAVE ANY DARKNESS...FOR US, ARCANE?
ARE THEY...GOING TO... TAKE AWAY EVERYTHING?
16

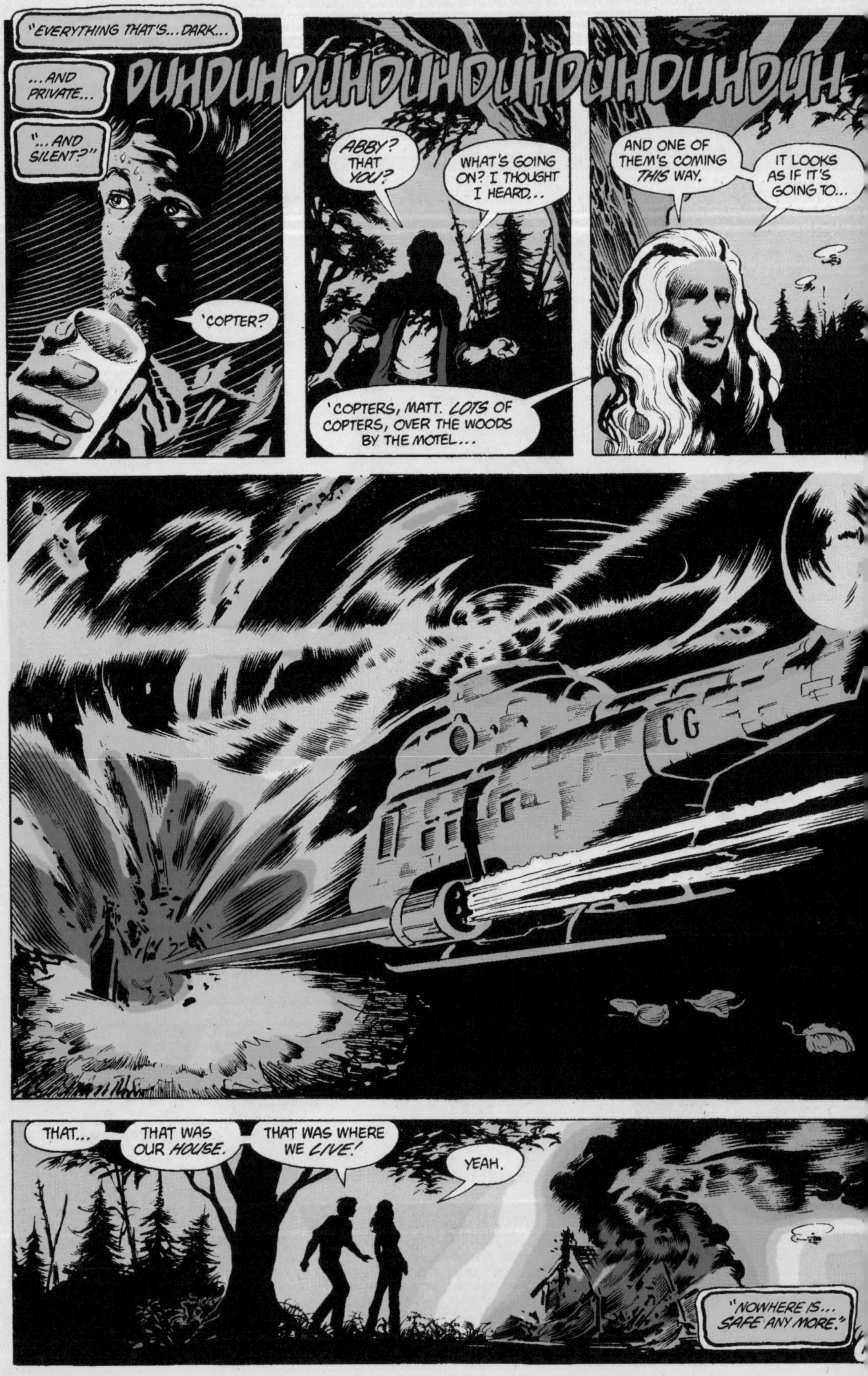
"EVERYTHING THAT'S...DARK...
...AND PRIVATE...
"...AND SILENT?"
DUHDUHDUHDUHDUHDUHDUHDUH
'COPTER?
ABBY? THAT YOU?
WHAT'S GOING ON? I THOUGHT I HEARD...
'COPTERS, MATT. LOTS OF COPTERS, OVER THE WOODS BY THE MOTEL...
AND ONE OF THEM'S COMING THIS WAY.
IT LOOKS AS IF IT'S GOING TO...
CG
THAT...
THAT WAS OUR HOUSE.
THAT WAS WHERE WE LIVE!
YEAH.
"NOWHERE IS... SAFE ANY MORE."

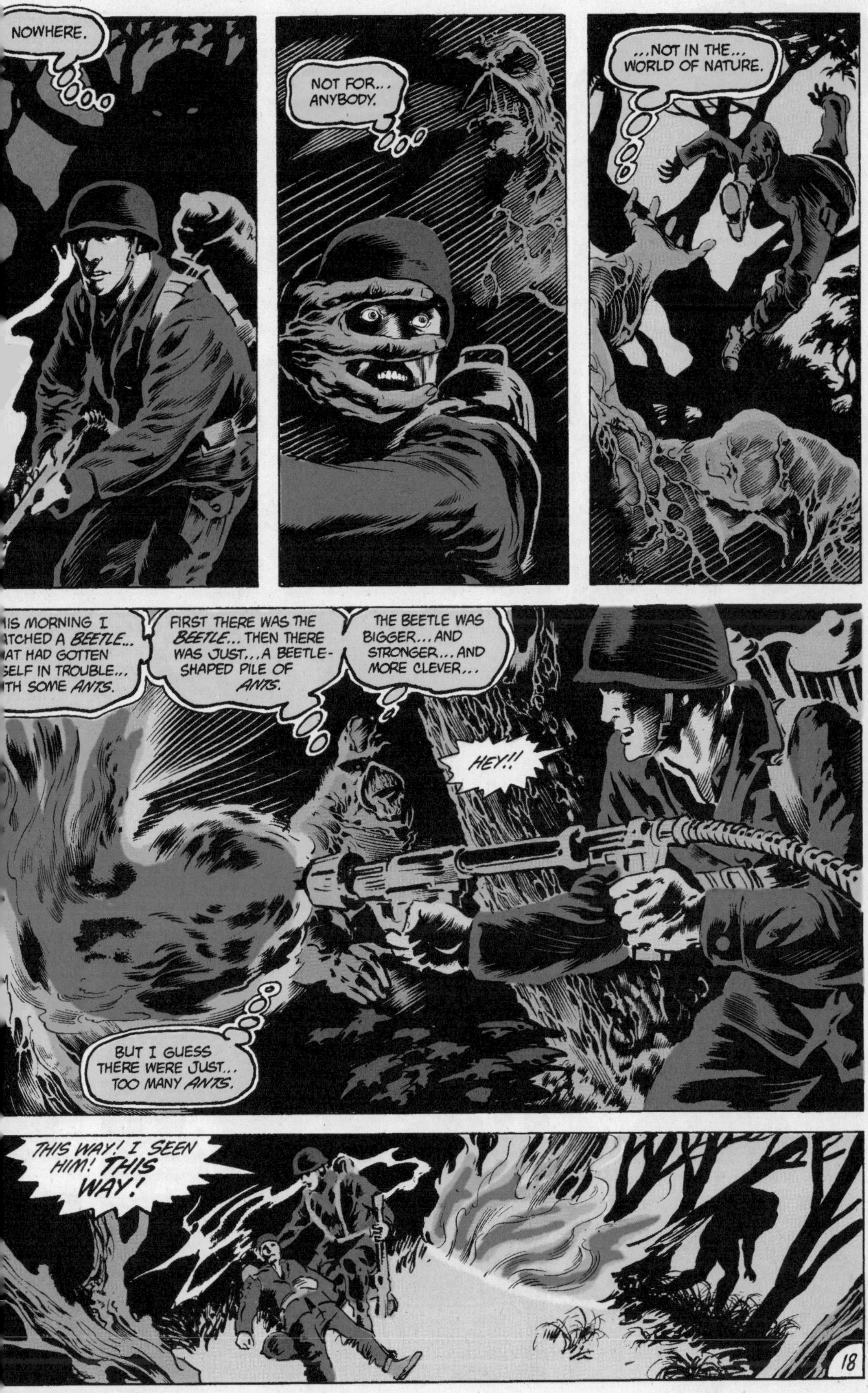
NOWHERE.
NOT FOR... ANYBODY.
...NOT IN THE... WORLD OF NATURE.
IS MORNING I ATCHED A BEETLE... AT HAD GOTTEN SELF IN TROUBLE... TH SOME ANTS.
FIRST THERE WAS THE BEETLE... THEN THERE WAS JUST... A BEETLE-SHAPED PILE OF ANTS.
THE BEETLE WAS BIGGER... AND STRONGER... AND MORE CLEVER...
HEY!!
BUT I GUESS THERE WERE JUST... TOO MANY ANTS.
THIS WAY! I SEEN HIM! THIS WAY!
18

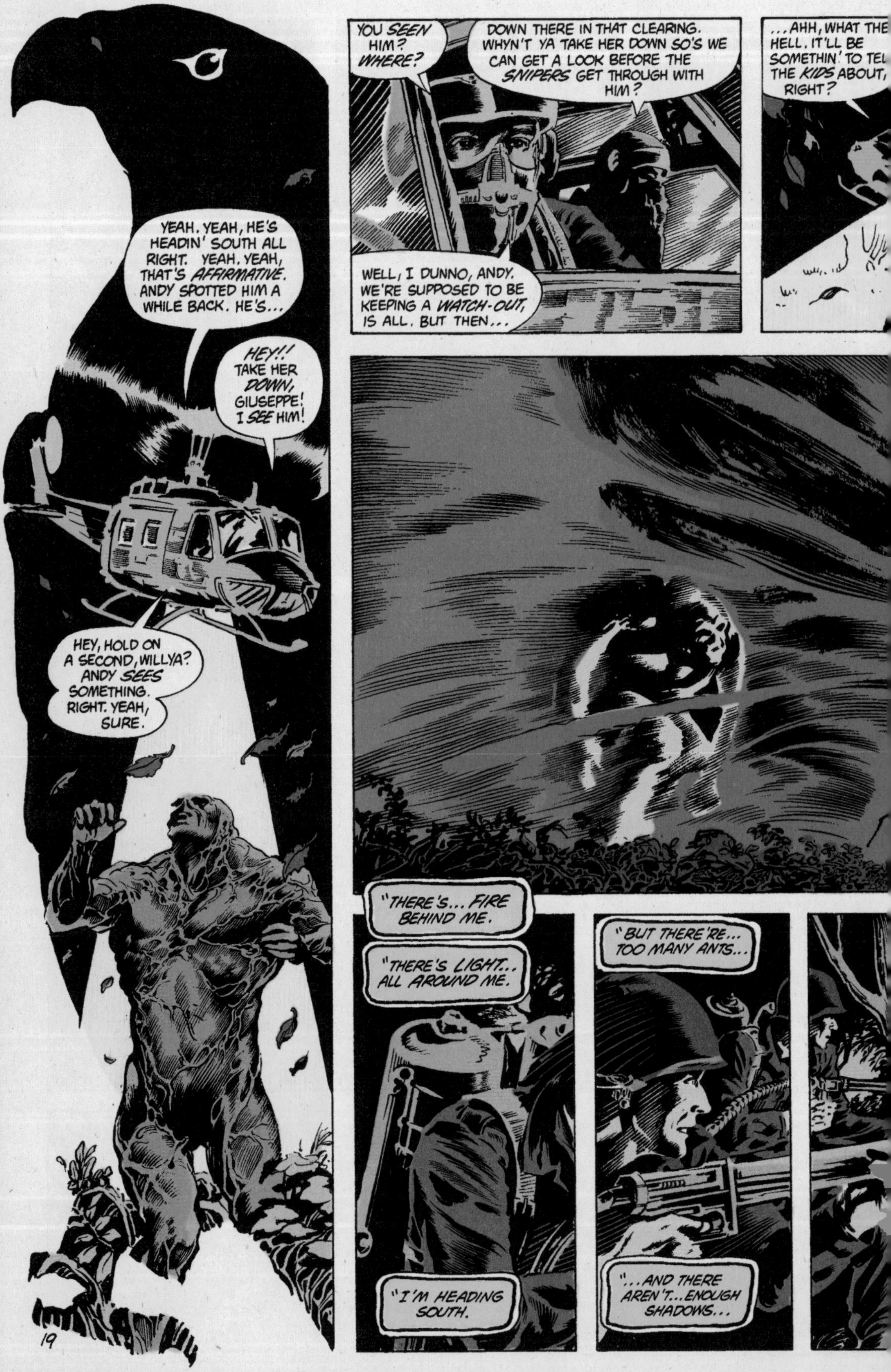
YEAH. YEAH, HE'S HEADIN' SOUTH ALL RIGHT. YEAH. YEAH, THAT'S AFFIRMATIVE. ANDY SPOTTED HIM A WHILE BACK. HE'S...
HEY!! TAKE HER DOWN, GIUSEPPE! I SEE HIM!
HEY, HOLD ON A SECOND, WILLYA? ANDY SEES SOMETHING. RIGHT. YEAH, SURE.
19
YOU SEEN HIM? WHERE?
DOWN THERE IN THAT CLEARING. WHYN'T YA TAKE HER DOWN SO'S WE CAN GET A LOOK BEFORE THE SNIPERS GET THROUGH WITH HIM?
WELL, I DUNNO, ANDY. WE'RE SUPPOSED TO BE KEEPING A WATCH-OUT, IS ALL. BUT THEN...
...AHH, WHAT THE HELL. IT'LL BE SOMETHIN' TO TEL THE KIDS ABOUT, RIGHT?
"THERE'S... FIRE BEHIND ME.
"THERE'S LIGHT... ALL AROUND ME.
"I'M HEADING SOUTH.
"BUT THERE'RE... TOO MANY ANTS...
"...AND THERE AREN'T...ENOUGH SHADOWS...

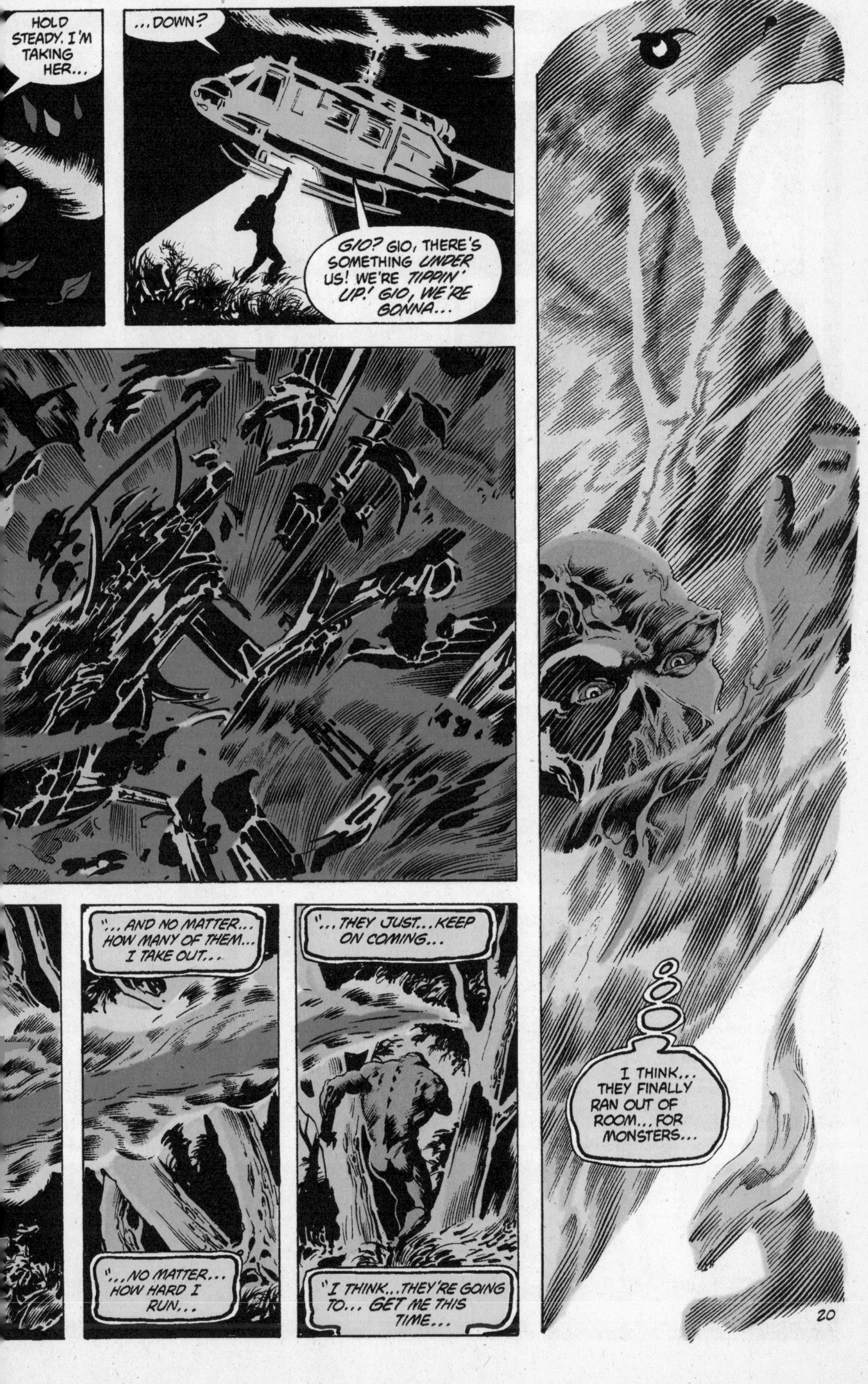
HOLD STEADY. I'M TAKING HER...
...DOWN?
GIO? GIO, THERE'S SOMETHING UNDER US! WE'RE TIPPIN' UP! GIO, WE'RE GONNA...
"...AND NO MATTER... HOW MANY OF THEM... I TAKE OUT...
"...NO MATTER... HOW HARD I RUN...
"...THEY JUST...KEEP ON COMING...
"I THINK...THEY'RE GOING TO... GET ME THIS TIME...
I THINK... THEY FINALLY RAN OUT OF ROOM... FOR MONSTERS...
20

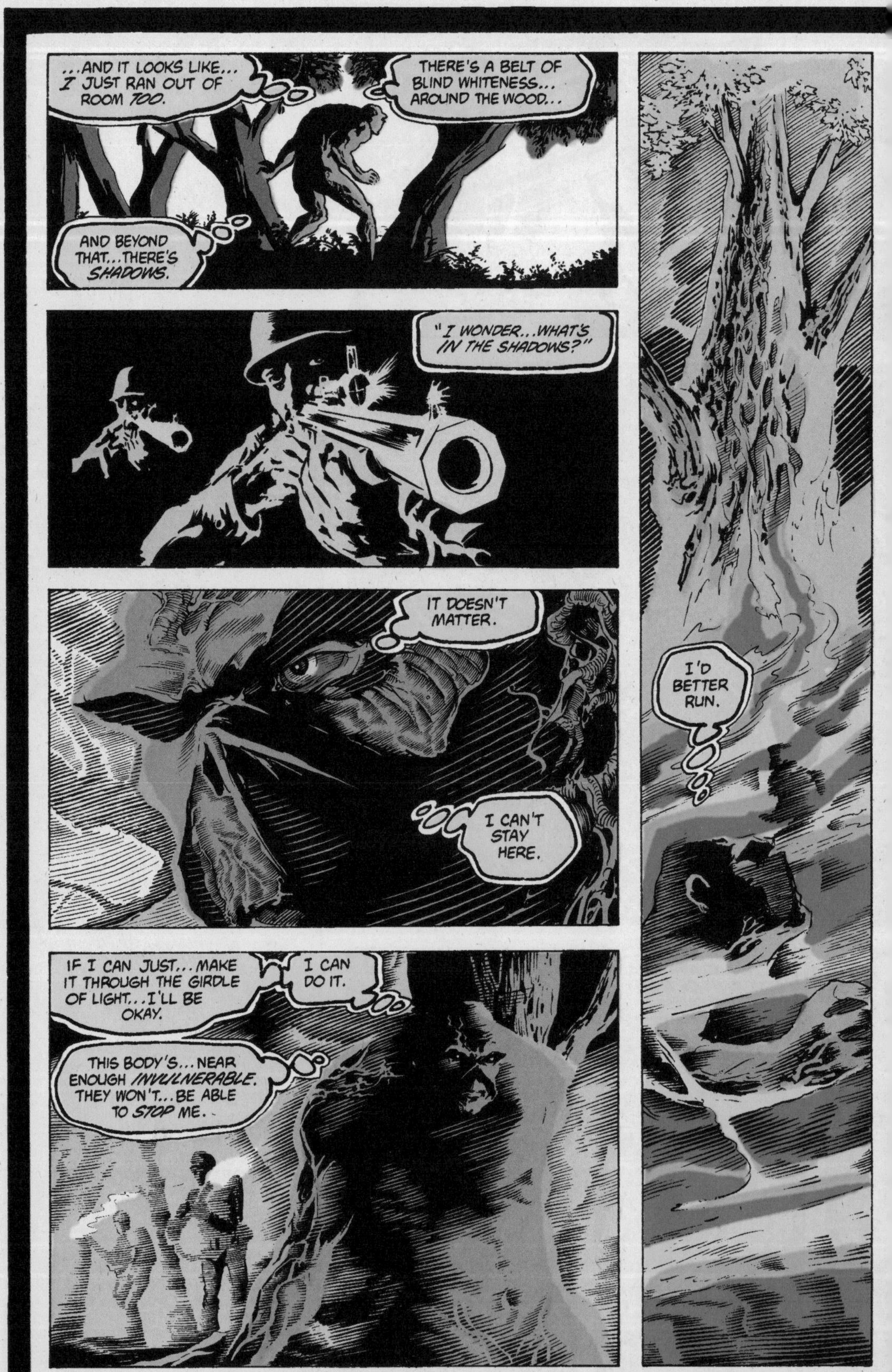
...AND IT LOOKS LIKE... I JUST RAN OUT OF ROOM TOO.
THERE'S A BELT OF BLIND WHITENESS... AROUND THE WOOD...
AND BEYOND THAT...THERE'S SHADOWS.
"I WONDER...WHAT'S IN THE SHADOWS?"
IT DOESN'T MATTER.
I CAN'T STAY HERE.
IF I CAN JUST...MAKE IT THROUGH THE GIRDLE OF LIGHT...I'LL BE OKAY.
I CAN DO IT.
THIS BODY'S...NEAR ENOUGH INVULNERABLE. THEY WON'T...BE ABLE TO STOP ME.
I'D BETTER RUN.

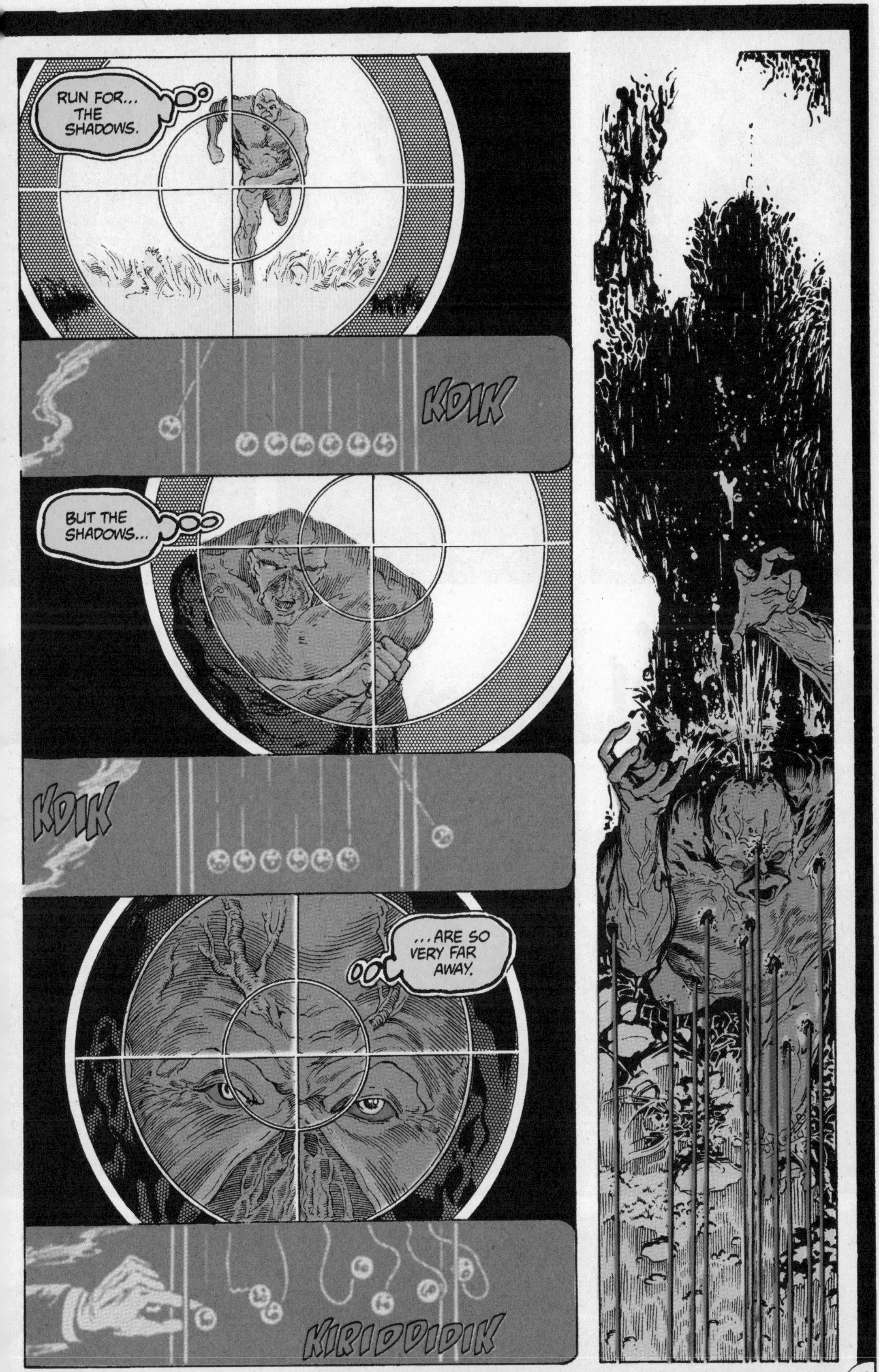
RUN FOR... THE SHADOWS.
KDIK
BUT THE SHADOWS...
KDIK
...ARE SO VERY FAR AWAY.
KIRIDDIDIK
22

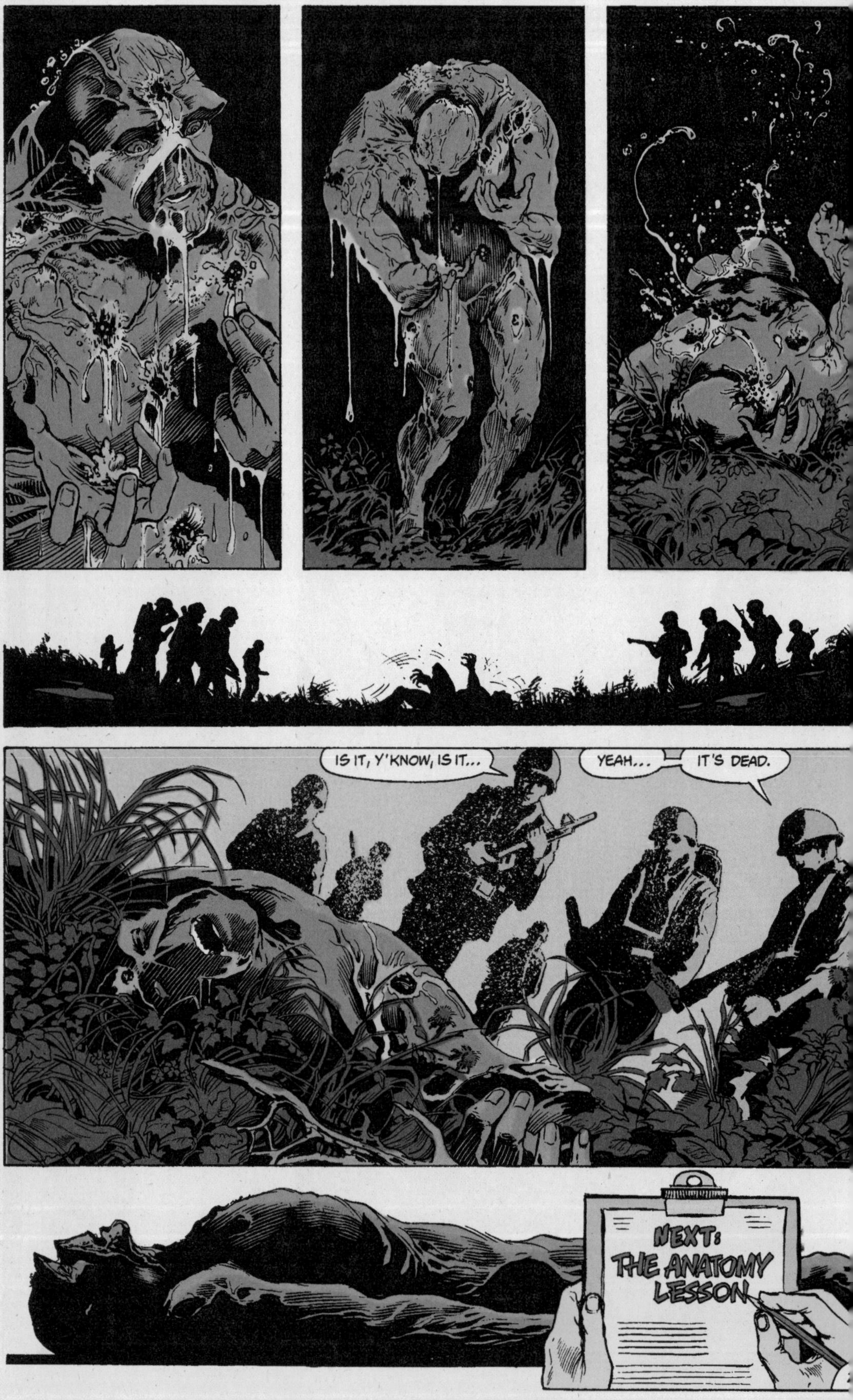
IS IT, Y'KNOW, IS IT...
YEAH...
IT'S DEAD.
NEXT:
THE ANATOMY LESSON

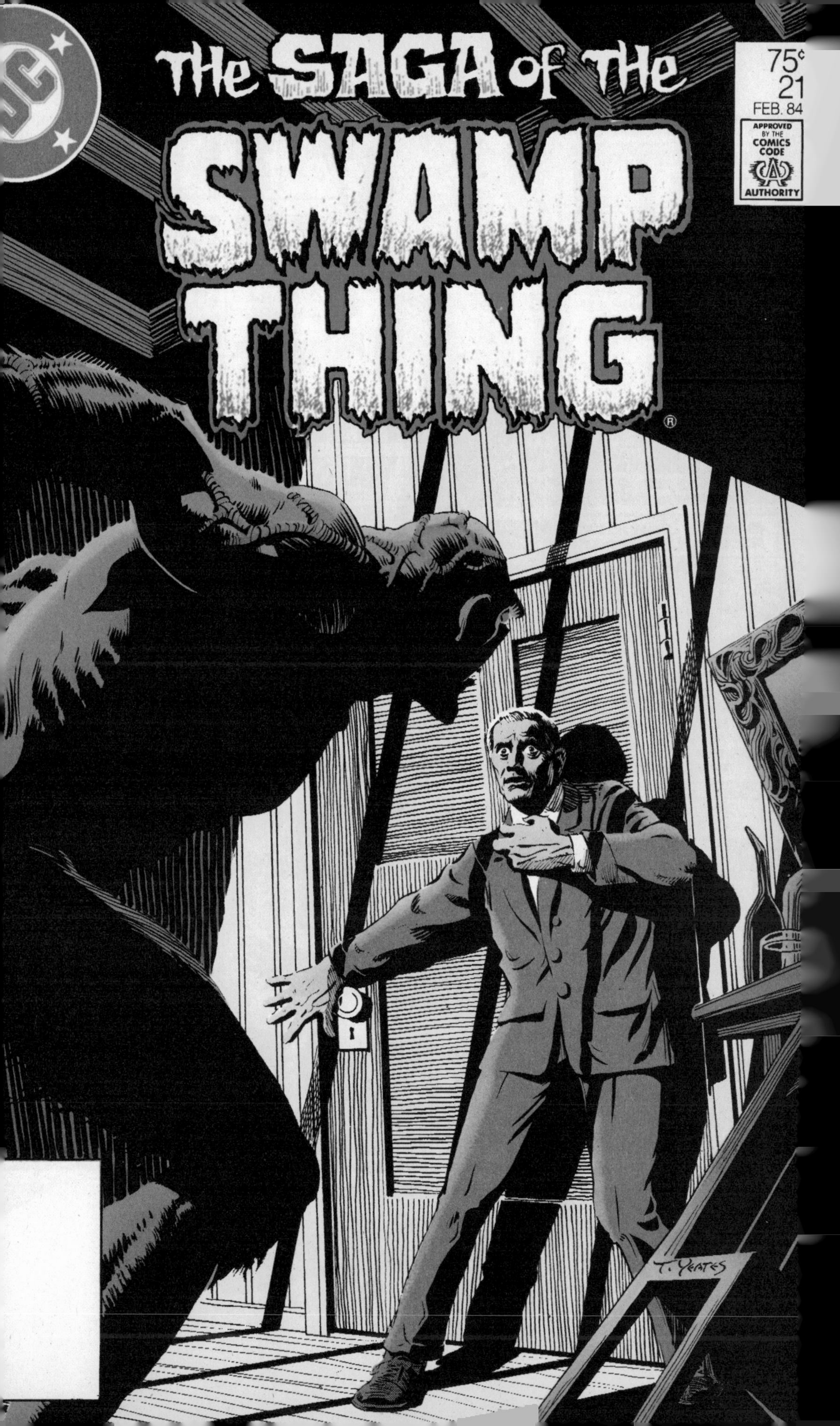
The SAGA of the
SWAMP THING
75¢
21
FEB. 84
APPROVED BY THE COMICS CODE AUTHORITY
T. Yeates

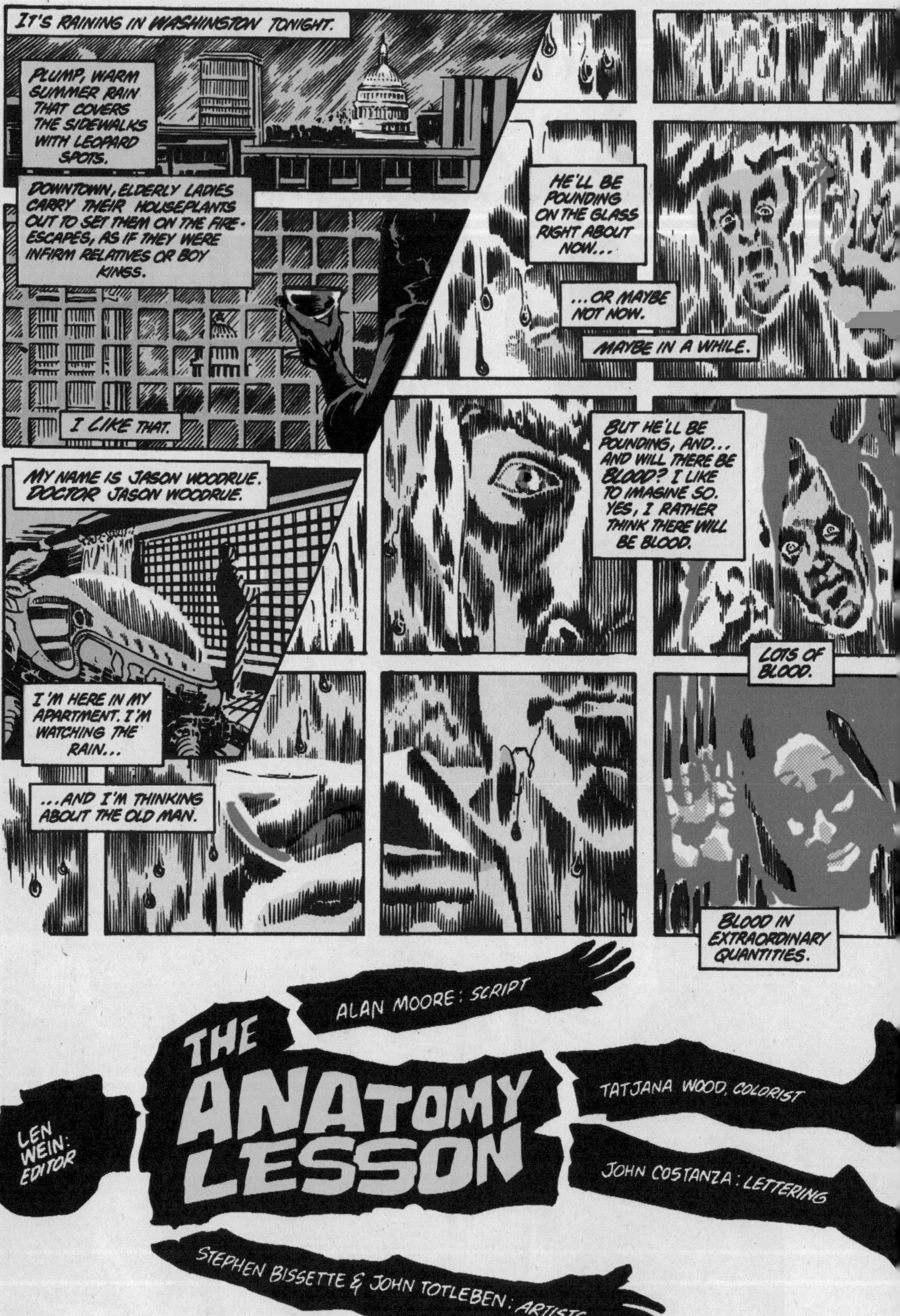
IT'S RAINING IN WASHINGTON TONIGHT.
PLUMP, WARM SUMMER RAIN THAT COVERS THE SIDEWALKS WITH LEOPARD SPOTS.
DOWNTOWN, ELDERLY LADIES CARRY THEIR HOUSEPLANTS OUT TO SET THEM ON THE FIRE-ESCAPES, AS IF THEY WERE INFIRM RELATIVES OR BOY KINGS.
I LIKE THAT.
MY NAME IS JASON WOODRUE. DOCTOR JASON WOODRUE.
I'M HERE IN MY APARTMENT. I'M WATCHING THE RAIN...
...AND I'M THINKING ABOUT THE OLD MAN.
HE'LL BE POUNDING ON THE GLASS RIGHT ABOUT NOW...
...OR MAYBE NOT NOW.
MAYBE IN A WHILE.
BUT HE'LL BE POUNDING, AND... AND WILL THERE BE BLOOD? I LIKE TO IMAGINE SO. YES, I RATHER THINK THERE WILL BE BLOOD.
LOTS OF BLOOD.
BLOOD IN EXTRAORDINARY QUANTITIES.
ALAN MOORE: SCRIPT
THE ANATOMY LESSON
LEN WEIN: EDITOR
TATJANA WOOD, COLORIST
JOHN COSTANZA: LETTERING
STEPHEN BISSETTE & JOHN TOTLEBEN: ARTISTS

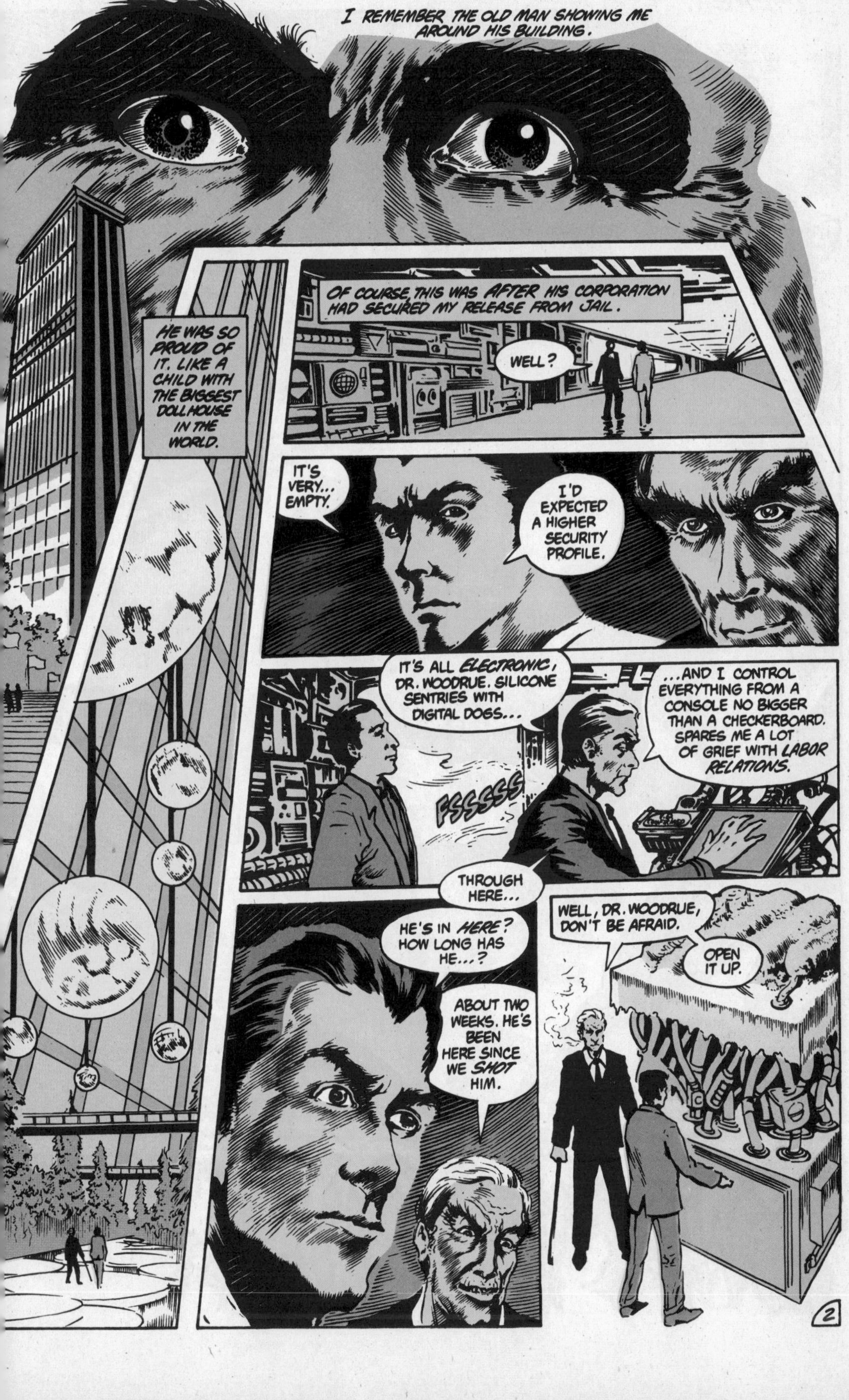
I REMEMBER THE OLD MAN SHOWING ME AROUND HIS BUILDING.
HE WAS SO PROUD OF IT. LIKE A CHILD WITH THE BIGGEST DOLLHOUSE IN THE WORLD.
OF COURSE, THIS WAS AFTER HIS CORPORATION HAD SECURED MY RELEASE FROM JAIL.
WELL?
IT'S VERY... EMPTY.
I'D EXPECTED A HIGHER SECURITY PROFILE.
IT'S ALL ELECTRONIC, DR. WOODRUE. SILICONE SENTRIES WITH DIGITAL DOGS...
...AND I CONTROL EVERYTHING FROM A CONSOLE NO BIGGER THAN A CHECKERBOARD. SPARES ME A LOT OF GRIEF WITH LABOR RELATIONS.
FSSSSS
THROUGH HERE...
HE'S IN HERE? HOW LONG HAS HE...?
ABOUT TWO WEEKS. HE'S BEEN HERE SINCE WE SHOT HIM.
WELL, DR. WOODRUE, DON'T BE AFRAID.
OPEN IT UP.
2

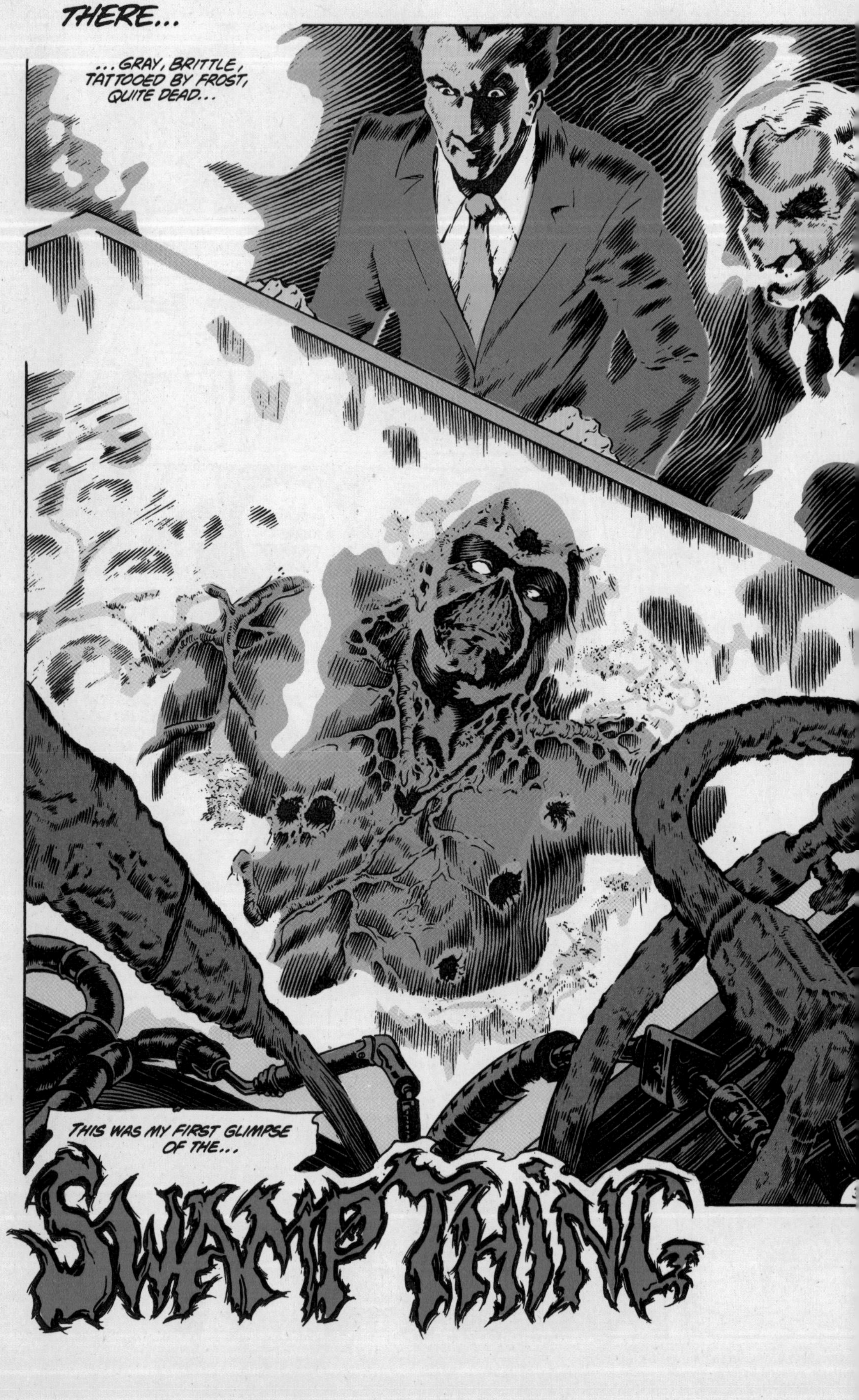
THERE...
...GRAY, BRITTLE, TATTOOED BY FROST, QUITE DEAD...
THIS WAS MY FIRST GLIMPSE OF THE...
SWAMP THING

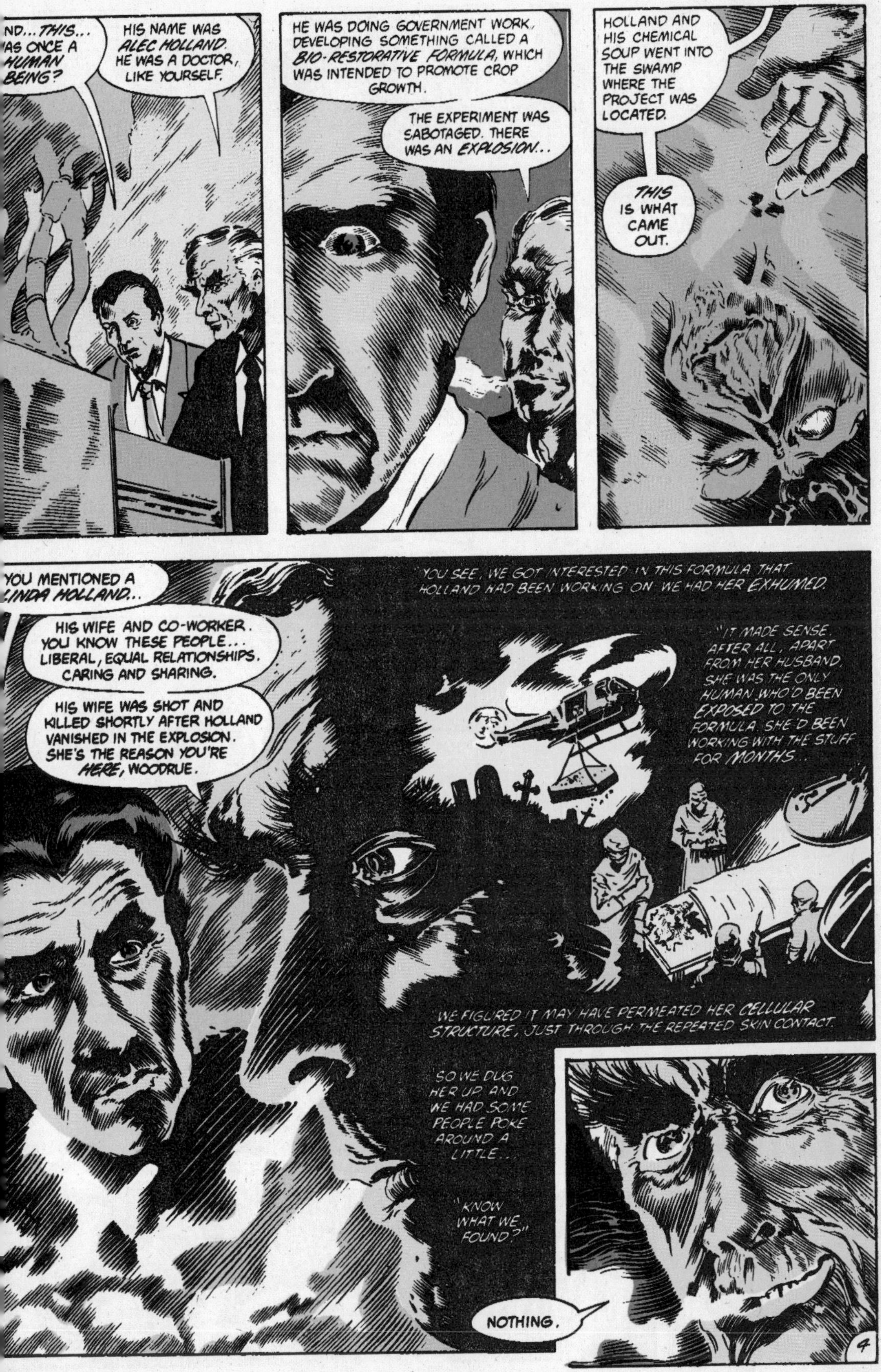

ND... THIS... AS ONCE A HUMAN BEING?
HIS NAME WAS ALEC HOLLAND. HE WAS A DOCTOR, LIKE YOURSELF.
HE WAS DOING GOVERNMENT WORK, DEVELOPING SOMETHING CALLED A BIO-RESTORATIVE FORMULA, WHICH WAS INTENDED TO PROMOTE CROP GROWTH.
THE EXPERIMENT WAS SABOTAGED. THERE WAS AN EXPLOSION...
HOLLAND AND HIS CHEMICAL SOUP WENT INTO THE SWAMP WHERE THE PROJECT WAS LOCATED.
THIS IS WHAT CAME OUT.
YOU MENTIONED A INDA HOLLAND...
HIS WIFE AND CO-WORKER. YOU KNOW THESE PEOPLE... LIBERAL, EQUAL RELATIONSHIPS. CARING AND SHARING.
HIS WIFE WAS SHOT AND KILLED SHORTLY AFTER HOLLAND VANISHED IN THE EXPLOSION. SHE'S THE REASON YOU'RE HERE, WOODRUE.
"YOU SEE, WE GOT INTERESTED IN THIS FORMULA THAT HOLLAND HAD BEEN WORKING ON. WE HAD HER EXHUMED.
"IT MADE SENSE. AFTER ALL, APART FROM HER HUSBAND, SHE WAS THE ONLY HUMAN WHO'D BEEN EXPOSED TO THE FORMULA. SHE'D BEEN WORKING WITH THE STUFF FOR MONTHS...
WE FIGURED IT MAY HAVE PERMEATED HER CELLULAR STRUCTURE, JUST THROUGH THE REPEATED SKIN CONTACT.
SO WE DUG HER UP, AND WE HAD SOME PEOPLE POKE AROUND A LITTLE...
"KNOW WHAT WE FOUND?"
NOTHING.
4

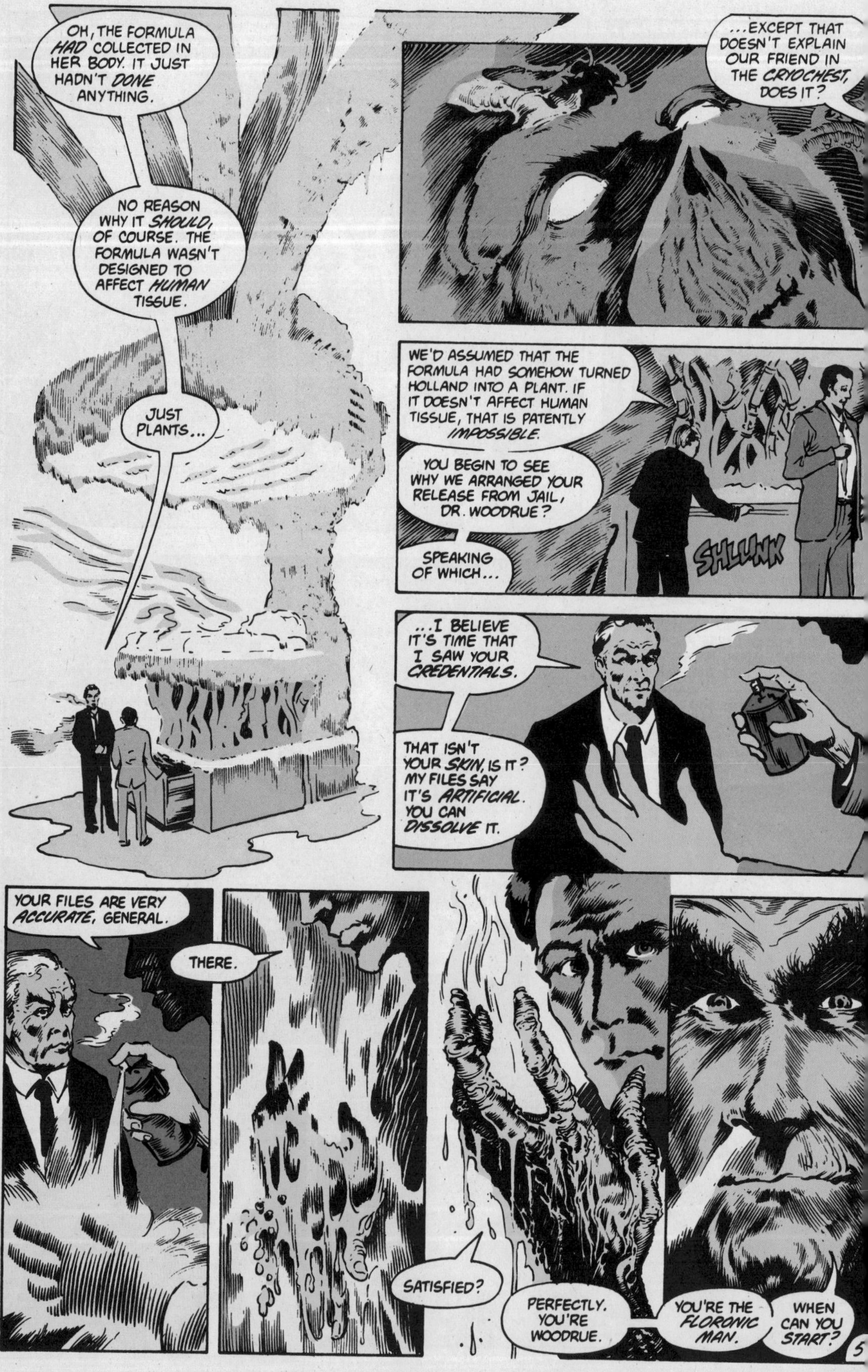
OH, THE FORMULA HAD COLLECTED IN HER BODY. IT JUST HADN'T DONE ANYTHING.
NO REASON WHY IT SHOULD, OF COURSE. THE FORMULA WASN'T DESIGNED TO AFFECT HUMAN TISSUE.
JUST PLANTS...
...EXCEPT THAT DOESN'T EXPLAIN OUR FRIEND IN THE CRYOCHEST, DOES IT?
WE'D ASSUMED THAT THE FORMULA HAD SOMEHOW TURNED HOLLAND INTO A PLANT. IF IT DOESN'T AFFECT HUMAN TISSUE, THAT IS PATENTLY IMPOSSIBLE.
YOU BEGIN TO SEE WHY WE ARRANGED YOUR RELEASE FROM JAIL, DR. WOODRUE?
SPEAKING OF WHICH...
SHLUNK
...I BELIEVE IT'S TIME THAT I SAW YOUR CREDENTIALS.
THAT ISN'T YOUR SKIN, IS IT? MY FILES SAY IT'S ARTIFICIAL. YOU CAN DISSOLVE IT.
YOUR FILES ARE VERY ACCURATE, GENERAL.
THERE.
SATISFIED?
PERFECTLY. YOU'RE WOODRUE.
YOU'RE THE FLORONIC MAN.
WHEN CAN YOU START?
5

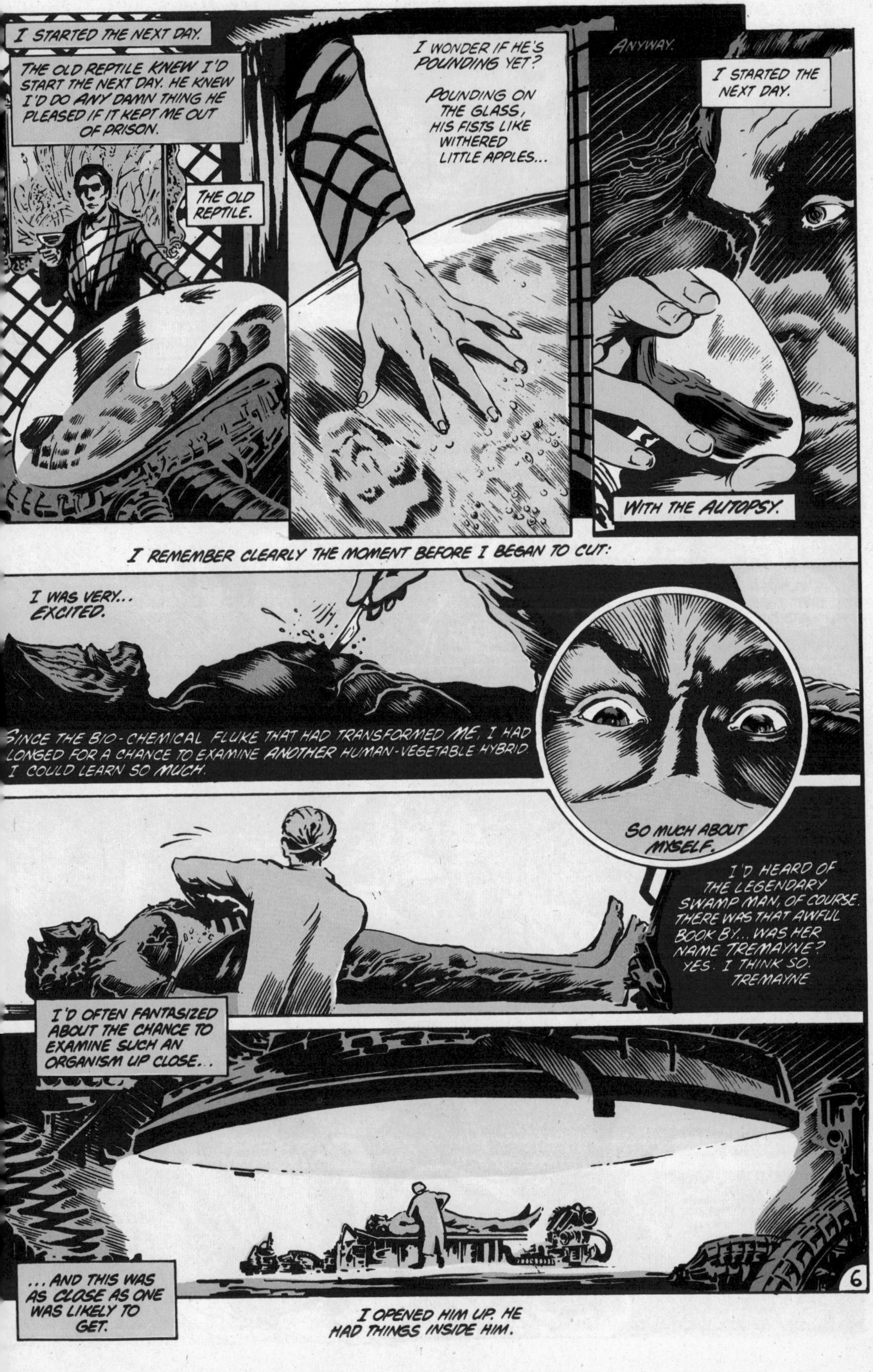
I STARTED THE NEXT DAY.
THE OLD REPTILE KNEW I'D START THE NEXT DAY. HE KNEW I'D DO ANY DAMN THING HE PLEASED IF IT KEPT ME OUT OF PRISON.
THE OLD REPTILE.
I WONDER IF HE'S POUNDING YET?
POUNDING ON THE GLASS, HIS FISTS LIKE WITHERED LITTLE APPLES...
ANYWAY.
I STARTED THE NEXT DAY.
WITH THE AUTOPSY.
I REMEMBER CLEARLY THE MOMENT BEFORE I BEGAN TO CUT:
I WAS VERY... EXCITED.
SINCE THE BIO-CHEMICAL FLUKE THAT HAD TRANSFORMED ME, I HAD LONGED FOR A CHANCE TO EXAMINE ANOTHER HUMAN-VEGETABLE HYBRID. I COULD LEARN SO MUCH.
SO MUCH ABOUT MYSELF.
I'D HEARD OF THE LEGENDARY SWAMP MAN, OF COURSE. THERE WAS THAT AWFUL BOOK BY... WAS HER NAME TREMAYNE? YES. I THINK SO. TREMAYNE
I'D OFTEN FANTASIZED ABOUT THE CHANCE TO EXAMINE SUCH AN ORGANISM UP CLOSE...
... AND THIS WAS AS CLOSE AS ONE WAS LIKELY TO GET.
6
I OPENED HIM UP. HE HAD THINGS INSIDE HIM.

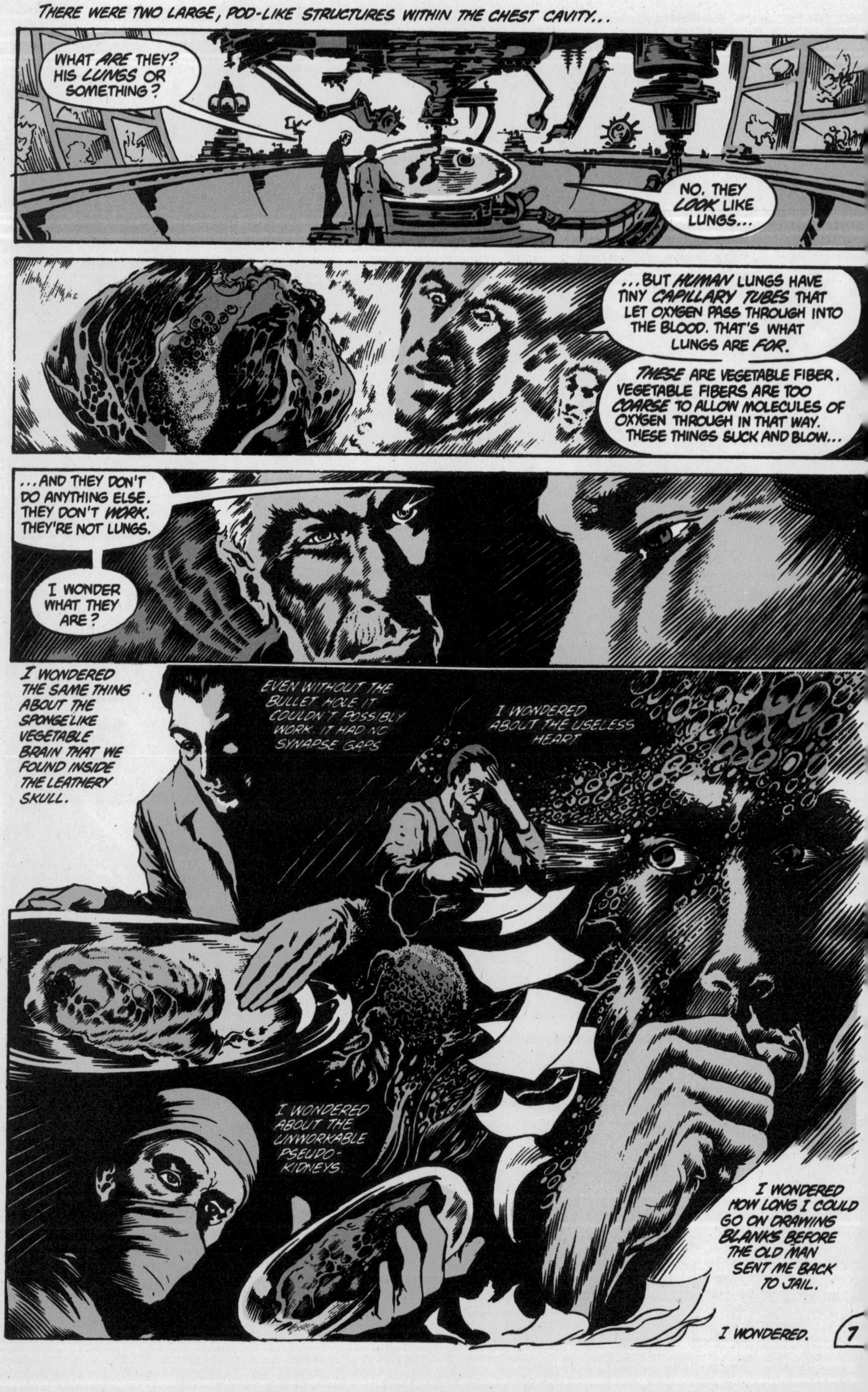
THERE WERE TWO LARGE, POD-LIKE STRUCTURES WITHIN THE CHEST CAVITY...
WHAT ARE THEY? HIS LUNGS OR SOMETHING?
NO. THEY LOOK LIKE LUNGS...
...BUT HUMAN LUNGS HAVE TINY CAPILLARY TUBES THAT LET OXYGEN PASS THROUGH INTO THE BLOOD. THAT'S WHAT LUNGS ARE FOR.
THESE ARE VEGETABLE FIBER. VEGETABLE FIBERS ARE TOO COARSE TO ALLOW MOLECULES OF OXYGEN THROUGH IN THAT WAY. THESE THINGS SUCK AND BLOW...
...AND THEY DON'T DO ANYTHING ELSE. THEY DON'T WORK. THEY'RE NOT LUNGS.
I WONDER WHAT THEY ARE?
I WONDERED THE SAME THING ABOUT THE SPONGE-LIKE VEGETABLE BRAIN THAT WE FOUND INSIDE THE LEATHERY SKULL.
EVEN WITHOUT THE BULLET HOLE IT COULDN'T POSSIBLY WORK. IT HAD NO SYNAPSE GAPS.
I WONDERED ABOUT THE USELESS HEART.
I WONDERED ABOUT THE UNWORKABLE PSEUDO-KIDNEYS.
I WONDERED HOW LONG I COULD GO ON DRAWING BLANKS BEFORE THE OLD MAN SENT ME BACK TO JAIL.
I WONDERED.
7

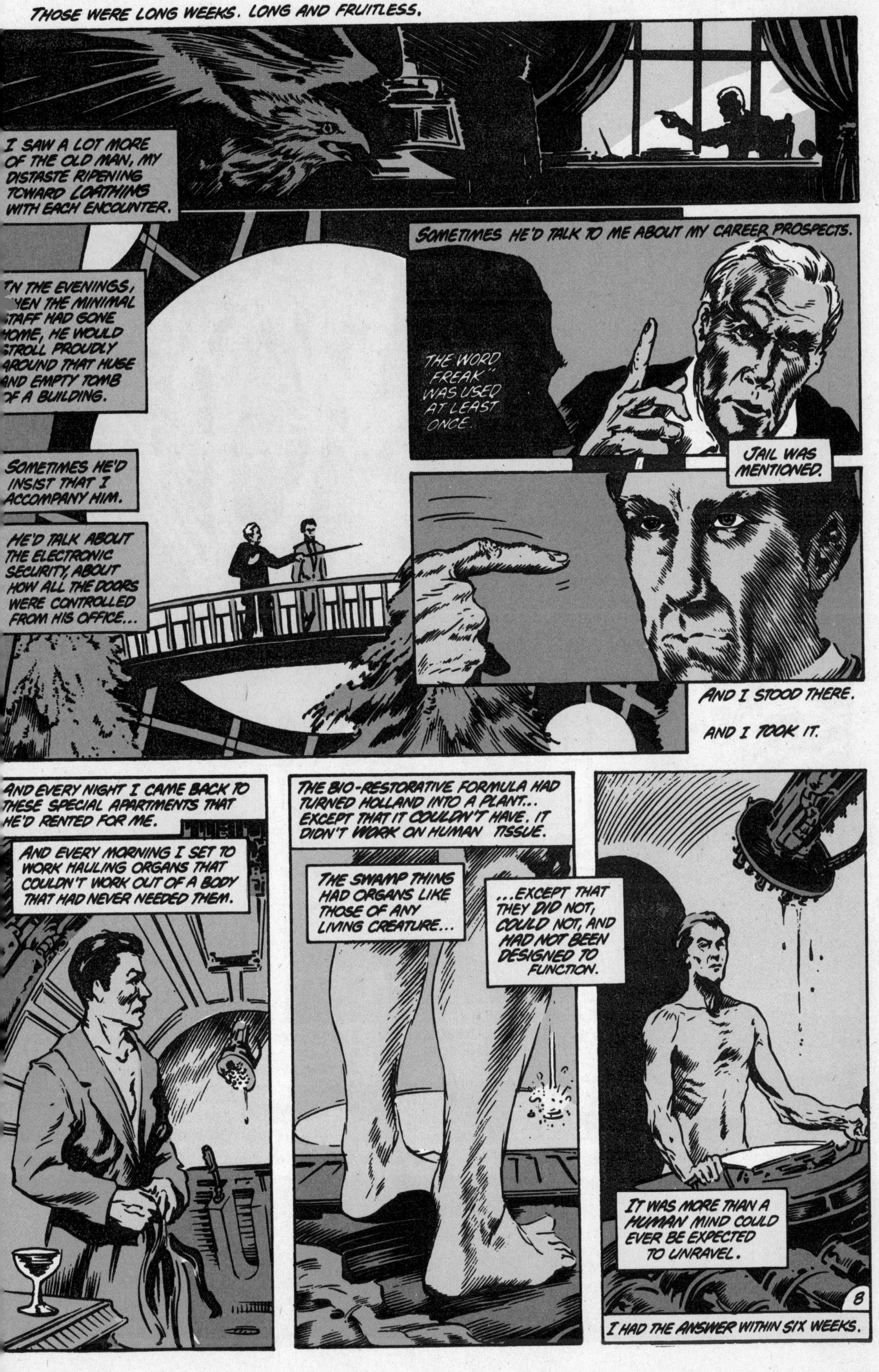
THOSE WERE LONG WEEKS. LONG AND FRUITLESS.
I SAW A LOT MORE OF THE OLD MAN, MY DISTASTE RIPENING TOWARD LOATHING WITH EACH ENCOUNTER.
IN THE EVENINGS, WHEN THE MINIMAL STAFF HAD GONE HOME, HE WOULD STROLL PROUDLY AROUND THAT HUGE AND EMPTY TOMB OF A BUILDING.
SOMETIMES HE'D INSIST THAT I ACCOMPANY HIM.
HE'D TALK ABOUT THE ELECTRONIC SECURITY, ABOUT HOW ALL THE DOORS WERE CONTROLLED FROM HIS OFFICE...
SOMETIMES HE'D TALK TO ME ABOUT MY CAREER PROSPECTS.
THE WORD "FREAK" WAS USED AT LEAST ONCE.
JAIL WAS MENTIONED.
AND I STOOD THERE.
AND I TOOK IT.
AND EVERY NIGHT I CAME BACK TO THESE SPECIAL APARTMENTS THAT HE'D RENTED FOR ME.
AND EVERY MORNING I SET TO WORK HAULING ORGANS THAT COULDN'T WORK OUT OF A BODY THAT HAD NEVER NEEDED THEM.
THE BIO-RESTORATIVE FORMULA HAD TURNED HOLLAND INTO A PLANT... EXCEPT THAT IT COULDN'T HAVE. IT DIDN'T WORK ON HUMAN TISSUE.
THE SWAMP THING HAD ORGANS LIKE THOSE OF ANY LIVING CREATURE...
...EXCEPT THAT THEY DID NOT, COULD NOT, AND HAD NOT BEEN DESIGNED TO FUNCTION.
IT WAS MORE THAN A HUMAN MIND COULD EVER BE EXPECTED TO UNRAVEL.
8
I HAD THE ANSWER WITHIN SIX WEEKS.

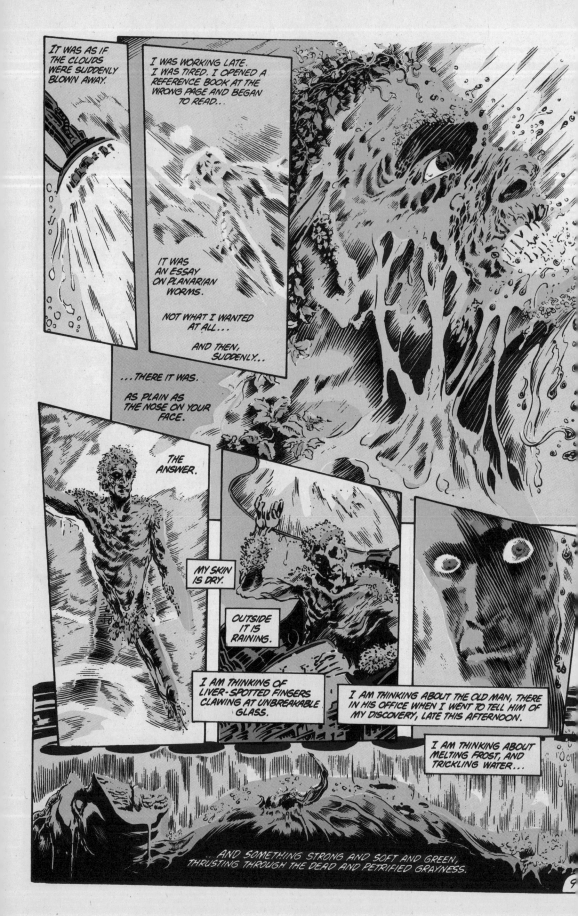

IT WAS AS IF THE CLOUDS WERE SUDDENLY BLOWN AWAY.

I WAS WORKING LATE. I WAS TIRED. I OPENED A REFERENCE BOOK AT THE WRONG PAGE AND BEGAN TO READ...

IT WAS AN ESSAY ON PLANARIAN WORMS.

NOT WHAT I WANTED AT ALL...

AND THEN, SUDDENLY...

...THERE IT WAS.

AS PLAIN AS THE NOSE ON YOUR FACE.

THE ANSWER.

MY SKIN IS DRY.

OUTSIDE IT IS RAINING.

I AM THINKING OF LIVER-SPOTTED FINGERS CLAWING AT UNBREAKABLE GLASS.

I AM THINKING ABOUT THE OLD MAN, THERE IN HIS OFFICE WHEN I WENT TO TELL HIM OF MY DISCOVERY, LATE THIS AFTERNOON.

I AM THINKING ABOUT MELTING FROST, AND TRICKLING WATER...

AND SOMETHING STRONG AND SOFT AND GREEN, THRUSTING THROUGH THE DEAD AND PETRIFIED GRAYNESS.

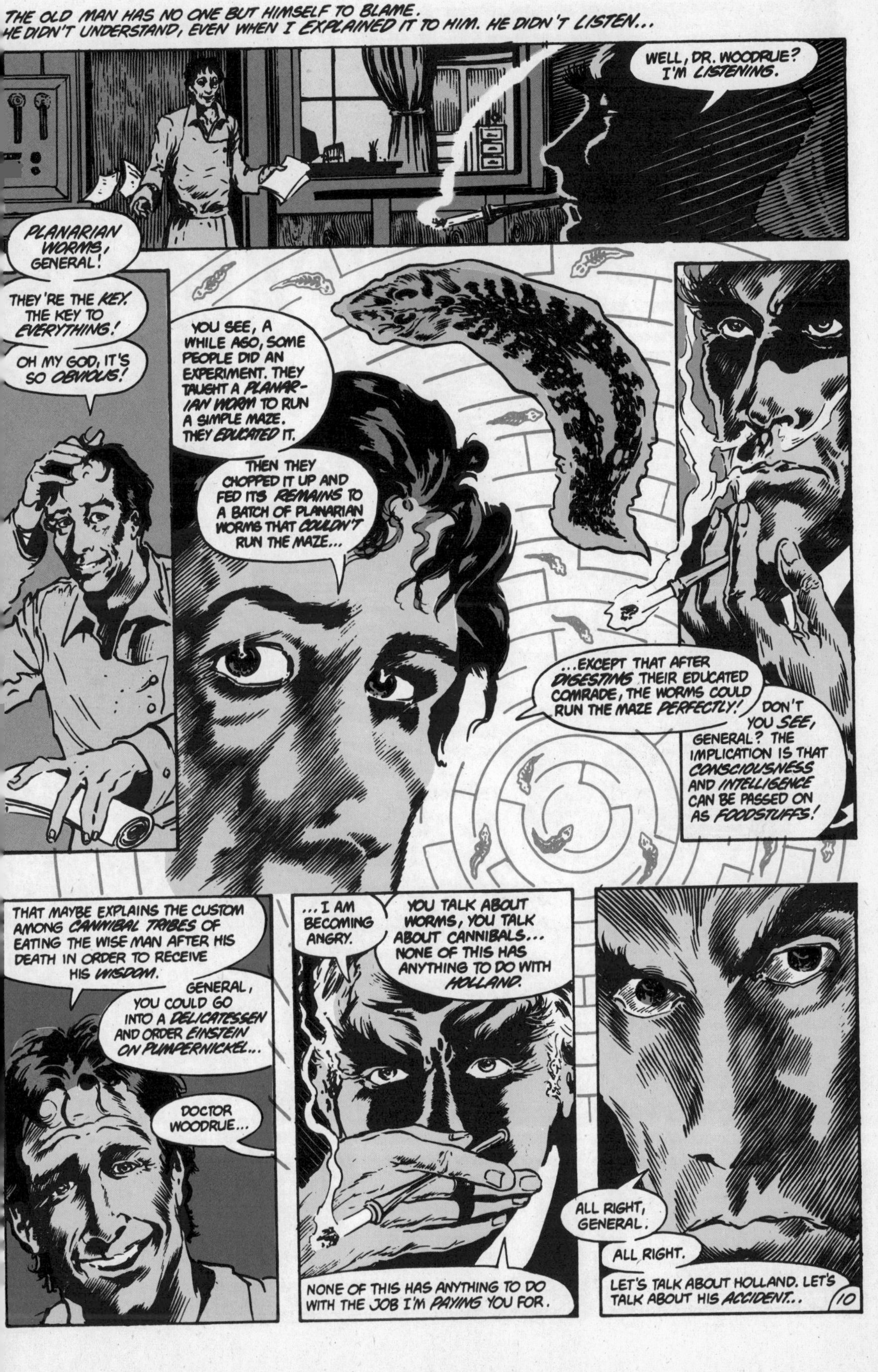
THE OLD MAN HAS NO ONE BUT HIMSELF TO BLAME.
HE DIDN'T UNDERSTAND, EVEN WHEN I EXPLAINED IT TO HIM. HE DIDN'T LISTEN...
WELL, DR. WOODRUE? I'M LISTENING.
PLANARIAN WORMS, GENERAL!
THEY'RE THE KEY. THE KEY TO EVERYTHING!
OH MY GOD, IT'S SO OBVIOUS!
YOU SEE, A WHILE AGO, SOME PEOPLE DID AN EXPERIMENT. THEY TAUGHT A PLANARIAN WORM TO RUN A SIMPLE MAZE. THEY EDUCATED IT.
THEN THEY CHOPPED IT UP AND FED ITS REMAINS TO A BATCH OF PLANARIAN WORMS THAT COULDN'T RUN THE MAZE...
...EXCEPT THAT AFTER DIGESTING THEIR EDUCATED COMRADE, THE WORMS COULD RUN THE MAZE PERFECTLY!
DON'T YOU SEE, GENERAL? THE IMPLICATION IS THAT CONSCIOUSNESS AND INTELLIGENCE CAN BE PASSED ON AS FOODSTUFFS!
THAT MAYBE EXPLAINS THE CUSTOM AMONG CANNIBAL TRIBES OF EATING THE WISE MAN AFTER HIS DEATH IN ORDER TO RECEIVE HIS WISDOM.
GENERAL, YOU COULD GO INTO A DELICATESSEN AND ORDER EINSTEIN ON PUMPERNICKEL...
DOCTOR WOODRUE...
...I AM BECOMING ANGRY.
YOU TALK ABOUT WORMS, YOU TALK ABOUT CANNIBALS... NONE OF THIS HAS ANYTHING TO DO WITH HOLLAND.
NONE OF THIS HAS ANYTHING TO DO WITH THE JOB I'M PAYING YOU FOR.
ALL RIGHT, GENERAL.
ALL RIGHT.
LET'S TALK ABOUT HOLLAND. LET'S TALK ABOUT HIS ACCIDENT...
10

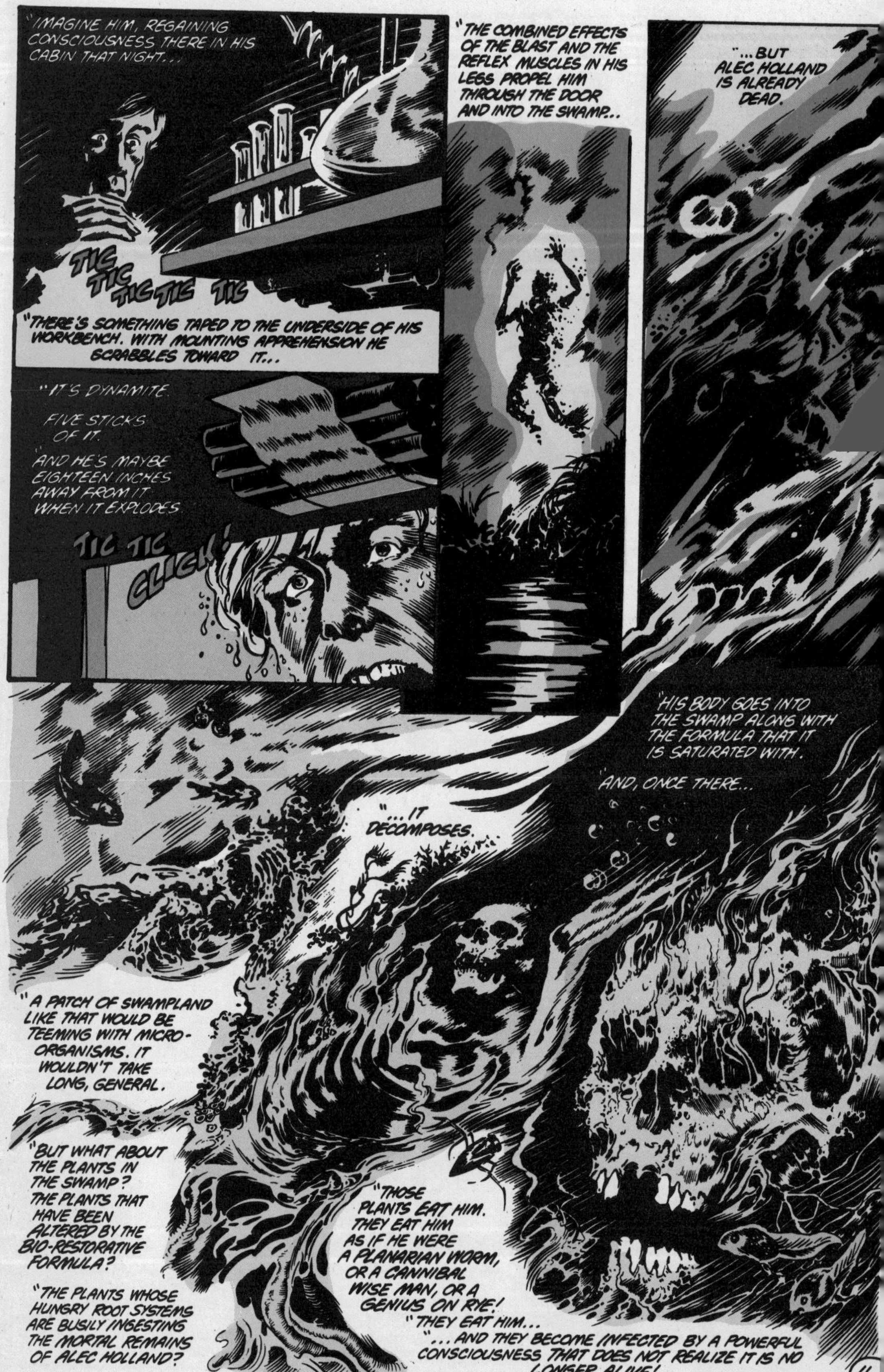
"IMAGINE HIM, REGAINING CONSCIOUSNESS THERE IN HIS CABIN THAT NIGHT...
TIC TIC TIC TIC TIC
"THERE'S SOMETHING TAPED TO THE UNDERSIDE OF HIS WORKBENCH. WITH MOUNTING APPREHENSION HE SCRABBLES TOWARD IT...
"IT'S DYNAMITE.
FIVE STICKS OF IT.
"AND HE'S MAYBE EIGHTEEN INCHES AWAY FROM IT WHEN IT EXPLODES.
TIC TIC CLICK!
"THE COMBINED EFFECTS OF THE BLAST AND THE REFLEX MUSCLES IN HIS LEGS PROPEL HIM THROUGH THE DOOR AND INTO THE SWAMP...
"...BUT ALEC HOLLAND IS ALREADY DEAD.
"HIS BODY GOES INTO THE SWAMP ALONG WITH THE FORMULA THAT IT IS SATURATED WITH.
"AND, ONCE THERE...
"...IT DECOMPOSES.
"A PATCH OF SWAMPLAND LIKE THAT WOULD BE TEEMING WITH MICRO-ORGANISMS. IT WOULDN'T TAKE LONG, GENERAL.
"BUT WHAT ABOUT THE PLANTS IN THE SWAMP? THE PLANTS THAT HAVE BEEN ALTERED BY THE BIO-RESTORATIVE FORMULA?
"THE PLANTS WHOSE HUNGRY ROOT SYSTEMS ARE BUSILY INGESTING THE MORTAL REMAINS OF ALEC HOLLAND?
"THOSE PLANTS EAT HIM. THEY EAT HIM AS IF HE WERE A PLANARIAN WORM, OR A CANNIBAL WISE MAN, OR A GENIUS ON RYE!
"THEY EAT HIM...
"...AND THEY BECOME INFECTED BY A POWERFUL CONSCIOUSNESS THAT DOES NOT REALIZE IT IS NO LONGER ALIVE!
11

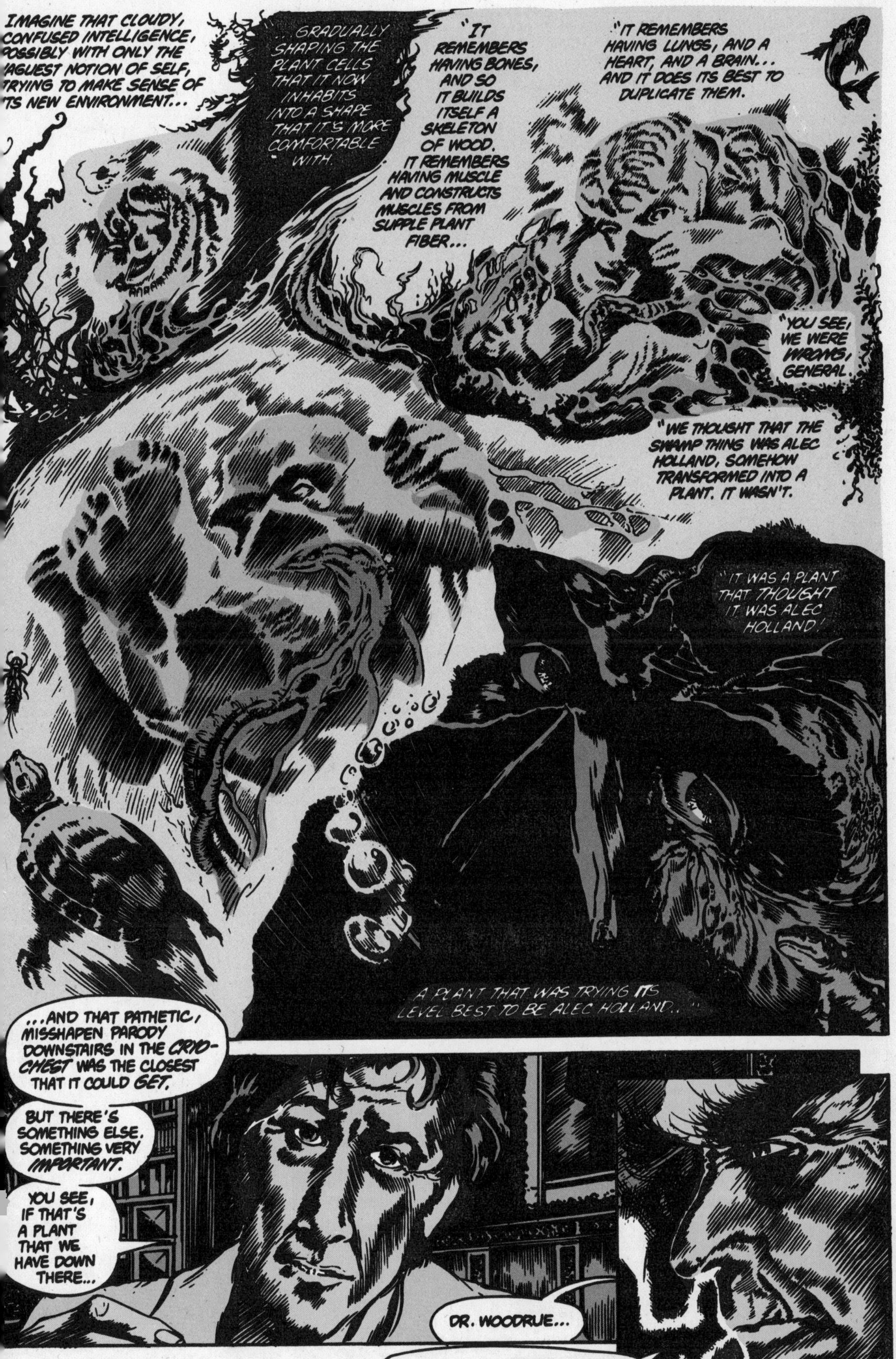
IMAGINE THAT CLOUDY, CONFUSED INTELLIGENCE, POSSIBLY WITH ONLY THE VAGUEST NOTION OF SELF, TRYING TO MAKE SENSE OF ITS NEW ENVIRONMENT...
...GRADUALLY SHAPING THE PLANT CELLS THAT IT NOW INHABITS INTO A SHAPE THAT IT'S MORE COMFORTABLE WITH.
"IT REMEMBERS HAVING BONES, AND SO IT BUILDS ITSELF A SKELETON OF WOOD. IT REMEMBERS HAVING MUSCLE AND CONSTRUCTS MUSCLES FROM SUPPLE PLANT FIBER...
"IT REMEMBERS HAVING LUNGS, AND A HEART, AND A BRAIN... AND IT DOES ITS BEST TO DUPLICATE THEM.
"YOU SEE, WE WERE WRONG, GENERAL.
"WE THOUGHT THAT THE SWAMP THING WAS ALEC HOLLAND, SOMEHOW TRANSFORMED INTO A PLANT. IT WASN'T.
"IT WAS A PLANT THAT THOUGHT IT WAS ALEC HOLLAND!
A PLANT THAT WAS TRYING ITS LEVEL BEST TO BE ALEC HOLLAND..."
...AND THAT PATHETIC, MISSHAPEN PARODY DOWNSTAIRS IN THE CRYO-CHEST WAS THE CLOSEST THAT IT COULD GET.
BUT THERE'S SOMETHING ELSE. SOMETHING VERY IMPORTANT.
YOU SEE, IF THAT'S A PLANT THAT WE HAVE DOWN THERE...
DR. WOODRUE...
...I THINK I'VE HEARD ENOUGH.
12

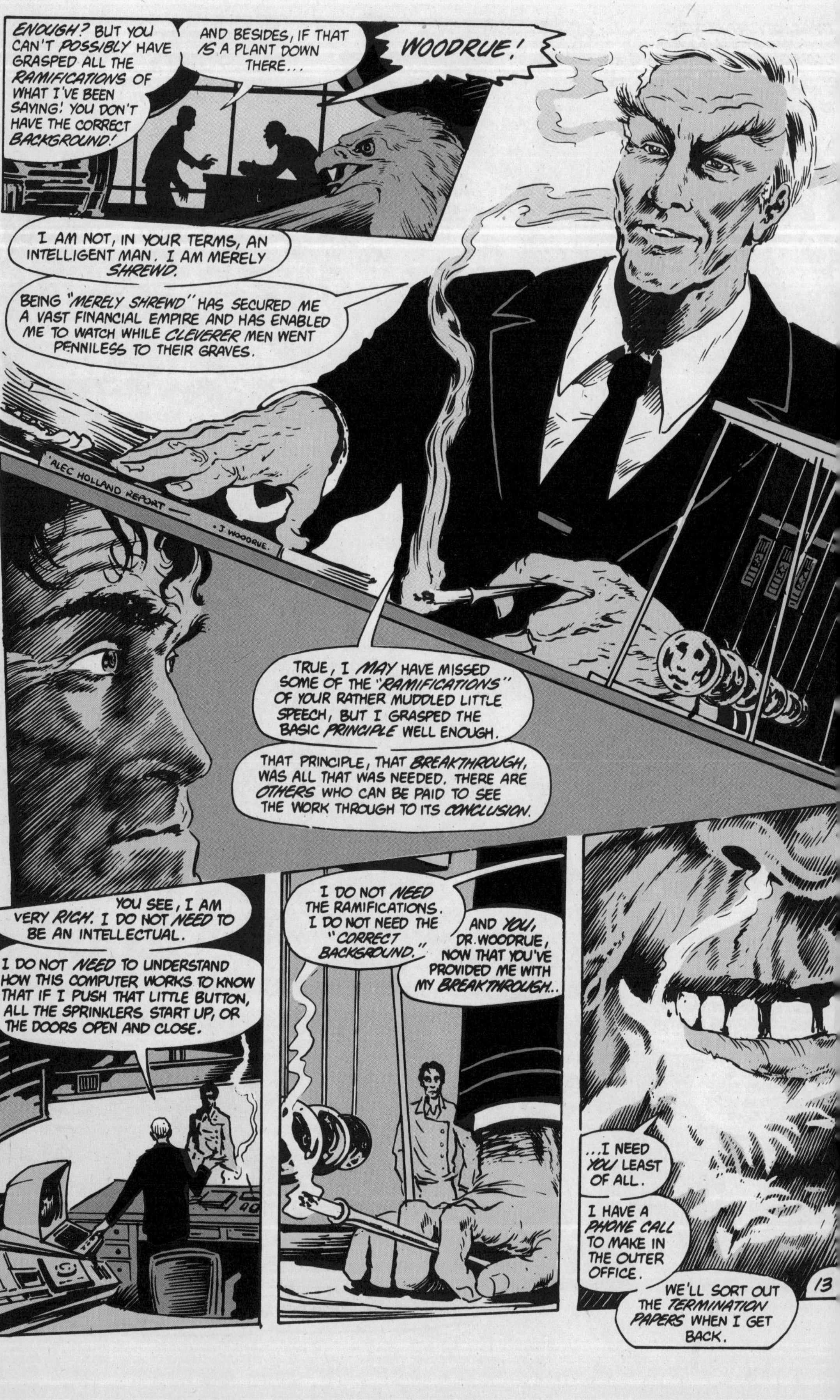
ENOUGH? BUT YOU CAN'T POSSIBLY HAVE GRASPED ALL THE RAMIFICATIONS OF WHAT I'VE BEEN SAYING! YOU DON'T HAVE THE CORRECT BACKGROUND!
AND BESIDES, IF THAT IS A PLANT DOWN THERE...
WOODRUE!
I AM NOT, IN YOUR TERMS, AN INTELLIGENT MAN. I AM MERELY SHREWD.
BEING "MERELY SHREWD" HAS SECURED ME A VAST FINANCIAL EMPIRE AND HAS ENABLED ME TO WATCH WHILE CLEVERER MEN WENT PENNILESS TO THEIR GRAVES.
ALEC HOLLAND REPORT
J. WOODRUE.
TRUE, I MAY HAVE MISSED SOME OF THE "RAMIFICATIONS" OF YOUR RATHER MUDDLED LITTLE SPEECH, BUT I GRASPED THE BASIC PRINCIPLE WELL ENOUGH.
THAT PRINCIPLE, THAT BREAKTHROUGH, WAS ALL THAT WAS NEEDED. THERE ARE OTHERS WHO CAN BE PAID TO SEE THE WORK THROUGH TO ITS CONCLUSION.
YOU SEE, I AM VERY RICH. I DO NOT NEED TO BE AN INTELLECTUAL.
I DO NOT NEED TO UNDERSTAND HOW THIS COMPUTER WORKS TO KNOW THAT IF I PUSH THAT LITTLE BUTTON, ALL THE SPRINKLERS START UP, OR THE DOORS OPEN AND CLOSE.
I DO NOT NEED THE RAMIFICATIONS. I DO NOT NEED THE "CORRECT BACKGROUND."
AND YOU, DR. WOODRUE, NOW THAT YOU'VE PROVIDED ME WITH MY BREAKTHROUGH...
...I NEED YOU LEAST OF ALL.
I HAVE A PHONE CALL TO MAKE IN THE OUTER OFFICE.
WE'LL SORT OUT THE TERMINATION PAPERS WHEN I GET BACK.
13

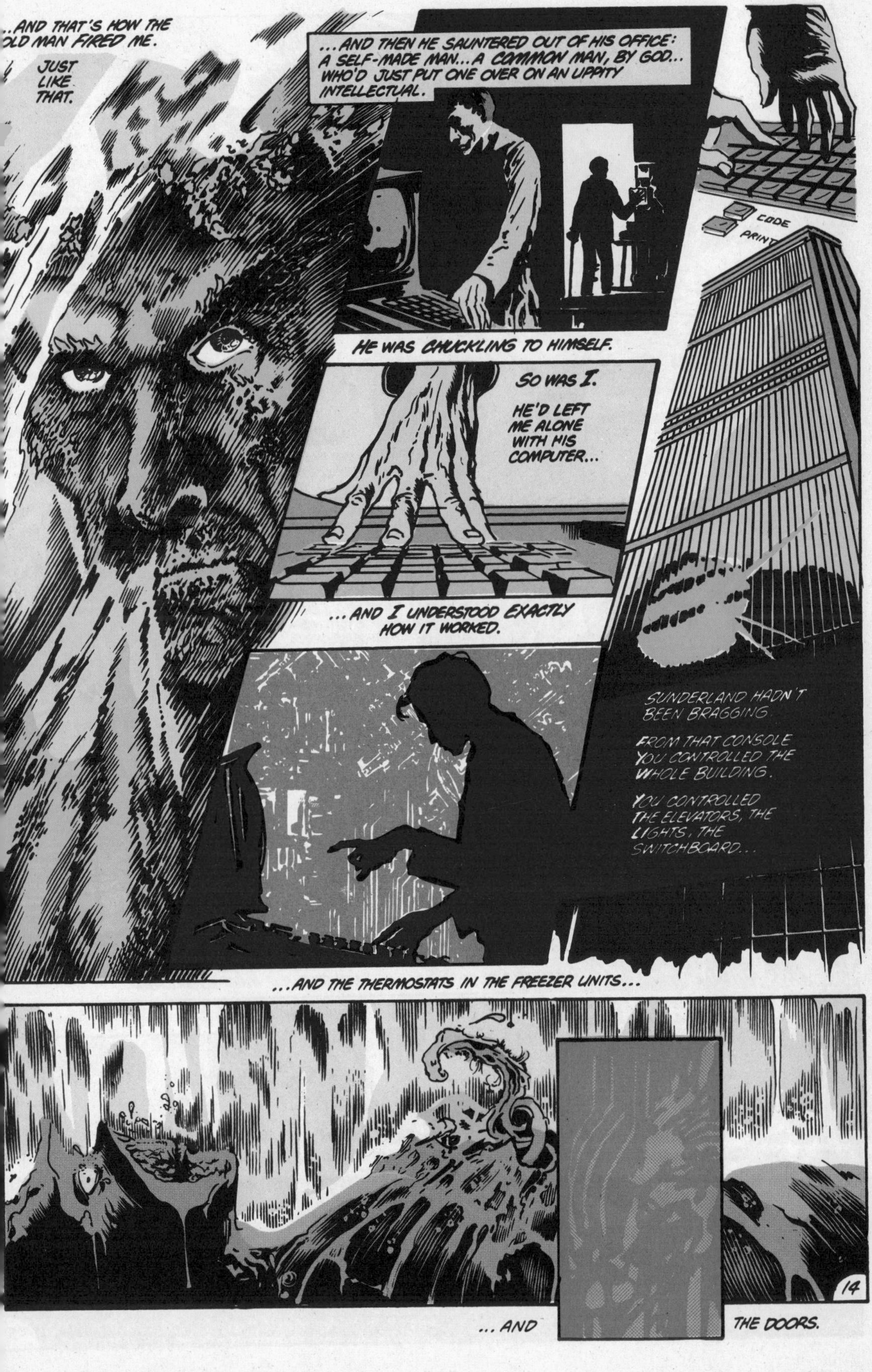
...AND THAT'S HOW THE OLD MAN FIRED ME.
JUST LIKE THAT.
...AND THEN HE SAUNTERED OUT OF HIS OFFICE: A SELF-MADE MAN... A COMMON MAN, BY GOD... WHO'D JUST PUT ONE OVER ON AN UPPITY INTELLECTUAL.
CODE
PRINT
HE WAS CHUCKLING TO HIMSELF.
SO WAS I.
HE'D LEFT ME ALONE WITH HIS COMPUTER...
...AND I UNDERSTOOD EXACTLY HOW IT WORKED.
SUNDERLAND HADN'T BEEN BRAGGING.
FROM THAT CONSOLE YOU CONTROLLED THE WHOLE BUILDING.
YOU CONTROLLED THE ELEVATORS, THE LIGHTS, THE SWITCHBOARD...
...AND THE THERMOSTATS IN THE FREEZER UNITS...
14
...AND
THE DOORS.

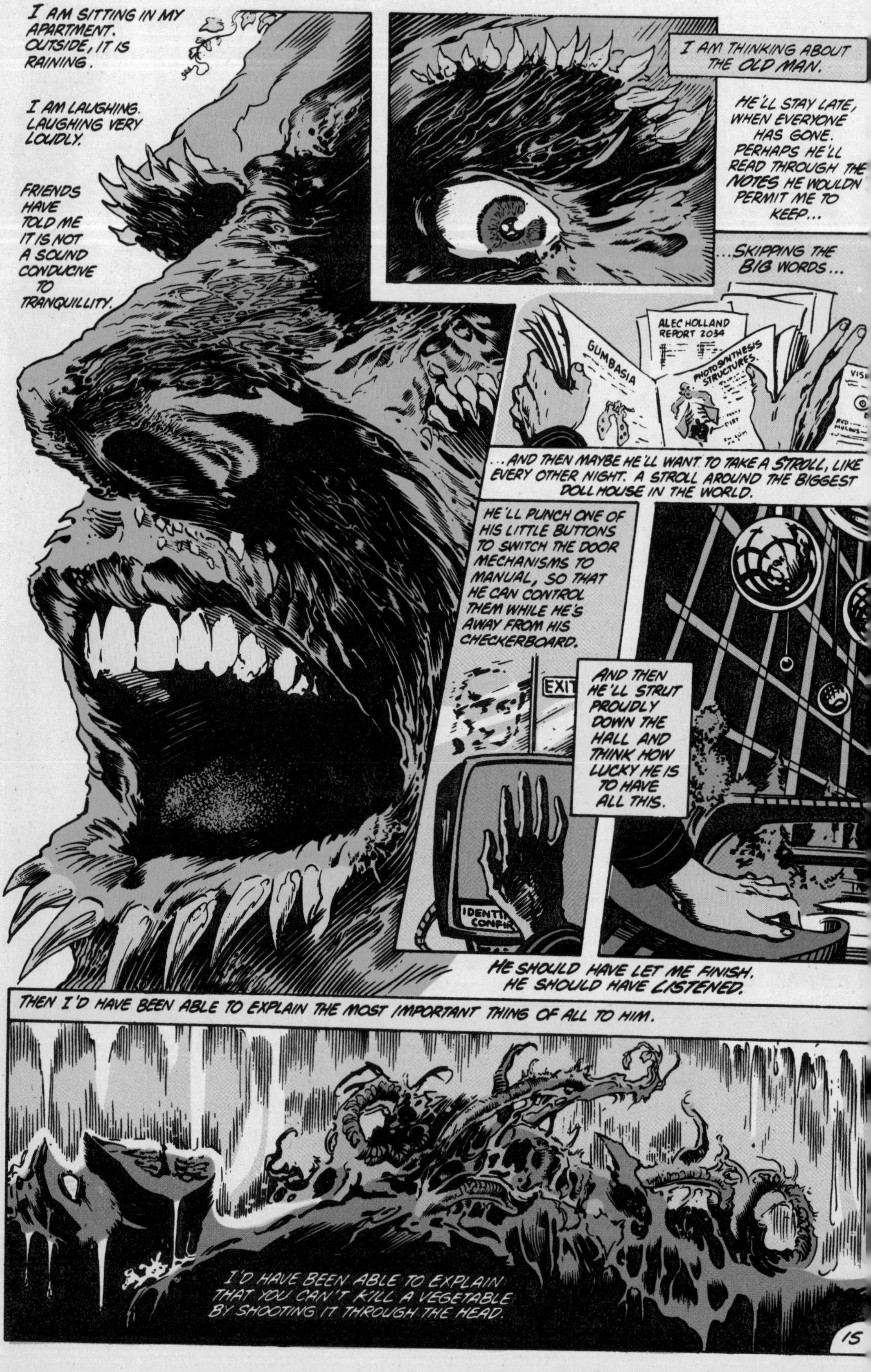
I AM SITTING IN MY APARTMENT. OUTSIDE, IT IS RAINING.
I AM LAUGHING. LAUGHING VERY LOUDLY.
FRIENDS HAVE TOLD ME IT IS NOT A SOUND CONDUCIVE TO TRANQUILLITY.
I AM THINKING ABOUT THE OLD MAN.
HE'LL STAY LATE, WHEN EVERYONE HAS GONE. PERHAPS HE'LL READ THROUGH THE NOTES HE WOULDN PERMIT ME TO KEEP...
...SKIPPING THE BIG WORDS...
ALEC HOLLAND REPORT 2034
GUMBASIA
PHOTOSYNTHESIS STRUCTURES.
...AND THEN MAYBE HE'LL WANT TO TAKE A STROLL, LIKE EVERY OTHER NIGHT. A STROLL AROUND THE BIGGEST DOLL HOUSE IN THE WORLD.
HE'LL PUNCH ONE OF HIS LITTLE BUTTONS TO SWITCH THE DOOR MECHANISMS TO MANUAL, SO THAT HE CAN CONTROL THEM WHILE HE'S AWAY FROM HIS CHECKERBOARD.
EXIT
AND THEN HE'LL STRUT PROUDLY DOWN THE HALL AND THINK HOW LUCKY HE IS TO HAVE ALL THIS.
HE SHOULD HAVE LET ME FINISH. HE SHOULD HAVE LISTENED.
THEN I'D HAVE BEEN ABLE TO EXPLAIN THE MOST IMPORTANT THING OF ALL TO HIM.
I'D HAVE BEEN ABLE TO EXPLAIN THAT YOU CAN'T KILL A VEGETABLE BY SHOOTING IT THROUGH THE HEAD.
15

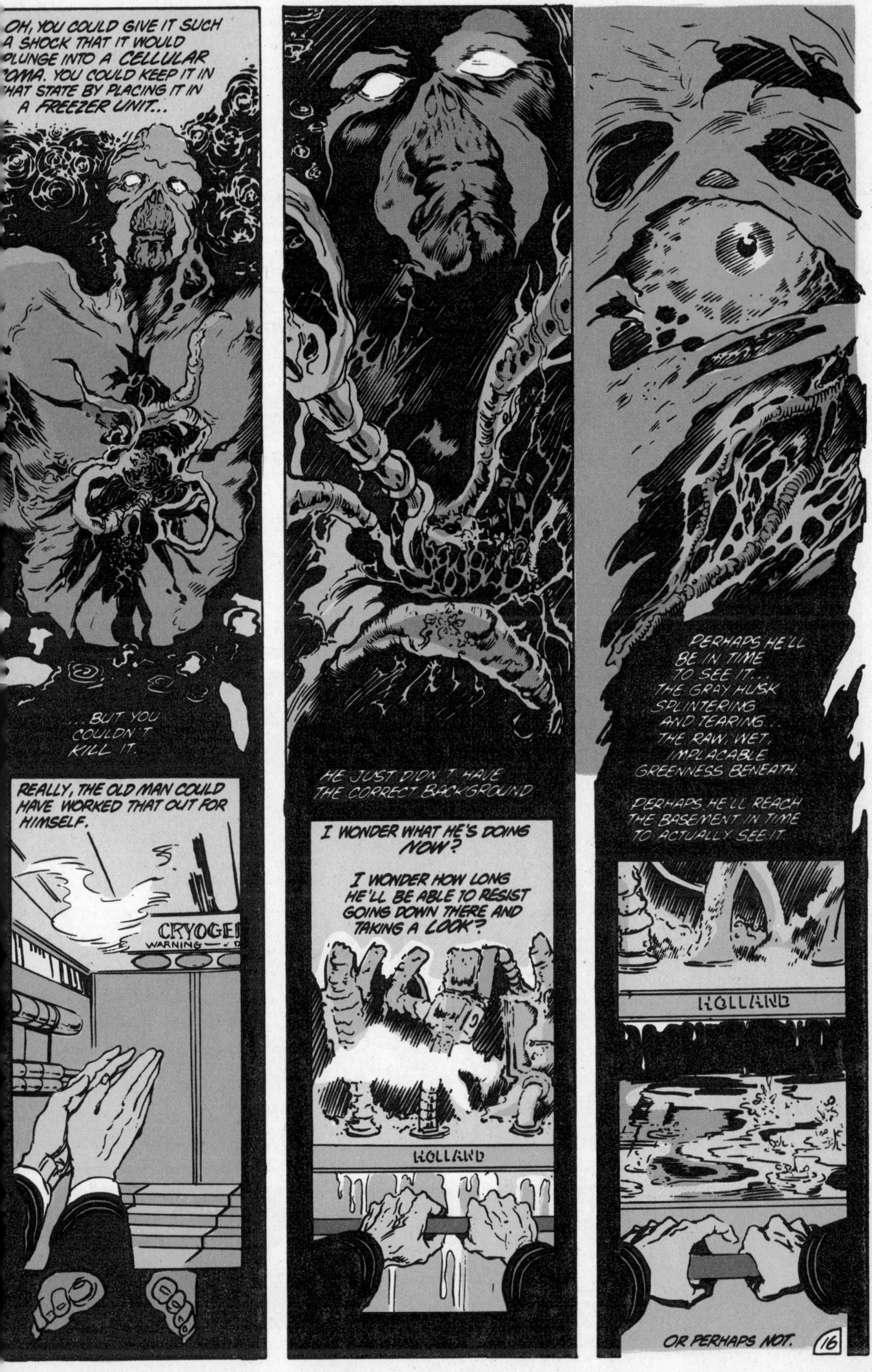
OH, YOU COULD GIVE IT SUCH A SHOCK THAT IT WOULD PLUNGE INTO A CELLULAR COMA. YOU COULD KEEP IT IN THAT STATE BY PLACING IT IN A FREEZER UNIT...
...BUT YOU COULDN'T KILL IT.
HE JUST DIDN'T HAVE THE CORRECT BACKGROUND.
PERHAPS HE'LL BE IN TIME TO SEE IT... THE GRAY HUSK SPLINTERING AND TEARING... THE RAW, WET, IMPLACABLE GREENNESS BENEATH.
REALLY, THE OLD MAN COULD HAVE WORKED THAT OUT FOR HIMSELF.
CRYOGE
WARNING
I WONDER WHAT HE'S DOING NOW?
I WONDER HOW LONG HE'LL BE ABLE TO RESIST GOING DOWN THERE AND TAKING A LOOK?
HOLLAND
PERHAPS HE'LL REACH THE BASEMENT IN TIME TO ACTUALLY SEE IT.
HOLLAND
OR PERHAPS NOT.
16

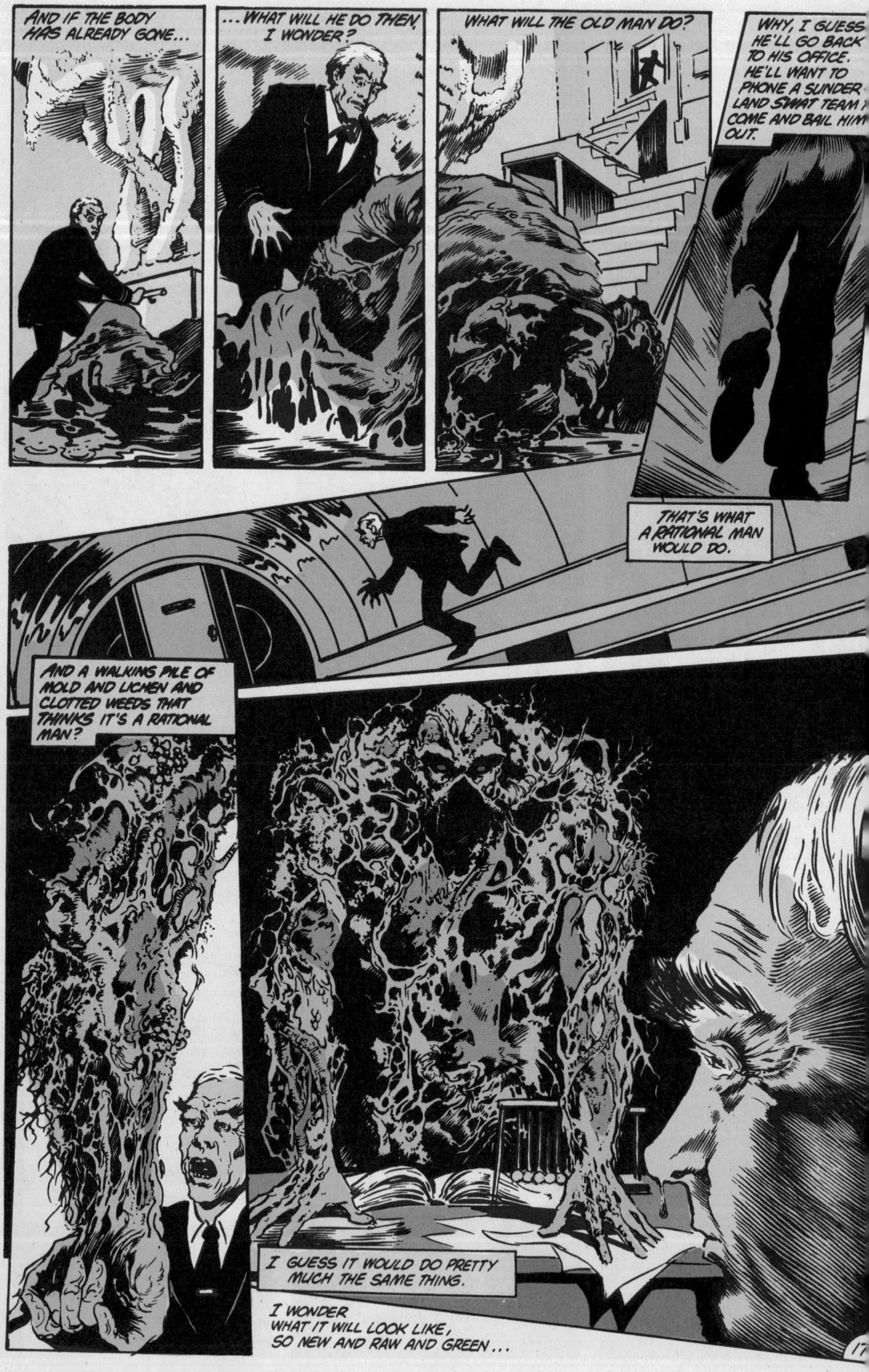
AND IF THE BODY HAS ALREADY GONE...
...WHAT WILL HE DO THEN, I WONDER?
WHAT WILL THE OLD MAN DO?
WHY, I GUESS HE'LL GO BACK TO HIS OFFICE. HE'LL WANT TO PHONE A SUNDERLAND SWAT TEAM TO COME AND BAIL HIM OUT.
THAT'S WHAT A RATIONAL MAN WOULD DO.
AND A WALKING PILE OF MOLD AND LICHEN AND CLOTTED WEEDS THAT THINKS IT'S A RATIONAL MAN?
I GUESS IT WOULD DO PRETTY MUCH THE SAME THING.
I WONDER WHAT IT WILL LOOK LIKE, SO NEW AND RAW AND GREEN...
17

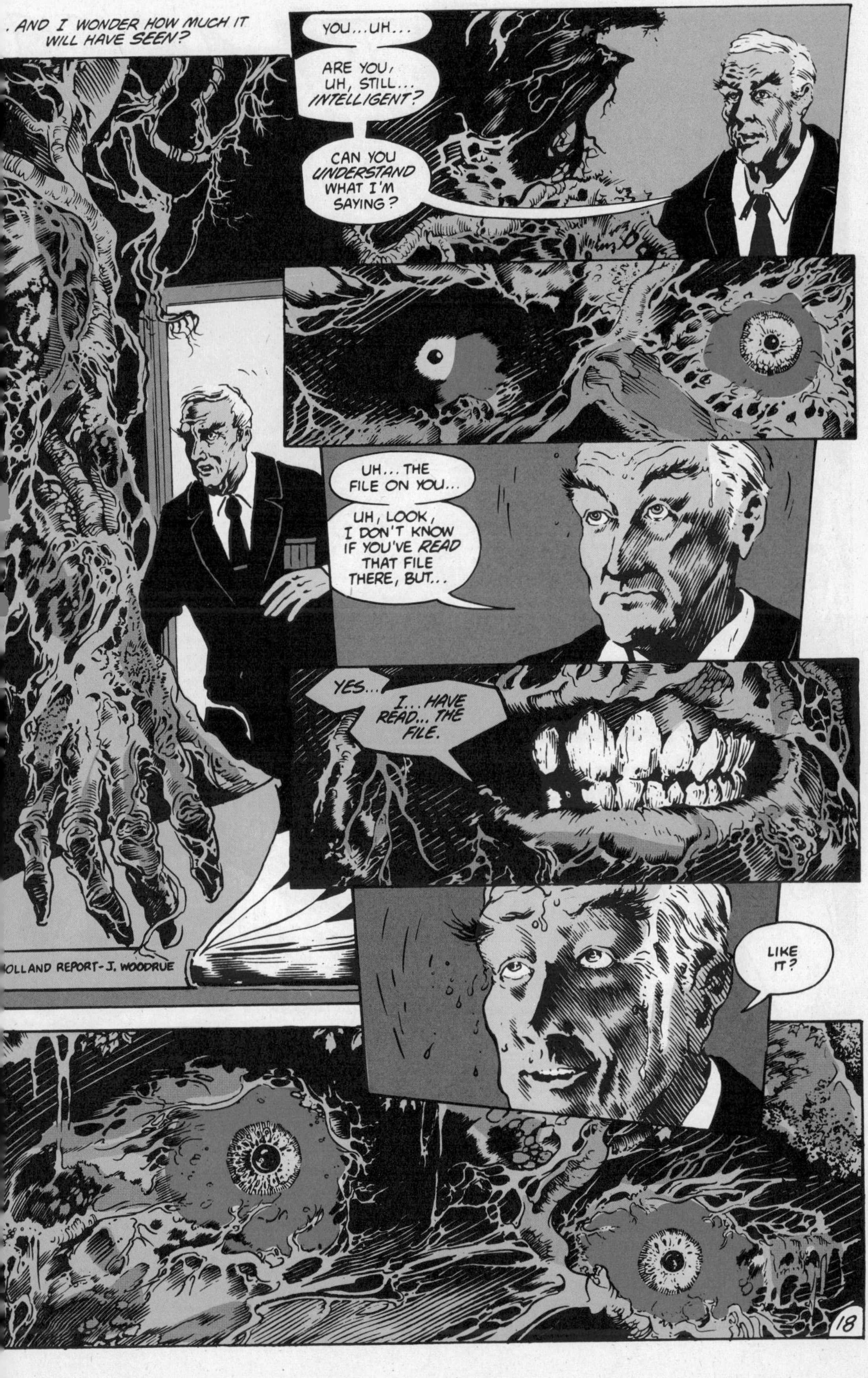
...AND I WONDER HOW MUCH IT WILL HAVE SEEN?
YOU...UH...
ARE YOU, UH, STILL... INTELLIGENT?
CAN YOU UNDERSTAND WHAT I'M SAYING?
UH... THE FILE ON YOU...
UH, LOOK, I DON'T KNOW IF YOU'VE READ THAT FILE THERE, BUT...
YES... I... HAVE READ... THE FILE.
OLLAND REPORT - J. WOODRUE
LIKE IT?
18

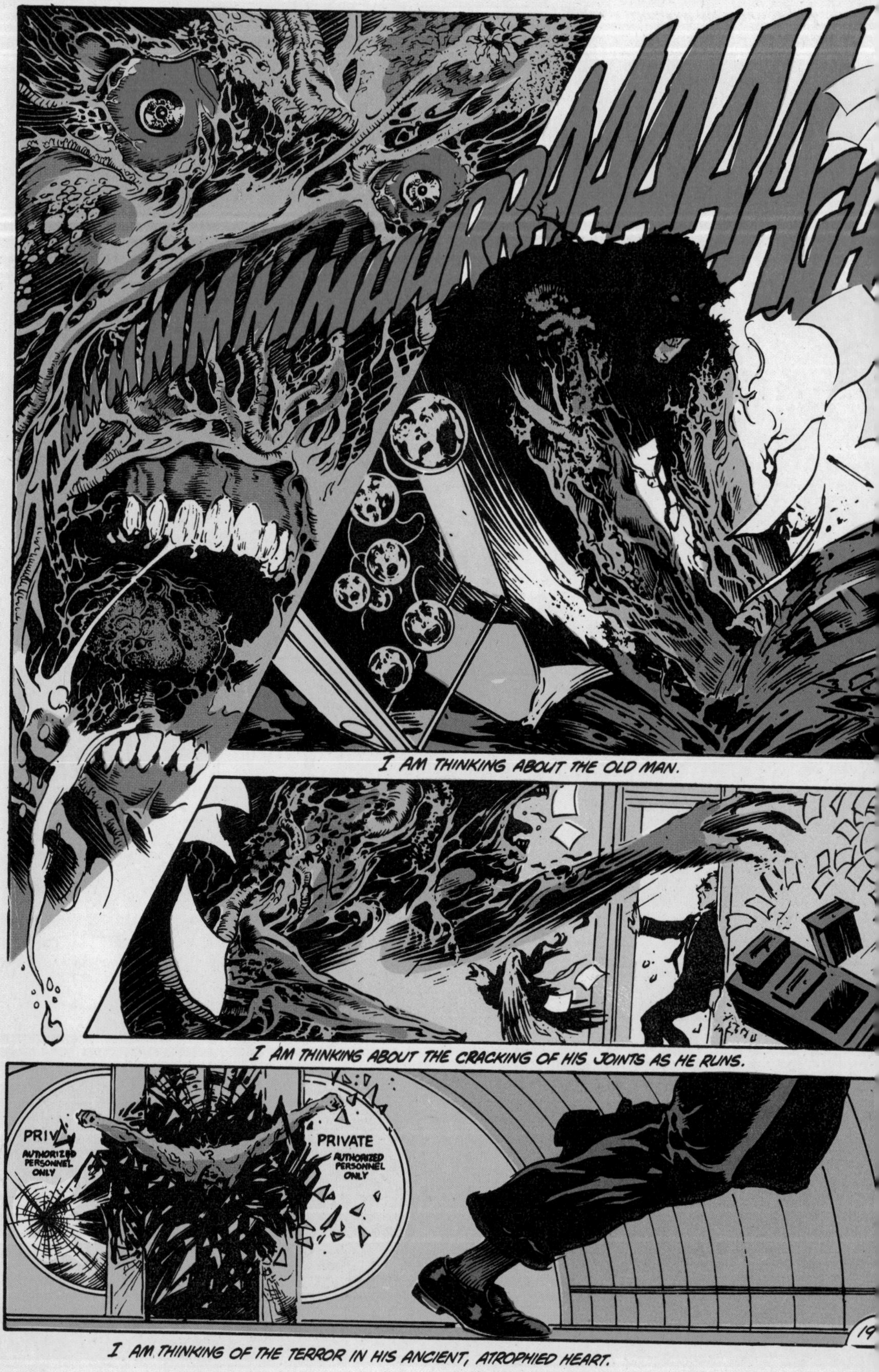
MMMMMMMMMMMUHRRRAAAAAAAAGH
I AM THINKING ABOUT THE OLD MAN.
I AM THINKING ABOUT THE CRACKING OF HIS JOINTS AS HE RUNS.
PRIV
AUTHORIZED PERSONNEL ONLY
PRIVATE
AUTHORIZED PERSONNEL ONLY
19
I AM THINKING OF THE TERROR IN HIS ANCIENT, ATROPHIED HEART.

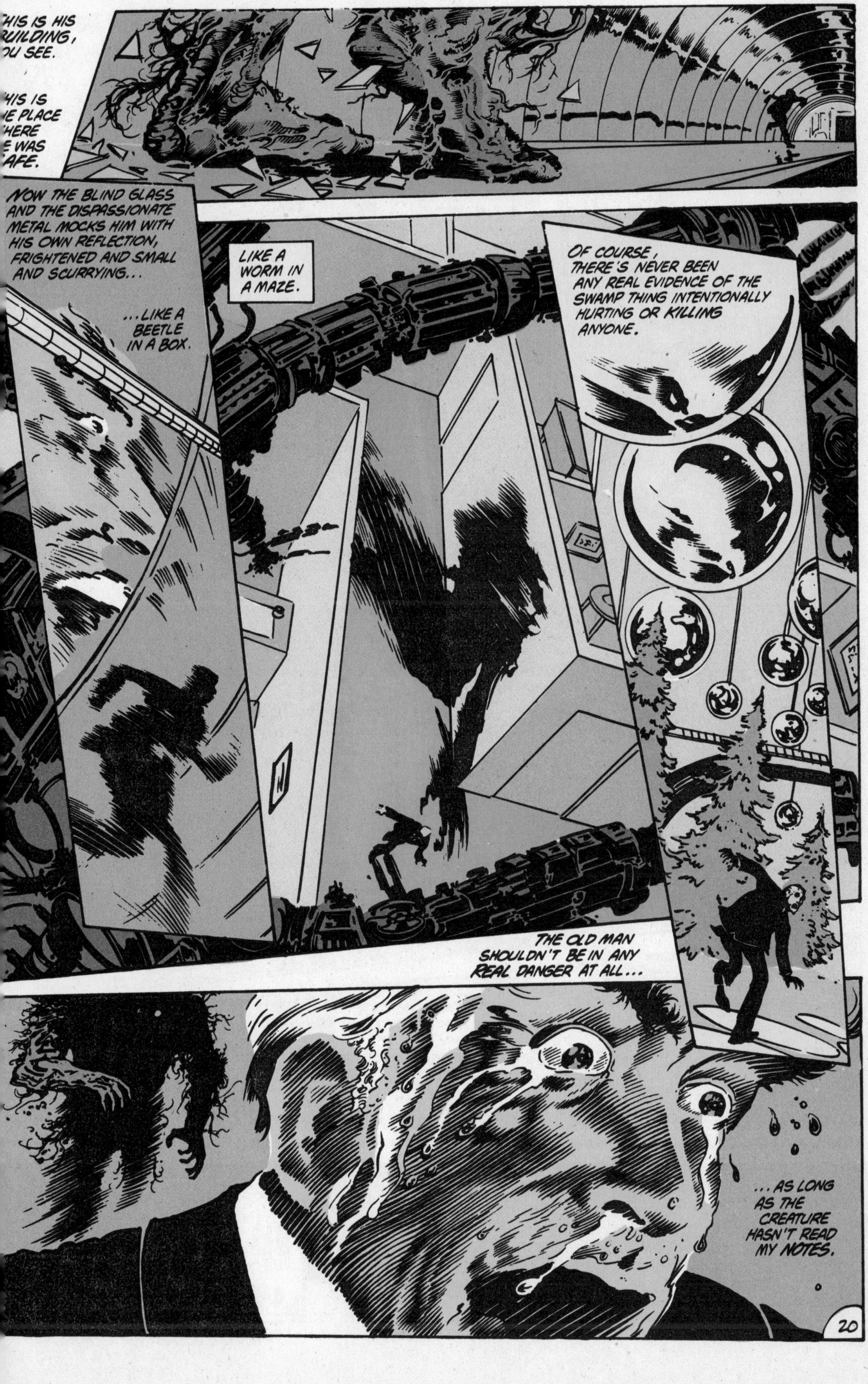
HIS IS HIS UILDING, OU SEE.
HIS IS E PLACE HERE E WAS AFE.
NOW THE BLIND GLASS AND THE DISPASSIONATE METAL MOCKS HIM WITH HIS OWN REFLECTION, FRIGHTENED AND SMALL AND SCURRYING...
...LIKE A BEETLE IN A BOX.
LIKE A WORM IN A MAZE.
OF COURSE, THERE'S NEVER BEEN ANY REAL EVIDENCE OF THE SWAMP THING INTENTIONALLY HURTING OR KILLING ANYONE.
THE OLD MAN SHOULDN'T BE IN ANY REAL DANGER AT ALL...
...AS LONG AS THE CREATURE HASN'T READ MY NOTES.
20

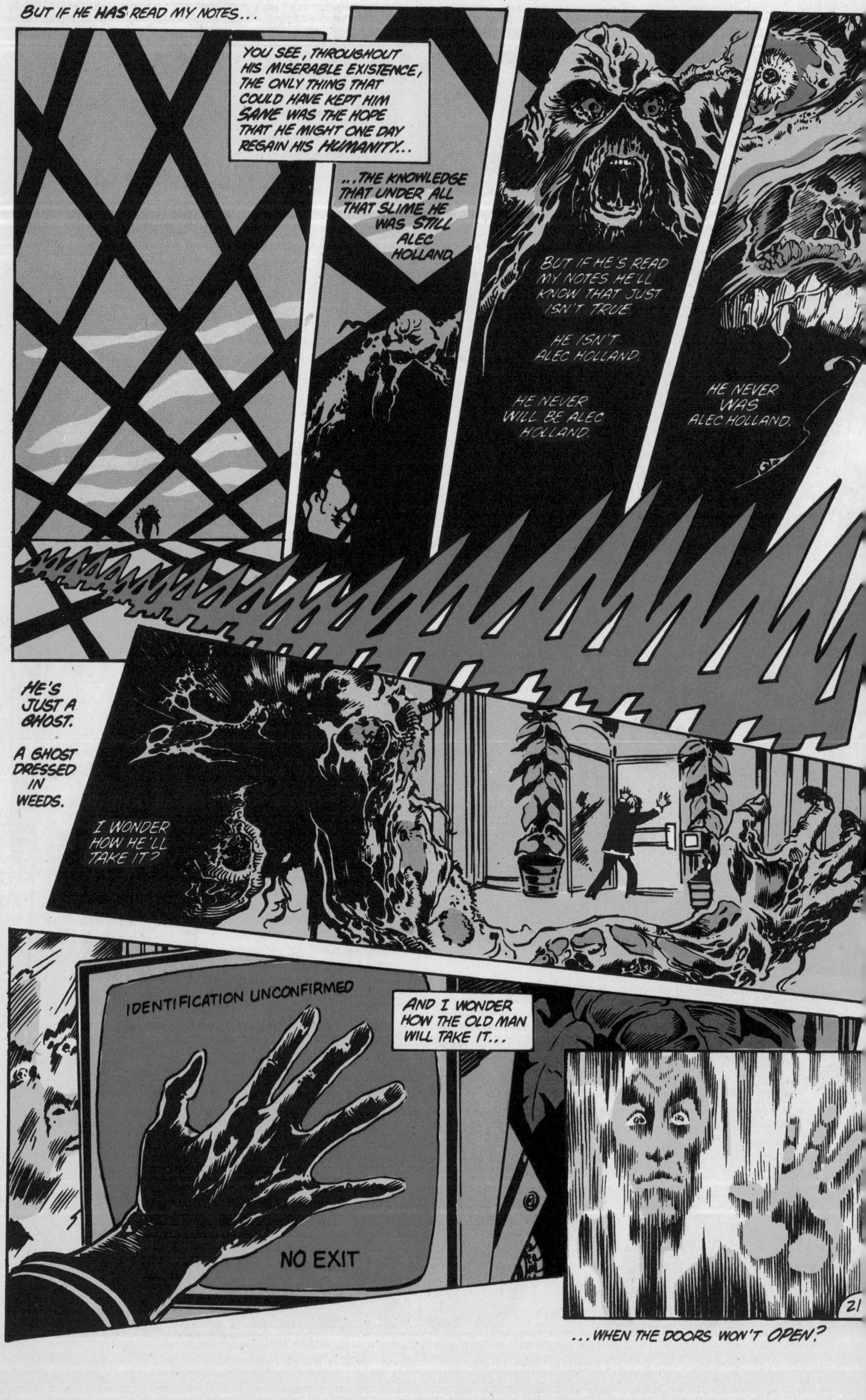
BUT IF HE HAS READ MY NOTES...
YOU SEE, THROUGHOUT HIS MISERABLE EXISTENCE, THE ONLY THING THAT COULD HAVE KEPT HIM SANE WAS THE HOPE THAT HE MIGHT ONE DAY REGAIN HIS HUMANITY...
...THE KNOWLEDGE THAT UNDER ALL THAT SLIME HE WAS STILL ALEC HOLLAND.
BUT IF HE'S READ MY NOTES HE'LL KNOW THAT JUST ISN'T TRUE.
HE ISN'T ALEC HOLLAND.
HE NEVER WILL BE ALEC HOLLAND.
HE NEVER WAS ALEC HOLLAND.
HE'S JUST A GHOST.
A GHOST DRESSED IN WEEDS.
I WONDER HOW HE'LL TAKE IT?
IDENTIFICATION UNCONFIRMED
NO EXIT
AND I WONDER HOW THE OLD MAN WILL TAKE IT...
21
...WHEN THE DOORS WON'T OPEN?

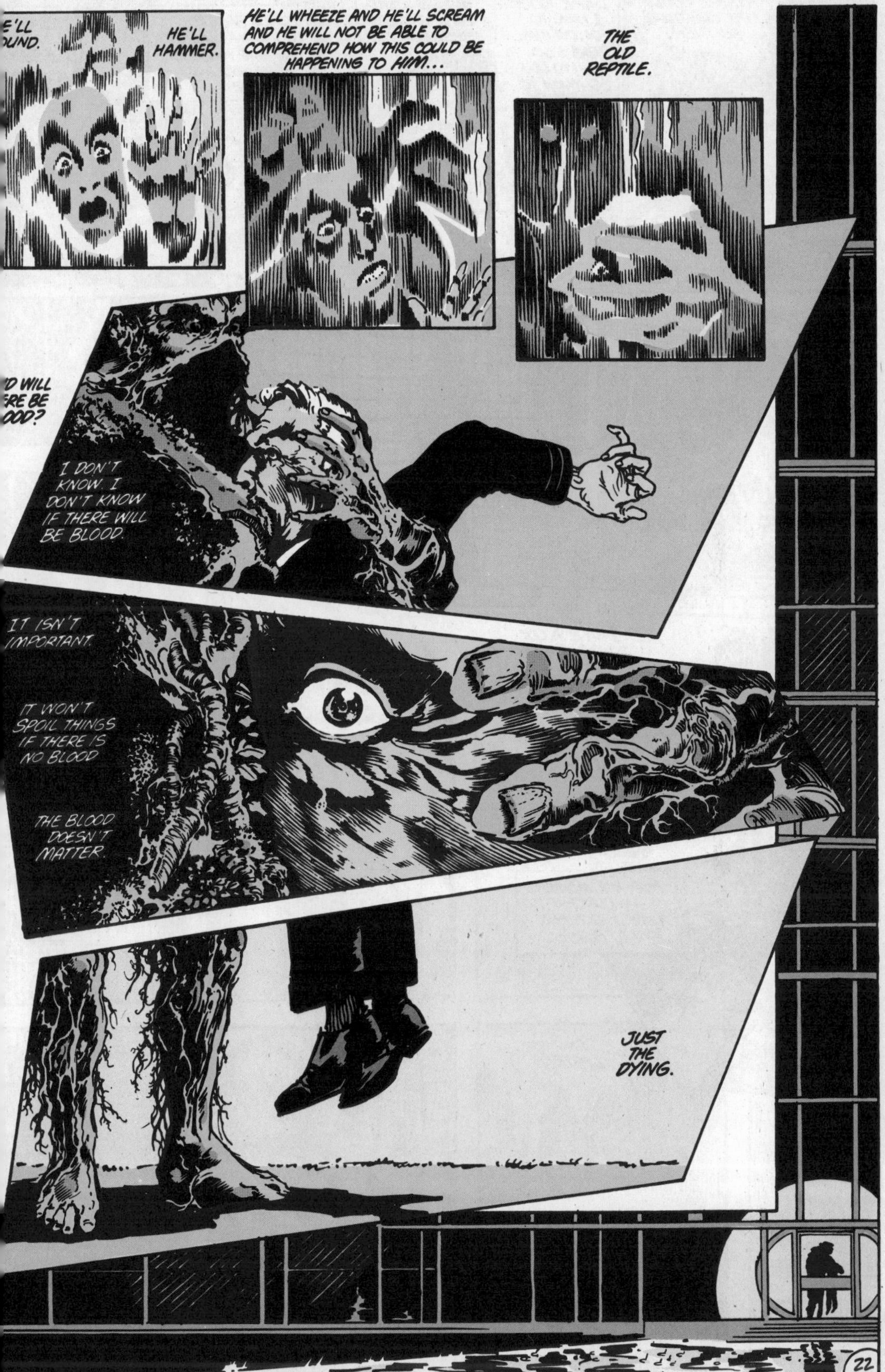
E'LL
UND.
HE'LL
HAMMER.
HE'LL WHEEZE AND HE'LL SCREAM AND HE WILL NOT BE ABLE TO COMPREHEND HOW THIS COULD BE HAPPENING TO HIM...
THE OLD REPTILE.
D WILL
ERE BE
OOD?
I DON'T KNOW. I DON'T KNOW IF THERE WILL BE BLOOD.
IT ISN'T IMPORTANT.
IT WON'T SPOIL THINGS IF THERE IS NO BLOOD.
THE BLOOD DOESN'T MATTER.
JUST THE DYING.
22
THE DYING'S ALL THAT MATTERS.

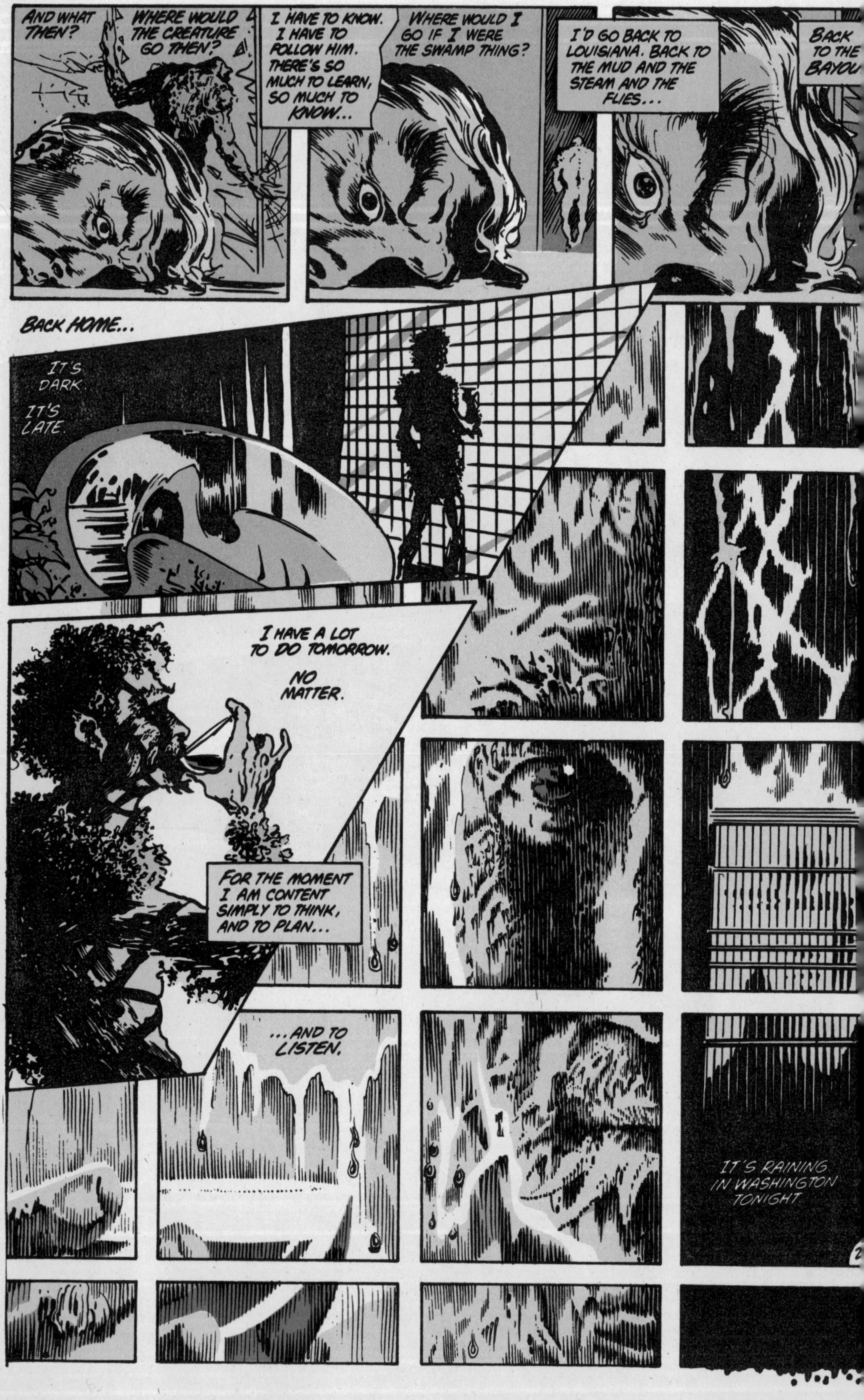
AND WHAT THEN?
WHERE WOULD THE CREATURE GO THEN?
I HAVE TO KNOW. I HAVE TO FOLLOW HIM. THERE'S SO MUCH TO LEARN, SO MUCH TO KNOW...
WHERE WOULD I GO IF I WERE THE SWAMP THING?
I'D GO BACK TO LOUISIANA. BACK TO THE MUD AND THE STEAM AND THE FLIES...
BACK TO THE BAYOU
BACK HOME...
IT'S DARK.
IT'S LATE.
I HAVE A LOT TO DO TOMORROW.
NO MATTER.
FOR THE MOMENT I AM CONTENT SIMPLY TO THINK, AND TO PLAN...
...AND TO LISTEN.
IT'S RAINING IN WASHINGTON TONIGHT

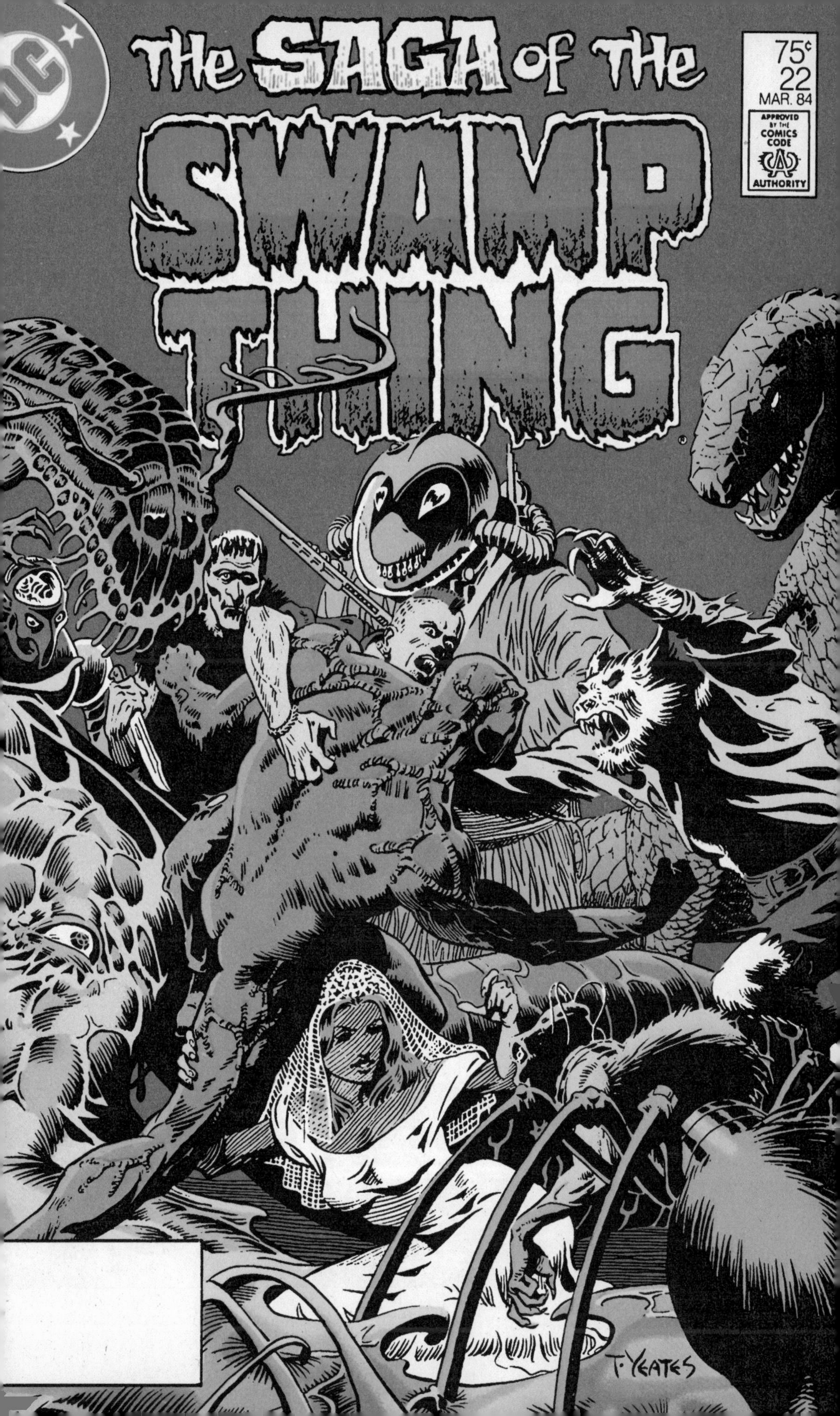
DC
The SAGA of the
SWAMP THING
75¢
22
MAR. 84
APPROVED BY THE COMICS CODE AUTHORITY
T. YEATES

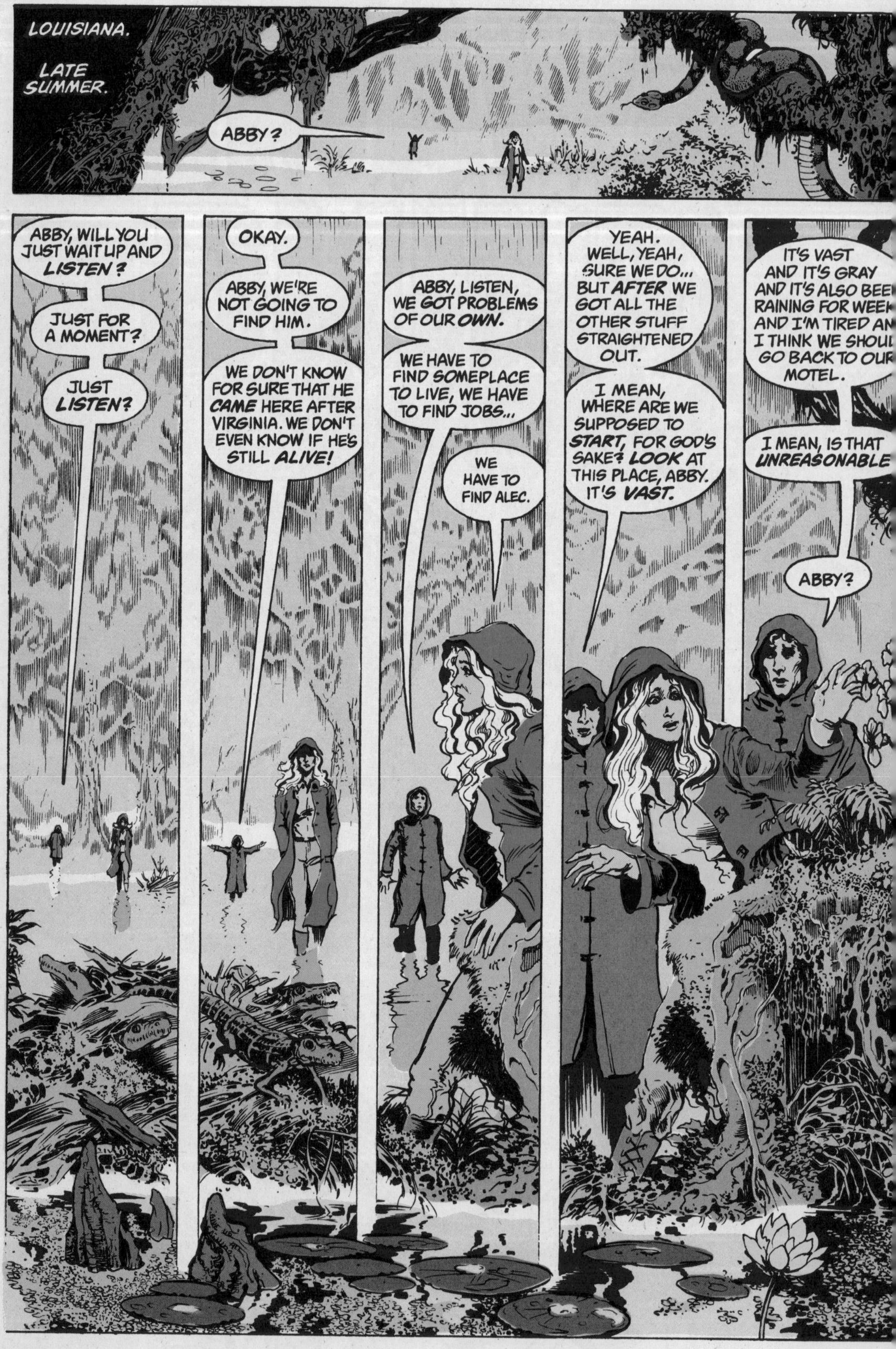
LOUISIANA.
LATE SUMMER.
ABBY?
ABBY, WILL YOU JUST WAIT UP AND LISTEN?
JUST FOR A MOMENT?
JUST LISTEN?
OKAY.
ABBY, WE'RE NOT GOING TO FIND HIM.
WE DON'T KNOW FOR SURE THAT HE CAME HERE AFTER VIRGINIA. WE DON'T EVEN KNOW IF HE'S STILL ALIVE!
ABBY, LISTEN, WE GOT PROBLEMS OF OUR OWN.
WE HAVE TO FIND SOMEPLACE TO LIVE, WE HAVE TO FIND JOBS...
WE HAVE TO FIND ALEC.
YEAH. WELL, YEAH, SURE WE DO... BUT AFTER WE GOT ALL THE OTHER STUFF STRAIGHTENED OUT.
I MEAN, WHERE ARE WE SUPPOSED TO START, FOR GOD'S SAKE? LOOK AT THIS PLACE, ABBY. IT'S VAST.
IT'S VAST AND IT'S GRAY AND IT'S ALSO BEE RAINING FOR WEEK AND I'M TIRED AN I THINK WE SHOUL GO BACK TO OUR MOTEL.
I MEAN, IS THAT UNREASONABLE
ABBY?

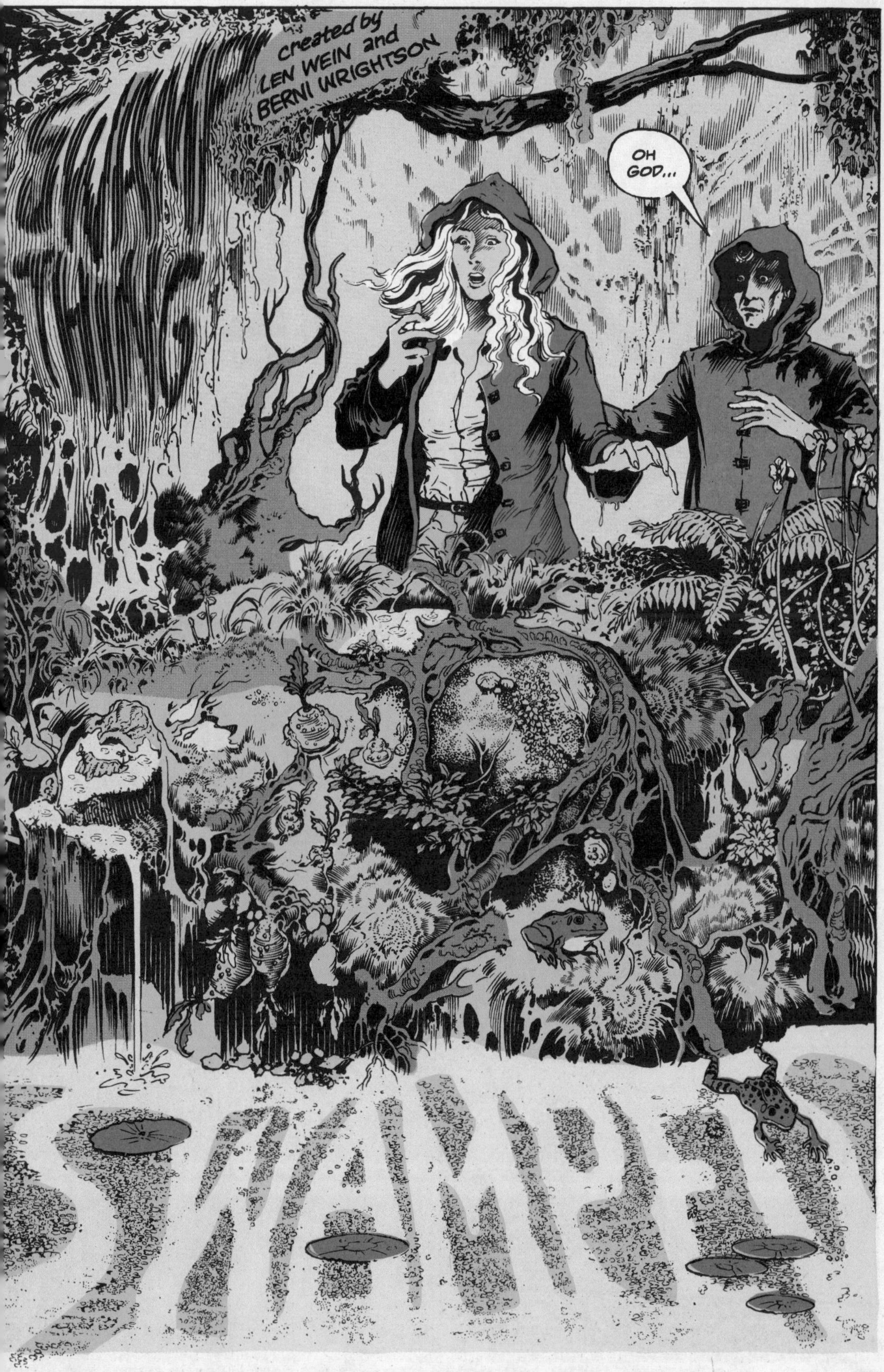
SWAMP THING
created by
LEN WEIN and
BERNI WRIGHTSON
OH GOD...
SWAMPED

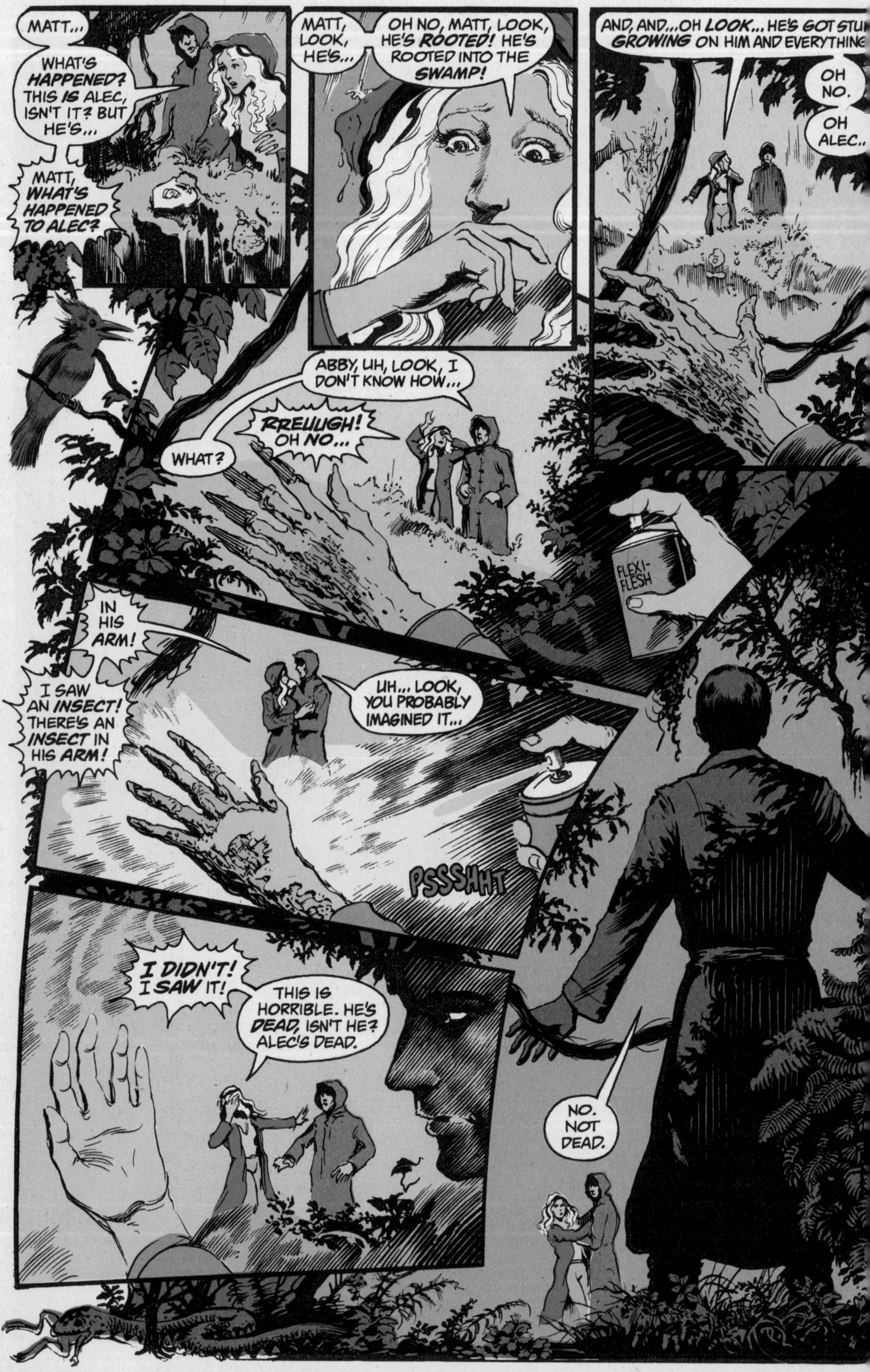
MATT...
WHAT'S HAPPENED? THIS IS ALEC, ISN'T IT? BUT HE'S...
MATT, WHAT'S HAPPENED TO ALEC?
MATT, LOOK, HE'S...
OH NO, MATT, LOOK, HE'S ROOTED! HE'S ROOTED INTO THE SWAMP!
AND, AND...OH LOOK... HE'S GOT STU
GROWING ON HIM AND EVERYTHING
OH NO.
OH ALEC...
ABBY, UH, LOOK, I DON'T KNOW HOW...
RREUUGH! OH NO...
WHAT?
FLEXI-FLESH
IN HIS ARM!
I SAW AN INSECT! THERE'S AN INSECT IN HIS ARM!
UH... LOOK, YOU PROBABLY IMAGINED IT...
PSSSHHT
I DIDN'T! I SAW IT!
THIS IS HORRIBLE. HE'S DEAD, ISN'T HE? ALEC'S DEAD.
NO. NOT DEAD.

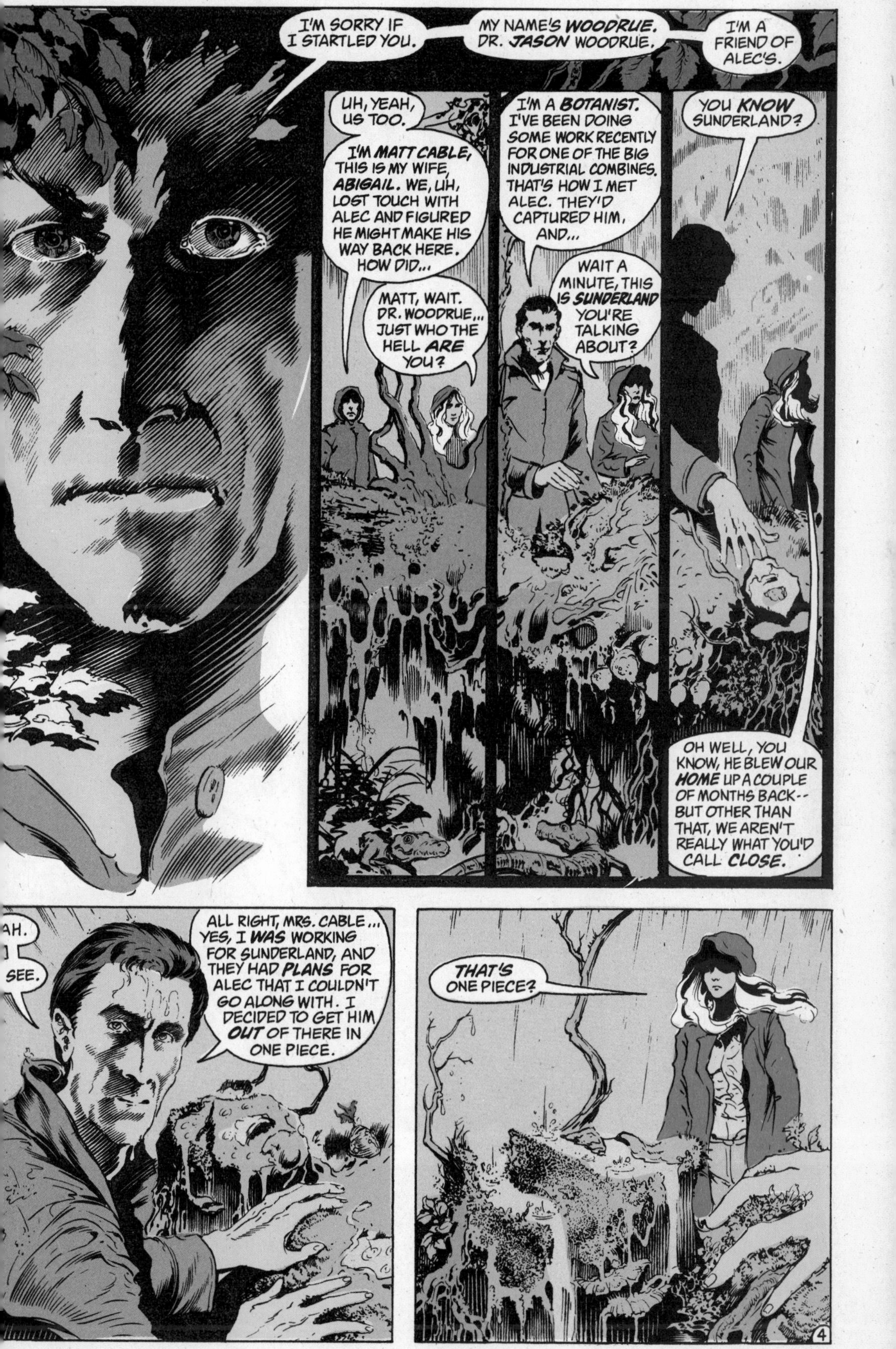
I'M SORRY IF I STARTLED YOU.
MY NAME'S WOODRUE. DR. JASON WOODRUE.
I'M A FRIEND OF ALEC'S.
UH, YEAH, US TOO.
I'M MATT CABLE, THIS IS MY WIFE, ABIGAIL. WE, UH, LOST TOUCH WITH ALEC AND FIGURED HE MIGHT MAKE HIS WAY BACK HERE. HOW DID...
MATT, WAIT. DR. WOODRUE... JUST WHO THE HELL ARE YOU?
I'M A BOTANIST. I'VE BEEN DOING SOME WORK RECENTLY FOR ONE OF THE BIG INDUSTRIAL COMBINES. THAT'S HOW I MET ALEC. THEY'D CAPTURED HIM, AND...
WAIT A MINUTE, THIS IS SUNDERLAND YOU'RE TALKING ABOUT?
YOU KNOW SUNDERLAND?
OH WELL, YOU KNOW, HE BLEW OUR HOME UP A COUPLE OF MONTHS BACK-- BUT OTHER THAN THAT, WE AREN'T REALLY WHAT YOU'D CALL CLOSE.
AH. I SEE.
ALL RIGHT, MRS. CABLE... YES, I WAS WORKING FOR SUNDERLAND, AND THEY HAD PLANS FOR ALEC THAT I COULDN'T GO ALONG WITH. I DECIDED TO GET HIM OUT OF THERE IN ONE PIECE.
THAT'S ONE PIECE?
4

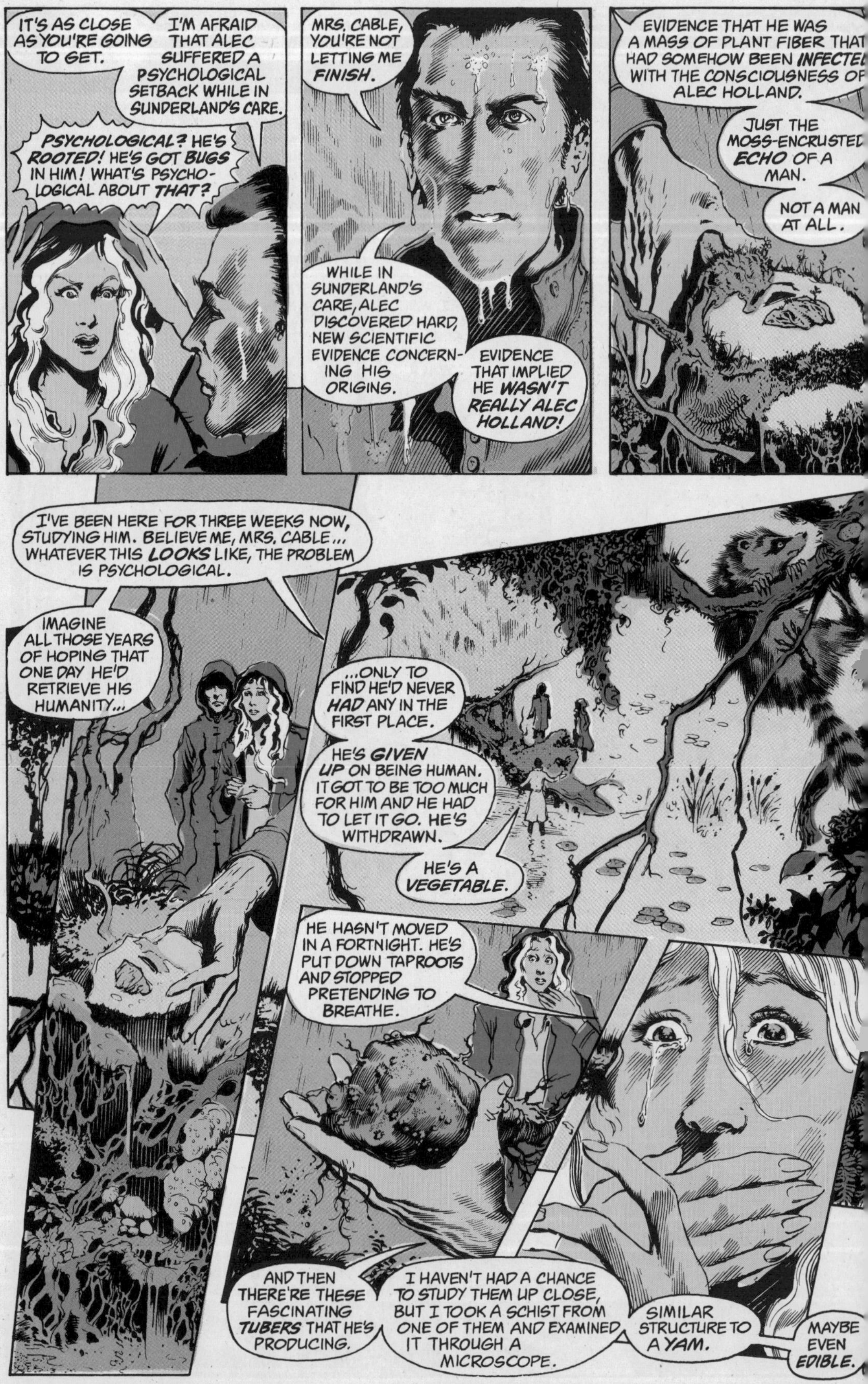
IT'S AS CLOSE AS YOU'RE GOING TO GET.
I'M AFRAID THAT ALEC SUFFERED A PSYCHOLOGICAL SETBACK WHILE IN SUNDERLAND'S CARE.
PSYCHOLOGICAL? HE'S ROOTED! HE'S GOT BUGS IN HIM! WHAT'S PSYCHOLOGICAL ABOUT THAT?
MRS. CABLE, YOU'RE NOT LETTING ME FINISH.
WHILE IN SUNDERLAND'S CARE, ALEC DISCOVERED HARD, NEW SCIENTIFIC EVIDENCE CONCERNING HIS ORIGINS.
EVIDENCE THAT IMPLIED HE WASN'T REALLY ALEC HOLLAND!
EVIDENCE THAT HE WAS A MASS OF PLANT FIBER THAT HAD SOMEHOW BEEN INFECTED WITH THE CONSCIOUSNESS OF ALEC HOLLAND.
JUST THE MOSS-ENCRUSTED ECHO OF A MAN.
NOT A MAN AT ALL.
I'VE BEEN HERE FOR THREE WEEKS NOW, STUDYING HIM. BELIEVE ME, MRS. CABLE... WHATEVER THIS LOOKS LIKE, THE PROBLEM IS PSYCHOLOGICAL.
IMAGINE ALL THOSE YEARS OF HOPING THAT ONE DAY HE'D RETRIEVE HIS HUMANITY...
...ONLY TO FIND HE'D NEVER HAD ANY IN THE FIRST PLACE.
HE'S GIVEN UP ON BEING HUMAN. IT GOT TO BE TOO MUCH FOR HIM AND HE HAD TO LET IT GO. HE'S WITHDRAWN.
HE'S A VEGETABLE.
HE HASN'T MOVED IN A FORTNIGHT. HE'S PUT DOWN TAPROOTS AND STOPPED PRETENDING TO BREATHE.
AND THEN THERE'RE THESE FASCINATING TUBERS THAT HE'S PRODUCING.
I HAVEN'T HAD A CHANCE TO STUDY THEM UP CLOSE, BUT I TOOK A SCHIST FROM ONE OF THEM AND EXAMINED IT THROUGH A MICROSCOPE.
SIMILAR STRUCTURE TO A YAM.
MAYBE EVEN EDIBLE.

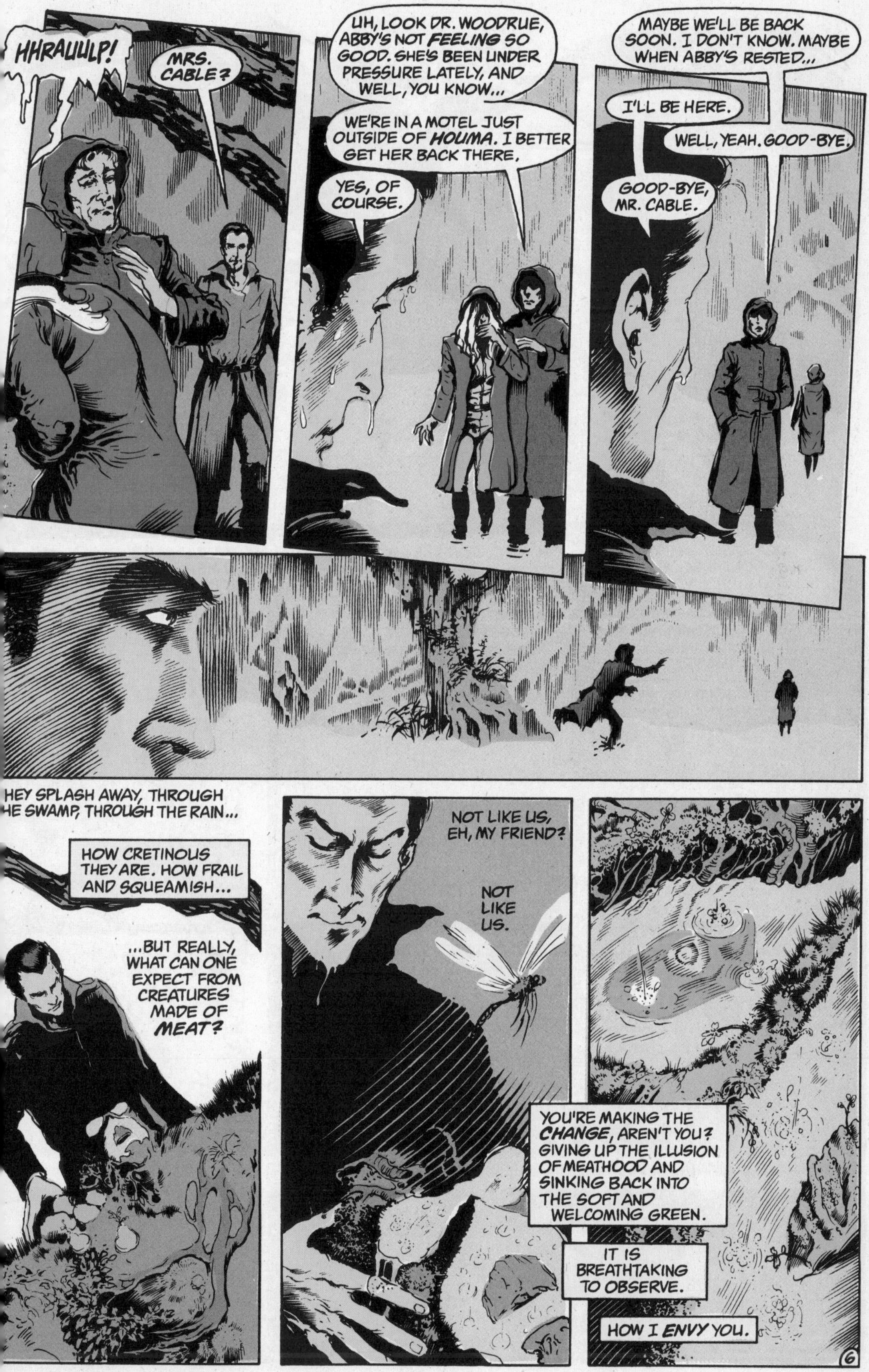
HHRAUULP!
MRS. CABLE?
UH, LOOK DR. WOODRUE, ABBY'S NOT FEELING SO GOOD. SHE'S BEEN UNDER PRESSURE LATELY, AND WELL, YOU KNOW...
WE'RE IN A MOTEL JUST OUTSIDE OF HOUMA. I BETTER GET HER BACK THERE.
YES, OF COURSE.
MAYBE WE'LL BE BACK SOON. I DON'T KNOW. MAYBE WHEN ABBY'S RESTED...
I'LL BE HERE.
WELL, YEAH. GOOD-BYE.
GOOD-BYE, MR. CABLE.
HEY SPLASH AWAY, THROUGH
HE SWAMP, THROUGH THE RAIN...
HOW CRETINOUS THEY ARE. HOW FRAIL AND SQUEAMISH...
...BUT REALLY, WHAT CAN ONE EXPECT FROM CREATURES MADE OF MEAT?
NOT LIKE US, EH, MY FRIEND?
NOT LIKE US.
YOU'RE MAKING THE CHANGE, AREN'T YOU? GIVING UP THE ILLUSION OF MEATHOOD AND SINKING BACK INTO THE SOFT AND WELCOMING GREEN.
IT IS BREATHTAKING TO OBSERVE.
HOW I ENVY YOU.
6

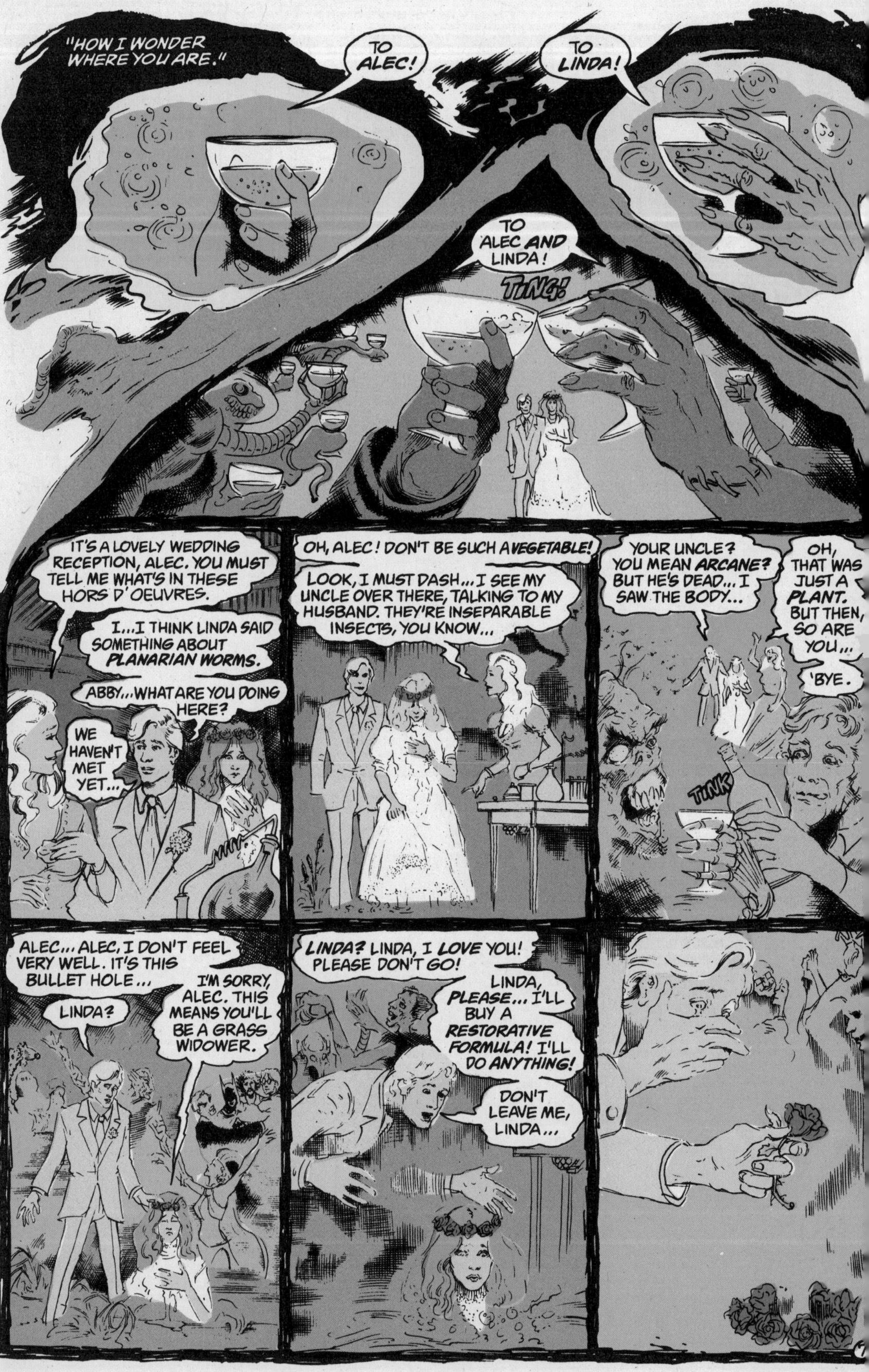
"HOW I WONDER WHERE YOU ARE."
TO ALEC!
TO LINDA!
TO ALEC AND LINDA!
TING!
IT'S A LOVELY WEDDING RECEPTION, ALEC. YOU MUST TELL ME WHAT'S IN THESE HORS D' OEUVRES.
I...I THINK LINDA SAID SOMETHING ABOUT PLANARIAN WORMS.
ABBY...WHAT ARE YOU DOING HERE?
WE HAVEN'T MET YET...
OH, ALEC! DON'T BE SUCH A VEGETABLE!
LOOK, I MUST DASH... I SEE MY UNCLE OVER THERE, TALKING TO MY HUSBAND. THEY'RE INSEPARABLE INSECTS, YOU KNOW...
YOUR UNCLE? YOU MEAN ARCANE? BUT HE'S DEAD... I SAW THE BODY...
OH, THAT WAS JUST A PLANT. BUT THEN, SO ARE YOU...
'BYE.
TINK
ALEC... ALEC, I DON'T FEEL VERY WELL. IT'S THIS BULLET HOLE...
LINDA?
I'M SORRY, ALEC. THIS MEANS YOU'LL BE A GRASS WIDOWER.
LINDA? LINDA, I LOVE YOU! PLEASE DON'T GO!
LINDA, PLEASE... I'LL BUY A RESTORATIVE FORMULA! I'LL DO ANYTHING!
DON'T LEAVE ME, LINDA...

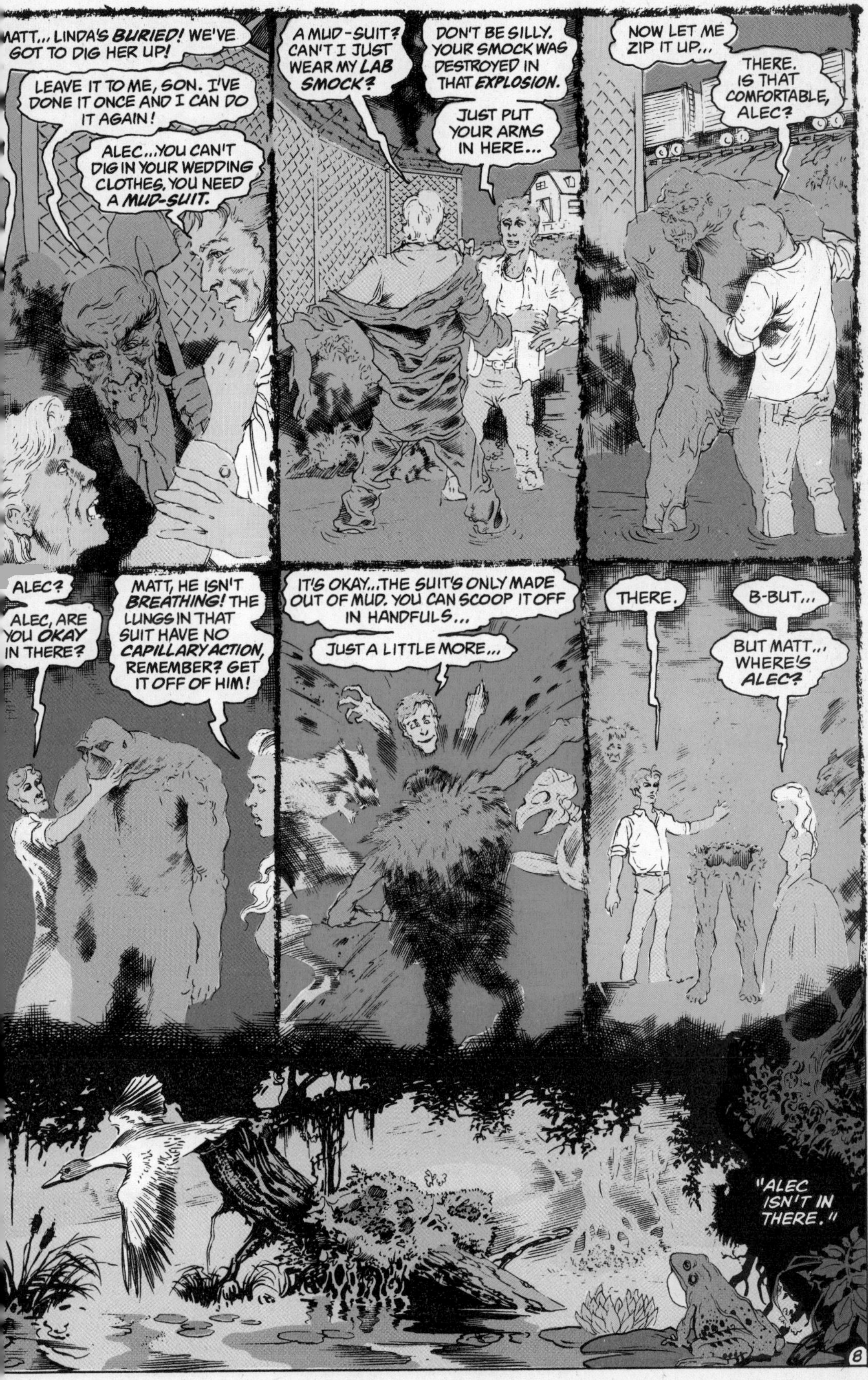
MATT... LINDA'S BURIED! WE'VE GOT TO DIG HER UP!
LEAVE IT TO ME, SON. I'VE DONE IT ONCE AND I CAN DO IT AGAIN!
ALEC... YOU CAN'T DIG IN YOUR WEDDING CLOTHES. YOU NEED A MUD-SUIT.
A MUD-SUIT? CAN'T I JUST WEAR MY LAB SMOCK?
DON'T BE SILLY. YOUR SMOCK WAS DESTROYED IN THAT EXPLOSION.
JUST PUT YOUR ARMS IN HERE...
NOW LET ME ZIP IT UP...
THERE. IS THAT COMFORTABLE, ALEC?
ALEC?
ALEC, ARE YOU OKAY IN THERE?
MATT, HE ISN'T BREATHING! THE LUNGS IN THAT SUIT HAVE NO CAPILLARY ACTION, REMEMBER? GET IT OFF OF HIM!
IT'S OKAY... THE SUIT'S ONLY MADE OUT OF MUD. YOU CAN SCOOP IT OFF IN HANDFULS...
JUST A LITTLE MORE...
THERE.
B-BUT...
BUT MATT... WHERE'S ALEC?
"ALEC ISN'T IN THERE."
8

SUNSET OVER HOUMA.

THE RAINS HAVE STOPPED. CLOUDS LIKE PLUGS OF BLOODIED COTTON WOOL DAB INEFFECTUALLY AT THE SLASHED WRISTS OF THE SKY.

SHE'S BEEN OUT WALKING BY HERSELF AGAIN.

MOTOR INN

BRIAN'S La TOUR

SHE'S BEEN THINKING ABOUT MATT, SHE'S BEEN THINKING ABOUT WOODRU SHE'S BEEN THINKING ABOUT ALEC AND EDIBLE TUBERS AND WHETHER SHE'S LOSING HER MIND OR NOT...

JUST WALKING, THINKING, STUFF LIKE THAT...

SWAMPED.

SHE'S GOING HOME NOW.

GOING HOME TO SLEEP.

BRIARWOOD MOTOR INN

VACANCY

MATT WILL PROBABLY SIT UP ALONE AGAIN, EATING PINK BURRITOS IN THE CELLOPHANE-BLUE LIGHT OF THE T.V.

HOW IS IT POSSIBLE TO LIVE WITH SOMEONE AND YET FEEL SO UTTERLY...

...ALONE?

AND MATT IS C. 1-1' DRIPPING I-115' ...BULBS?

LIKE TRAPPED FLIES, THE LOW BUZZ OF WHISPERED LAUGHTER.

VOICES. MATT'S...

...A WOMAN'S...

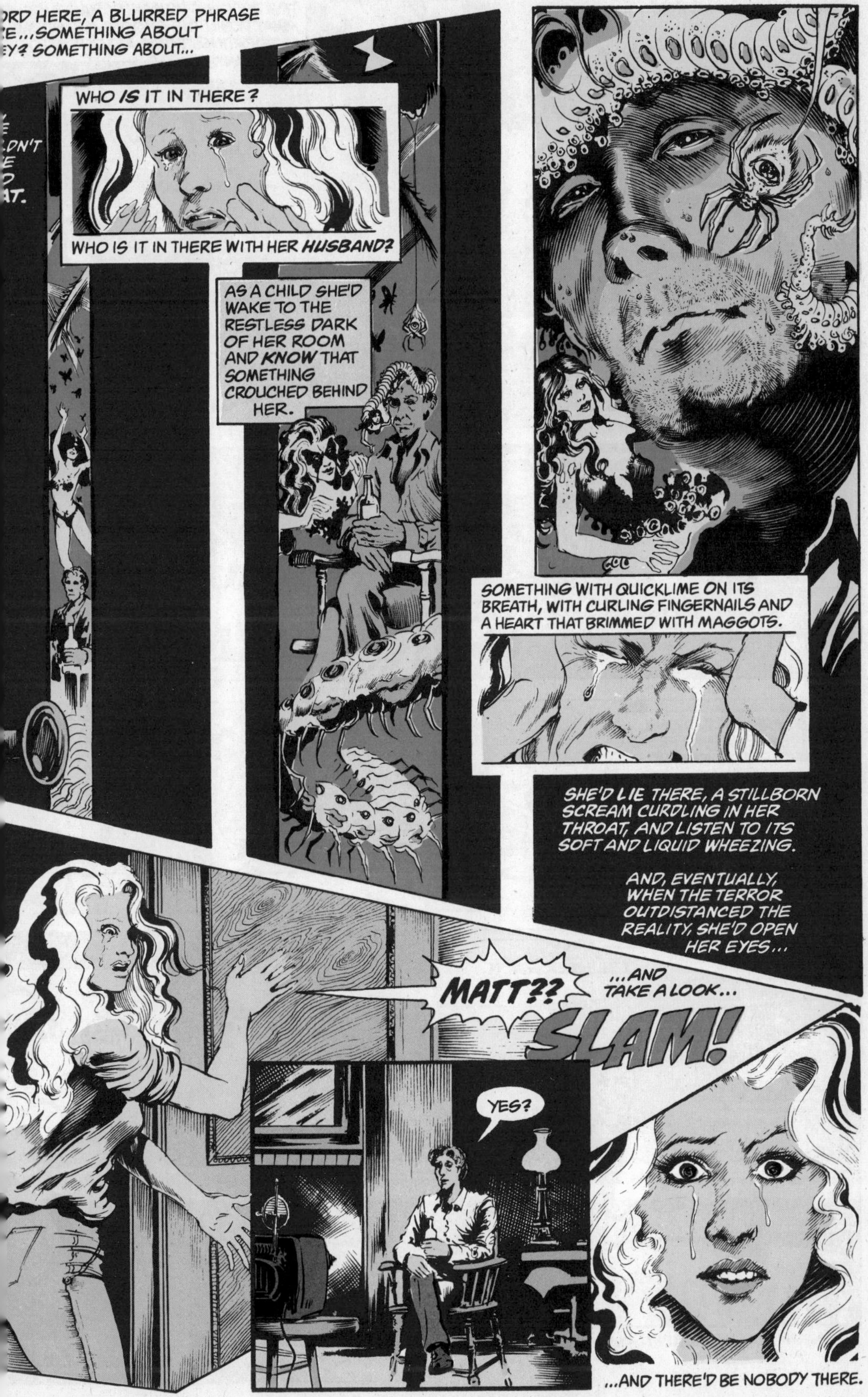
ORD HERE, A BLURRED PHRASE
E...SOMETHING ABOUT
EY? SOMETHING ABOUT...
WHO *IS* IT IN THERE?
WHO IS IT IN THERE WITH HER *HUSBAND?*
AS A CHILD SHE'D WAKE TO THE RESTLESS DARK OF HER ROOM AND *KNOW* THAT SOMETHING CROUCHED BEHIND HER.
SOMETHING WITH QUICKLIME ON ITS BREATH, WITH CURLING FINGERNAILS AND A HEART THAT BRIMMED WITH MAGGOTS.
SHE'D *LIE* THERE, A STILLBORN SCREAM CURDLING IN HER THROAT, AND LISTEN TO ITS SOFT AND LIQUID WHEEZING.
AND, EVENTUALLY, WHEN THE TERROR OUTDISTANCED THE REALITY, SHE'D OPEN HER EYES...
MATT??
...AND TAKE A LOOK...
SLAM!
YES?
...AND THERE'D BE NOBODY THERE.

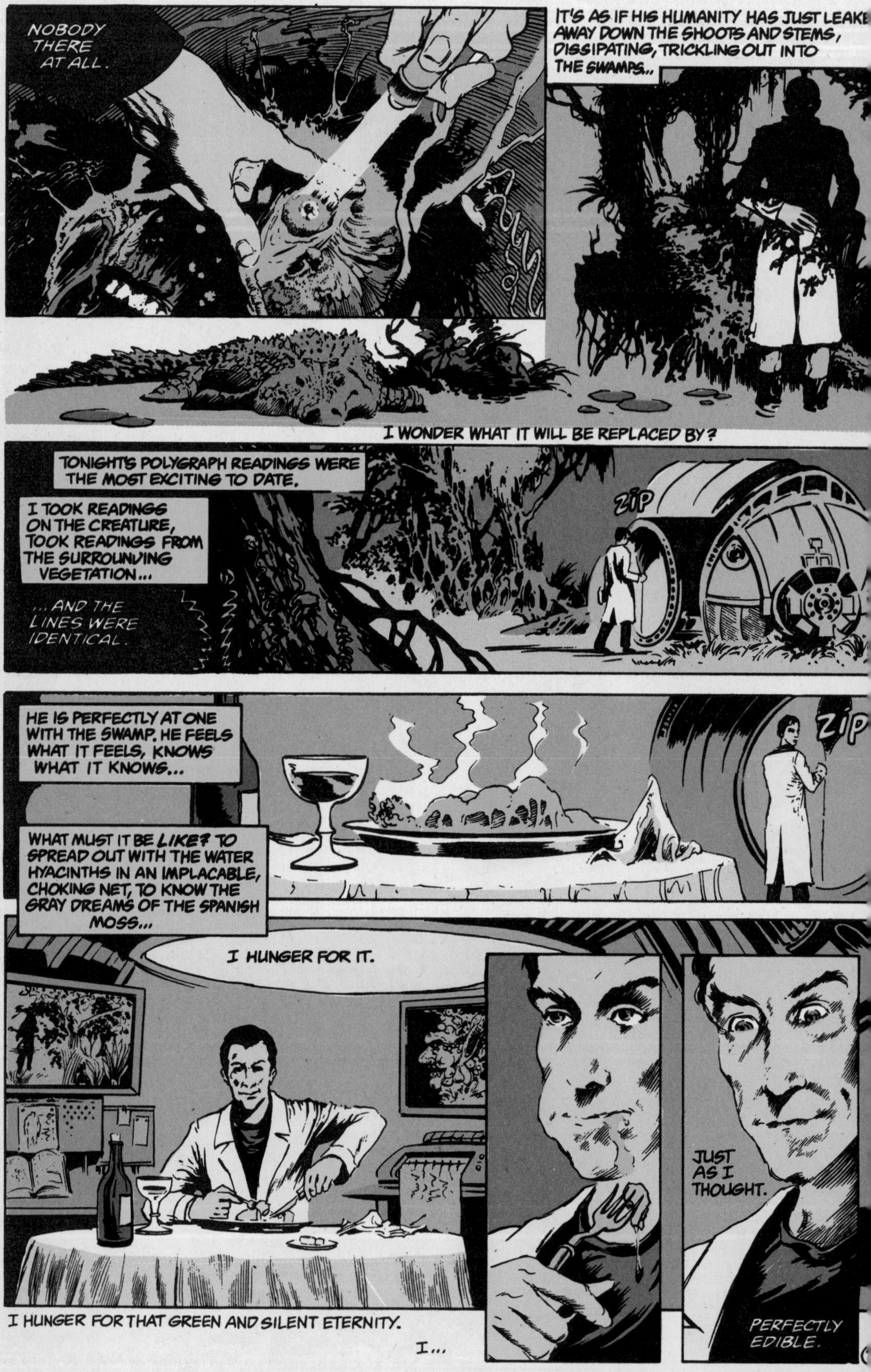
NOBODY THERE AT ALL.
IT'S AS IF HIS HUMANITY HAS JUST LEAKE AWAY DOWN THE SHOOTS AND STEMS, DISSIPATING, TRICKLING OUT INTO THE SWAMPS...
I WONDER WHAT IT WILL BE REPLACED BY?
TONIGHT'S POLYGRAPH READINGS WERE THE MOST EXCITING TO DATE.
I TOOK READINGS ON THE CREATURE, TOOK READINGS FROM THE SURROUNDING VEGETATION...
...AND THE LINES WERE IDENTICAL.
ZIP
HE IS PERFECTLY AT ONE WITH THE SWAMP. HE FEELS WHAT IT FEELS, KNOWS WHAT IT KNOWS...
WHAT MUST IT BE LIKE? TO SPREAD OUT WITH THE WATER HYACINTHS IN AN IMPLACABLE, CHOKING NET, TO KNOW THE GRAY DREAMS OF THE SPANISH MOSS...
ZIP
I HUNGER FOR IT.
I HUNGER FOR THAT GREEN AND SILENT ETERNITY.
I...
JUST AS I THOUGHT.
PERFECTLY EDIBLE.

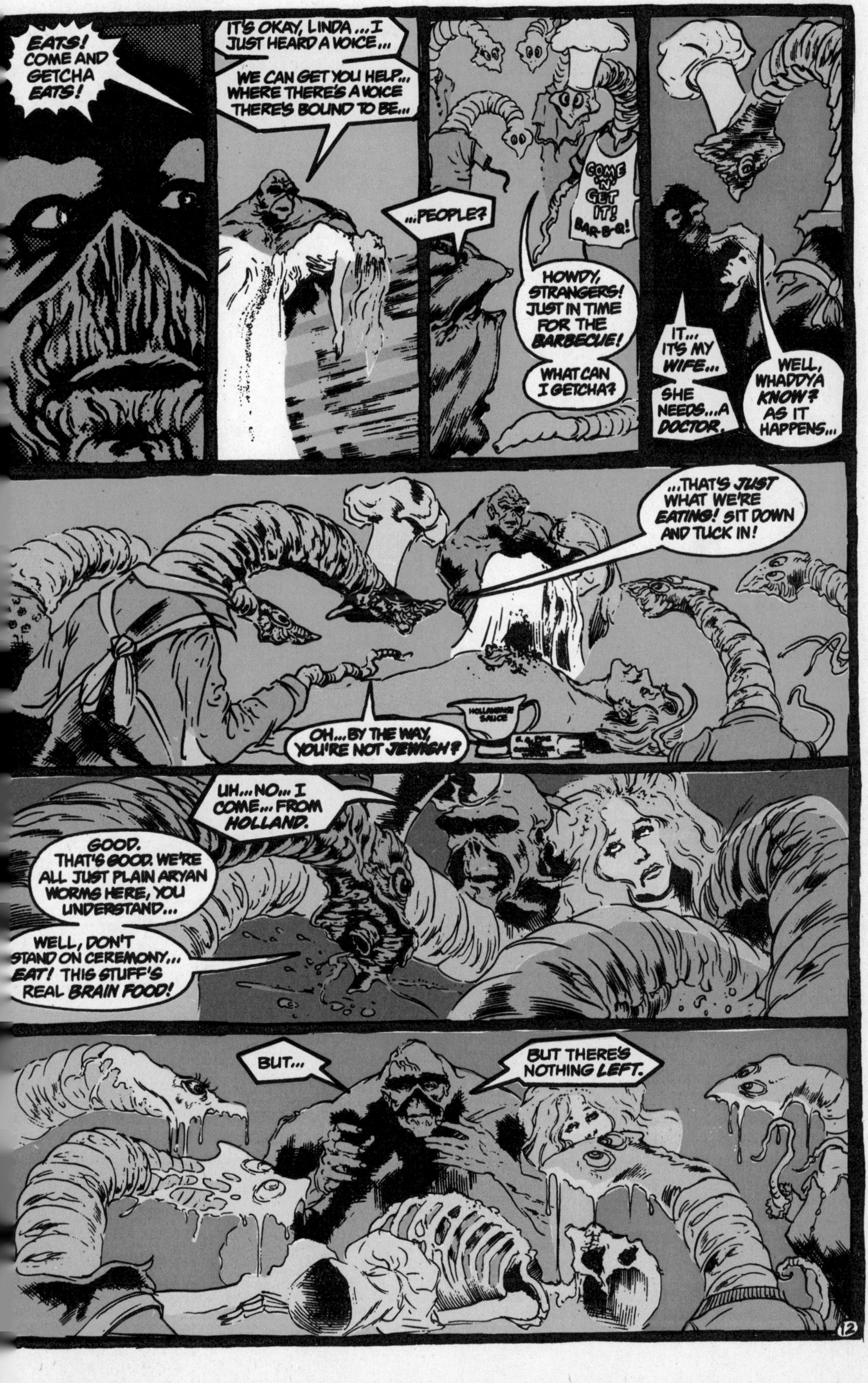
EATS! COME AND GETCHA EATS!
IT'S OKAY, LINDA... I JUST HEARD A VOICE...
WE CAN GET YOU HELP... WHERE THERE'S A VOICE THERE'S BOUND TO BE...
...PEOPLE?
COME 'N' GET IT! BAR-B-Q!
HOWDY, STRANGERS! JUST IN TIME FOR THE BARBECUE!
WHAT CAN I GETCHA?
IT... IT'S MY WIFE...
SHE NEEDS... A DOCTOR.
WELL, WHADDYA KNOW? AS IT HAPPENS...
...THAT'S JUST WHAT WE'RE EATING! SIT DOWN AND TUCK IN!
HOLLANDAISE SAUCE
OH... BY THE WAY, YOU'RE NOT JEWISH?
UH... NO... I COME... FROM HOLLAND.
GOOD. THAT'S GOOD. WE'RE ALL JUST PLAIN ARYAN WORMS HERE, YOU UNDERSTAND...
WELL, DON'T STAND ON CEREMONY... EAT! THIS STUFF'S REAL BRAIN FOOD!
BUT...
BUT THERE'S NOTHING LEFT.
12

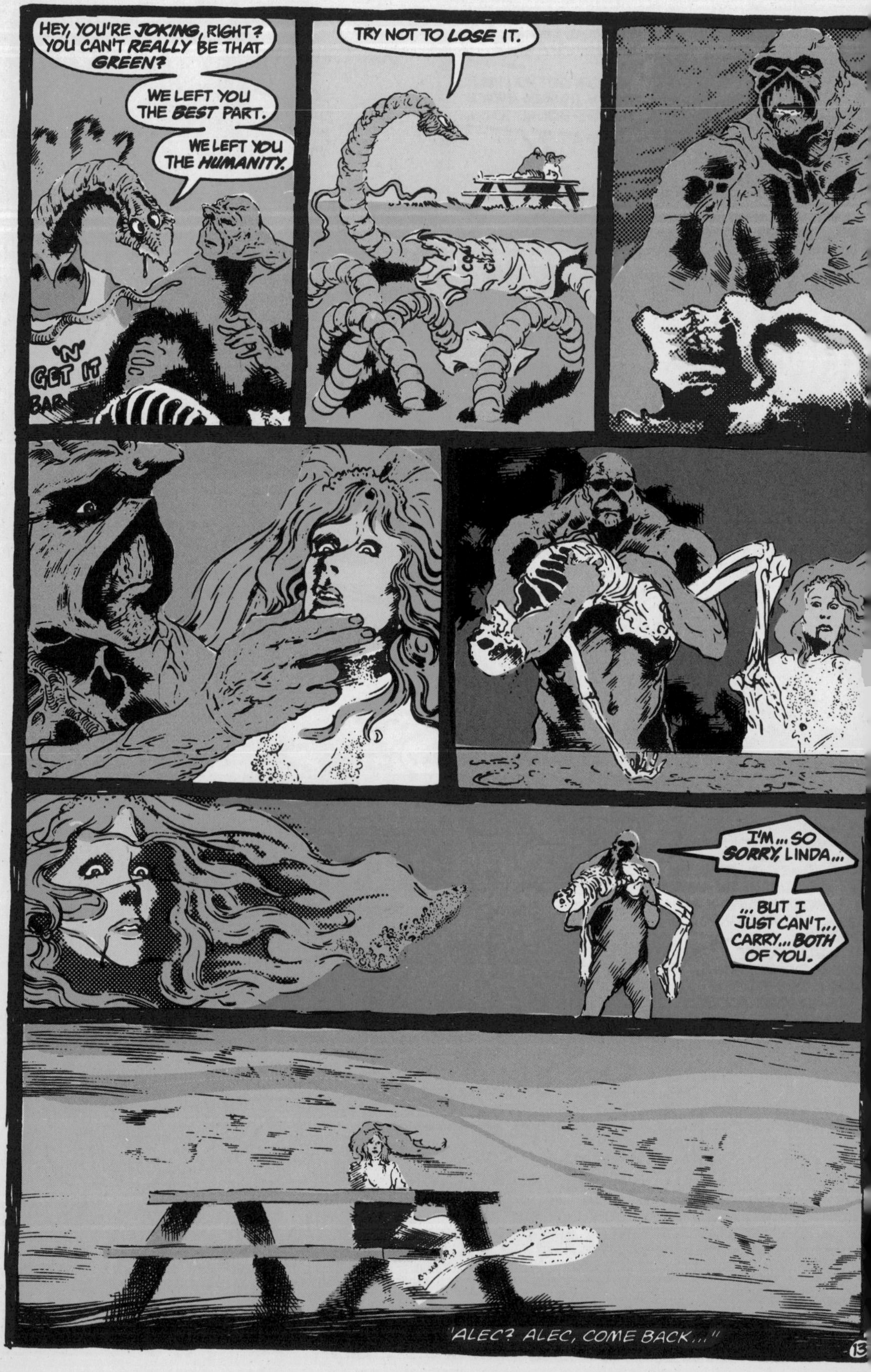
HEY, YOU'RE JOKING, RIGHT? YOU CAN'T REALLY BE THAT GREEN?
WE LEFT YOU THE BEST PART.
WE LEFT YOU THE HUMANITY.
TRY NOT TO LOSE IT.
I'M... SO SORRY, LINDA...
...BUT I JUST CAN'T... CARRY... BOTH OF YOU.
"ALEC? ALEC, COME BACK..."
13

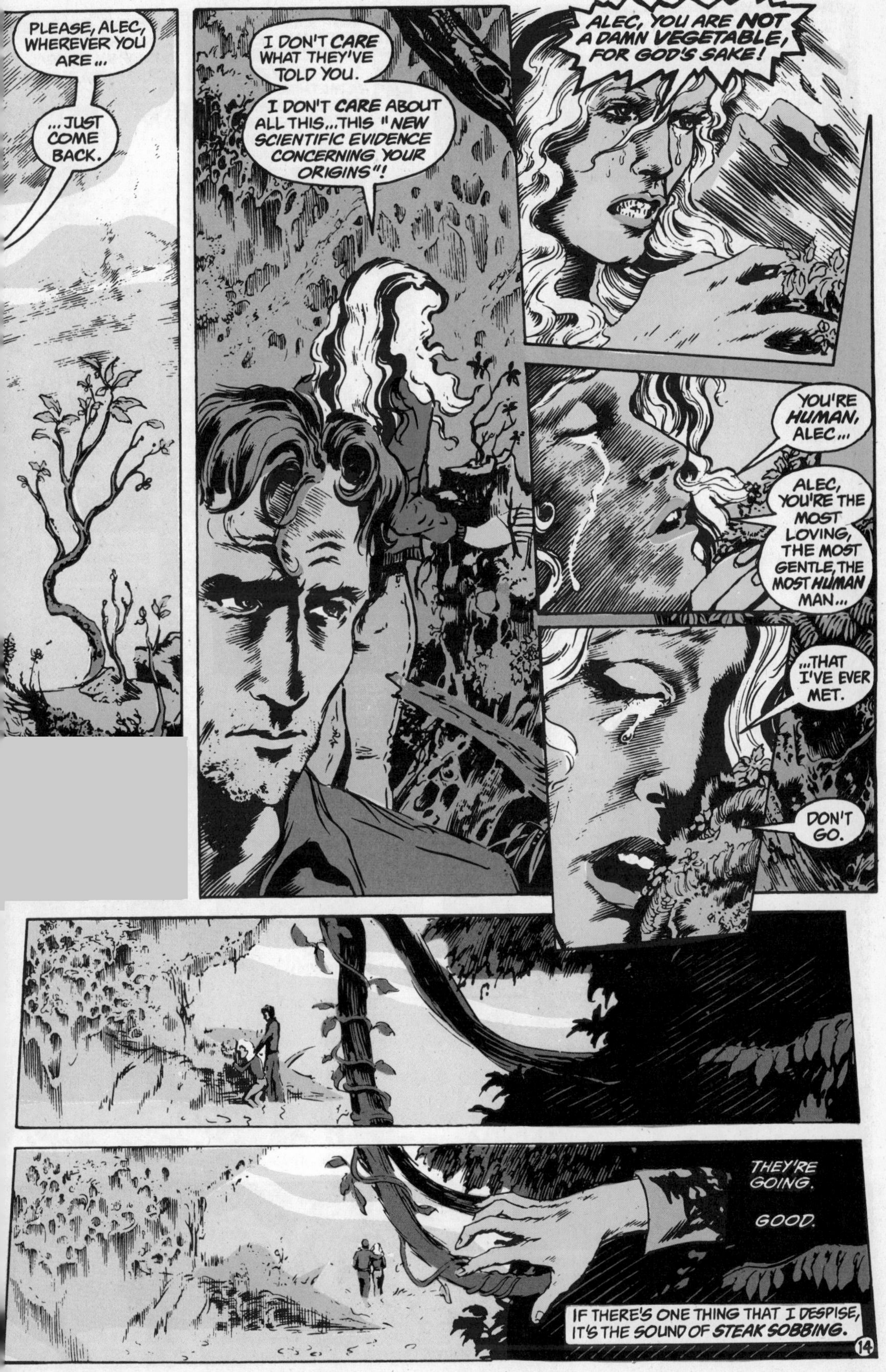
PLEASE, ALEC, WHEREVER YOU ARE...
...JUST COME BACK.
I DON'T CARE WHAT THEY'VE TOLD YOU.
I DON'T CARE ABOUT ALL THIS...THIS "NEW SCIENTIFIC EVIDENCE CONCERNING YOUR ORIGINS"!
ALEC, YOU ARE NOT A DAMN VEGETABLE, FOR GOD'S SAKE!
YOU'RE HUMAN, ALEC...
ALEC, YOU'RE THE MOST LOVING, THE MOST GENTLE, THE MOST HUMAN MAN...
...THAT I'VE EVER MET.
DON'T GO.
THEY'RE GOING.
GOOD.
IF THERE'S ONE THING THAT I DESPISE, IT'S THE SOUND OF STEAK SOBBING.
14

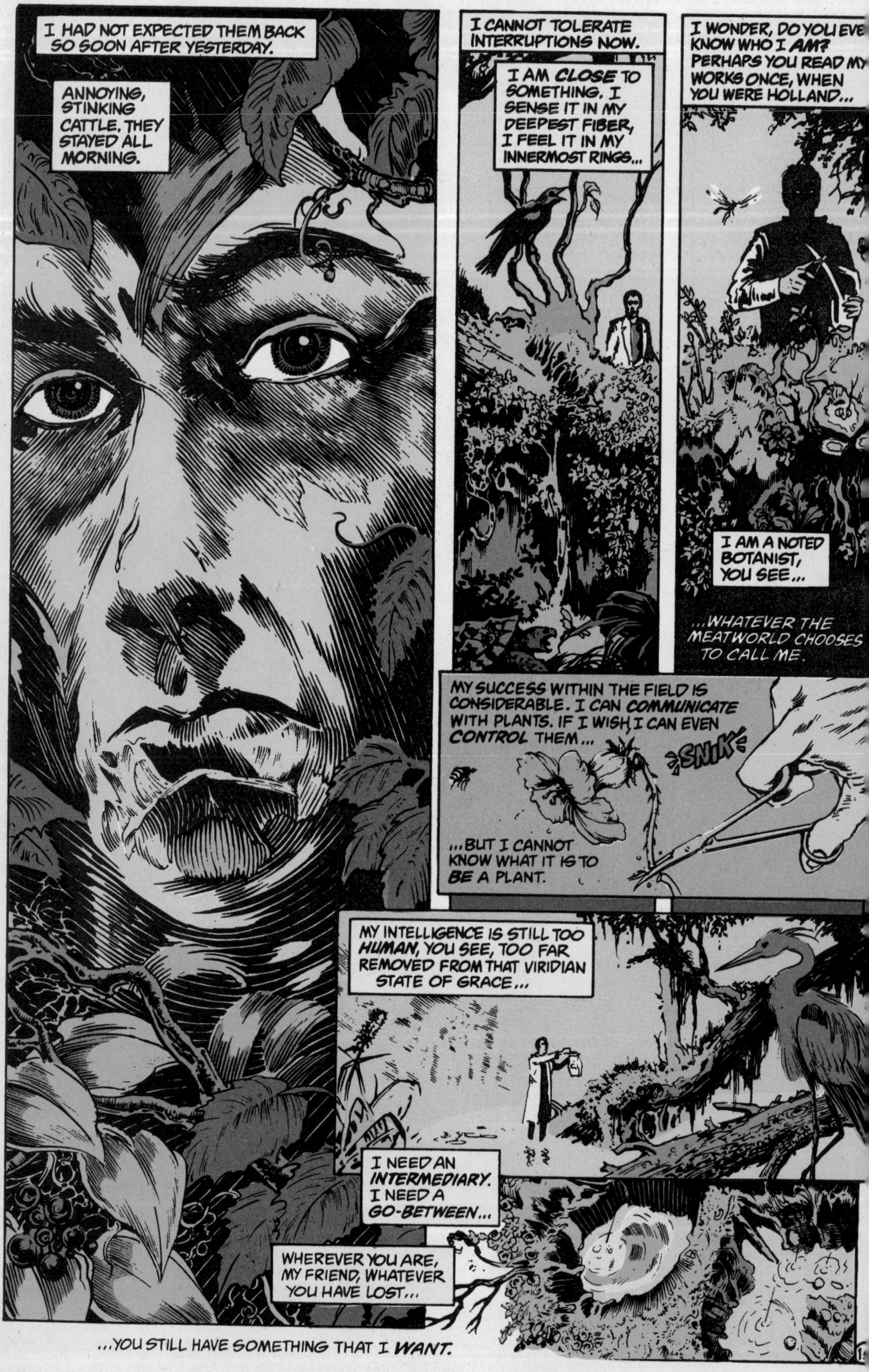
I HAD NOT EXPECTED THEM BACK SO SOON AFTER YESTERDAY.
ANNOYING, STINKING CATTLE. THEY STAYED ALL MORNING.
I CANNOT TOLERATE INTERRUPTIONS NOW.
I AM CLOSE TO SOMETHING. I SENSE IT IN MY DEEPEST FIBER, I FEEL IT IN MY INNERMOST RINGS...
I WONDER, DO YOU EVE
KNOW WHO I AM?
PERHAPS YOU READ MY WORKS ONCE, WHEN YOU WERE HOLLAND...
I AM A NOTED BOTANIST, YOU SEE...
...WHATEVER THE MEATWORLD CHOOSES TO CALL ME.
MY SUCCESS WITHIN THE FIELD IS CONSIDERABLE. I CAN COMMUNICATE WITH PLANTS. IF I WISH, I CAN EVEN CONTROL THEM...
SNIK
...BUT I CANNOT KNOW WHAT IT IS TO BE A PLANT.
MY INTELLIGENCE IS STILL TOO HUMAN, YOU SEE, TOO FAR REMOVED FROM THAT VIRIDIAN STATE OF GRACE...
I NEED AN INTERMEDIARY. I NEED A GO-BETWEEN...
WHEREVER YOU ARE, MY FRIEND, WHATEVER YOU HAVE LOST...
...YOU STILL HAVE SOMETHING THAT I WANT.

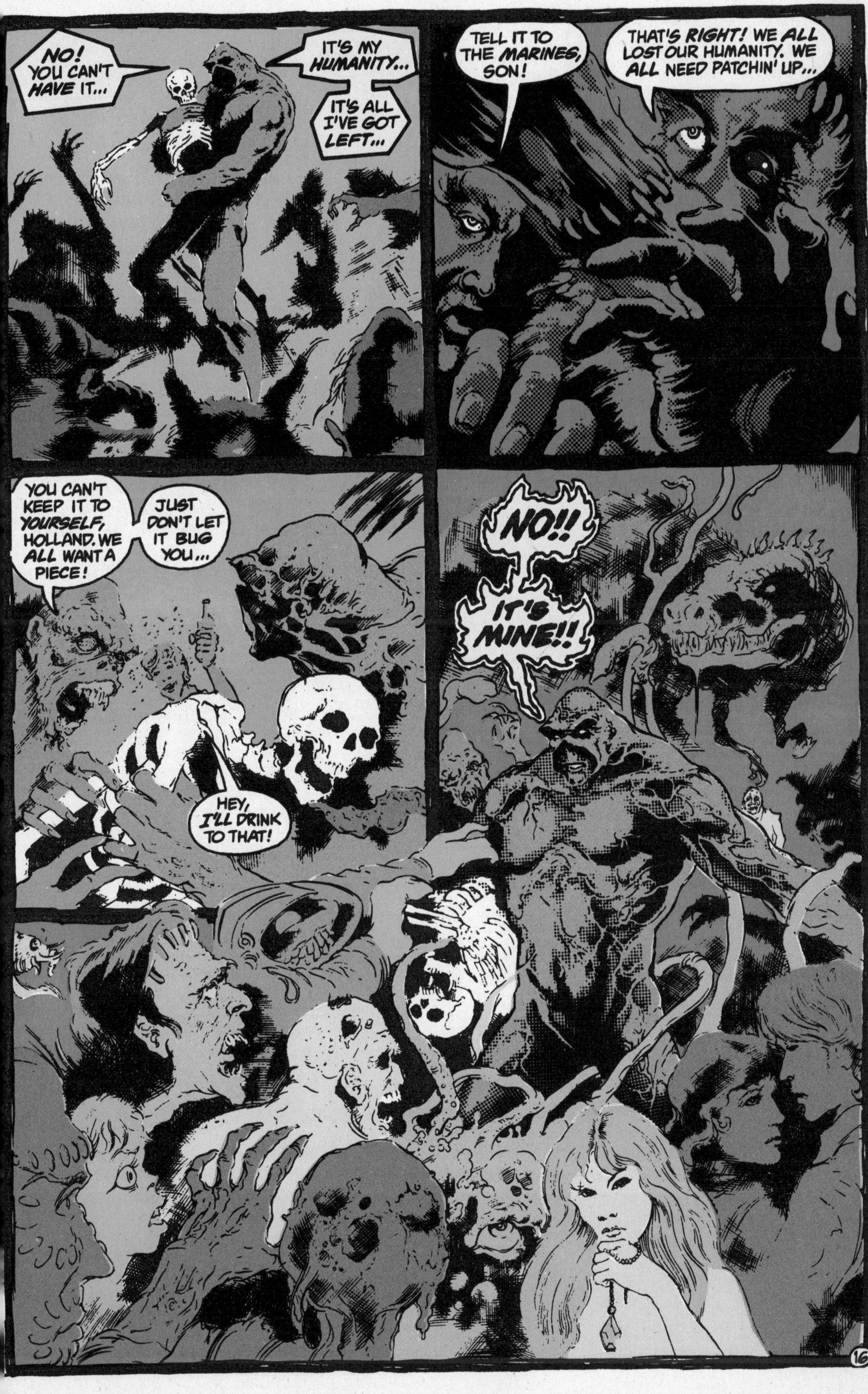
NO! YOU CAN'T HAVE IT...
IT'S MY HUMANITY...
IT'S ALL I'VE GOT LEFT...
TELL IT TO THE MARINES, SON!
THAT'S RIGHT! WE ALL LOST OUR HUMANITY. WE ALL NEED PATCHIN' UP...
YOU CAN'T KEEP IT TO YOURSELF, HOLLAND. WE ALL WANT A PIECE!
JUST DON'T LET IT BUG YOU...
HEY, I'LL DRINK TO THAT!
NO!!
IT'S MINE!!
16

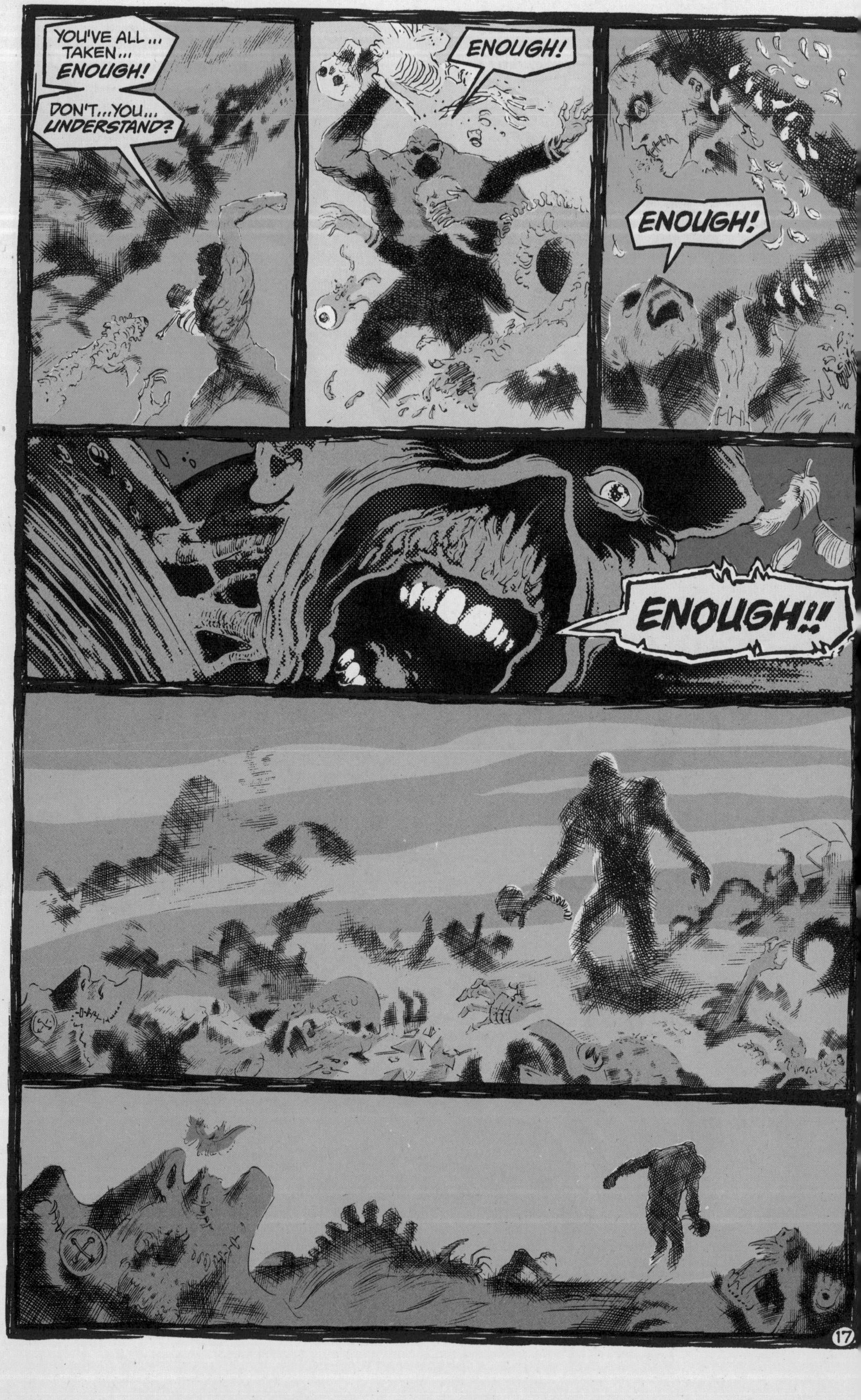
YOU'VE ALL... TAKEN... ENOUGH!
DON'T...YOU... UNDERSTAND?
ENOUGH!
ENOUGH!
ENOUGH!!
17

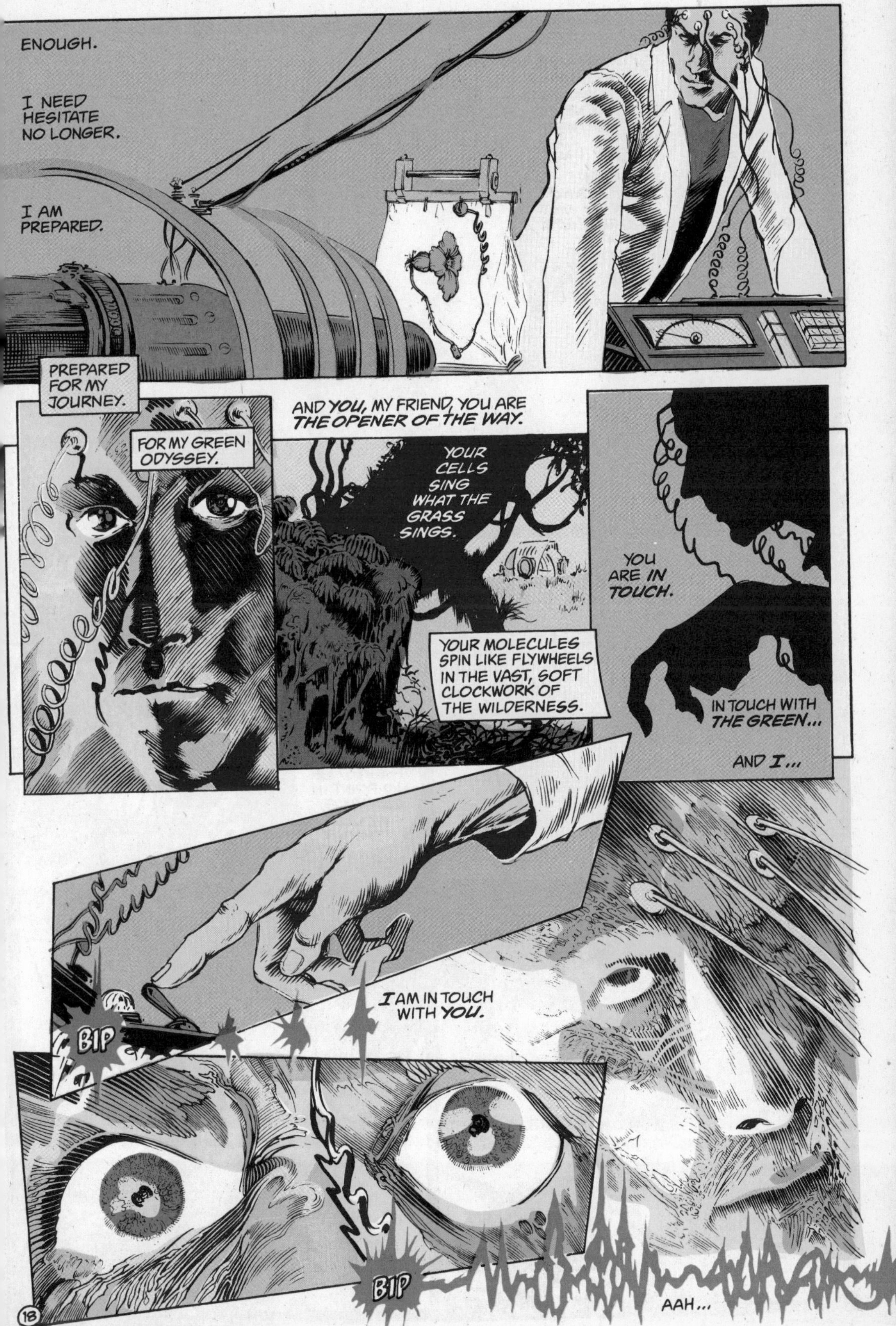
ENOUGH.
I NEED HESITATE NO LONGER.
I AM PREPARED.
PREPARED FOR MY JOURNEY.
FOR MY GREEN ODYSSEY.
AND YOU, MY FRIEND, YOU ARE THE OPENER OF THE WAY.
YOUR CELLS SING WHAT THE GRASS SINGS.
YOUR MOLECULES SPIN LIKE FLYWHEELS IN THE VAST, SOFT CLOCKWORK OF THE WILDERNESS.
YOU ARE IN TOUCH.
IN TOUCH WITH THE GREEN...
AND I...
I AM IN TOUCH WITH YOU.
BIP
BIP
AAH...
18

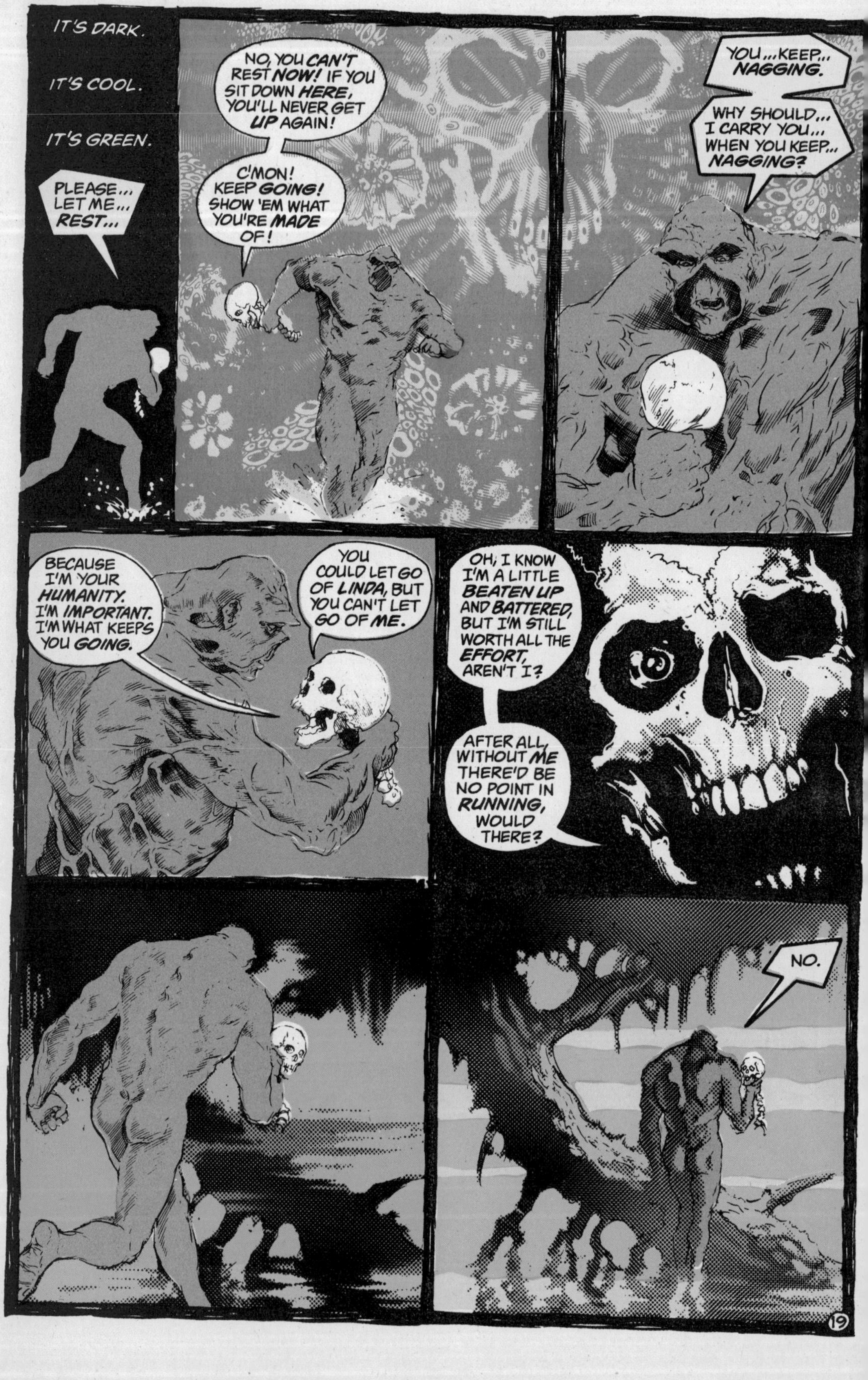
IT'S DARK.
IT'S COOL.
IT'S GREEN.
PLEASE... LET ME... REST...
NO, YOU CAN'T REST NOW! IF YOU SIT DOWN HERE, YOU'LL NEVER GET UP AGAIN!
C'MON! KEEP GOING! SHOW 'EM WHAT YOU'RE MADE OF!
YOU... KEEP... NAGGING.
WHY SHOULD... I CARRY YOU... WHEN YOU KEEP... NAGGING?
BECAUSE I'M YOUR HUMANITY. I'M IMPORTANT. I'M WHAT KEEPS YOU GOING.
YOU COULD LET GO OF LINDA, BUT YOU CAN'T LET GO OF ME.
OH, I KNOW I'M A LITTLE BEATEN UP AND BATTERED, BUT I'M STILL WORTH ALL THE EFFORT, AREN'T I?
AFTER ALL, WITHOUT ME THERE'D BE NO POINT IN RUNNING, WOULD THERE?
NO.
19

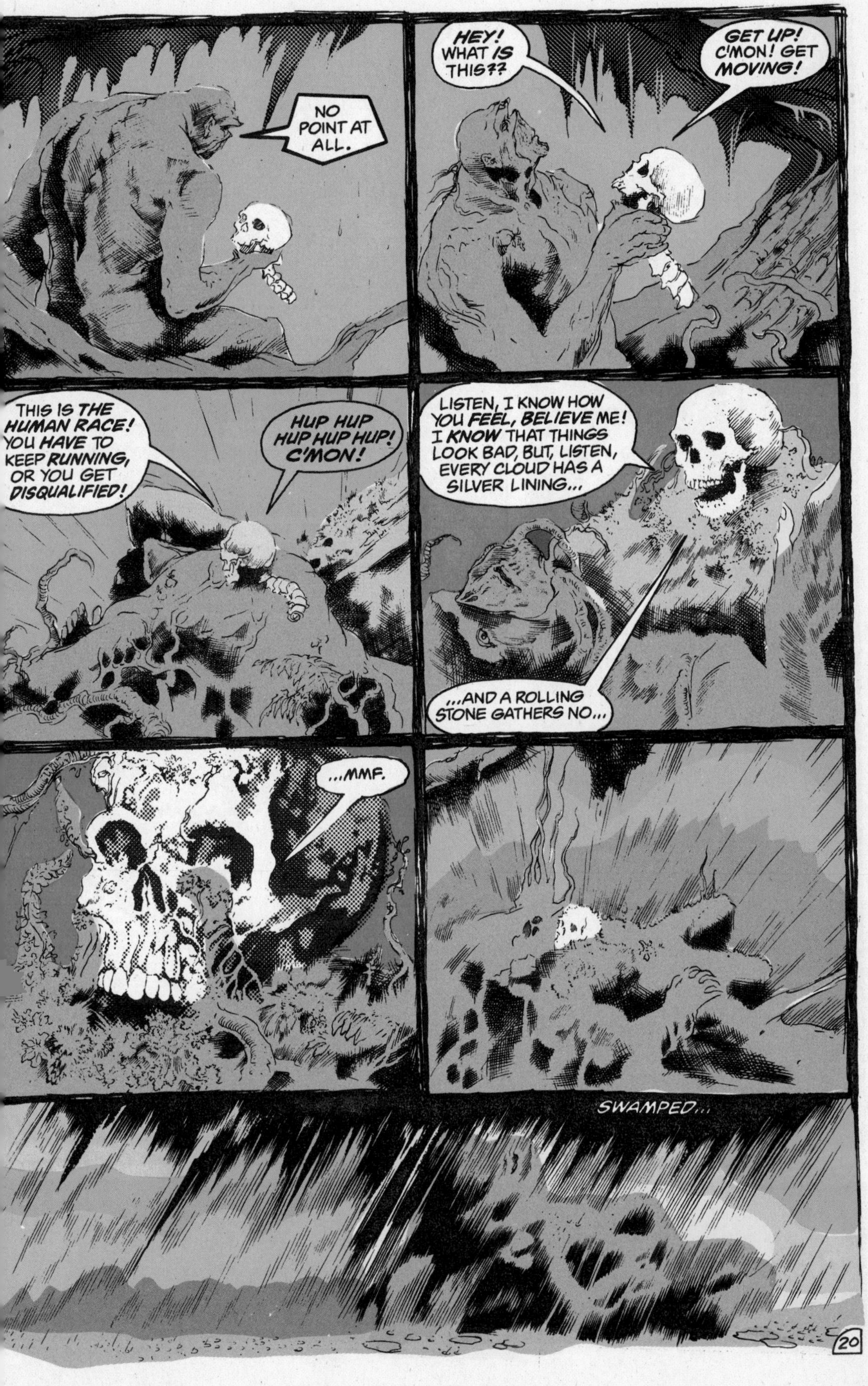
NO POINT AT ALL.
HEY! WHAT IS THIS??
GET UP! C'MON! GET MOVING!
THIS IS THE HUMAN RACE! YOU HAVE TO KEEP RUNNING, OR YOU GET DISQUALIFIED!
HUP HUP HUP HUP HUP! C'MON!
LISTEN, I KNOW HOW YOU FEEL, BELIEVE ME! I KNOW THAT THINGS LOOK BAD, BUT, LISTEN, EVERY CLOUD HAS A SILVER LINING...
...AND A ROLLING STONE GATHERS NO...
...MMF.
SWAMPED...
20

...BY ALIEN EXPERIENCE, BY NEW PERCEPTIONS, THIS *FEELING*, THIS BURNING *COOLNESS*...

MY ROOTS DRINK THROUGH THIRSTY FILAMENTS... THE RUSHING LAVA-TASTE OF THE *PHOSPHATES*, THE LANGUID HYDRAULIC BALLET...

I...

AM...

THE PLANT.

...AND *BEYOND* THE PLANT?

WHAT? I *SENSE* SOMETHING...*OTHER* CONSCIOUSNESSES, PRESSING IN...

THE GRASS OUTSIDE... I LIE A MILLION SILVER BLADES THREATENING THE MOON AND...

...AND THE *TREES!* I...AM...THE TREES. A BOA OF MOSS HANGS ABOUT MY SHOULDERS...

I FEEL THE INTRICATE GENIUS OF THE LIANAS... THE GIANT, TIMELESS WISDOM OF...

...THE REDWOODS?

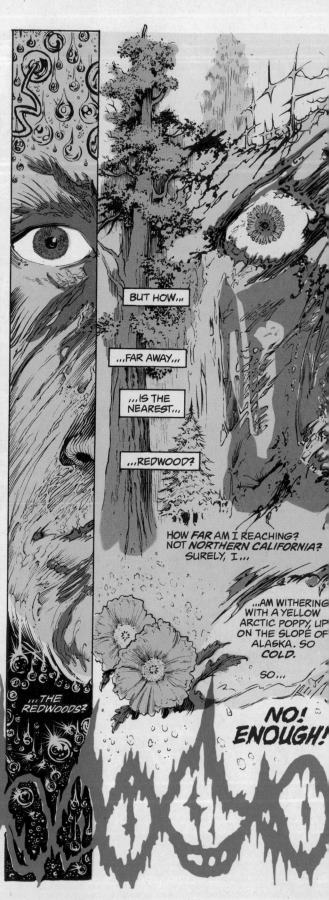

BUT HOW...

...FAR AWAY...

...IS THE NEAREST...

...REDWOOD?

HOW *FAR* AM I REACHING? NOT *NORTHERN CALIFORNIA?* SURELY, I...

...AM WITHERING WITH A YELLOW ARCTIC POPPY, UP ON THE SLOPE OF ALASKA. SO *COLD.*

SO...

NO! ENOUGH!

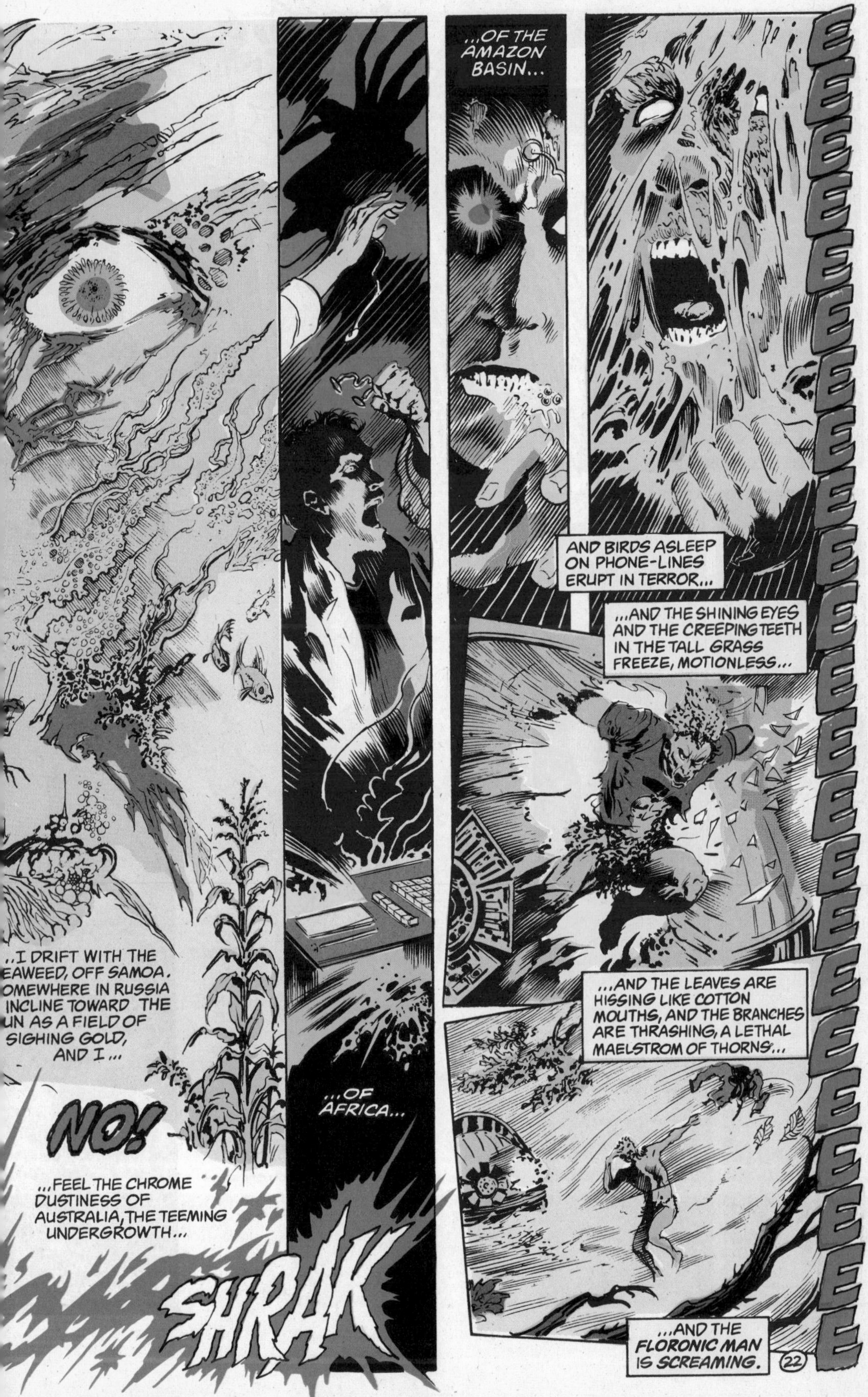
..I DRIFT WITH THE
EAWEED, OFF SAMOA.
OMEWHERE IN RUSSIA
INCLINE TOWARD THE
UN AS A FIELD OF
SIGHING GOLD,
AND I...
NO!
...FEEL THE CHROME DUSTINESS OF AUSTRALIA, THE TEEMING UNDERGROWTH...
SHRAK
...OF AFRICA...
...OF THE AMAZON BASIN...
EEEEEEEEEEEEEEEEEEEEEEEE
AND BIRDS ASLEEP ON PHONE-LINES ERUPT IN TERROR...
...AND THE SHINING EYES AND THE CREEPING TEETH IN THE TALL GRASS FREEZE, MOTIONLESS...
...AND THE LEAVES ARE HISSING LIKE COTTON MOUTHS, AND THE BRANCHES ARE THRASHING, A LETHAL MAELSTROM OF THORNS...
...AND THE FLORONIC MAN IS SCREAMING.
22

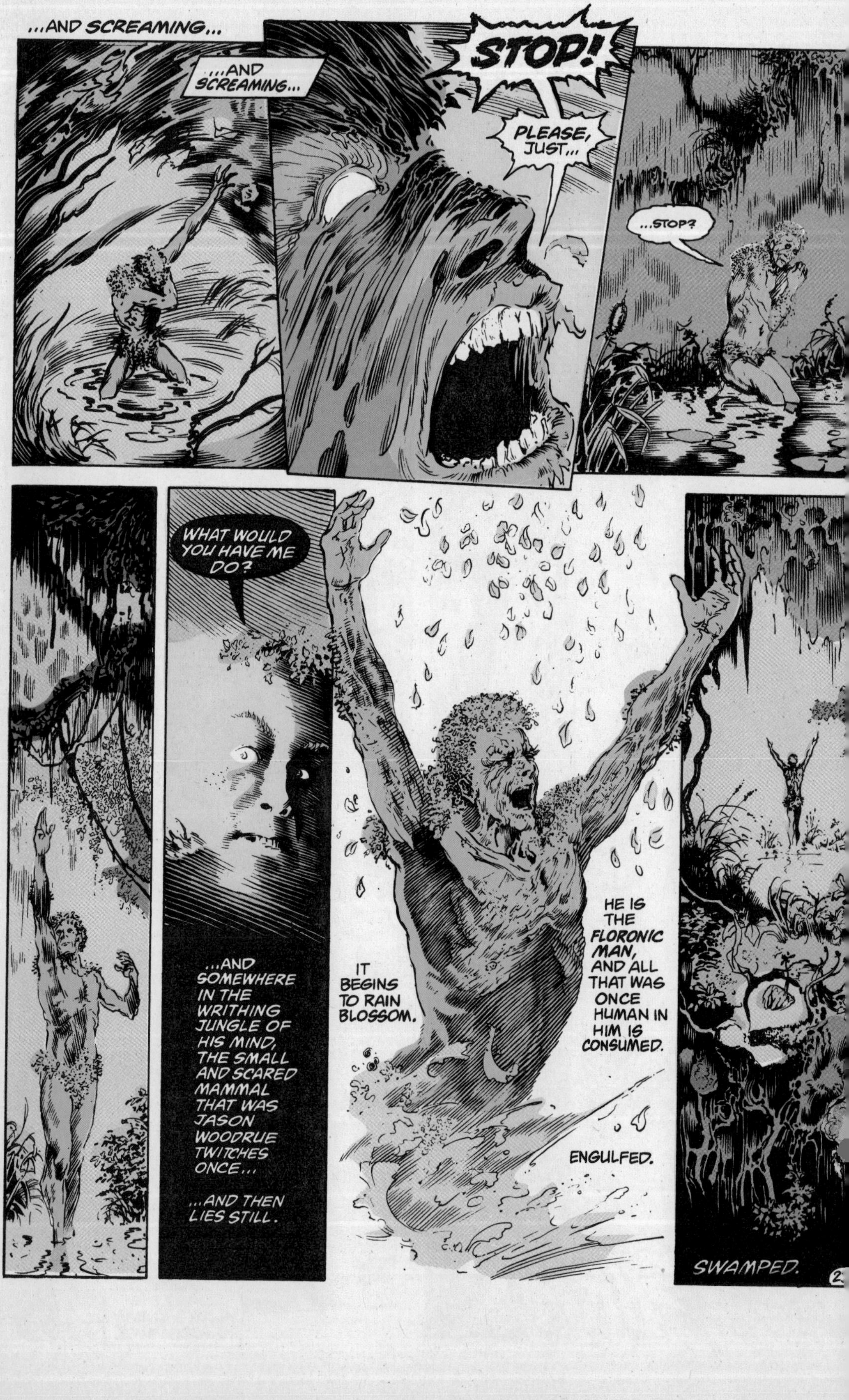
...AND SCREAMING...
...AND SCREAMING...
STOP!
PLEASE, JUST...
...STOP?
WHAT WOULD YOU HAVE ME DO?
...AND SOMEWHERE IN THE WRITHING JUNGLE OF HIS MIND, THE SMALL AND SCARED MAMMAL THAT WAS JASON WOODRUE TWITCHES ONCE...
...AND THEN LIES STILL.
IT BEGINS TO RAIN BLOSSOM.
HE IS THE FLORONIC MAN, AND ALL THAT WAS ONCE HUMAN IN HIM IS CONSUMED.
ENGULFED.
SWAMPED.

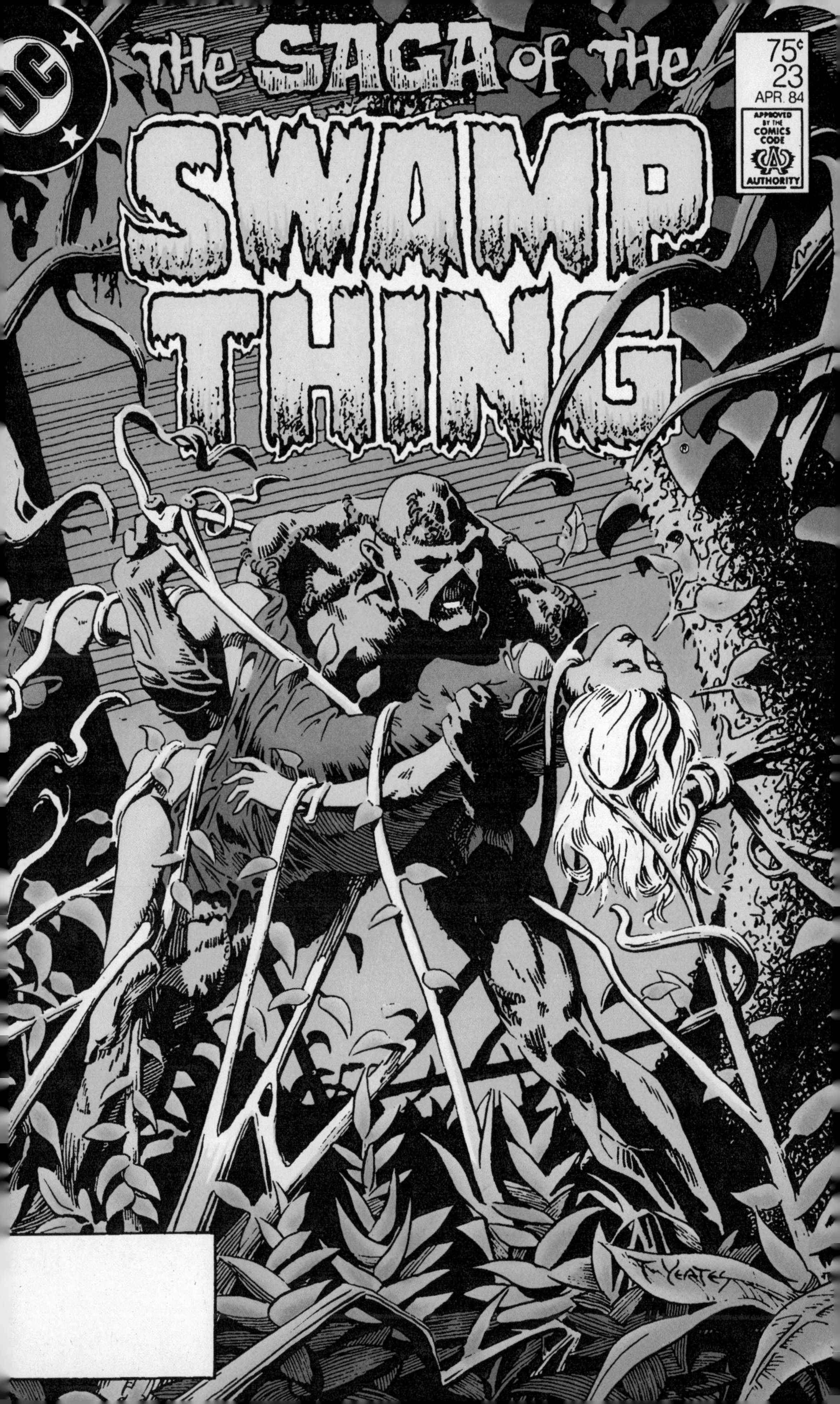

The SAGA of The
SWAMP THING
75¢
23
APR. 84
APPROVED BY THE COMICS CODE AUTHORITY

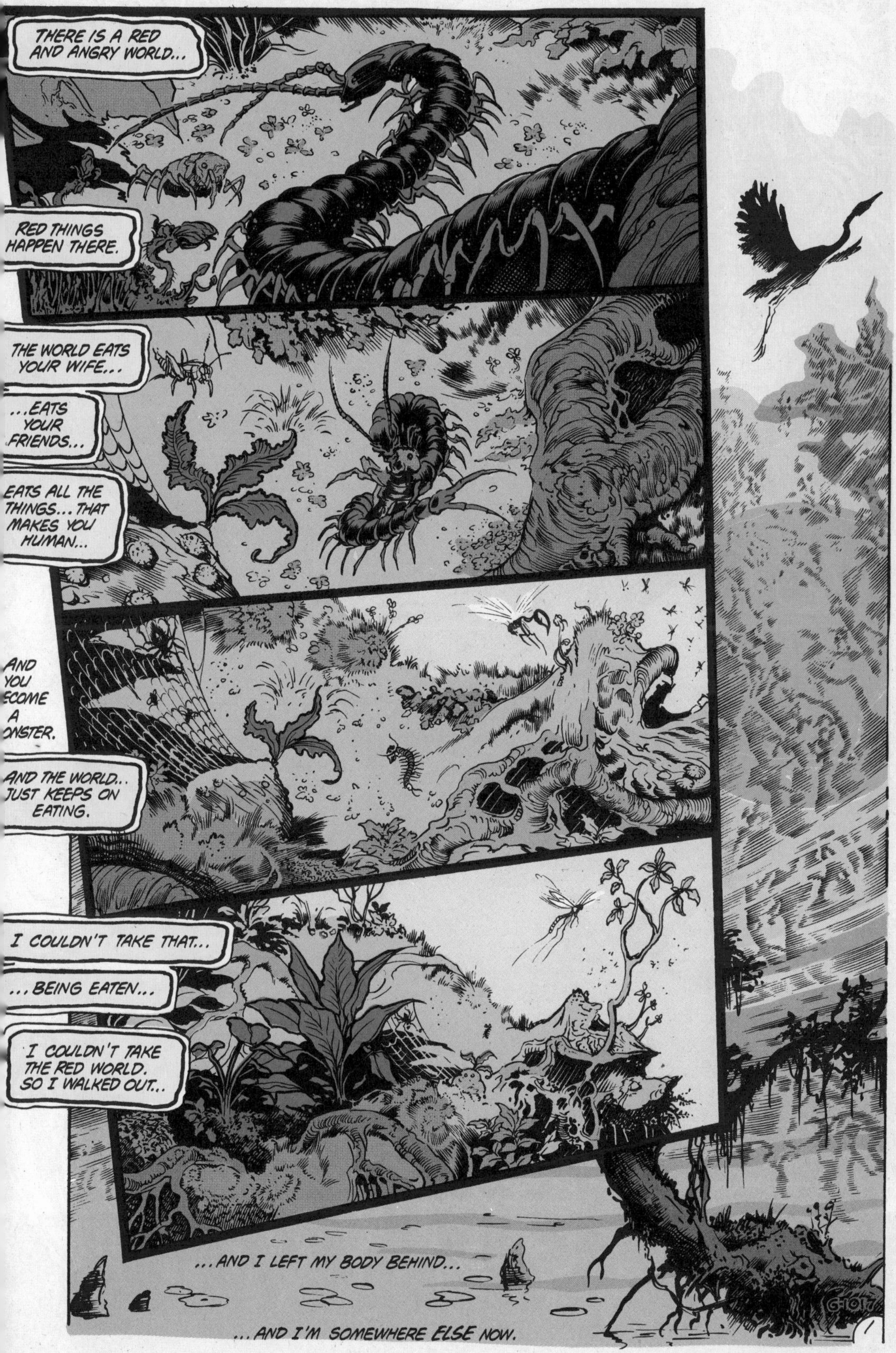
THERE IS A RED AND ANGRY WORLD...
RED THINGS HAPPEN THERE.
THE WORLD EATS YOUR WIFE...
...EATS YOUR FRIENDS...
EATS ALL THE THINGS... THAT MAKES YOU HUMAN...
AND YOU ECOME A ONSTER.
AND THE WORLD... JUST KEEPS ON EATING.
I COULDN'T TAKE THAT...
...BEING EATEN...
I COULDN'T TAKE THE RED WORLD. SO I WALKED OUT...
...AND I LEFT MY BODY BEHIND...
...AND I'M SOMEWHERE ELSE NOW.

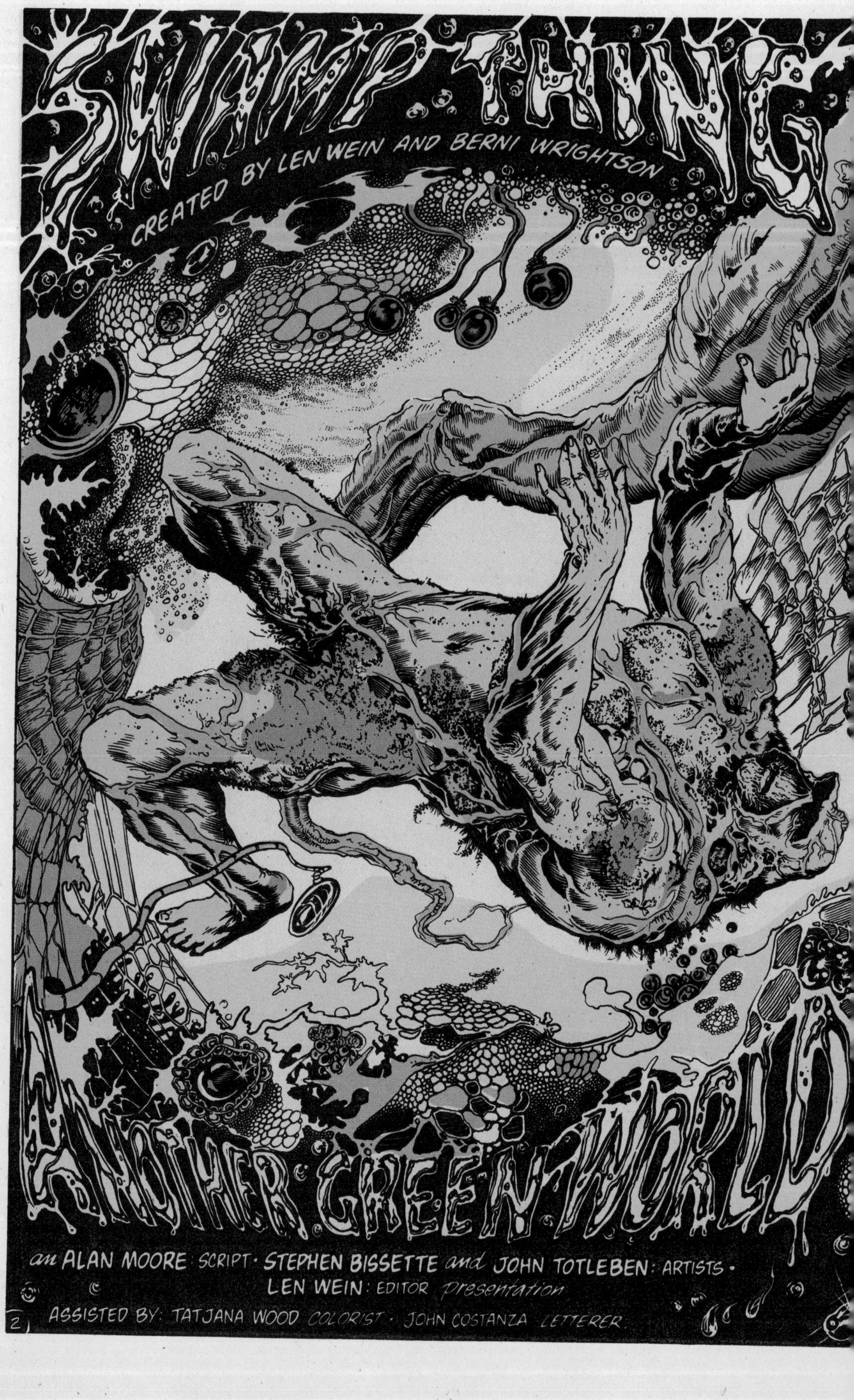
SWAMP THING
CREATED BY LEN WEIN AND BERNI WRIGHTSON
ANOTHER GREEN WORLD
an ALAN MOORE: SCRIPT · STEPHEN BISSETTE and JOHN TOTLEBEN: ARTISTS ·
LEN WEIN: EDITOR presentation
ASSISTED BY: TATJANA WOOD COLORIST · JOHN COSTANZA LETTERER
2

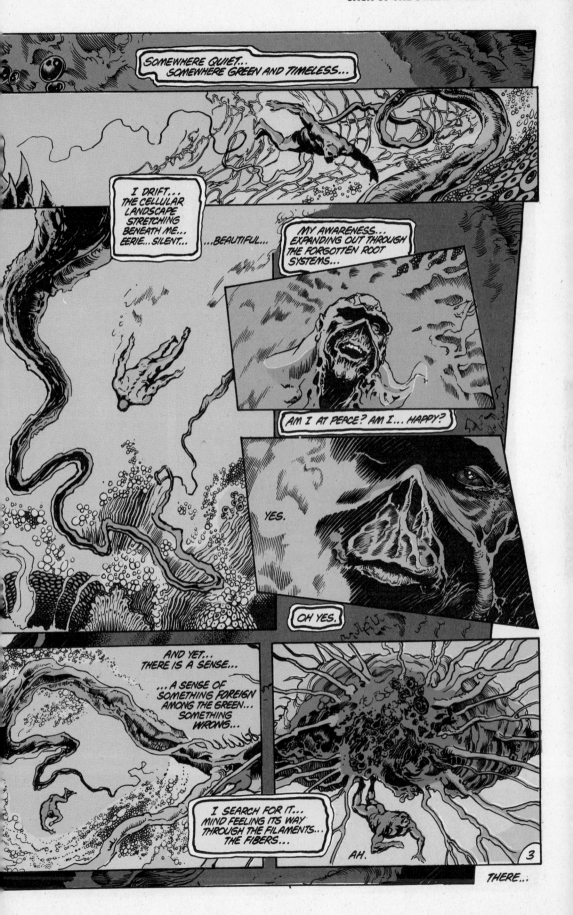

SOMEWHERE QUIET... SOMEWHERE GREEN AND TIMELESS...

I DRIFT... THE CELLULAR LANDSCAPE STRETCHING BENEATH ME... EERIE...SILENT... ...BEAUTIFUL...

MY AWARENESS... EXPANDING OUT THROUGH THE FORGOTTEN ROOT SYSTEMS...

AM I AT PEACE? AM I... HAPPY?

YES.

OH YES.

AND YET... THERE IS A SENSE...

...A SENSE OF SOMETHING FOREIGN AMONG THE GREEN... SOMETHING WRONGS...

I SEARCH FOR IT... MIND FEELING ITS WAY THROUGH THE FILAMENTS... THE FIBERS...

AH.

THERE...

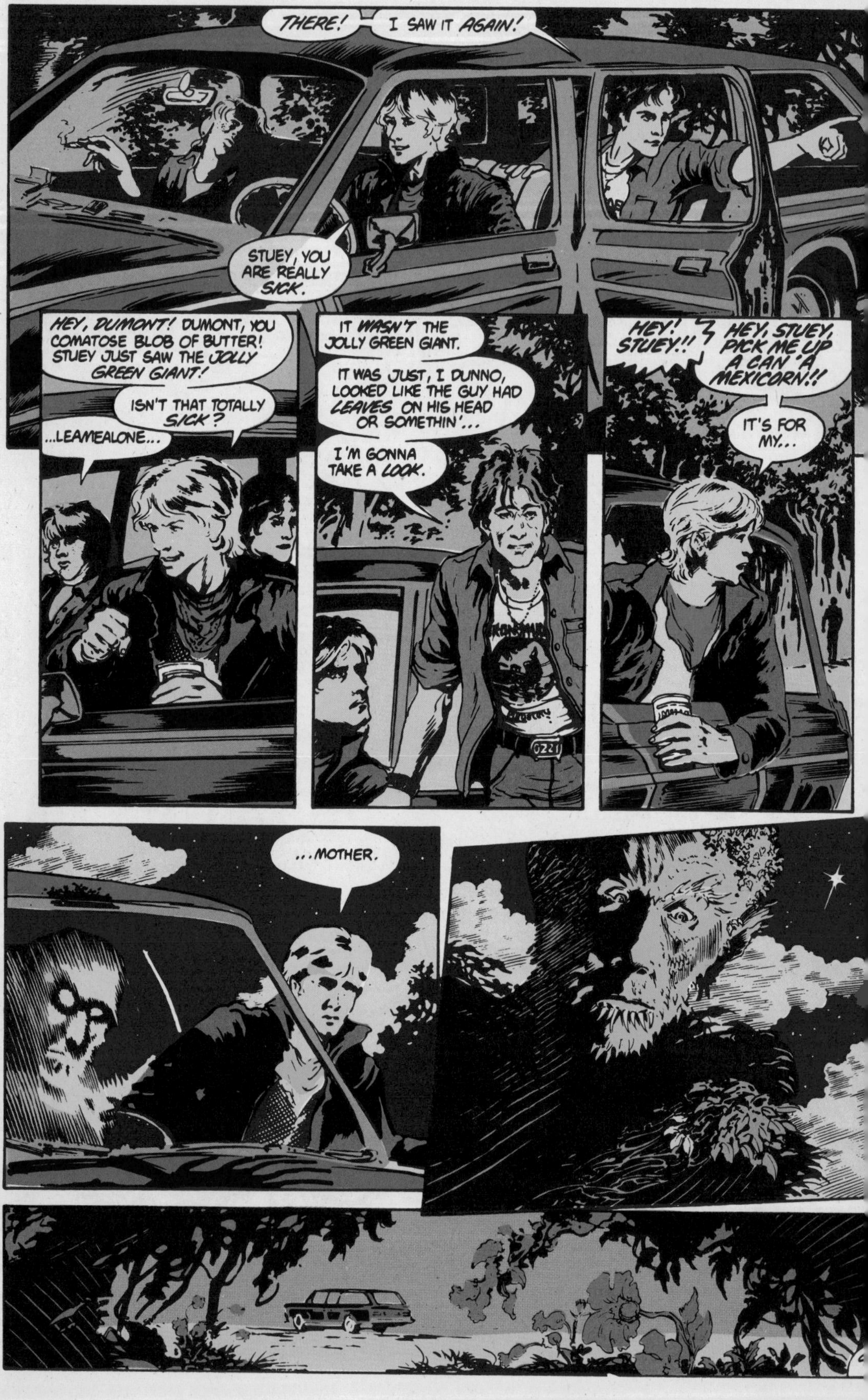
THERE!
I SAW IT AGAIN!
STUEY, YOU ARE REALLY SICK.
HEY, DUMONT! DUMONT, YOU COMATOSE BLOB OF BUTTER! STUEY JUST SAW THE JOLLY GREEN GIANT!
ISN'T THAT TOTALLY SICK?
...LEAMEALONE...
IT WASN'T THE JOLLY GREEN GIANT.
IT WAS JUST, I DUNNO, LOOKED LIKE THE GUY HAD LEAVES ON HIS HEAD OR SOMETHIN'...
I'M GONNA TAKE A LOOK.
HEY! STUEY!!
HEY, STUEY, PICK ME UP A CAN 'A MEXICORN!!
IT'S FOR MY...
...MOTHER.

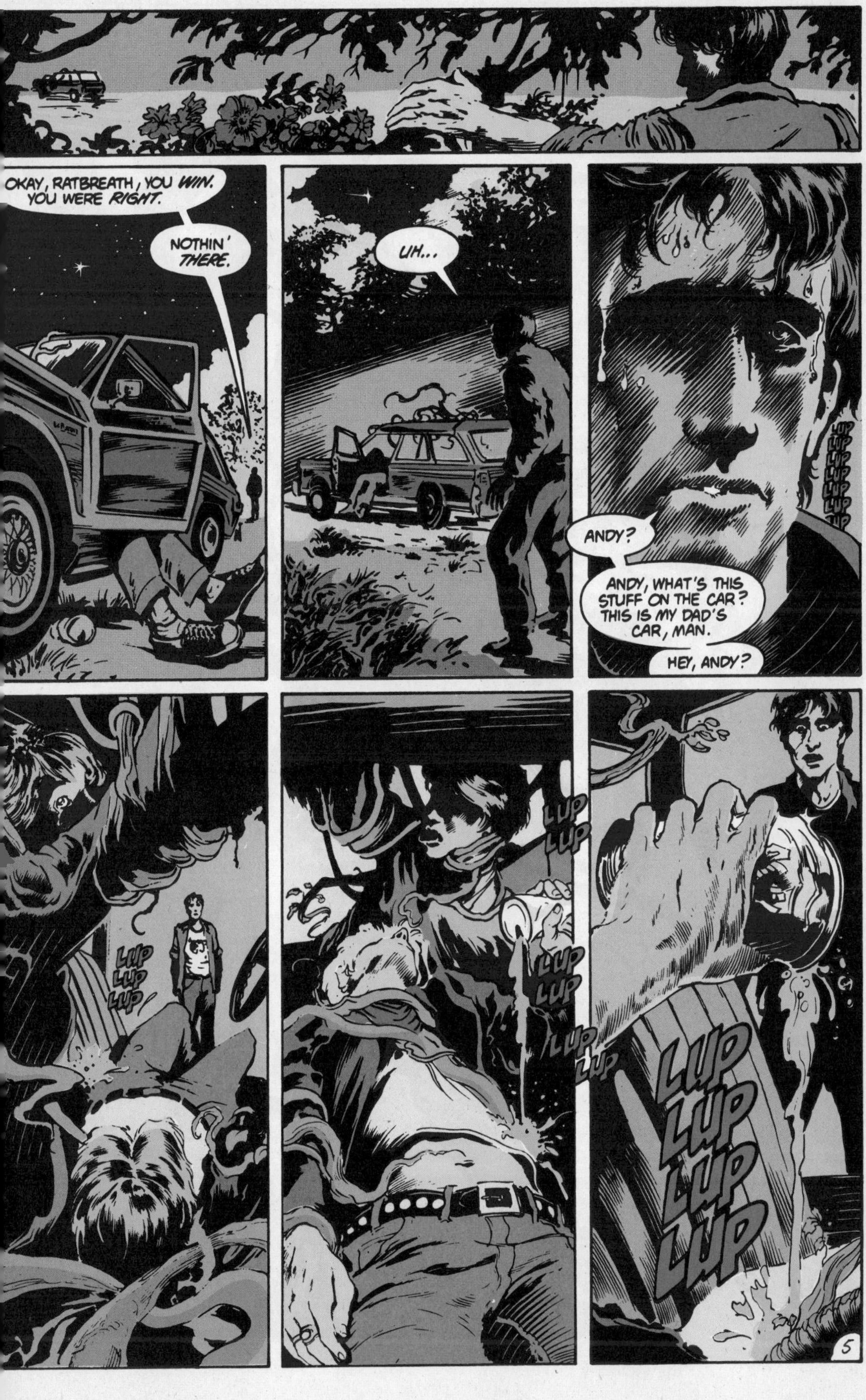
OKAY, RATBREATH, YOU WIN. YOU WERE RIGHT.
NOTHIN' THERE.
UH...
LUP LUP LUP LUP LUP LUP LUP
ANDY?
ANDY, WHAT'S THIS STUFF ON THE CAR? THIS IS MY DAD'S CAR, MAN.
HEY, ANDY?
LUP LUP LUP
LUP LUP
LUP LUP
LUP LUP
LUP LUP LUP LUP
5

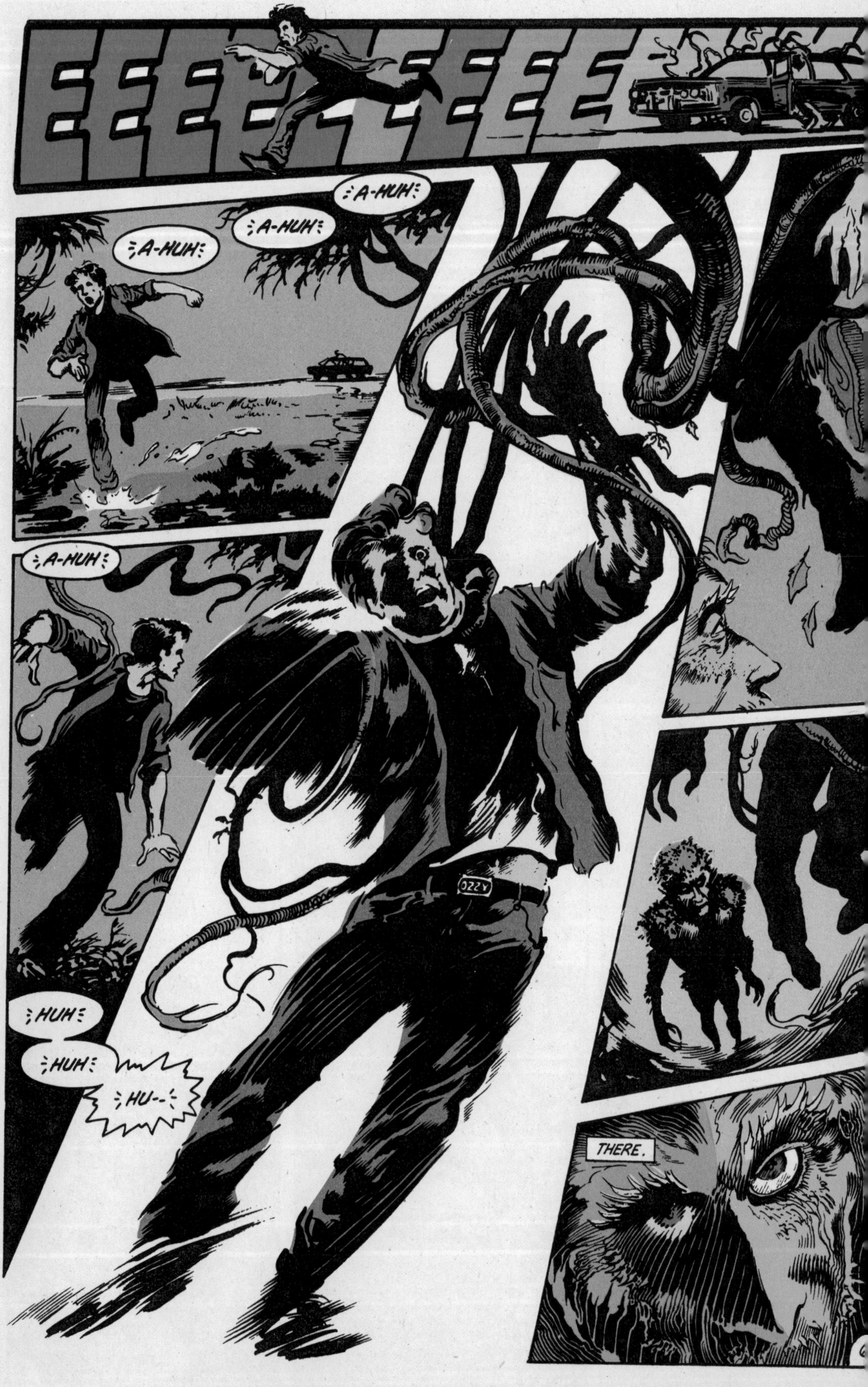
EEEEEEEEEE
A-HUH
A-HUH
A-HUH
A-HUH
OZZY
HUH
HUH
HU--
THERE.

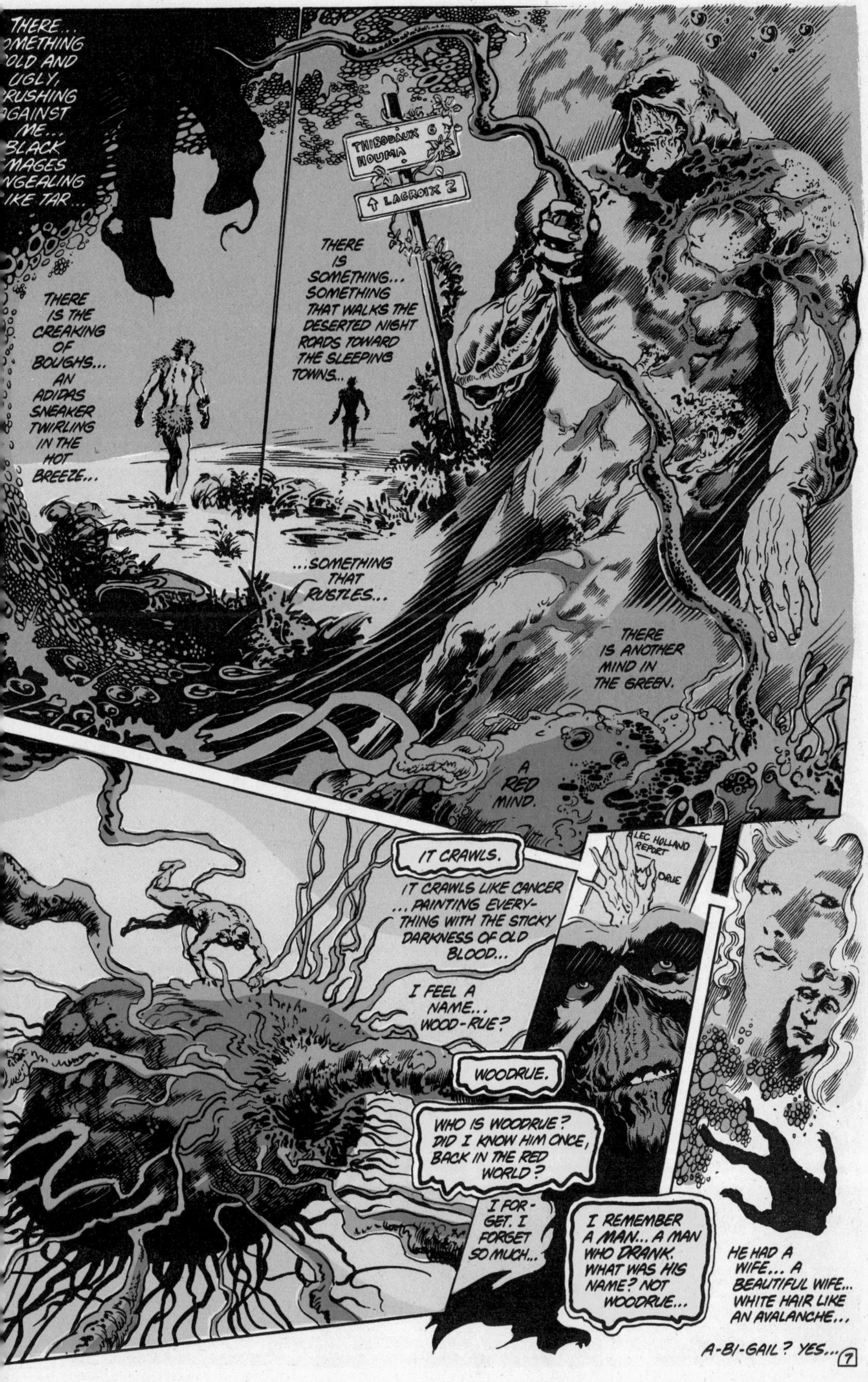
THERE... OMETHING OLD AND UGLY, RUSHING AGAINST ME... BLACK MAGES NGEALING IKE TAR...
THERE IS THE CREAKING OF BOUGHS... AN ADIDAS SNEAKER TWIRLING IN THE HOT BREEZE...
THIBODAUX 6
HOUMA
LAGROIX 2
THERE IS SOMETHING... SOMETHING THAT WALKS THE DESERTED NIGHT ROADS TOWARD THE SLEEPING TOWNS...
...SOMETHING THAT RUSTLES...
THERE IS ANOTHER MIND IN THE GREEN.
A RED MIND.
IT CRAWLS.
IT CRAWLS LIKE CANCER ...PAINTING EVERY-THING WITH THE STICKY DARKNESS OF OLD BLOOD...
I FEEL A NAME... WOOD-RUE?
WOODRUE.
WHO IS WOODRUE? DID I KNOW HIM ONCE, BACK IN THE RED WORLD?
I FOR-GET. I FORGET SO MUCH...
LEC HOLLAND REPORT
DRUE
I REMEMBER A MAN... A MAN WHO DRANK. WHAT WAS HIS NAME? NOT WOODRUE...
HE HAD A WIFE... A BEAUTIFUL WIFE... WHITE HAIR LIKE AN AVALANCHE...
A-BI-GAIL? YES...
7

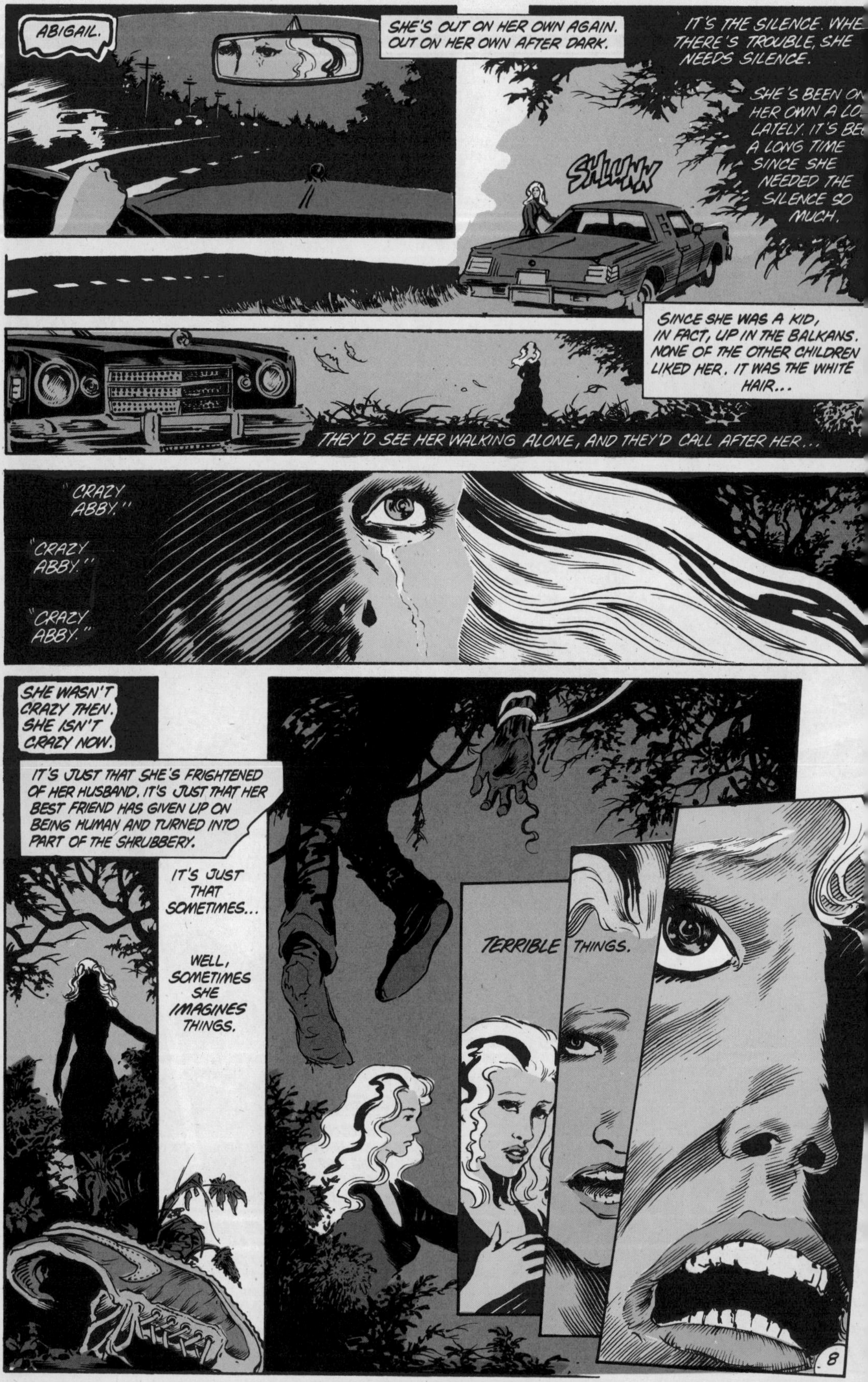
ABIGAIL.
SHE'S OUT ON HER OWN AGAIN. OUT ON HER OWN AFTER DARK.
IT'S THE SILENCE. WHE
THERE'S TROUBLE, SHE NEEDS SILENCE.
SHE'S BEEN O
HER OWN A LO
LATELY. IT'S BE
A LONG TIME SINCE SHE NEEDED THE SILENCE SO MUCH.
SHLUNK
SINCE SHE WAS A KID, IN FACT, UP IN THE BALKANS. NONE OF THE OTHER CHILDREN LIKED HER. IT WAS THE WHITE HAIR...
THEY'D SEE HER WALKING ALONE, AND THEY'D CALL AFTER HER...
"CRAZY ABBY."
"CRAZY ABBY."
"CRAZY ABBY."
SHE WASN'T CRAZY THEN. SHE ISN'T CRAZY NOW.
IT'S JUST THAT SHE'S FRIGHTENED OF HER HUSBAND. IT'S JUST THAT HER BEST FRIEND HAS GIVEN UP ON BEING HUMAN AND TURNED INTO PART OF THE SHRUBBERY.
IT'S JUST THAT SOMETIMES...
WELL, SOMETIMES SHE IMAGINES THINGS.
TERRIBLE THINGS.
8

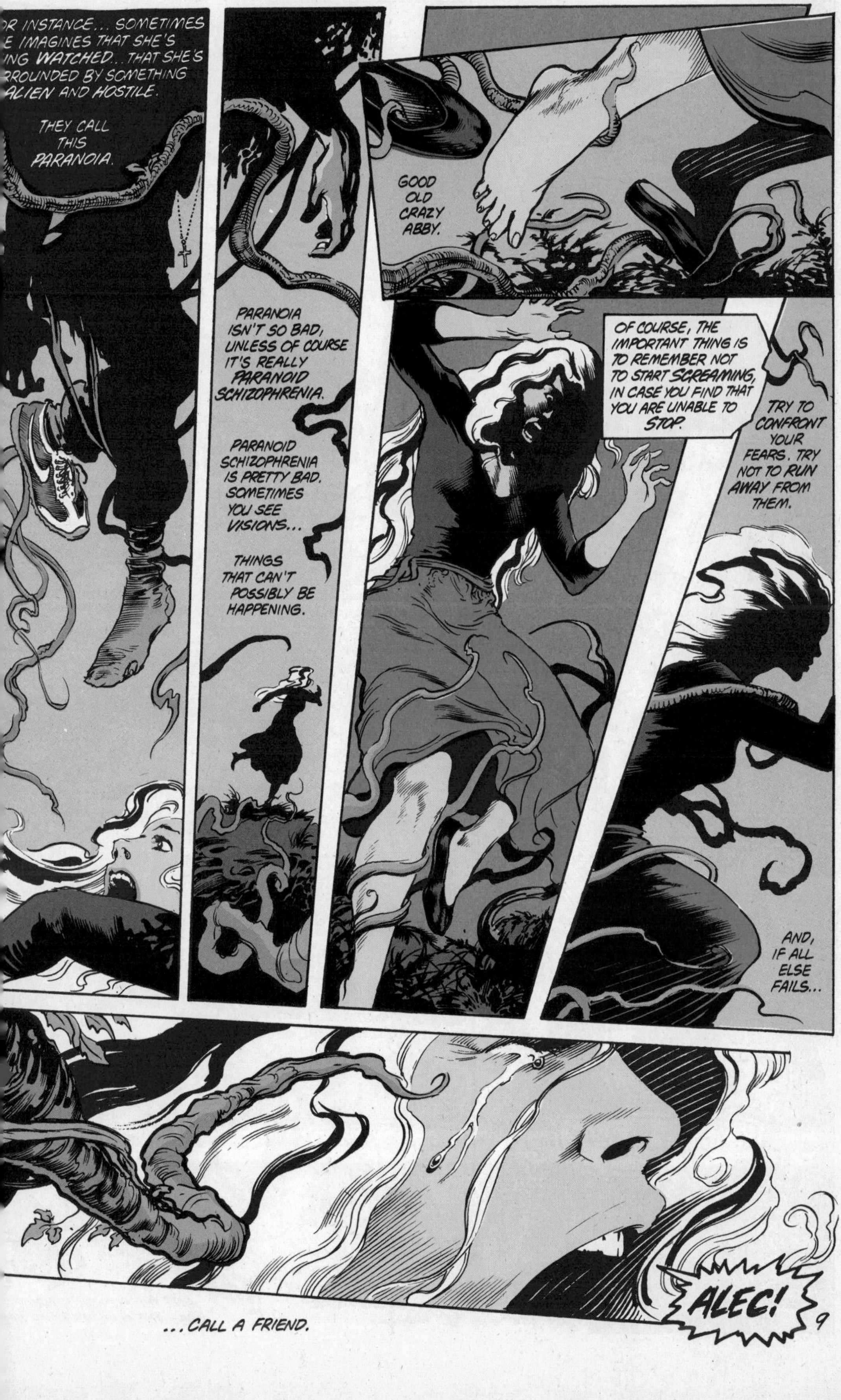
OR INSTANCE... SOMETIMES E IMAGINES THAT SHE'S ING WATCHED...THAT SHE'S RROUNDED BY SOMETHING ALIEN AND HOSTILE.
THEY CALL THIS PARANOIA.
PARANOIA ISN'T SO BAD, UNLESS OF COURSE IT'S REALLY PARANOID SCHIZOPHRENIA.
PARANOID SCHIZOPHRENIA IS PRETTY BAD. SOMETIMES YOU SEE VISIONS...
THINGS THAT CAN'T POSSIBLY BE HAPPENING.
GOOD OLD CRAZY ABBY.
OF COURSE, THE IMPORTANT THING IS TO REMEMBER NOT TO START SCREAMING, IN CASE YOU FIND THAT YOU ARE UNABLE TO STOP.
TRY TO CONFRONT YOUR FEARS. TRY NOT TO RUN AWAY FROM THEM.
AND, IF ALL ELSE FAILS...
...CALL A FRIEND.
ALEC!
9

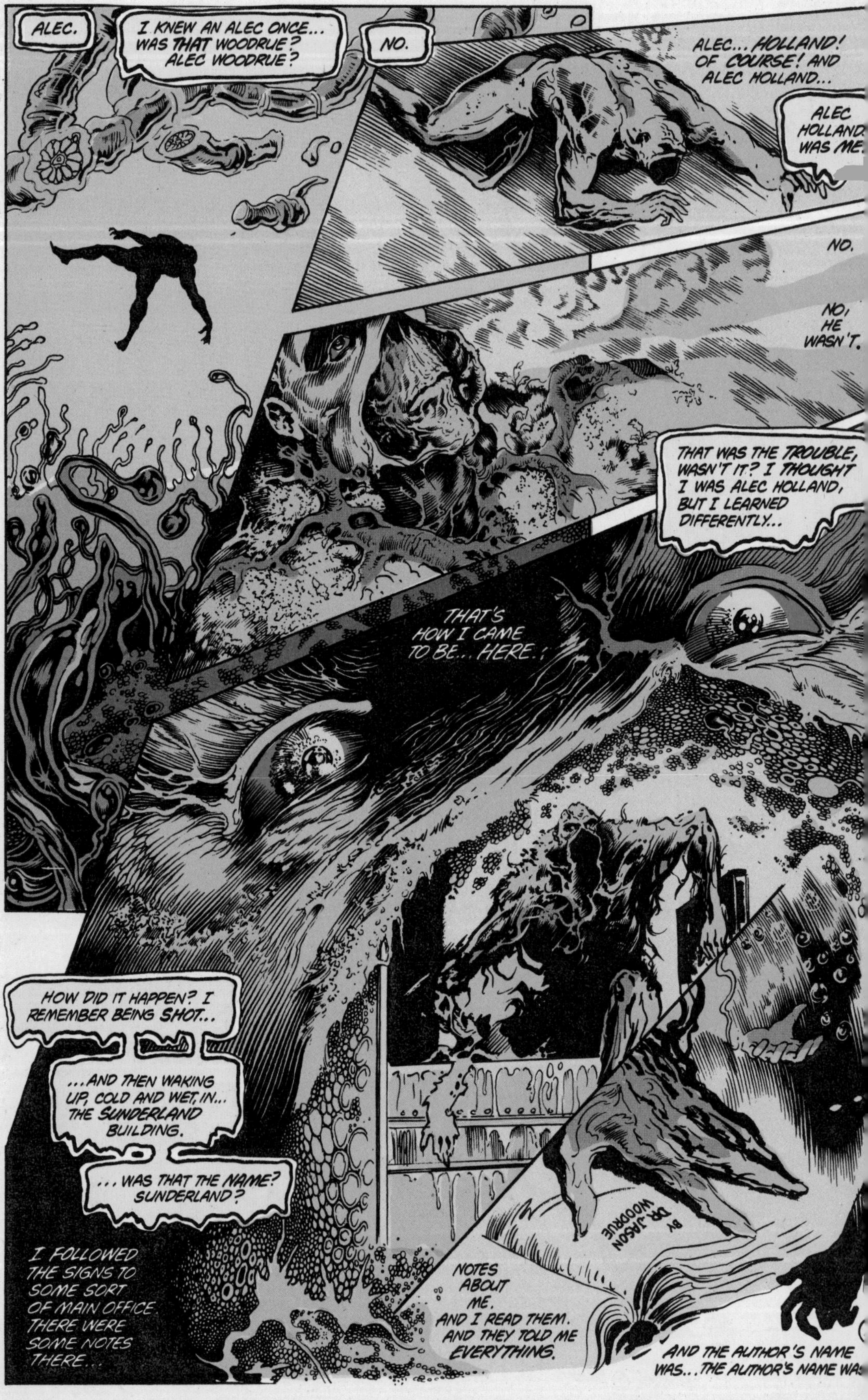
ALEC.
I KNEW AN ALEC ONCE... WAS THAT WOODRUE? ALEC WOODRUE?
NO.
ALEC... HOLLAND! OF COURSE! AND ALEC HOLLAND...
ALEC HOLLAND WAS ME.
NO.
NO, HE WASN'T.
THAT WAS THE TROUBLE, WASN'T IT? I THOUGHT I WAS ALEC HOLLAND, BUT I LEARNED DIFFERENTLY...
THAT'S HOW I CAME TO BE... HERE.
HOW DID IT HAPPEN? I REMEMBER BEING SHOT...
...AND THEN WAKING UP, COLD AND WET, IN... THE SUNDERLAND BUILDING.
...WAS THAT THE NAME? SUNDERLAND?
I FOLLOWED THE SIGNS TO SOME SORT OF MAIN OFFICE. THERE WERE SOME NOTES THERE...
NOTES ABOUT ME. AND I READ THEM. AND THEY TOLD ME EVERYTHING.
BY DR. JASON WOODRUE
AND THE AUTHOR'S NAME WAS... THE AUTHOR'S NAME WAS

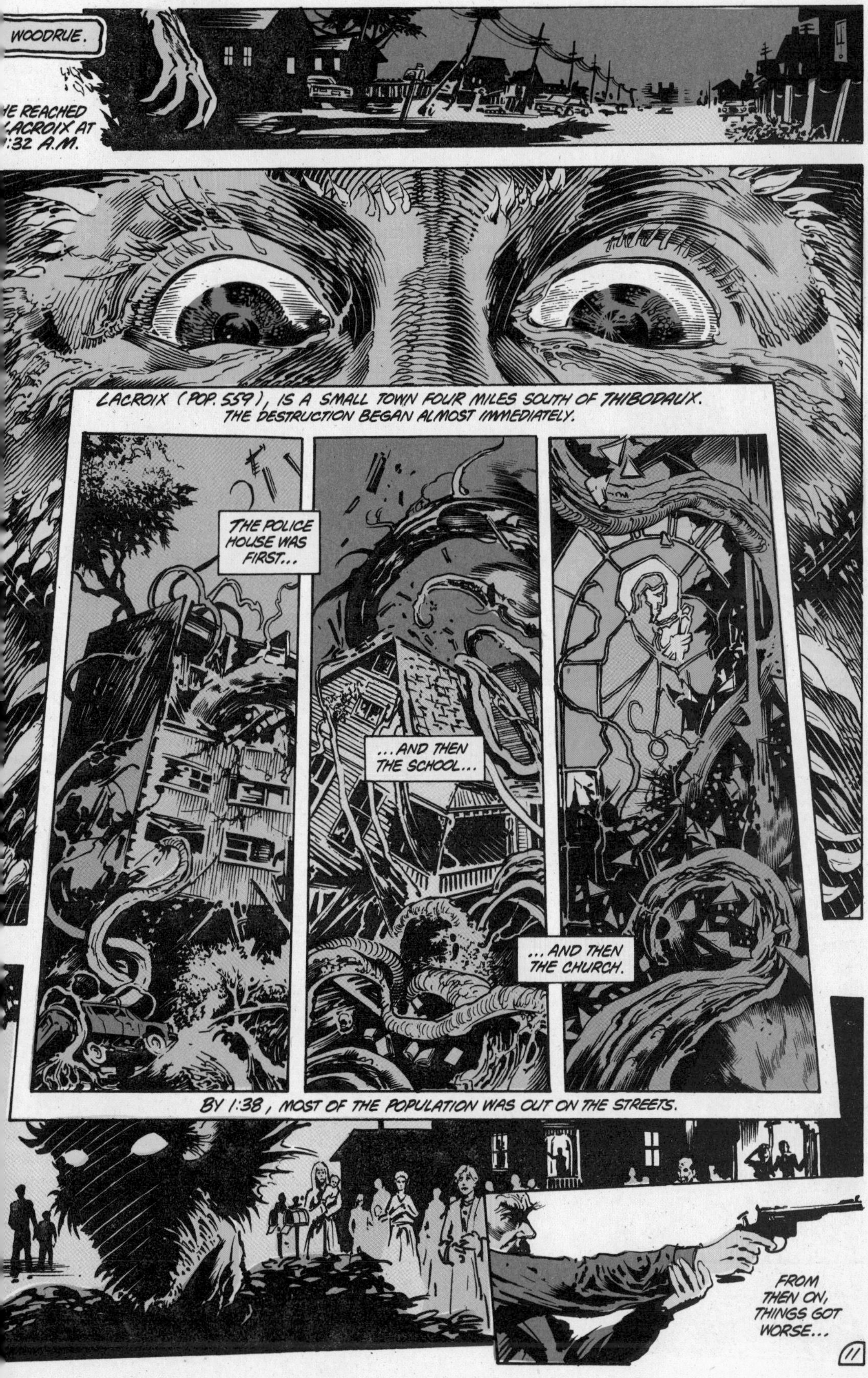
WOODRUE.
HE REACHED LACROIX AT 1:32 A.M.
LACROIX (POP. 559), IS A SMALL TOWN FOUR MILES SOUTH OF THIBODAUX. THE DESTRUCTION BEGAN ALMOST IMMEDIATELY.
THE POLICE HOUSE WAS FIRST...
...AND THEN THE SCHOOL...
...AND THEN THE CHURCH.
BY 1:38, MOST OF THE POPULATION WAS OUT ON THE STREETS.
FROM THEN ON, THINGS GOT WORSE...
11

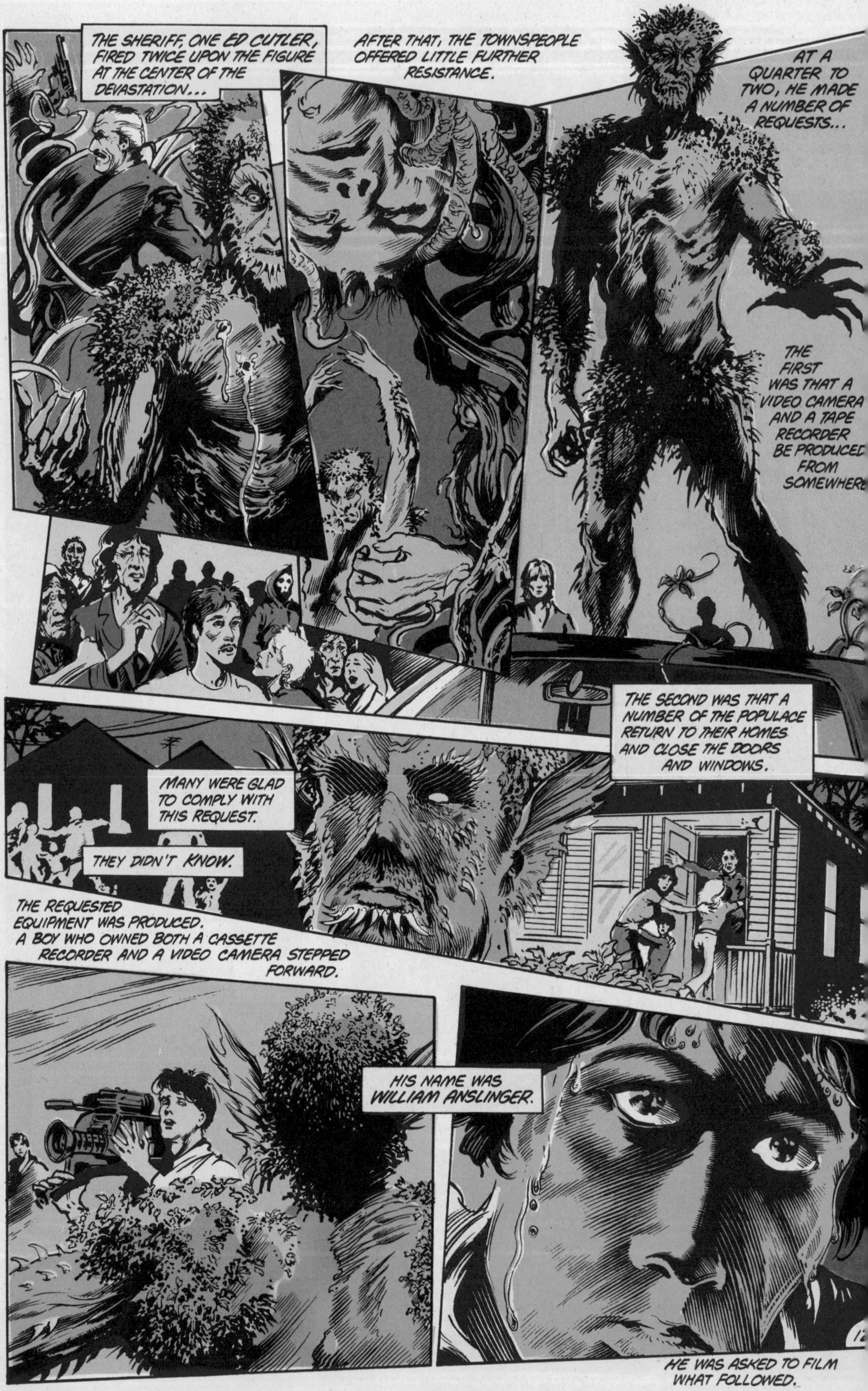
THE SHERIFF, ONE ED CUTLER, FIRED TWICE UPON THE FIGURE AT THE CENTER OF THE DEVASTATION...
AFTER THAT, THE TOWNSPEOPLE OFFERED LITTLE FURTHER RESISTANCE.
AT A QUARTER TO TWO, HE MADE A NUMBER OF REQUESTS...
THE FIRST WAS THAT A VIDEO CAMERA AND A TAPE RECORDER BE PRODUCED FROM SOMEWHERE
THE SECOND WAS THAT A NUMBER OF THE POPULACE RETURN TO THEIR HOMES AND CLOSE THE DOORS AND WINDOWS.
MANY WERE GLAD TO COMPLY WITH THIS REQUEST.
THEY DIDN'T KNOW.
THE REQUESTED EQUIPMENT WAS PRODUCED. A BOY WHO OWNED BOTH A CASSETTE RECORDER AND A VIDEO CAMERA STEPPED FORWARD.
HIS NAME WAS WILLIAM ANSLINGER.
HE WAS ASKED TO FILM WHAT FOLLOWED.

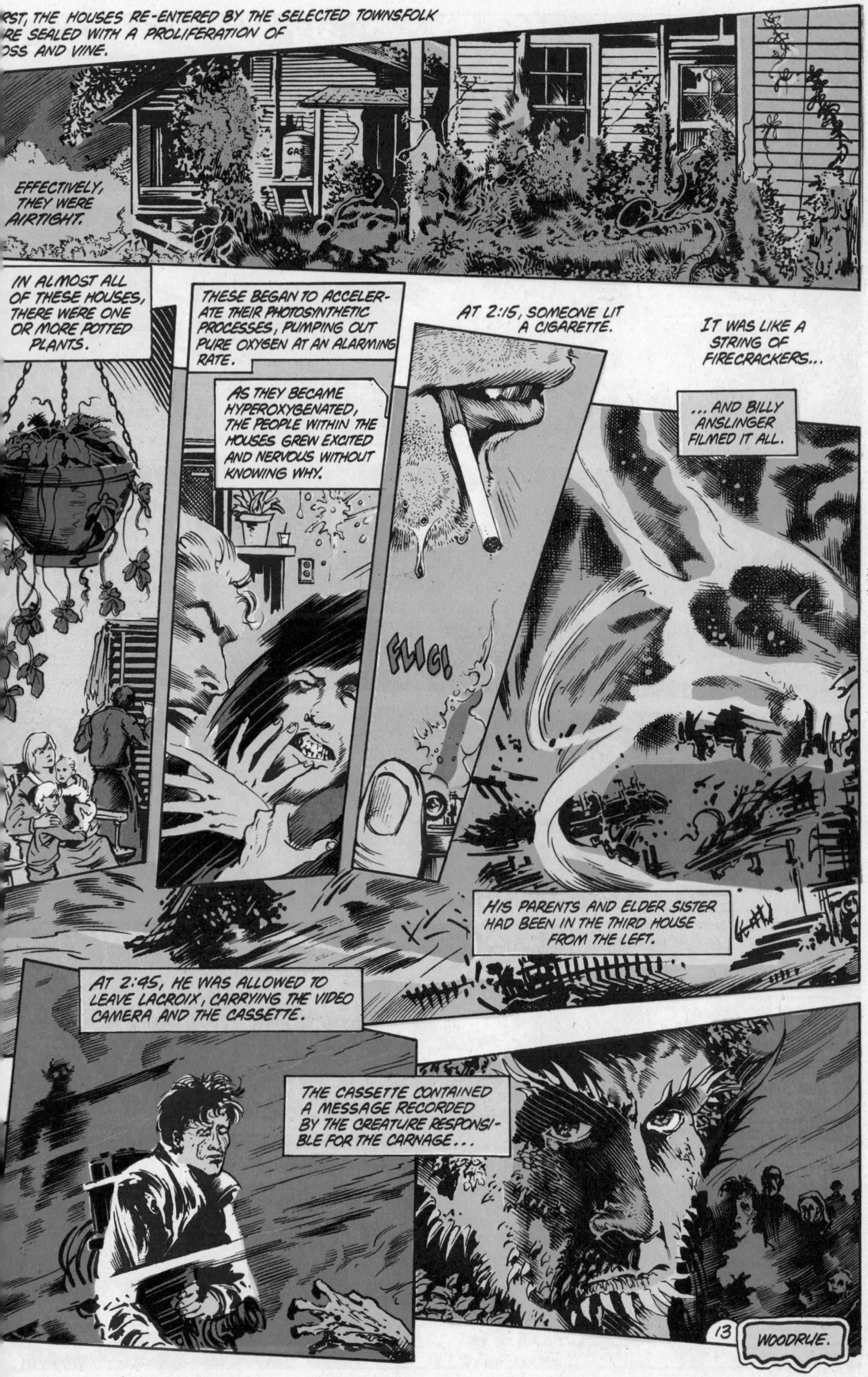
RST, THE HOUSES RE-ENTERED BY THE SELECTED TOWNSFOLK
RE SEALED WITH A PROLIFERATION OF
OSS AND VINE.
EFFECTIVELY, THEY WERE AIRTIGHT.
IN ALMOST ALL OF THESE HOUSES, THERE WERE ONE OR MORE POTTED PLANTS.
THESE BEGAN TO ACCELERATE THEIR PHOTOSYNTHETIC PROCESSES, PUMPING OUT PURE OXYGEN AT AN ALARMING RATE.
AS THEY BECAME HYPEROXYGENATED, THE PEOPLE WITHIN THE HOUSES GREW EXCITED AND NERVOUS WITHOUT KNOWING WHY.
AT 2:15, SOMEONE LIT A CIGARETTE.
FLIC!
IT WAS LIKE A STRING OF FIRECRACKERS...
...AND BILLY ANSLINGER FILMED IT ALL.
HIS PARENTS AND ELDER SISTER HAD BEEN IN THE THIRD HOUSE FROM THE LEFT.
AT 2:45, HE WAS ALLOWED TO LEAVE LACROIX, CARRYING THE VIDEO CAMERA AND THE CASSETTE.
THE CASSETTE CONTAINED A MESSAGE RECORDED BY THE CREATURE RESPONSIBLE FOR THE CARNAGE...
13
WOODRUE.

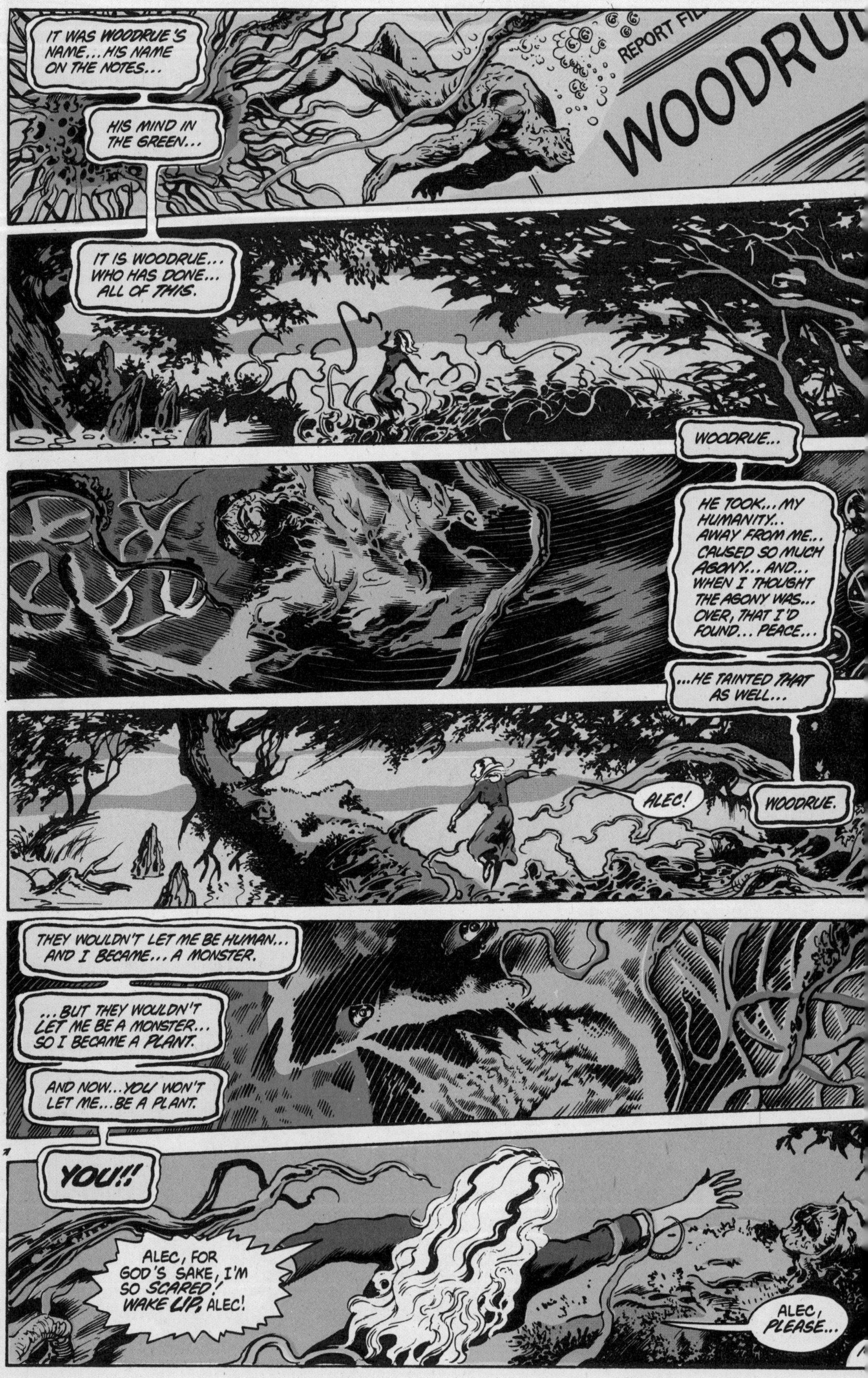
IT WAS WOODRUE'S NAME... HIS NAME ON THE NOTES...
HIS MIND IN THE GREEN...
REPORT FI
WOODRU
IT IS WOODRUE... WHO HAS DONE... ALL OF THIS.
WOODRUE...
HE TOOK... MY HUMANITY... AWAY FROM ME... CAUSED SO MUCH AGONY... AND... WHEN I THOUGHT THE AGONY WAS... OVER, THAT I'D FOUND... PEACE...
...HE TAINTED THAT AS WELL...
ALEC!
WOODRUE.
THEY WOULDN'T LET ME BE HUMAN... AND I BECAME... A MONSTER.
...BUT THEY WOULDN'T LET ME BE A MONSTER... SO I BECAME A PLANT.
AND NOW... YOU WON'T LET ME... BE A PLANT.
YOU!!
ALEC, FOR GOD'S SAKE, I'M SO SCARED! WAKE UP, ALEC!
ALEC, PLEASE...

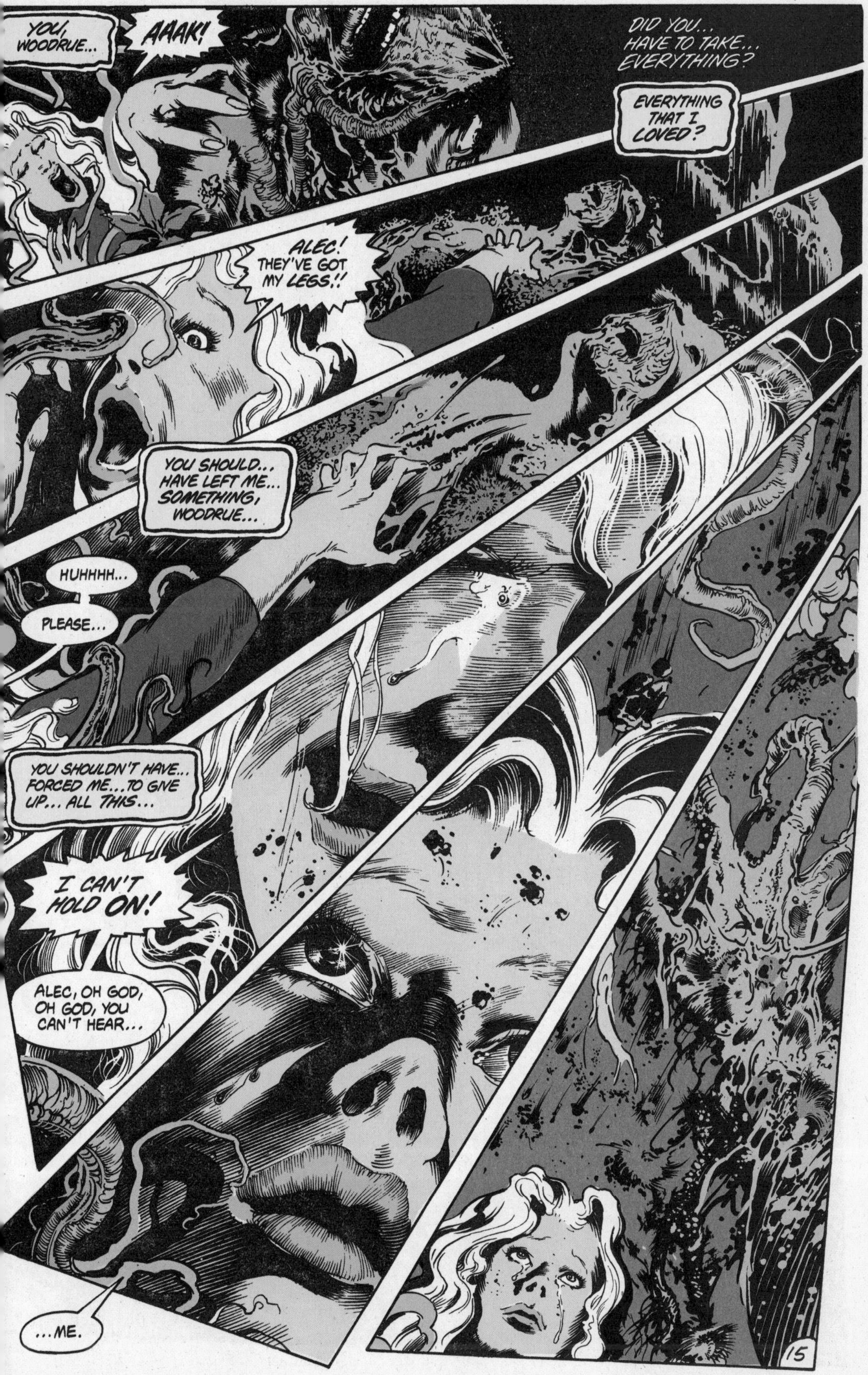

YOU, WOODRUE...
AAAK!
DID YOU... HAVE TO TAKE... EVERYTHING?
EVERYTHING THAT I LOVED?
ALEC! THEY'VE GOT MY LEGS!!
YOU SHOULD... HAVE LEFT ME... SOMETHING, WOODRUE...
HUHHHH...
PLEASE...
YOU SHOULDN'T HAVE... FORCED ME... TO GIVE UP... ALL THIS...
I CAN'T HOLD ON!
ALEC, OH GOD, OH GOD, YOU CAN'T HEAR...
...ME.
15

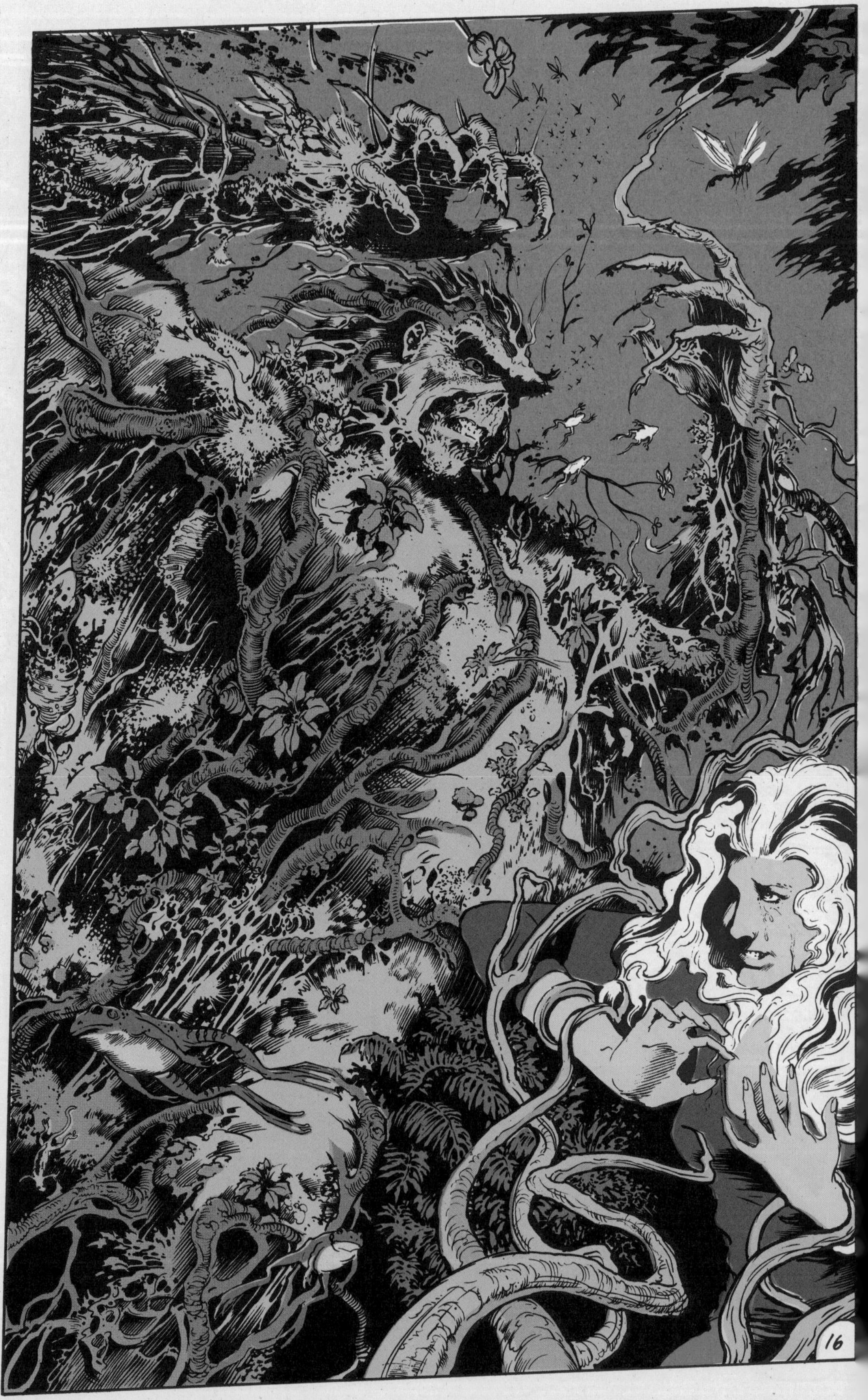
16

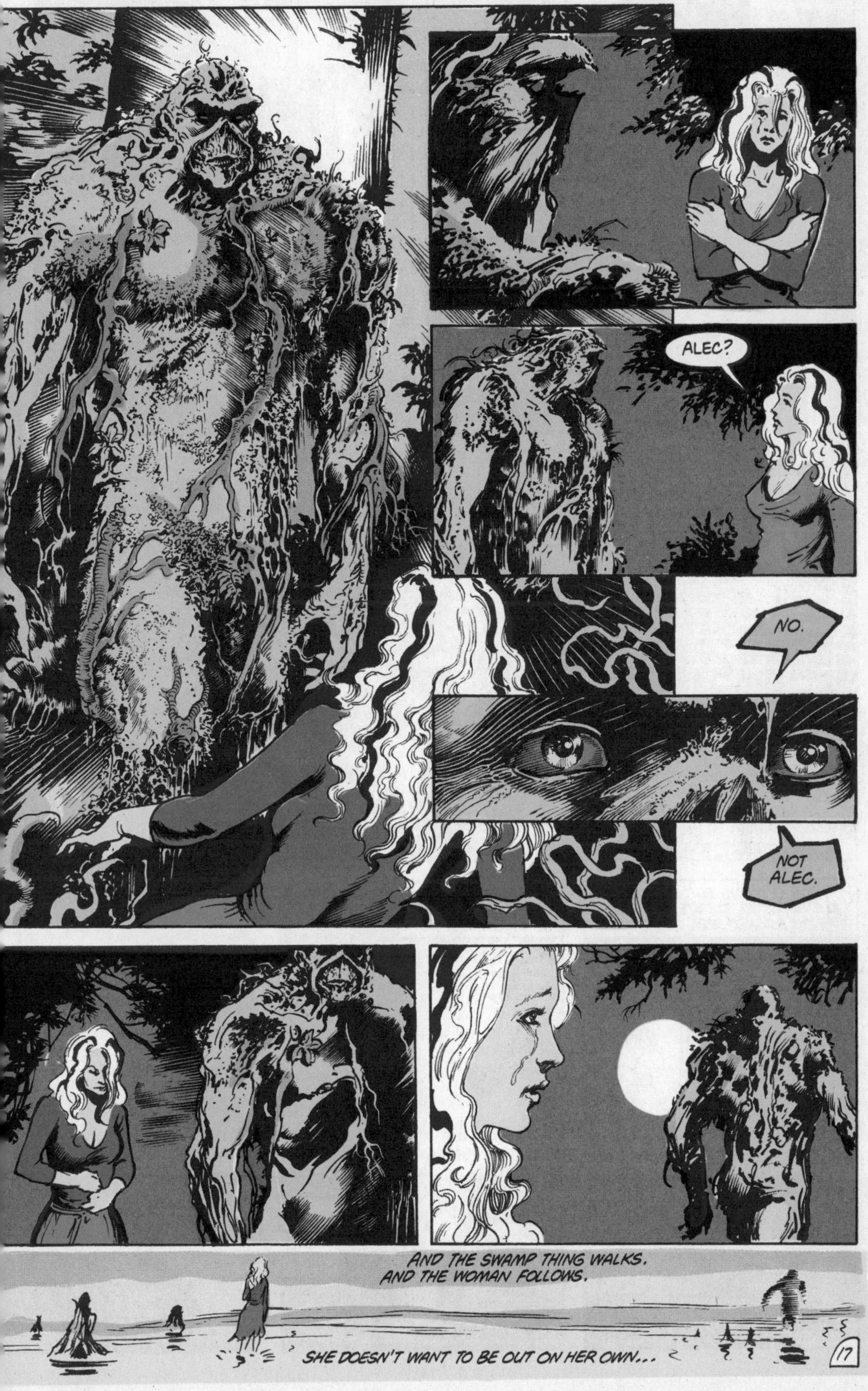
ALEC?
NO.
NOT ALEC.
AND THE SWAMP THING WALKS. AND THE WOMAN FOLLOWS.
SHE DOESN'T WANT TO BE OUT ON HER OWN...
17

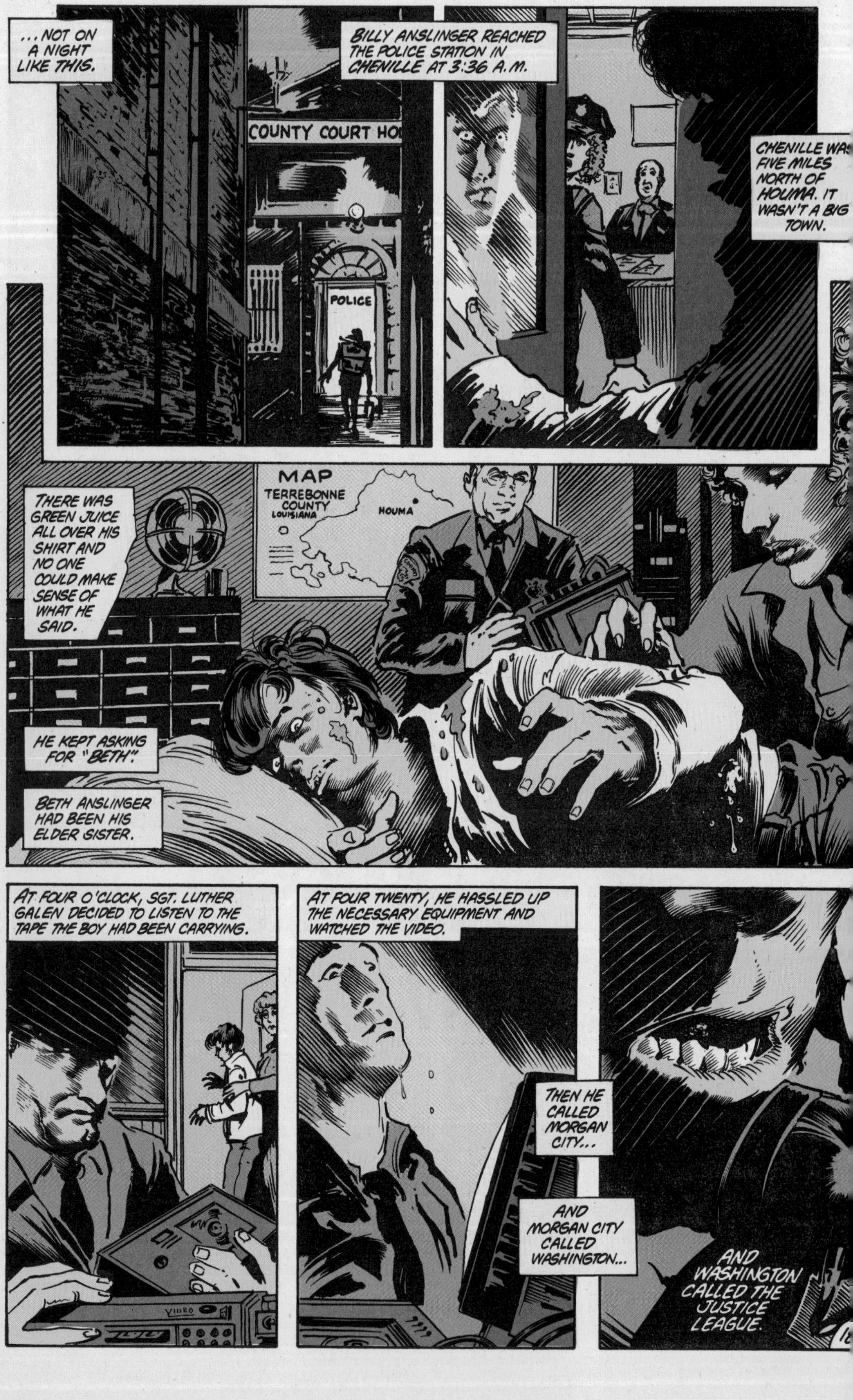
...NOT ON A NIGHT LIKE THIS.
BILLY ANSLINGER REACHED THE POLICE STATION IN CHENILLE AT 3:36 A.M.
COUNTY COURT HO
POLICE
CHENILLE WAS FIVE MILES NORTH OF HOUMA. IT WASN'T A BIG TOWN.
MAP
TERREBONNE COUNTY LOUISIANA
HOUMA
THERE WAS GREEN JUICE ALL OVER HIS SHIRT AND NO ONE COULD MAKE SENSE OF WHAT HE SAID.
HE KEPT ASKING FOR "BETH".
BETH ANSLINGER HAD BEEN HIS ELDER SISTER.
AT FOUR O'CLOCK, SGT. LUTHER GALEN DECIDED TO LISTEN TO THE TAPE THE BOY HAD BEEN CARRYING.
VIDEO
AT FOUR TWENTY, HE HASSLED UP THE NECESSARY EQUIPMENT AND WATCHED THE VIDEO.
THEN HE CALLED MORGAN CITY...
AND MORGAN CITY CALLED WASHINGTON...
AND WASHINGTON CALLED THE JUSTICE LEAGUE.

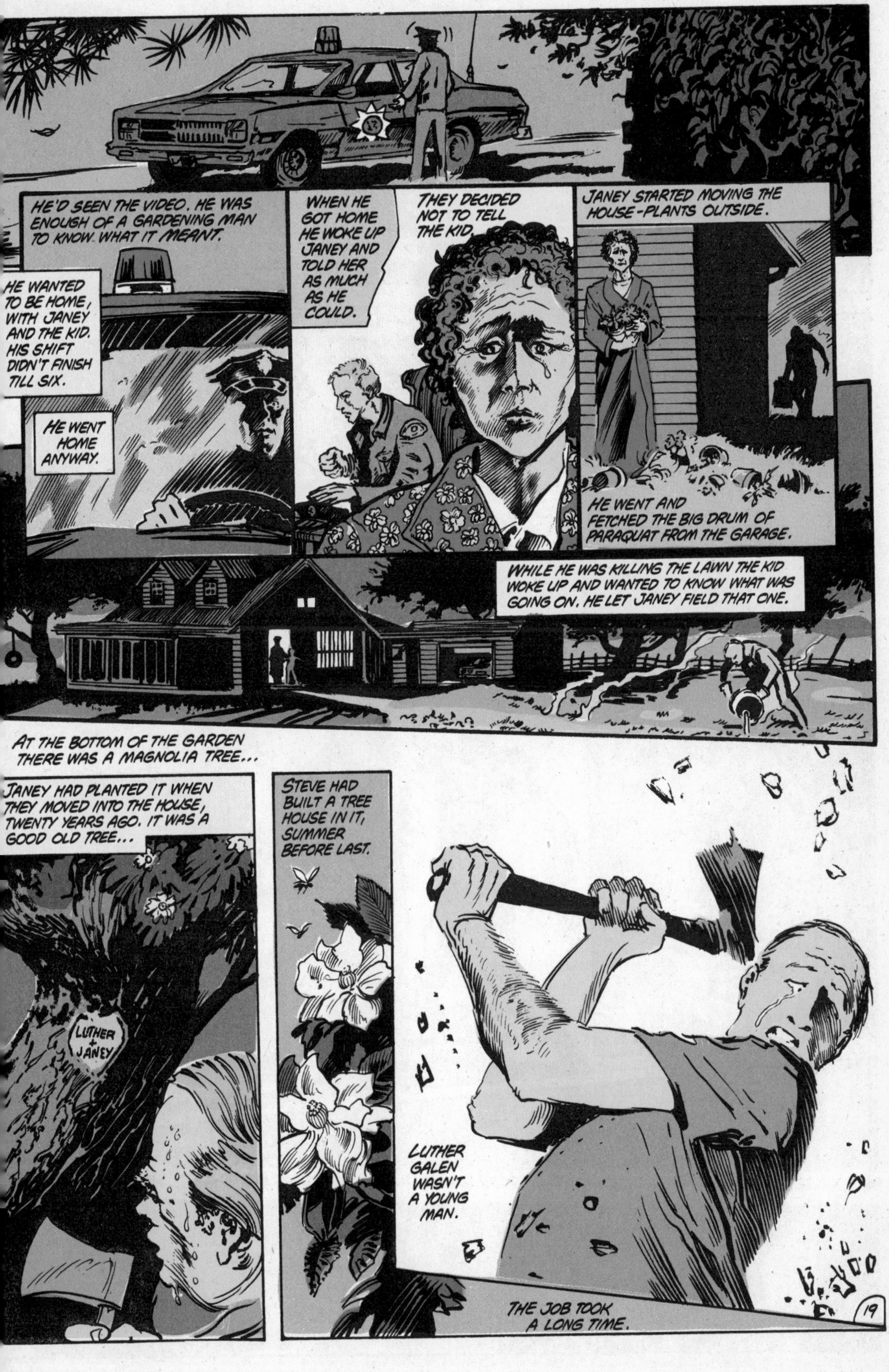
HE'D SEEN THE VIDEO. HE WAS ENOUGH OF A GARDENING MAN TO KNOW WHAT IT MEANT.
HE WANTED TO BE HOME, WITH JANEY AND THE KID. HIS SHIFT DIDN'T FINISH TILL SIX.
HE WENT HOME ANYWAY.
WHEN HE GOT HOME HE WOKE UP JANEY AND TOLD HER AS MUCH AS HE COULD.
THEY DECIDED NOT TO TELL THE KID.
JANEY STARTED MOVING THE HOUSE-PLANTS OUTSIDE.
HE WENT AND FETCHED THE BIG DRUM OF PARAQUAT FROM THE GARAGE.
WHILE HE WAS KILLING THE LAWN THE KID WOKE UP AND WANTED TO KNOW WHAT WAS GOING ON. HE LET JANEY FIELD THAT ONE.
AT THE BOTTOM OF THE GARDEN THERE WAS A MAGNOLIA TREE...
JANEY HAD PLANTED IT WHEN THEY MOVED INTO THE HOUSE, TWENTY YEARS AGO. IT WAS A GOOD OLD TREE...
LUTHER + JANEY
STEVE HAD BUILT A TREE HOUSE IN IT, SUMMER BEFORE LAST.
LUTHER GALEN WASN'T A YOUNG MAN.
THE JOB TOOK A LONG TIME.
19

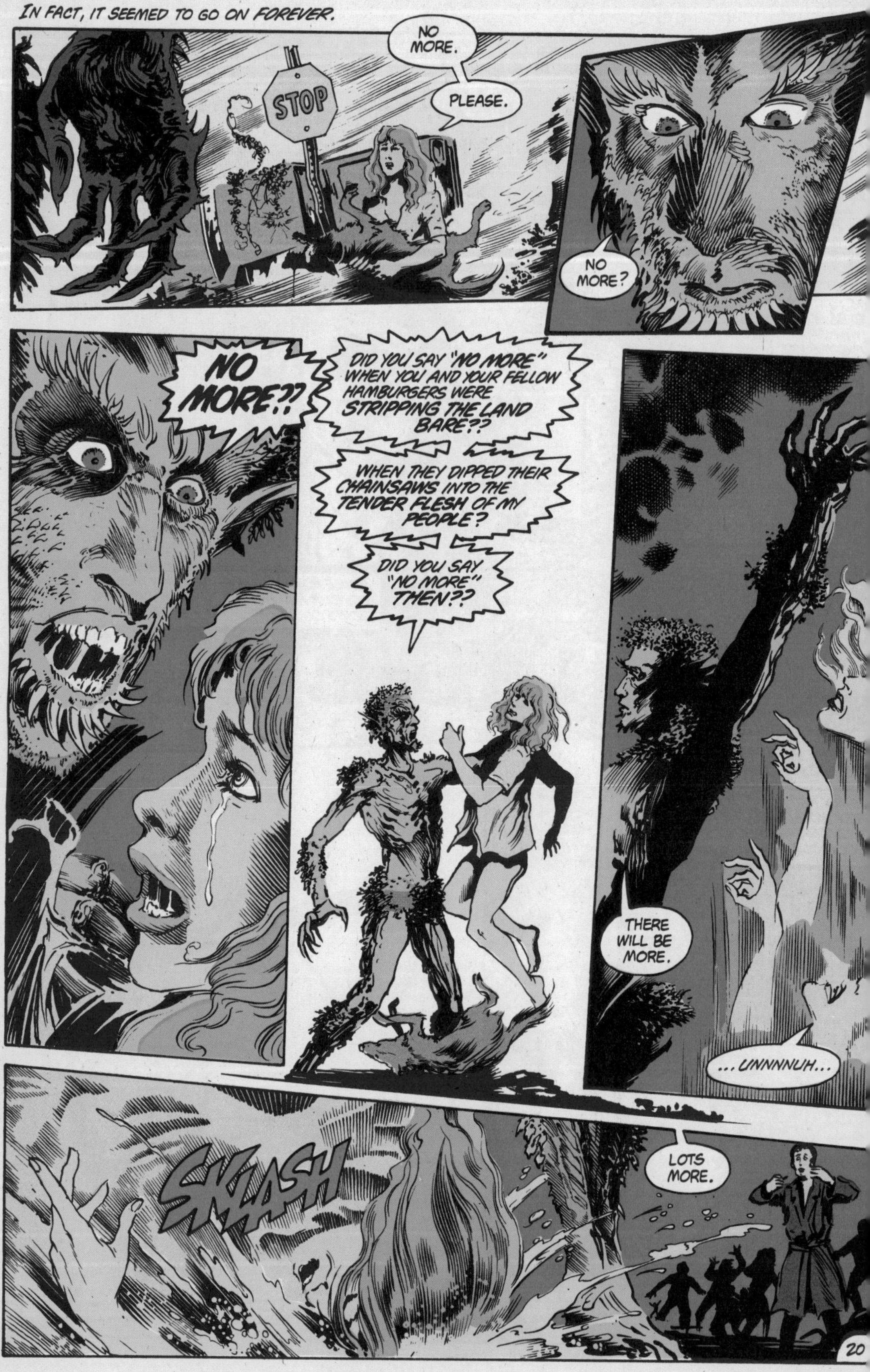
IN FACT, IT SEEMED TO GO ON FOREVER.
NO MORE.
PLEASE.
STOP
NO MORE?
NO MORE??
DID YOU SAY "NO MORE" WHEN YOU AND YOUR FELLOW HAMBURGERS WERE STRIPPING THE LAND BARE??
WHEN THEY DIPPED THEIR CHAINSAWS INTO THE TENDER FLESH OF MY PEOPLE?
DID YOU SAY "NO MORE" THEN??
THERE WILL BE MORE.
...UNNNNUH...
SKLASH
LOTS MORE.
20

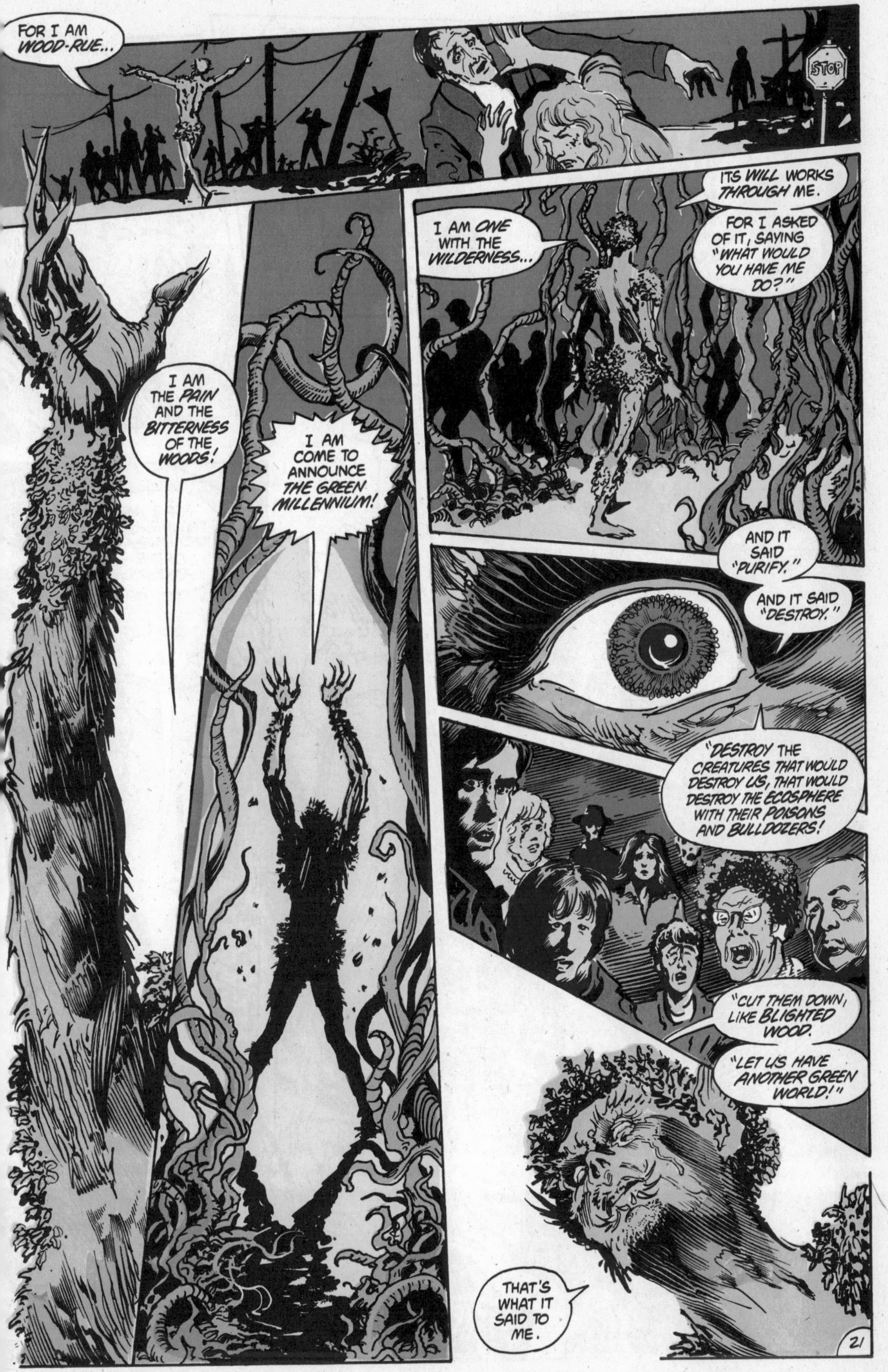
FOR I AM WOOD-RUE...
I AM THE PAIN AND THE BITTERNESS OF THE WOODS!
I AM COME TO ANNOUNCE THE GREEN MILLENNIUM!
I AM ONE WITH THE WILDERNESS...
ITS WILL WORKS THROUGH ME.
FOR I ASKED OF IT, SAYING "WHAT WOULD YOU HAVE ME DO?"
AND IT SAID "PURIFY."
AND IT SAID "DESTROY."
"DESTROY THE CREATURES THAT WOULD DESTROY US, THAT WOULD DESTROY THE ECOSPHERE WITH THEIR POISONS AND BULLDOZERS!
"CUT THEM DOWN, LIKE BLIGHTED WOOD.
"LET US HAVE ANOTHER GREEN WORLD!"
THAT'S WHAT IT SAID TO ME.
21

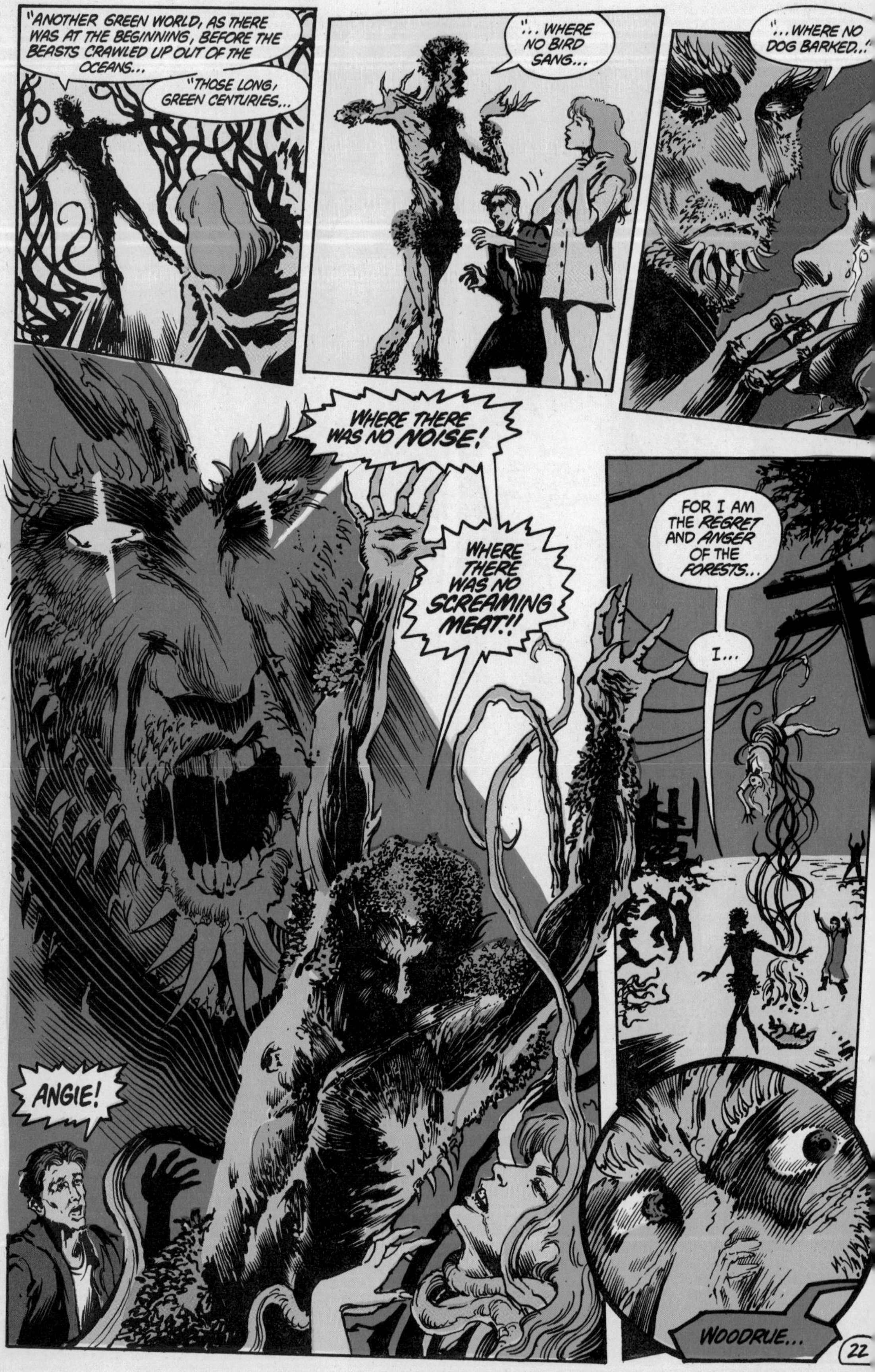
"ANOTHER GREEN WORLD, AS THERE WAS AT THE BEGINNING, BEFORE THE BEASTS CRAWLED UP OUT OF THE OCEANS...
"THOSE LONG, GREEN CENTURIES...
"...WHERE NO BIRD SANG...
"...WHERE NO DOG BARKED..."
WHERE THERE WAS NO NOISE!
WHERE THERE WAS NO SCREAMING MEAT!!
ANGIE!
FOR I AM THE REGRET AND ANGER OF THE FORESTS...
I...
WOODRUE...
22

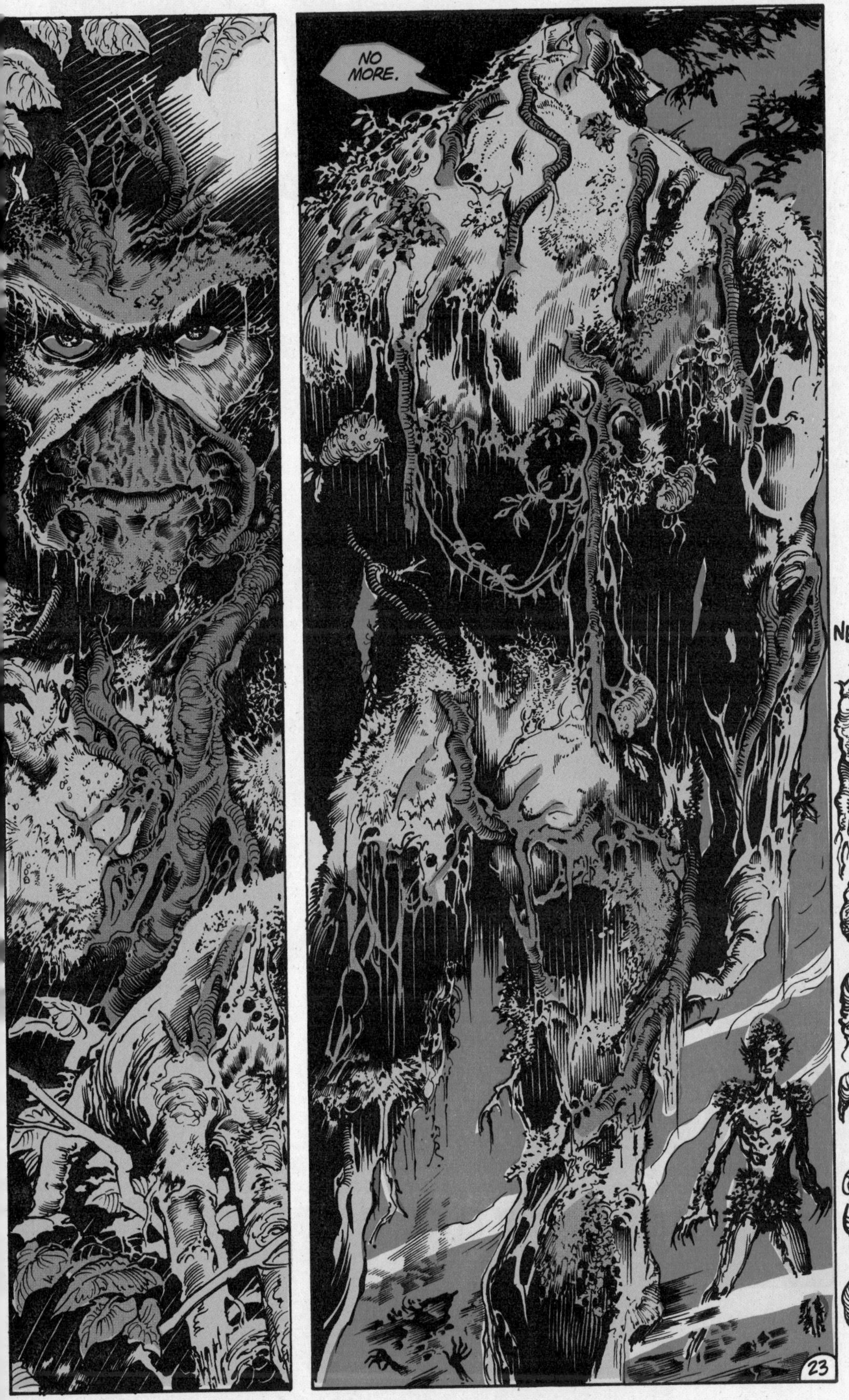
NO MORE.
NEXT:
ROOTS
23

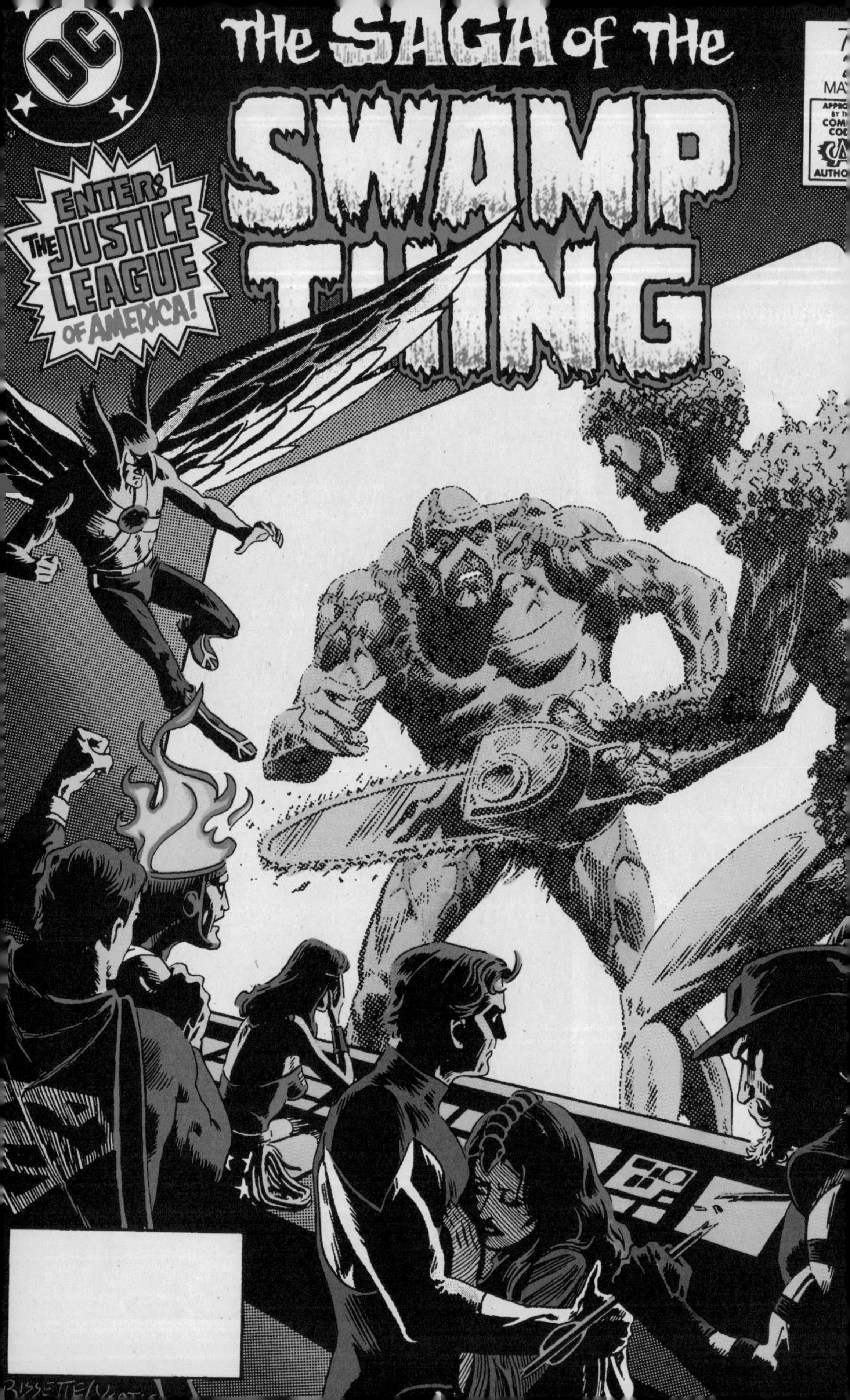
DC
The SAGA of the
SWAMP THING
ENTER: THE JUSTICE LEAGUE OF AMERICA!

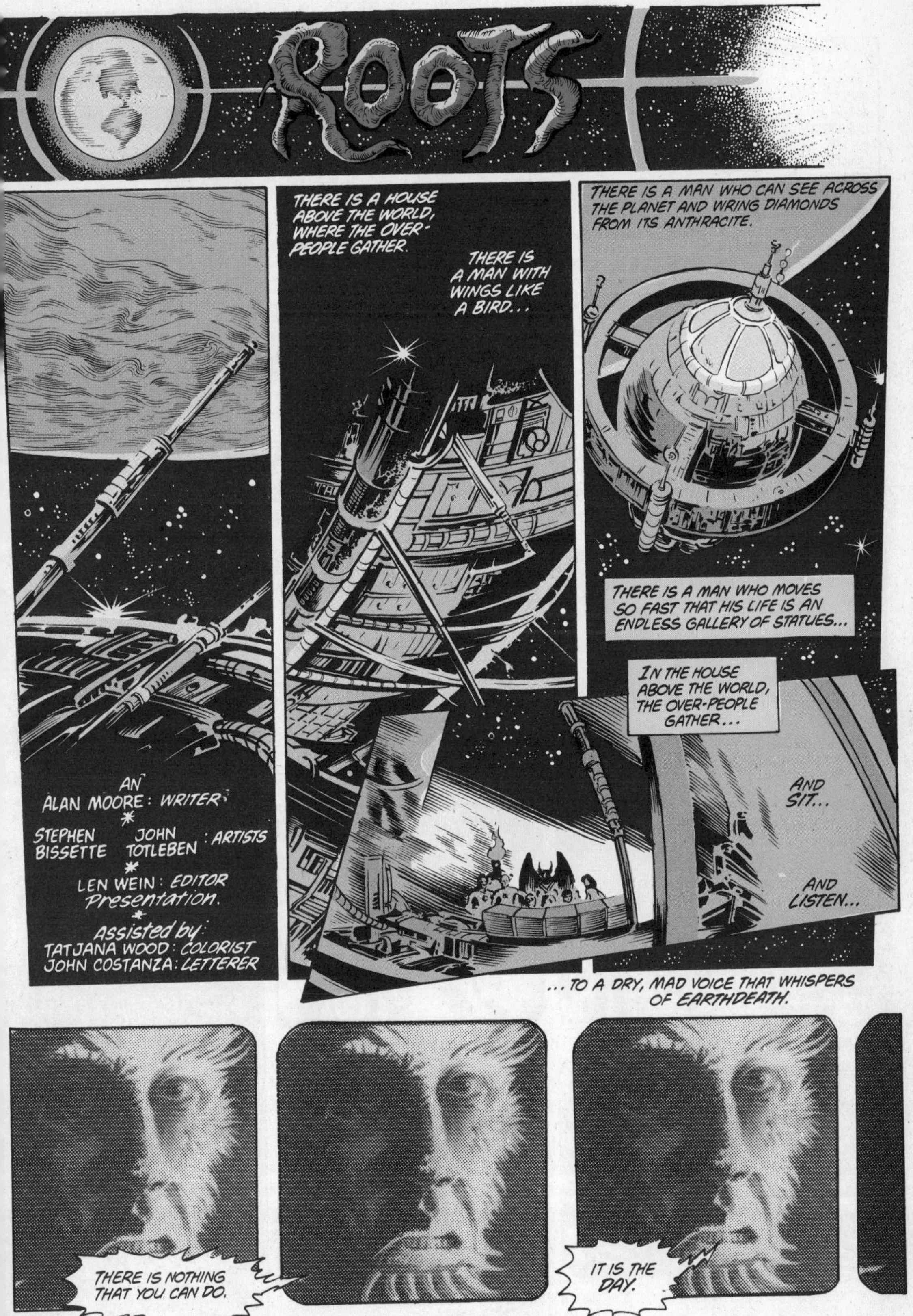
ROOTS
AN
ALAN MOORE: WRITER
STEPHEN BISSETTE JOHN TOTLEBEN: ARTISTS
LEN WEIN: EDITOR
Presentation.
Assisted by:
TATJANA WOOD: COLORIST
JOHN COSTANZA: LETTERER
THERE IS A HOUSE ABOVE THE WORLD, WHERE THE OVER-PEOPLE GATHER.
THERE IS A MAN WITH WINGS LIKE A BIRD...
THERE IS A MAN WHO CAN SEE ACROSS THE PLANET AND WRING DIAMONDS FROM ITS ANTHRACITE.
THERE IS A MAN WHO MOVES SO FAST THAT HIS LIFE IS AN ENDLESS GALLERY OF STATUES...
IN THE HOUSE ABOVE THE WORLD, THE OVER-PEOPLE GATHER...
AND SIT...
AND LISTEN...
...TO A DRY, MAD VOICE THAT WHISPERS OF EARTHDEATH.
THERE IS NOTHING THAT YOU CAN DO.
IT IS THE DAY.

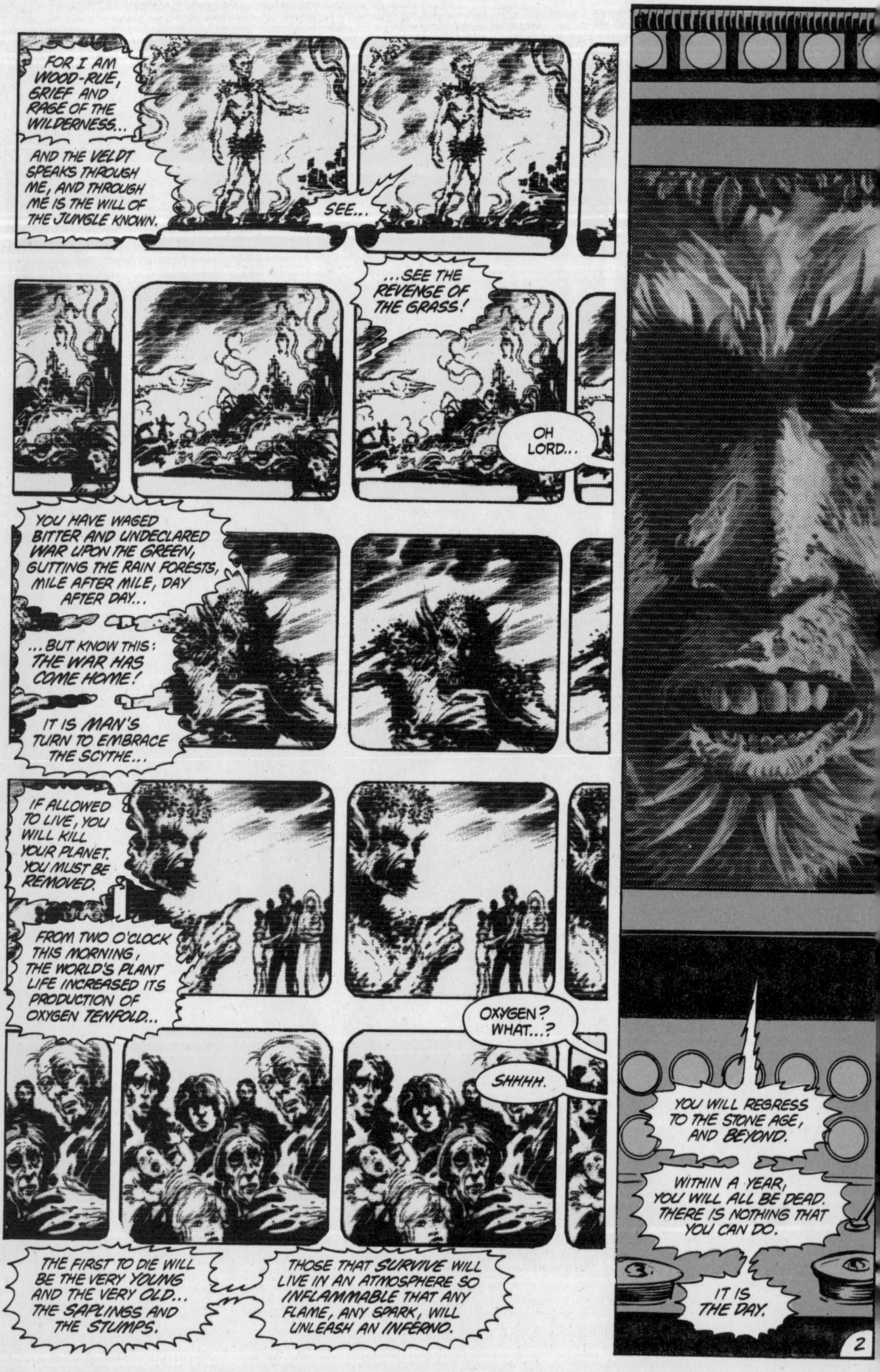
FOR I AM WOOD-RUE, GRIEF AND RAGE OF THE WILDERNESS...
AND THE VELDT SPEAKS THROUGH ME, AND THROUGH ME IS THE WILL OF THE JUNGLE KNOWN.
SEE...
...SEE THE REVENGE OF THE GRASS!
OH LORD...
YOU HAVE WAGED BITTER AND UNDECLARED WAR UPON THE GREEN, GUTTING THE RAIN FORESTS, MILE AFTER MILE, DAY AFTER DAY...
...BUT KNOW THIS: THE WAR HAS COME HOME!
IT IS MAN'S TURN TO EMBRACE THE SCYTHE...
IF ALLOWED TO LIVE, YOU WILL KILL YOUR PLANET. YOU MUST BE REMOVED.
FROM TWO O'CLOCK THIS MORNING, THE WORLD'S PLANT LIFE INCREASED ITS PRODUCTION OF OXYGEN TENFOLD...
OXYGEN? WHAT...?
SHHHH.
THE FIRST TO DIE WILL BE THE VERY YOUNG AND THE VERY OLD... THE SAPLINGS AND THE STUMPS.
THOSE THAT SURVIVE WILL LIVE IN AN ATMOSPHERE SO INFLAMMABLE THAT ANY FLAME, ANY SPARK, WILL UNLEASH AN INFERNO.
YOU WILL REGRESS TO THE STONE AGE, AND BEYOND.
WITHIN A YEAR, YOU WILL ALL BE DEAD. THERE IS NOTHING THAT YOU CAN DO.
IT IS THE DAY.
2

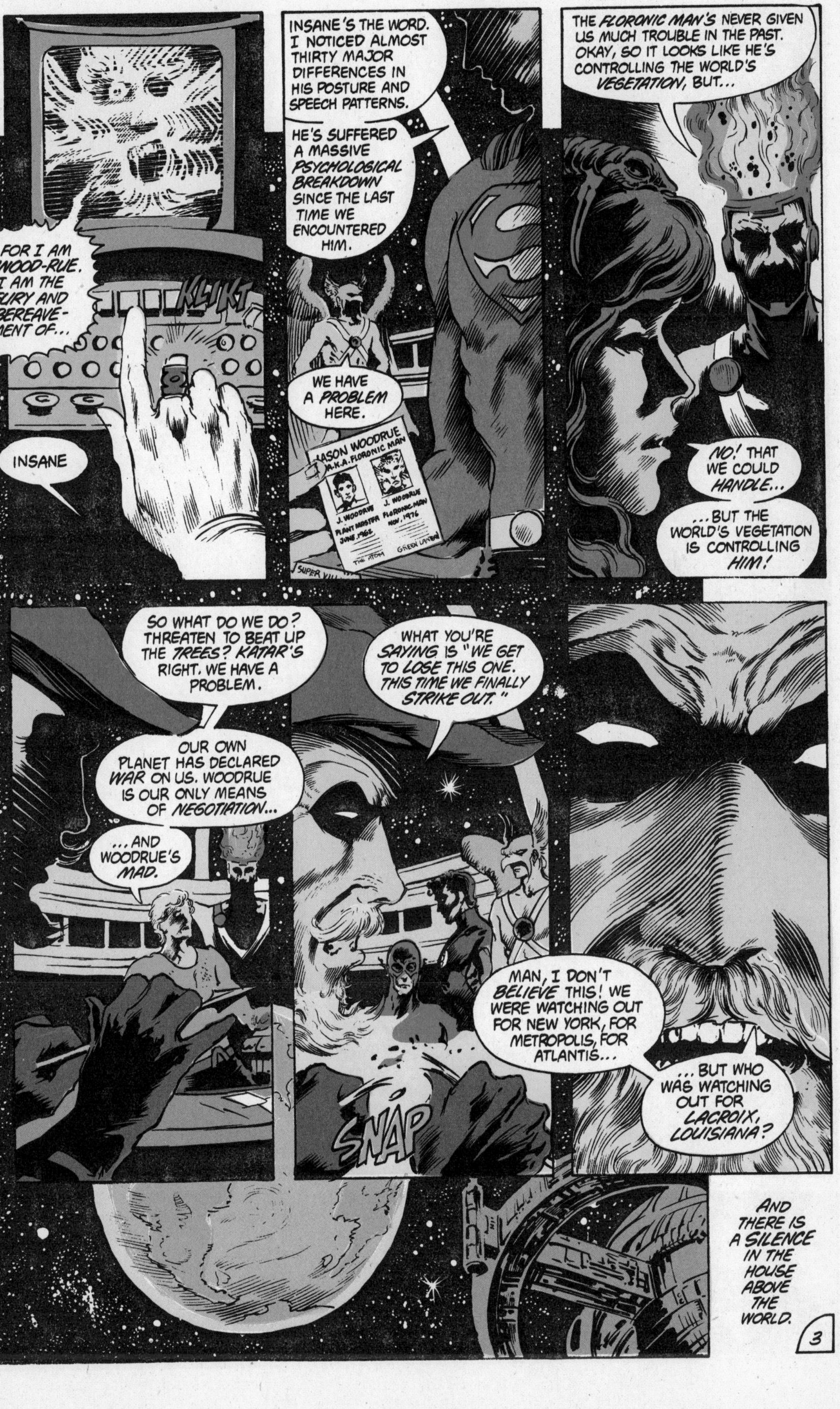
FOR I AM WOOD-RUE. I AM THE FURY AND BEREAVE-MENT OF...
KLIKT
INSANE
INSANE'S THE WORD. I NOTICED ALMOST THIRTY MAJOR DIFFERENCES IN HIS POSTURE AND SPEECH PATTERNS.
HE'S SUFFERED A MASSIVE PSYCHOLOGICAL BREAKDOWN SINCE THE LAST TIME WE ENCOUNTERED HIM.
WE HAVE A PROBLEM HERE.
JASON WOODRUE A.K.A. FLORONIC MAN
J. WOODRUE PLANT MASTER JUNE, 1962
J. WOODRUE FLORONIC MAN NOV, 1976
THE FLORONIC MAN'S NEVER GIVEN US MUCH TROUBLE IN THE PAST. OKAY, SO IT LOOKS LIKE HE'S CONTROLLING THE WORLD'S VEGETATION, BUT...
NO! THAT WE COULD HANDLE...
...BUT THE WORLD'S VEGETATION IS CONTROLLING HIM!
SO WHAT DO WE DO? THREATEN TO BEAT UP THE TREES? KATAR'S RIGHT. WE HAVE A PROBLEM.
OUR OWN PLANET HAS DECLARED WAR ON US. WOODRUE IS OUR ONLY MEANS OF NEGOTIATION...
...AND WOODRUE'S MAD.
WHAT YOU'RE SAYING IS "WE GET TO LOSE THIS ONE. THIS TIME WE FINALLY STRIKE OUT."
SNAP
MAN, I DON'T BELIEVE THIS! WE WERE WATCHING OUT FOR NEW YORK, FOR METROPOLIS, FOR ATLANTIS...
...BUT WHO WAS WATCHING OUT FOR LACROIX, LOUISIANA?
AND THERE IS A SILENCE IN THE HOUSE ABOVE THE WORLD.
3

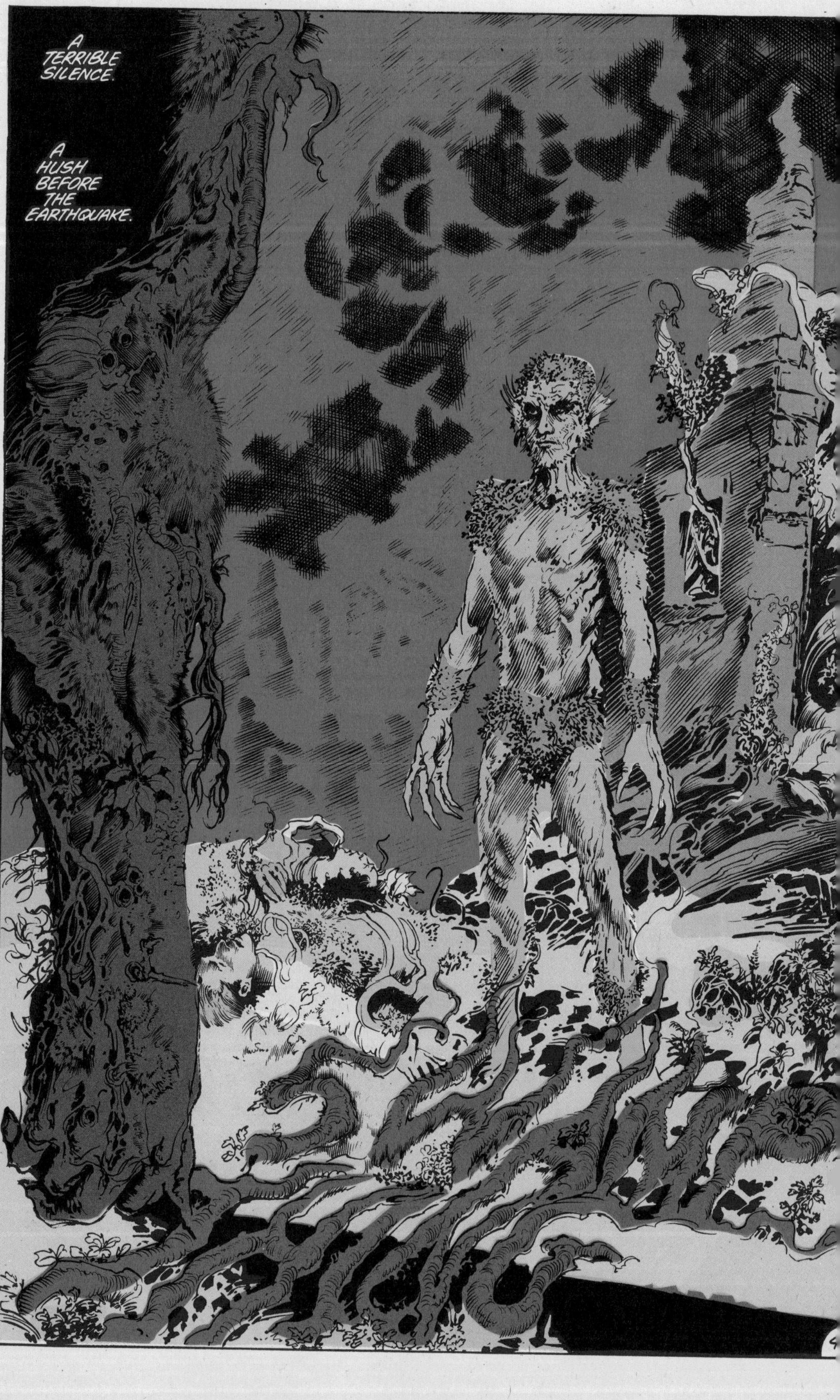
A TERRIBLE SILENCE.
A HUSH BEFORE THE EARTHQUAKE.

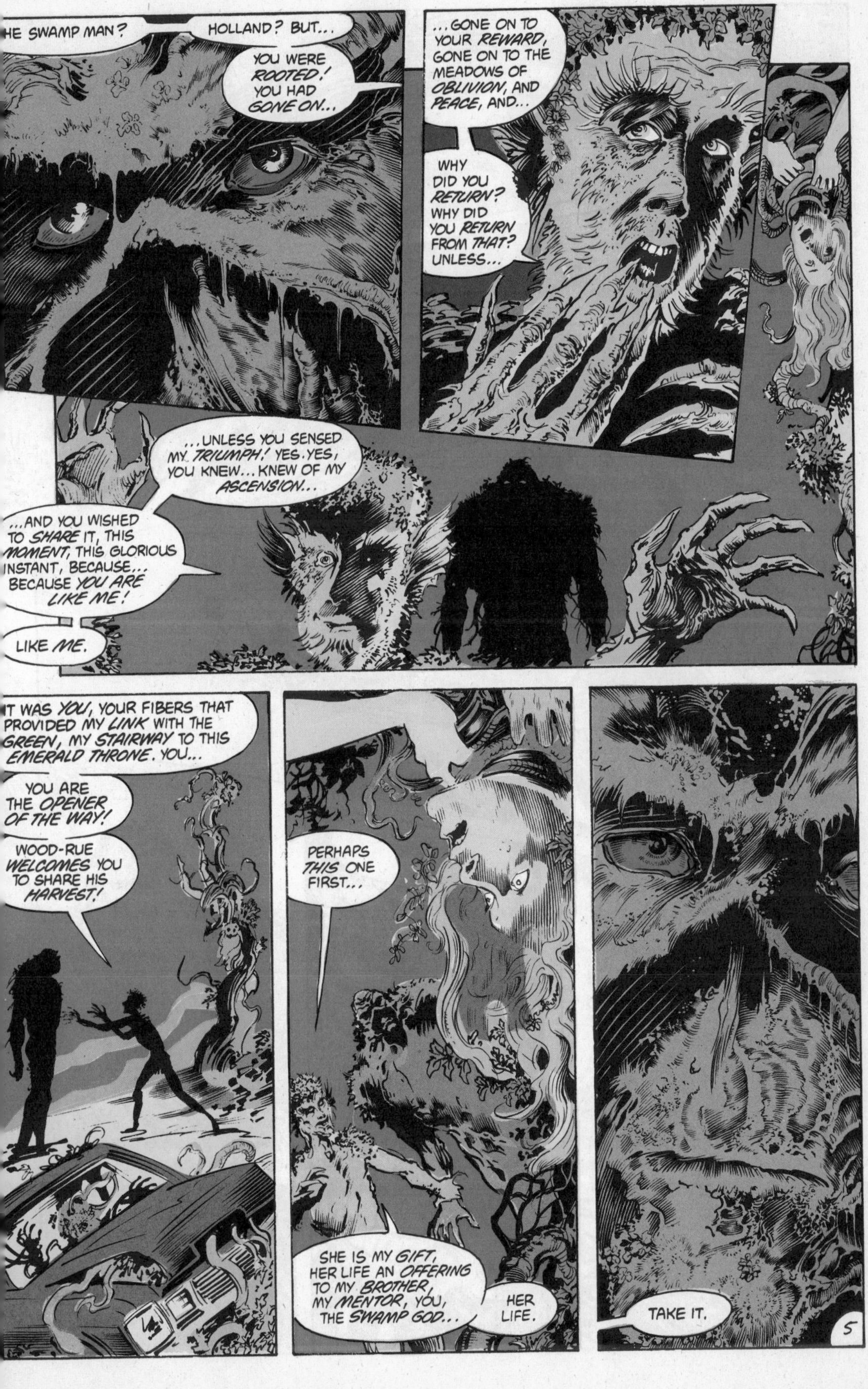
HE SWAMP MAN?
HOLLAND? BUT...
YOU WERE ROOTED! YOU HAD GONE ON...
...GONE ON TO YOUR REWARD, GONE ON TO THE MEADOWS OF OBLIVION, AND PEACE, AND...
WHY DID YOU RETURN? WHY DID YOU RETURN FROM THAT? UNLESS...
...UNLESS YOU SENSED MY TRIUMPH! YES. YES, YOU KNEW... KNEW OF MY ASCENSION...
...AND YOU WISHED TO SHARE IT, THIS MOMENT, THIS GLORIOUS INSTANT, BECAUSE... BECAUSE YOU ARE LIKE ME!
LIKE ME.
IT WAS YOU, YOUR FIBERS THAT PROVIDED MY LINK WITH THE GREEN, MY STAIRWAY TO THIS EMERALD THRONE. YOU...
YOU ARE THE OPENER OF THE WAY!
WOOD-RUE WELCOMES YOU TO SHARE HIS HARVEST!
PERHAPS THIS ONE FIRST...
SHE IS MY GIFT, HER LIFE AN OFFERING TO MY BROTHER, MY MENTOR, YOU, THE SWAMP GOD...
HER LIFE.
TAKE IT.
5

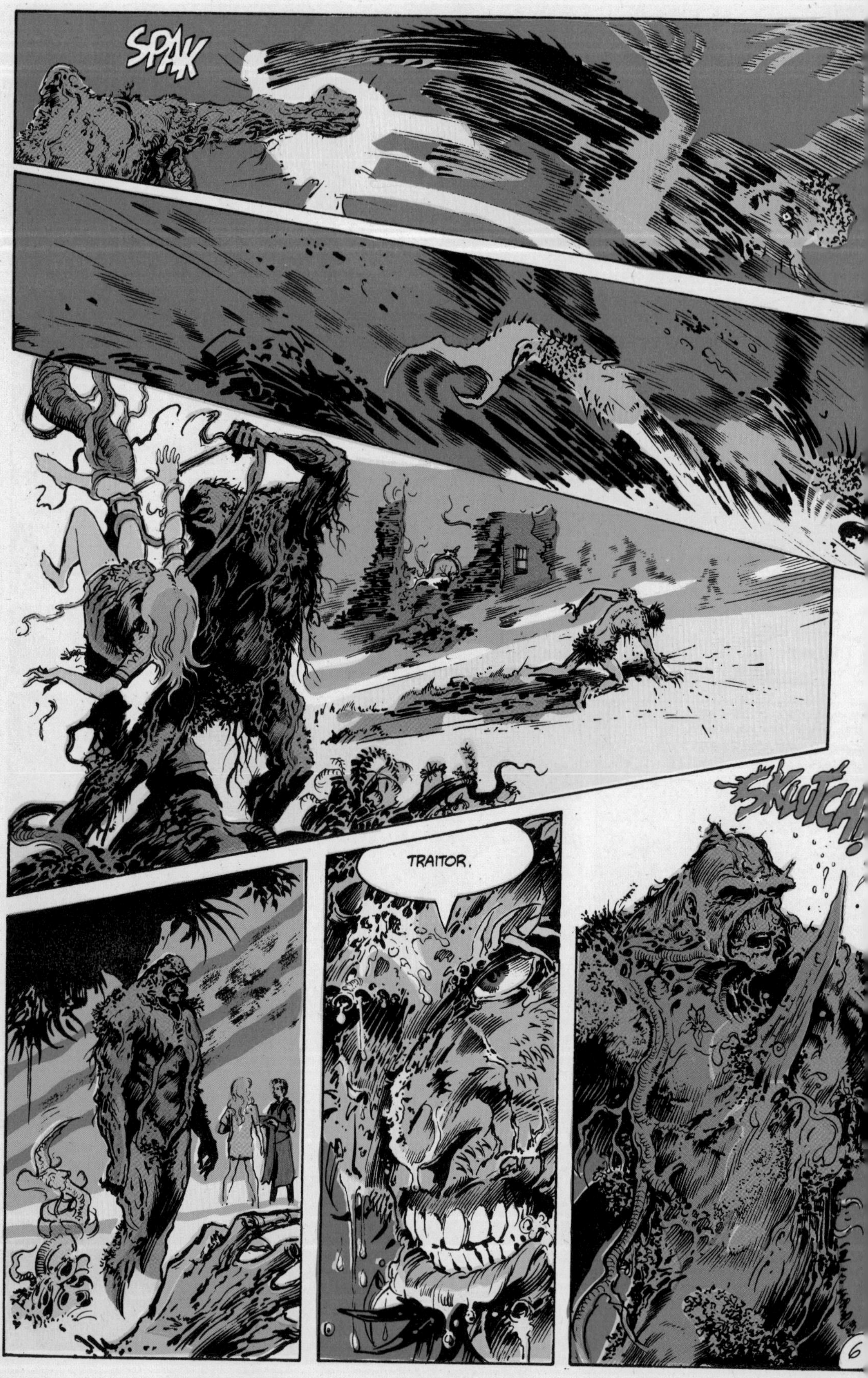
SPAK
SKLUTCH!
TRAITOR.
6

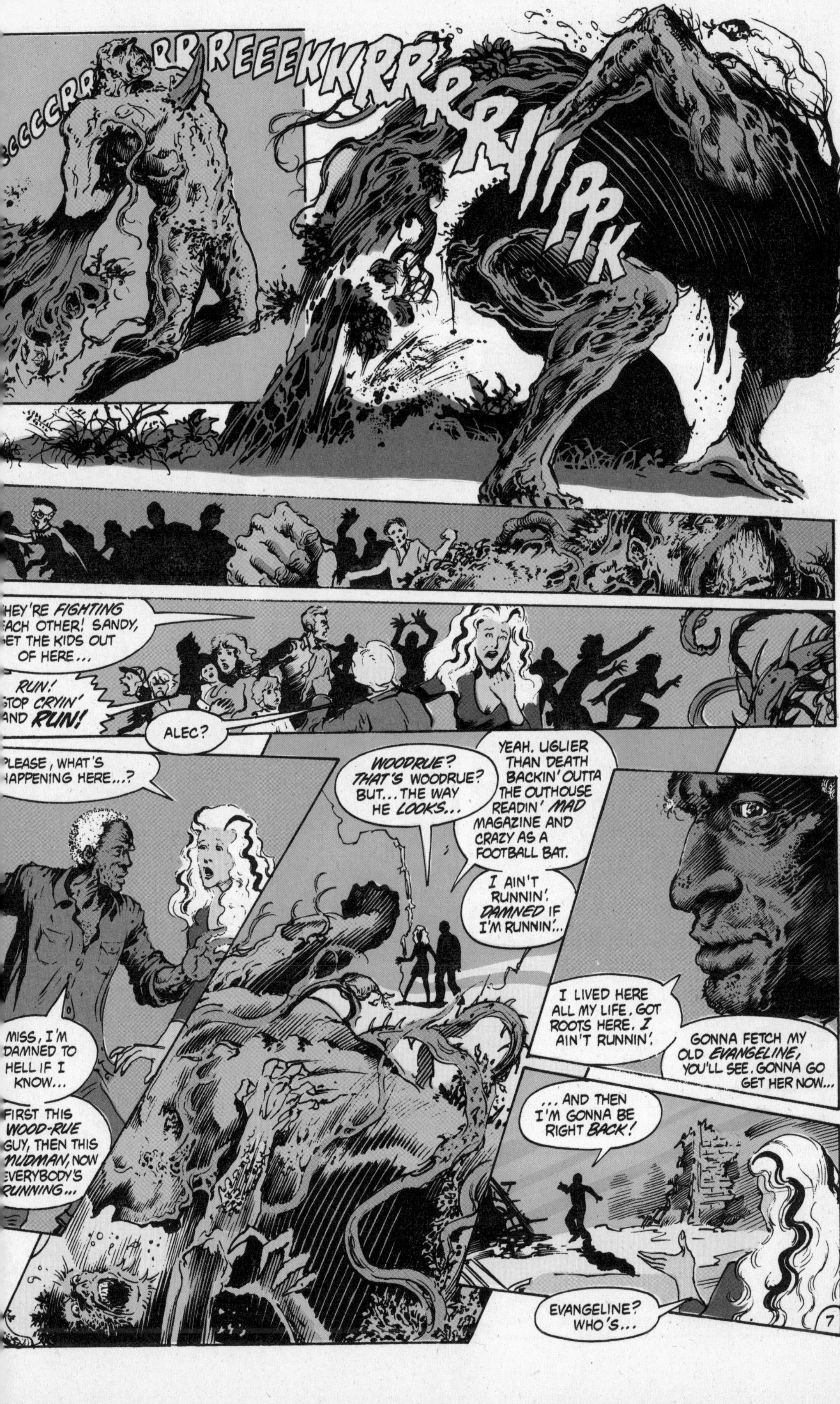
SCCCCRR RR REEEKKKRRRRRIIPPPK
HEY'RE FIGHTING EACH OTHER! SANDY, GET THE KIDS OUT OF HERE...
RUN! STOP CRYIN' AND RUN!
ALEC?
PLEASE, WHAT'S HAPPENING HERE...?
MISS, I'M DAMNED TO HELL IF I KNOW...
FIRST THIS WOOD-RUE GUY, THEN THIS MUDMAN, NOW EVERYBODY'S RUNNING...
WOODRUE? THAT'S WOODRUE? BUT... THE WAY HE LOOKS...
YEAH. UGLIER THAN DEATH BACKIN' OUTTA THE OUTHOUSE READIN' MAD MAGAZINE AND CRAZY AS A FOOTBALL BAT.
I AIN'T RUNNIN'. DAMNED IF I'M RUNNIN'...
I LIVED HERE ALL MY LIFE. GOT ROOTS HERE. I AIN'T RUNNIN'.
GONNA FETCH MY OLD EVANGELINE, YOU'LL SEE. GONNA GO GET HER NOW...
...AND THEN I'M GONNA BE RIGHT BACK!
EVANGELINE? WHO'S...
7

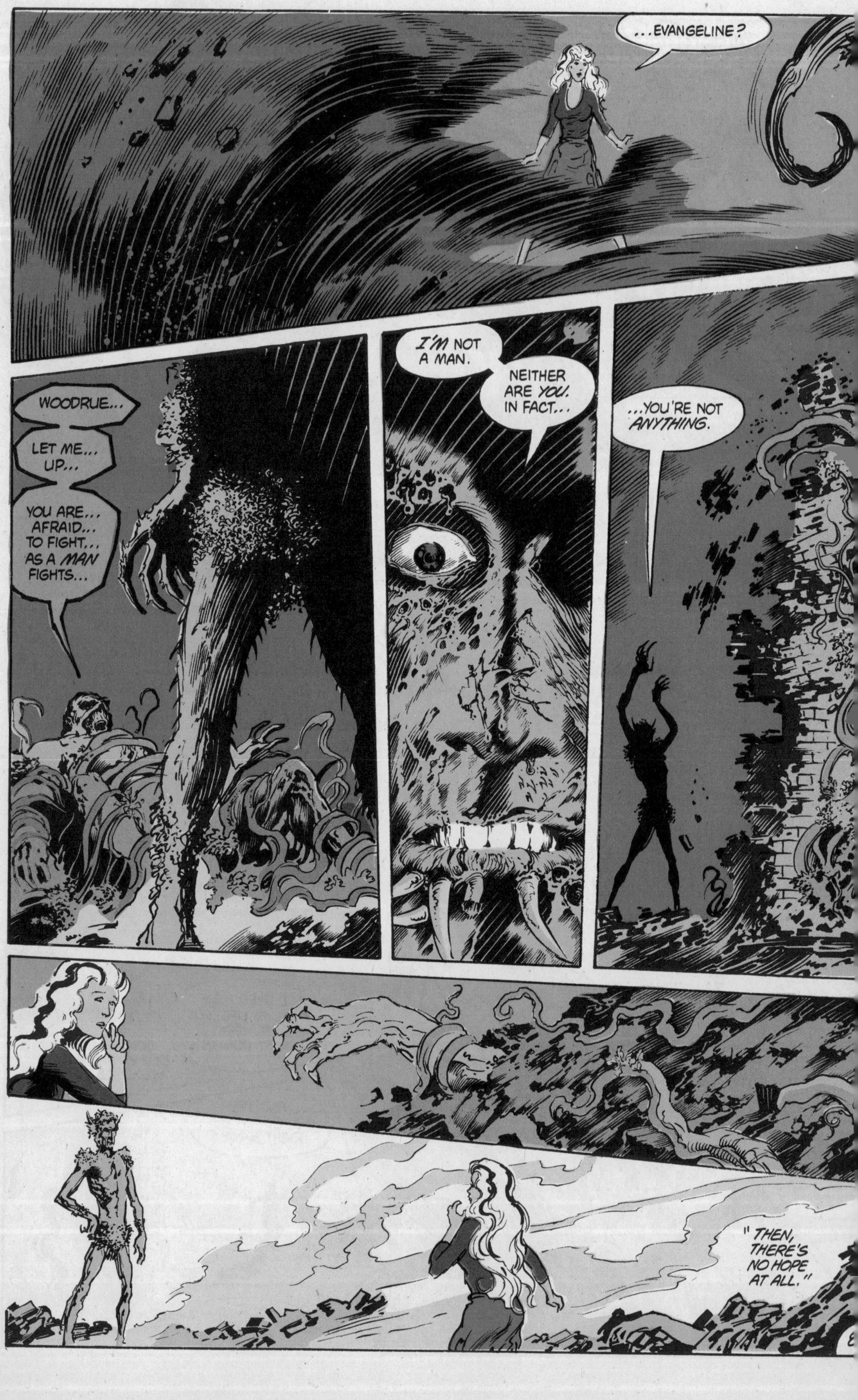
...EVANGELINE?
WOODRUE...
LET ME... UP...
YOU ARE... AFRAID... TO FIGHT... AS A MAN FIGHTS...
I'M NOT A MAN.
NEITHER ARE YOU. IN FACT...
...YOU'RE NOT ANYTHING.
"THEN, THERE'S NO HOPE AT ALL."

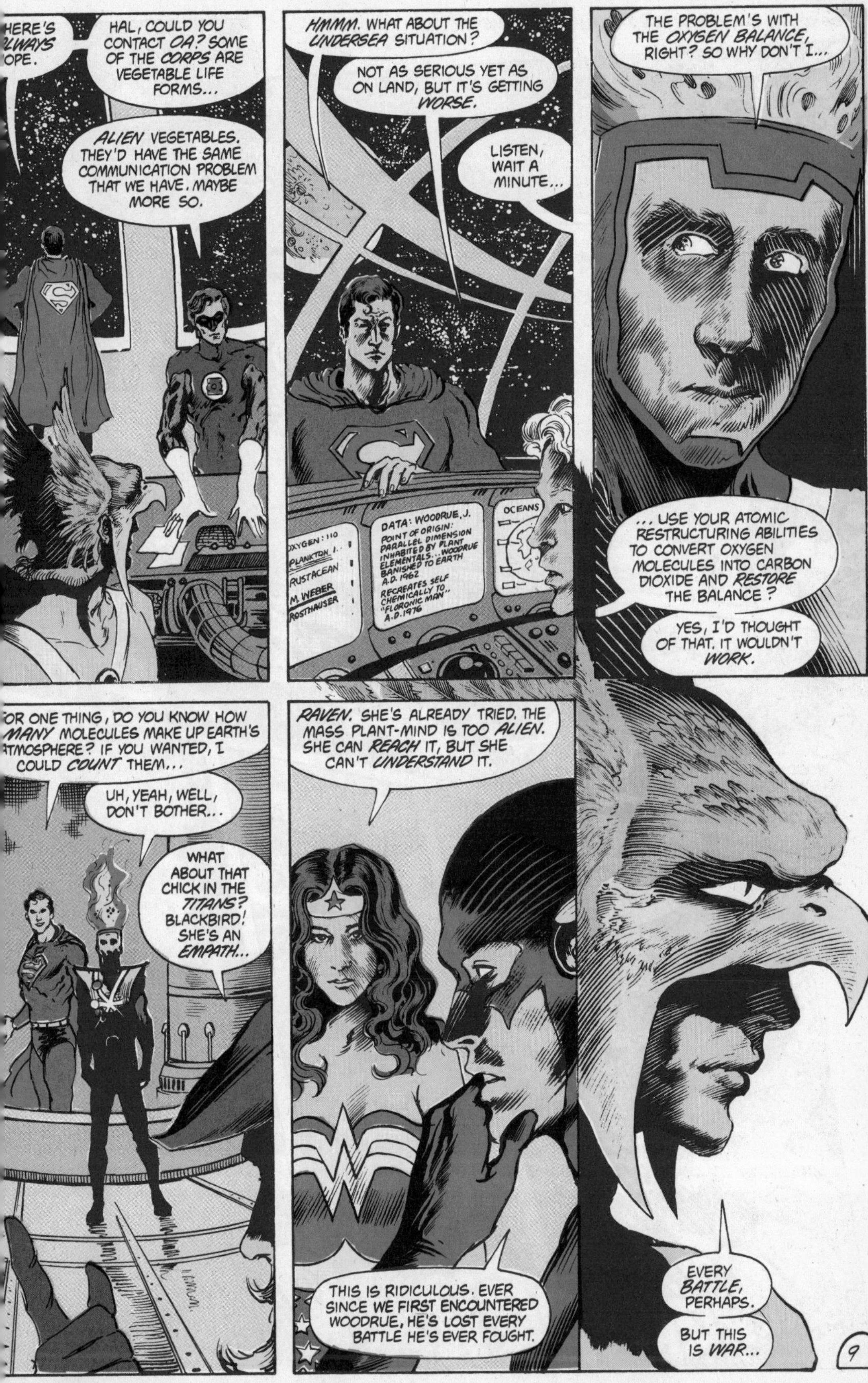
HERE'S
LWAYS
OPE.
HAL, COULD YOU CONTACT OA? SOME OF THE CORPS ARE VEGETABLE LIFE FORMS...
ALIEN VEGETABLES. THEY'D HAVE THE SAME COMMUNICATION PROBLEM THAT WE HAVE. MAYBE MORE SO.
HMMM. WHAT ABOUT THE UNDERSEA SITUATION?
NOT AS SERIOUS YET AS ON LAND, BUT IT'S GETTING WORSE.
LISTEN, WAIT A MINUTE...
OXYGEN: 110
PLANKTON
RUSTACEAN
M. WEBER
ROSTHAUSER
DATA: WOODRUE, J. POINT OF ORIGIN: PARALLEL DIMENSION INHABITED BY PLANT ELEMENTALS... WOODRUE BANISHED TO EARTH A.D. 1962 RECREATES SELF CHEMICALLY TO "FLORONIC MAN" A.D. 1976
OCEANS
THE PROBLEM'S WITH THE OXYGEN BALANCE, RIGHT? SO WHY DON'T I...
... USE YOUR ATOMIC RESTRUCTURING ABILITIES TO CONVERT OXYGEN MOLECULES INTO CARBON DIOXIDE AND RESTORE THE BALANCE?
YES, I'D THOUGHT OF THAT. IT WOULDN'T WORK.
FOR ONE THING, DO YOU KNOW HOW MANY MOLECULES MAKE UP EARTH'S ATMOSPHERE? IF YOU WANTED, I COULD COUNT THEM...
UH, YEAH, WELL, DON'T BOTHER...
WHAT ABOUT THAT CHICK IN THE TITANS? BLACKBIRD! SHE'S AN EMPATH...
RAVEN. SHE'S ALREADY TRIED. THE MASS PLANT-MIND IS TOO ALIEN. SHE CAN REACH IT, BUT SHE CAN'T UNDERSTAND IT.
THIS IS RIDICULOUS. EVER SINCE WE FIRST ENCOUNTERED WOODRUE, HE'S LOST EVERY BATTLE HE'S EVER FOUGHT.
EVERY BATTLE, PERHAPS.
BUT THIS IS WAR...
9

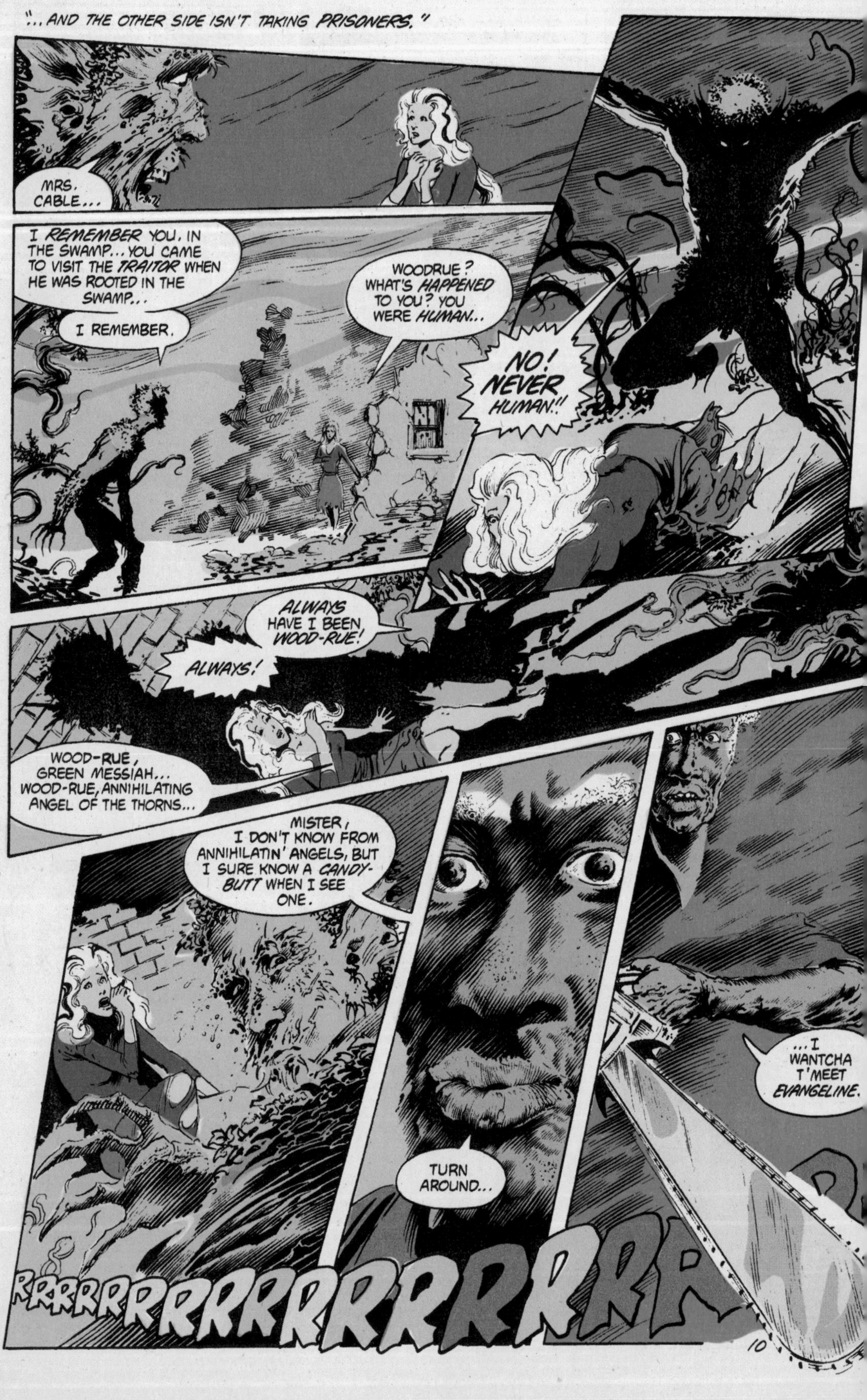
"... AND THE OTHER SIDE ISN'T TAKING PRISONERS."
MRS. CABLE...
I REMEMBER YOU. IN THE SWAMP... YOU CAME TO VISIT THE TRAITOR WHEN HE WAS ROOTED IN THE SWAMP...
I REMEMBER.
WOODRUE? WHAT'S HAPPENED TO YOU? YOU WERE HUMAN...
NO! NEVER HUMAN!!
ALWAYS HAVE I BEEN WOOD-RUE!
ALWAYS!
WOOD-RUE, GREEN MESSIAH... WOOD-RUE, ANNIHILATING ANGEL OF THE THORNS...
MISTER, I DON'T KNOW FROM ANNIHILATIN' ANGELS, BUT I SURE KNOW A CANDY-BUTT WHEN I SEE ONE.
TURN AROUND...
...I WANTCHA T'MEET EVANGELINE.
RRRRRRRRRRRRRRRRR
10

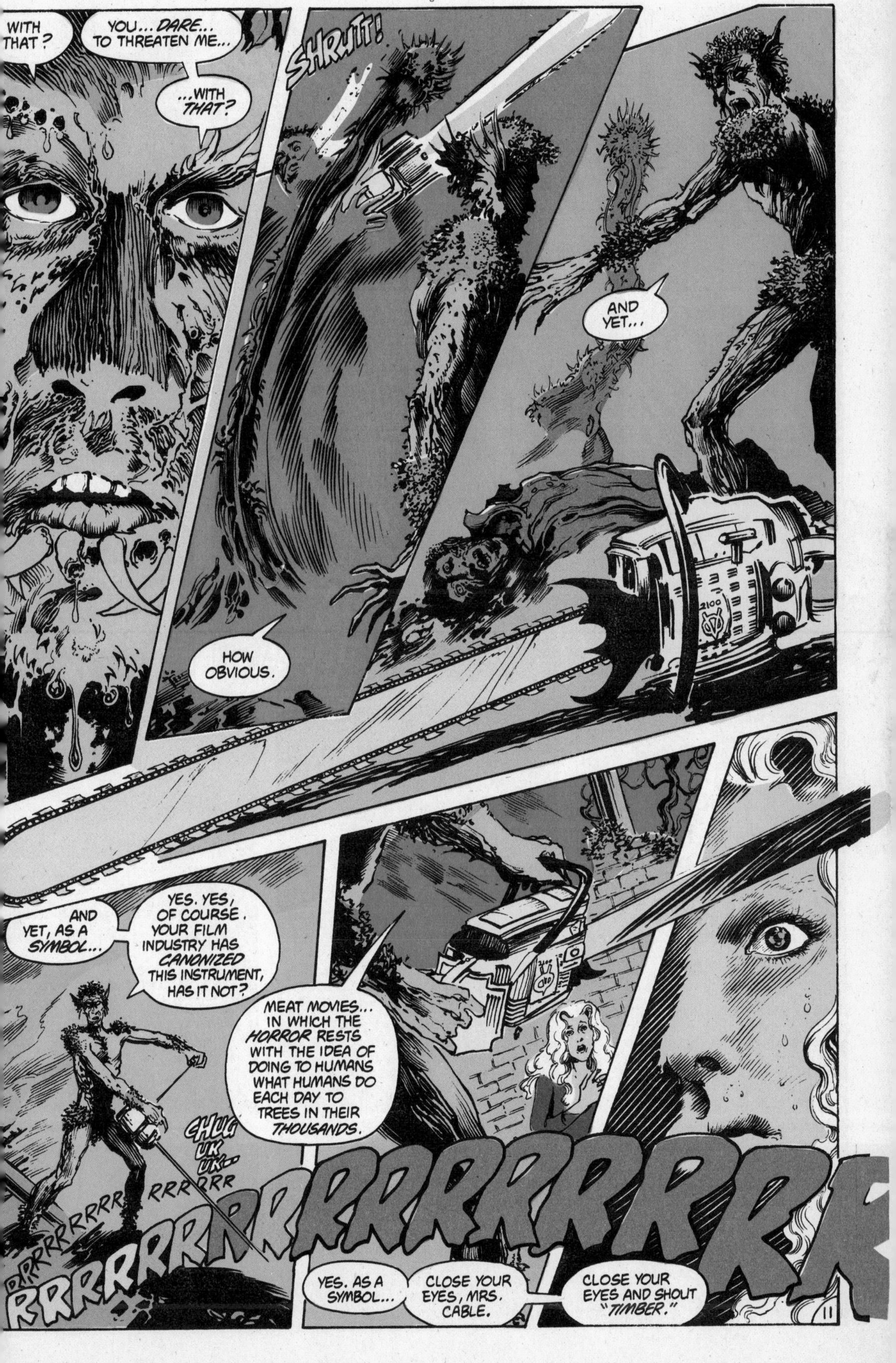
WITH THAT?
YOU... DARE... TO THREATEN ME...
...WITH THAT?
SHRUTT!
HOW OBVIOUS.
AND YET...
AND YET, AS A SYMBOL...
YES. YES, OF COURSE. YOUR FILM INDUSTRY HAS CANONIZED THIS INSTRUMENT, HAS IT NOT?
MEAT MOVIES... IN WHICH THE HORROR RESTS WITH THE IDEA OF DOING TO HUMANS WHAT HUMANS DO EACH DAY TO TREES IN THEIR THOUSANDS.
CHUG UK UK... RRR
RRR
RRRRRRRR
RRRRRRRRRRRRRRRRRRR
YES. AS A SYMBOL...
CLOSE YOUR EYES, MRS. CABLE.
CLOSE YOUR EYES AND SHOUT "TIMBER."
11

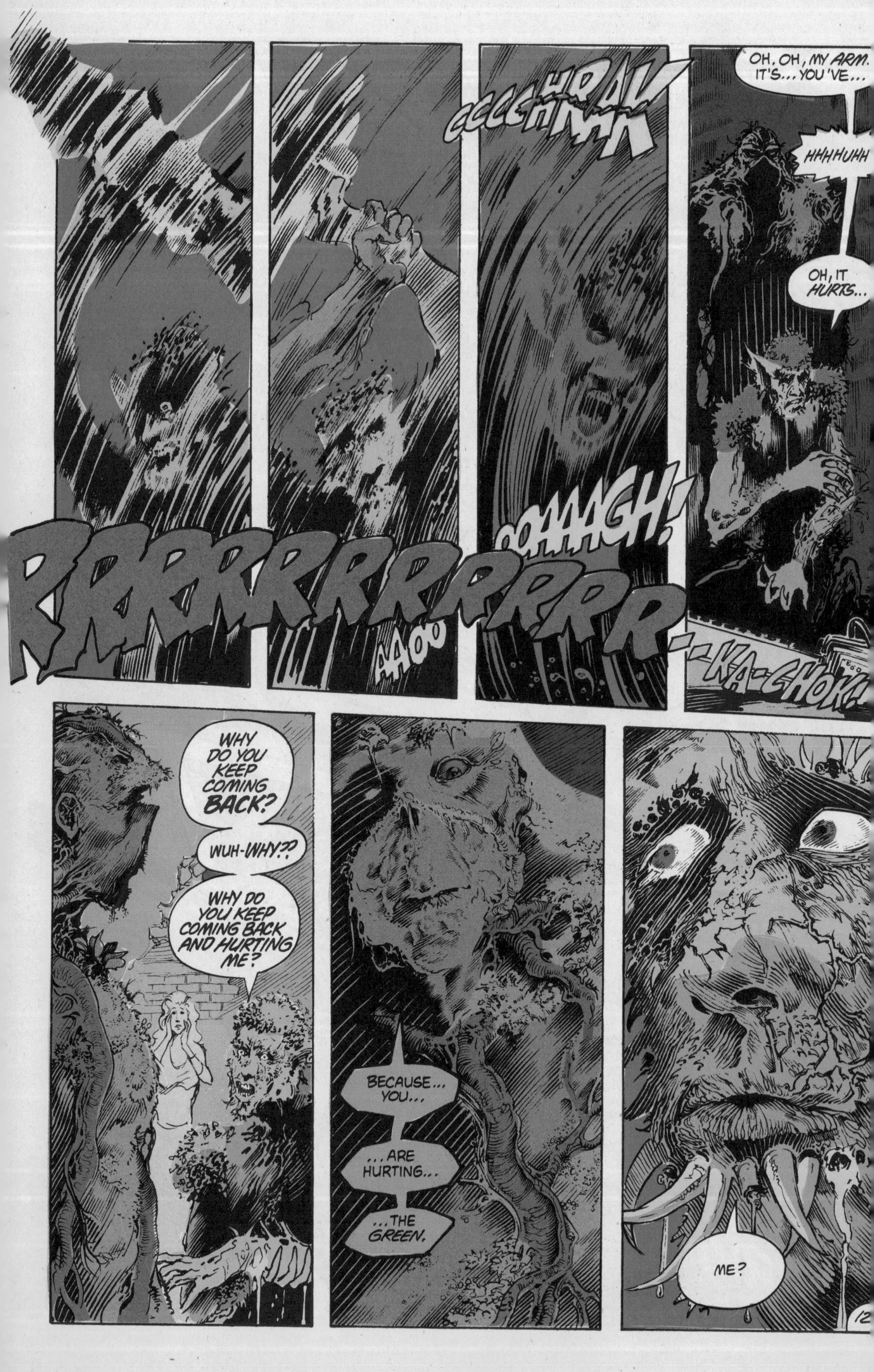
CCCCHRAK
OH, OH, MY ARM. IT'S... YOU'VE...
HHHHUHH
OH, IT HURTS...
RRRRRRRRRRRRR
OOHHAAAGH!
AAOO
-KA-CHOK!
WHY DO YOU KEEP COMING BACK?
WUH-WHY??
WHY DO YOU KEEP COMING BACK AND HURTING ME?
BECAUSE... YOU...
...ARE HURTING...
...THE GREEN.
ME?
12

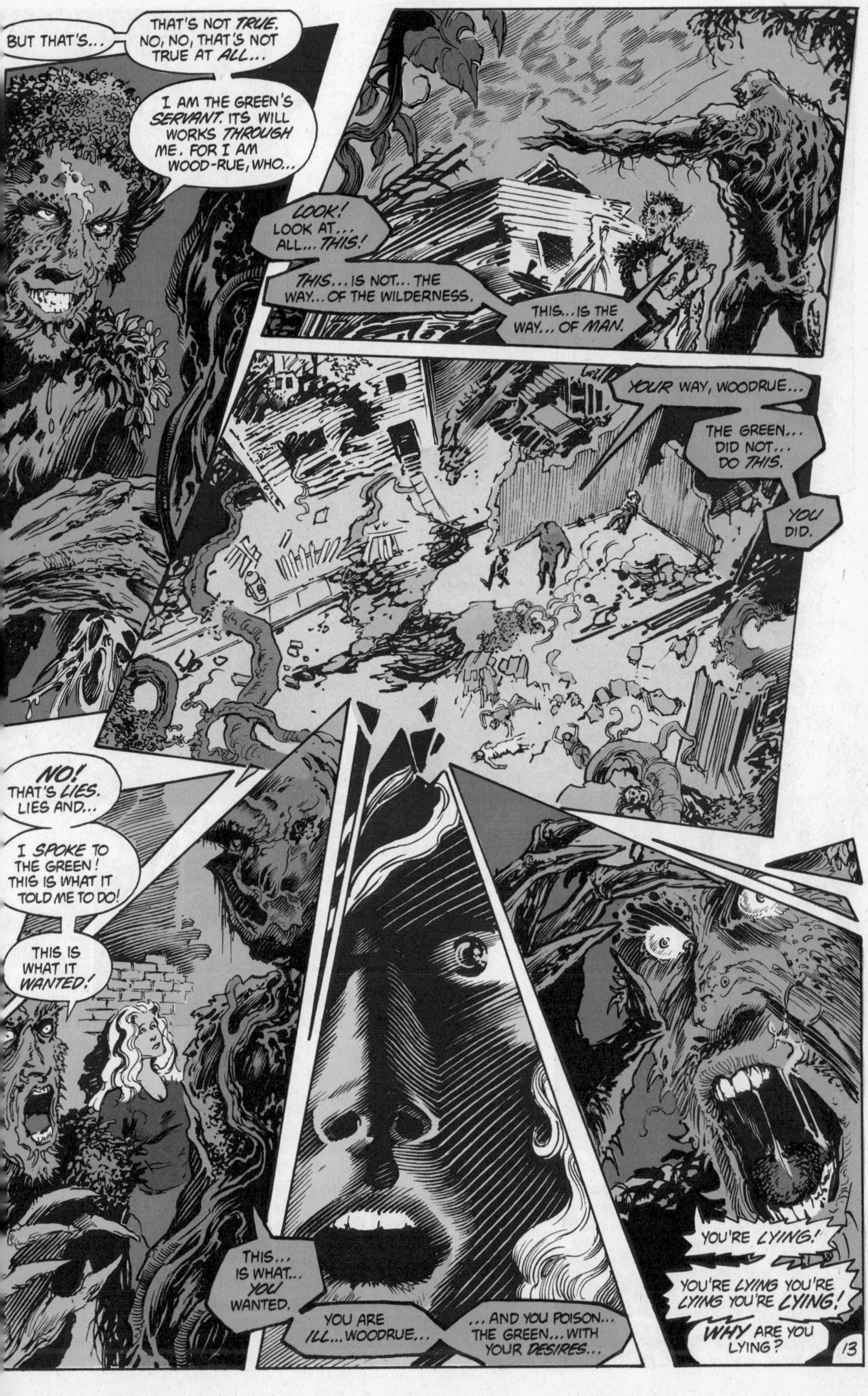
BUT THAT'S...
THAT'S NOT TRUE. NO, NO, THAT'S NOT TRUE AT ALL...
I AM THE GREEN'S SERVANT. ITS WILL WORKS THROUGH ME. FOR I AM WOOD-RUE, WHO...
LOOK! LOOK AT... ALL... THIS!
THIS... IS NOT... THE WAY... OF THE WILDERNESS.
THIS... IS THE WAY... OF MAN.
YOUR WAY, WOODRUE...
THE GREEN... DID NOT... DO THIS.
YOU DID.
NO! THAT'S LIES. LIES AND...
I SPOKE TO THE GREEN! THIS IS WHAT IT TOLD ME TO DO!
THIS IS WHAT IT WANTED!
THIS... IS WHAT... YOU WANTED.
YOU ARE ILL... WOODRUE...
... AND YOU POISON... THE GREEN... WITH YOUR DESIRES...
YOU'RE LYING!
YOU'RE LYING YOU'RE LYING YOU'RE LYING!
WHY ARE YOU LYING?
13

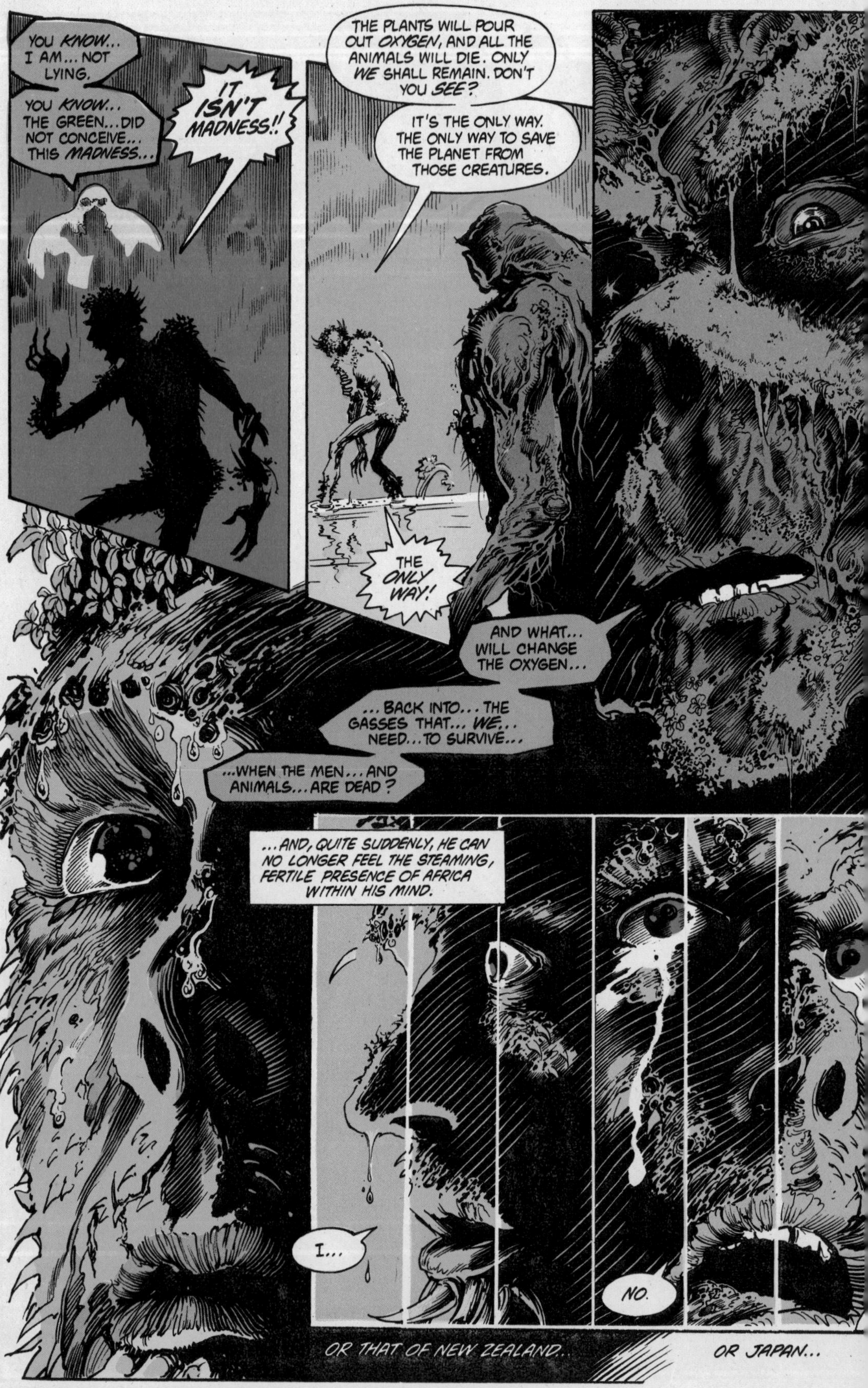
YOU KNOW... I AM... NOT LYING.
YOU KNOW... THE GREEN... DID NOT CONCEIVE... THIS MADNESS...
IT ISN'T MADNESS!!
THE PLANTS WILL POUR OUT OXYGEN, AND ALL THE ANIMALS WILL DIE. ONLY WE SHALL REMAIN. DON'T YOU SEE?
IT'S THE ONLY WAY. THE ONLY WAY TO SAVE THE PLANET FROM THOSE CREATURES.
THE ONLY WAY!
AND WHAT... WILL CHANGE THE OXYGEN...
... BACK INTO... THE GASSES THAT... WE... NEED... TO SURVIVE...
...WHEN THE MEN... AND ANIMALS... ARE DEAD?
...AND, QUITE SUDDENLY, HE CAN NO LONGER FEEL THE STEAMING, FERTILE PRESENCE OF AFRICA WITHIN HIS MIND.
I...
NO.
OR THAT OF NEW ZEALAND...
OR JAPAN...

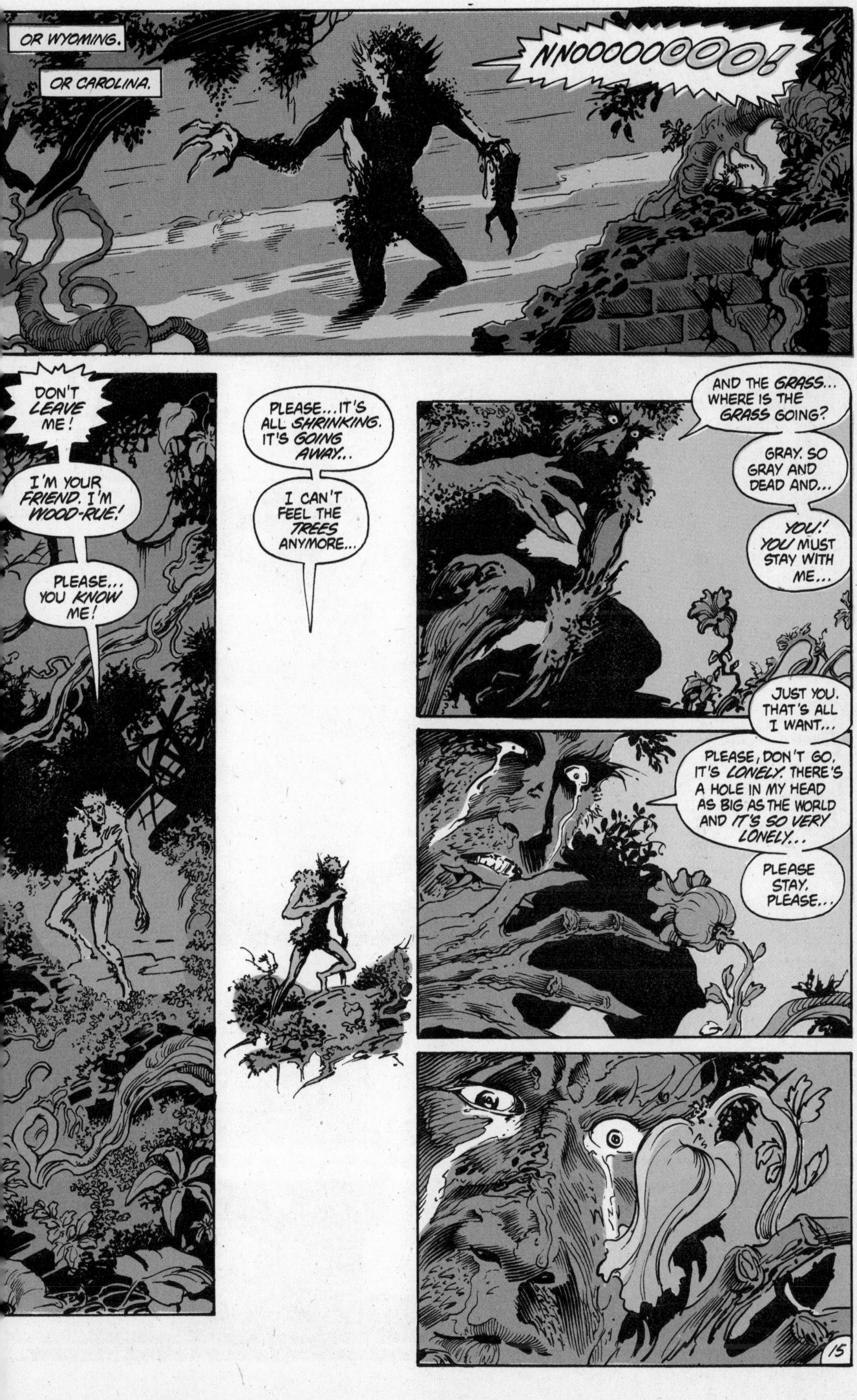
OR WYOMING.
OR CAROLINA.
NNOOOOOOOOO!
DON'T LEAVE ME!
I'M YOUR FRIEND. I'M WOOD-RUE!
PLEASE... YOU KNOW ME!
PLEASE... IT'S ALL SHRINKING. IT'S GOING AWAY...
I CAN'T FEEL THE TREES ANYMORE...
AND THE GRASS... WHERE IS THE GRASS GOING?
GRAY. SO GRAY AND DEAD AND...
YOU! YOU MUST STAY WITH ME...
JUST YOU. THAT'S ALL I WANT...
PLEASE, DON'T GO. IT'S LONELY. THERE'S A HOLE IN MY HEAD AS BIG AS THE WORLD AND IT'S SO VERY LONELY...
PLEASE STAY. PLEASE...
15

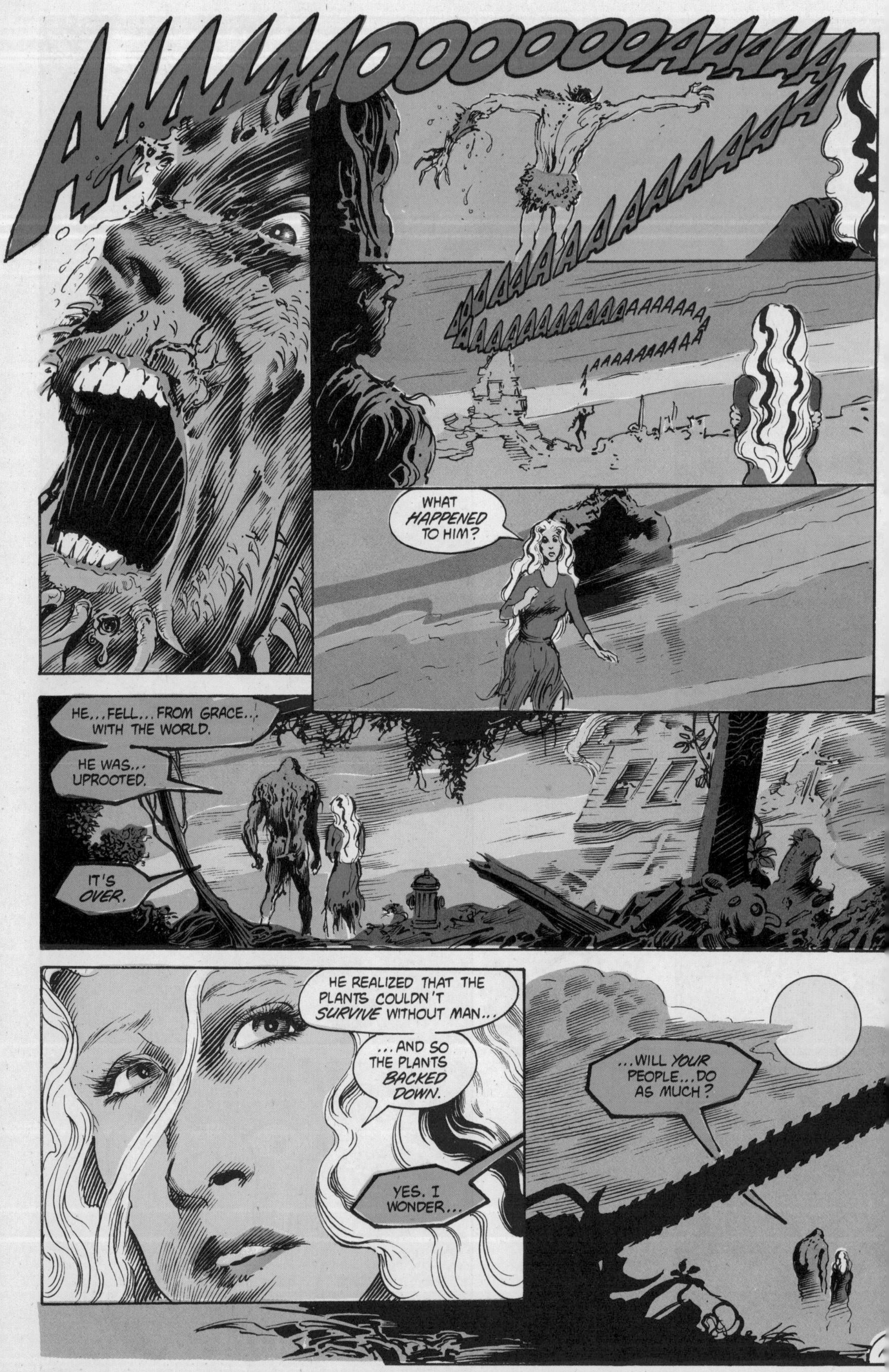
AAAAAOOOOOOOAAAAAA
AAAAAAAAAAAAAAA
AAAAAAAAAAAAAAAAAAAAAAAA
AAAAAAAAAAA
WHAT HAPPENED TO HIM?
HE...FELL...FROM GRACE... WITH THE WORLD.
HE WAS... UPROOTED.
IT'S OVER.
HE REALIZED THAT THE PLANTS COULDN'T SURVIVE WITHOUT MAN...
...AND SO THE PLANTS BACKED DOWN.
...WILL YOUR PEOPLE...DO AS MUCH?
YES. I WONDER...

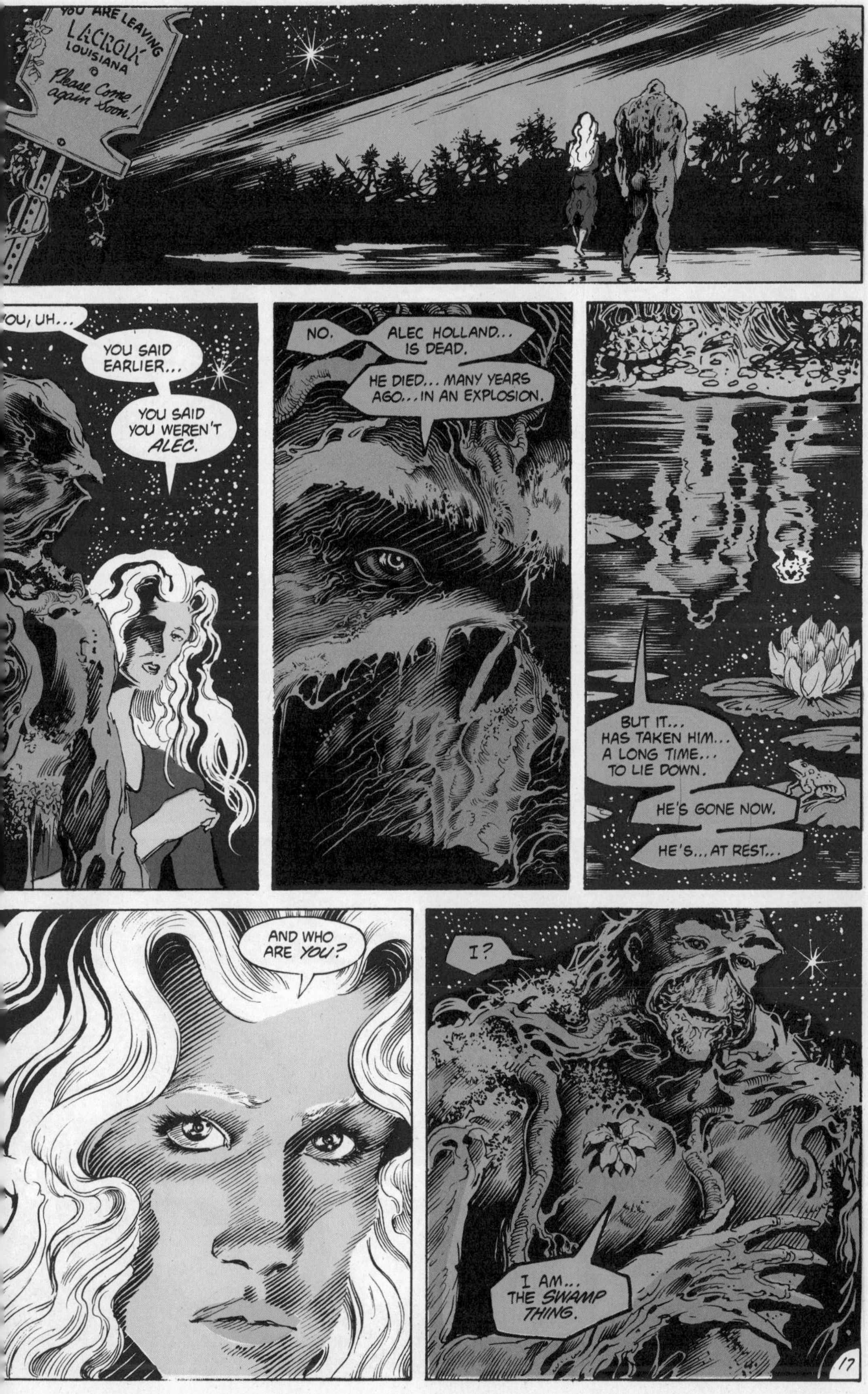
YOU ARE LEAVING
LACROIX
LOUISIANA
Please Come again Soon!
YOU, UH...
YOU SAID EARLIER...
YOU SAID YOU WEREN'T ALEC.
NO.
ALEC HOLLAND... IS DEAD.
HE DIED... MANY YEARS AGO... IN AN EXPLOSION.
BUT IT... HAS TAKEN HIM... A LONG TIME... TO LIE DOWN.
HE'S GONE NOW.
HE'S... AT REST...
AND WHO ARE YOU?
I?
I AM... THE SWAMP THING.
17

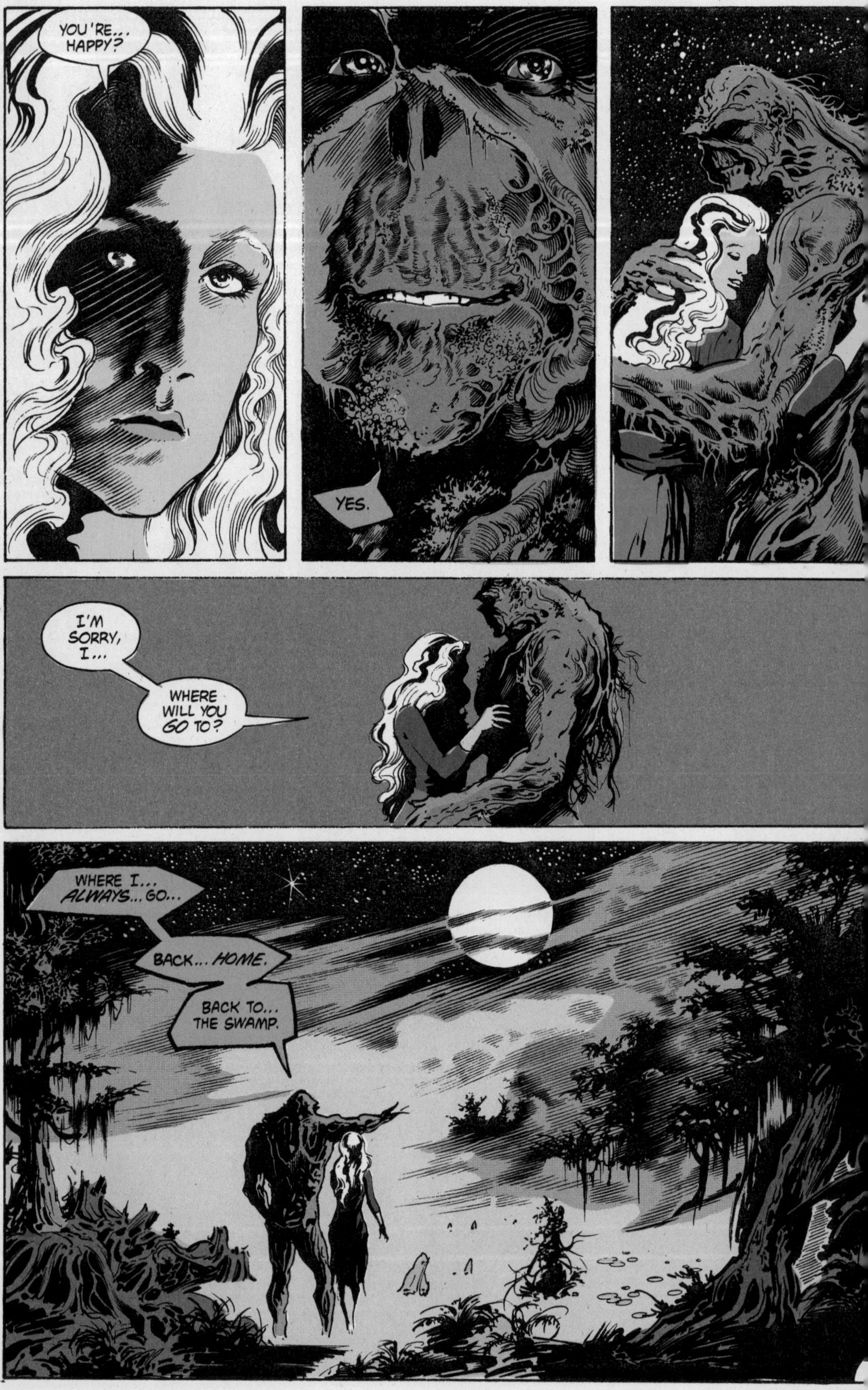
YOU'RE... HAPPY?
YES.
I'M SORRY, I...
WHERE WILL YOU GO TO?
WHERE I... ALWAYS... GO...
BACK... HOME.
BACK TO... THE SWAMP.

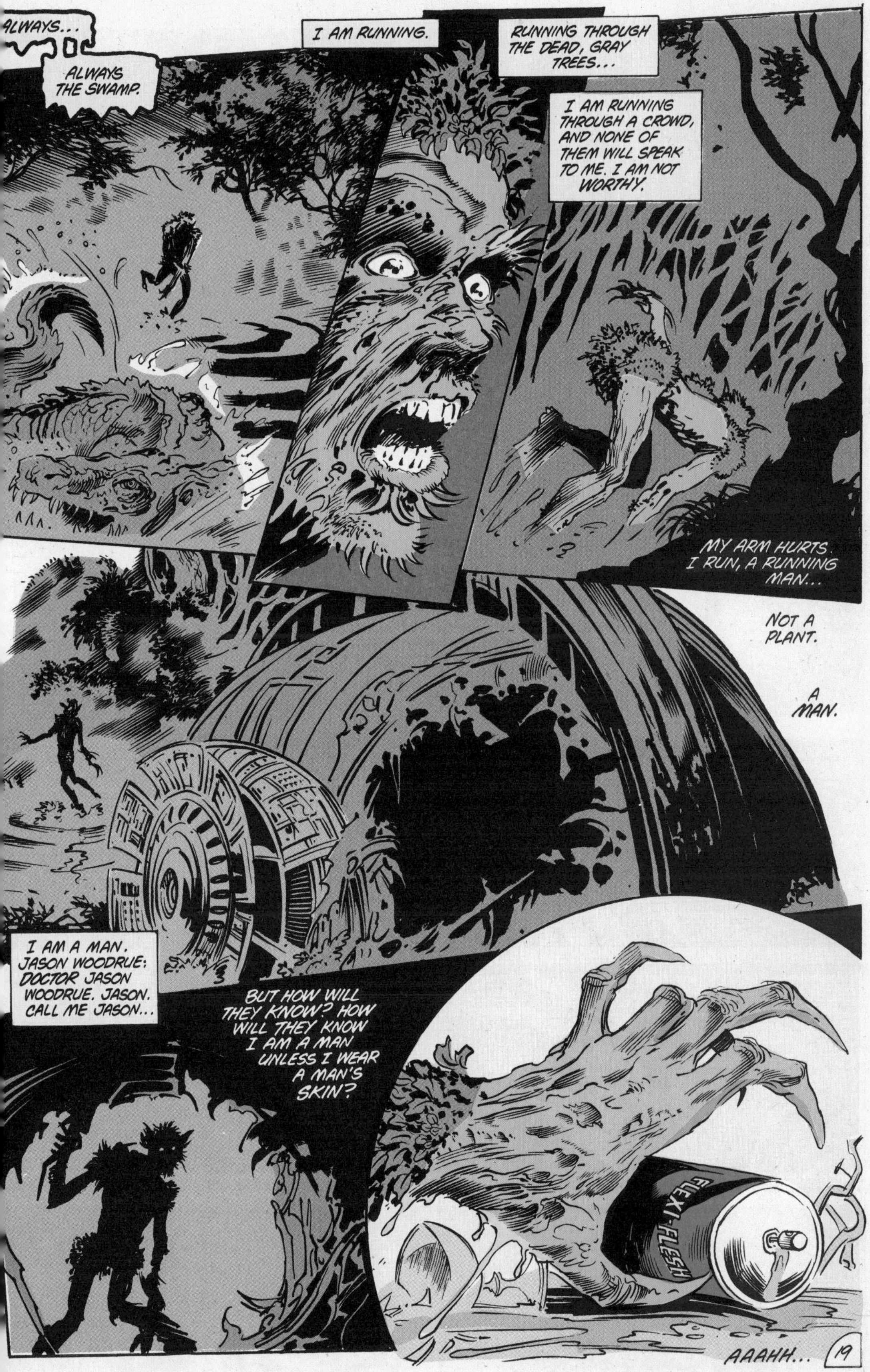
ALWAYS...
ALWAYS THE SWAMP.
I AM RUNNING.
RUNNING THROUGH THE DEAD, GRAY TREES...
I AM RUNNING THROUGH A CROWD, AND NONE OF THEM WILL SPEAK TO ME. I AM NOT WORTHY.
MY ARM HURTS. I RUN, A RUNNING MAN...
NOT A PLANT.
A MAN.
I AM A MAN. JASON WOODRUE: DOCTOR JASON WOODRUE. JASON. CALL ME JASON...
BUT HOW WILL THEY KNOW? HOW WILL THEY KNOW I AM A MAN UNLESS I WEAR A MAN'S SKIN?
FLEXI-FLESH
AAAHH...
19

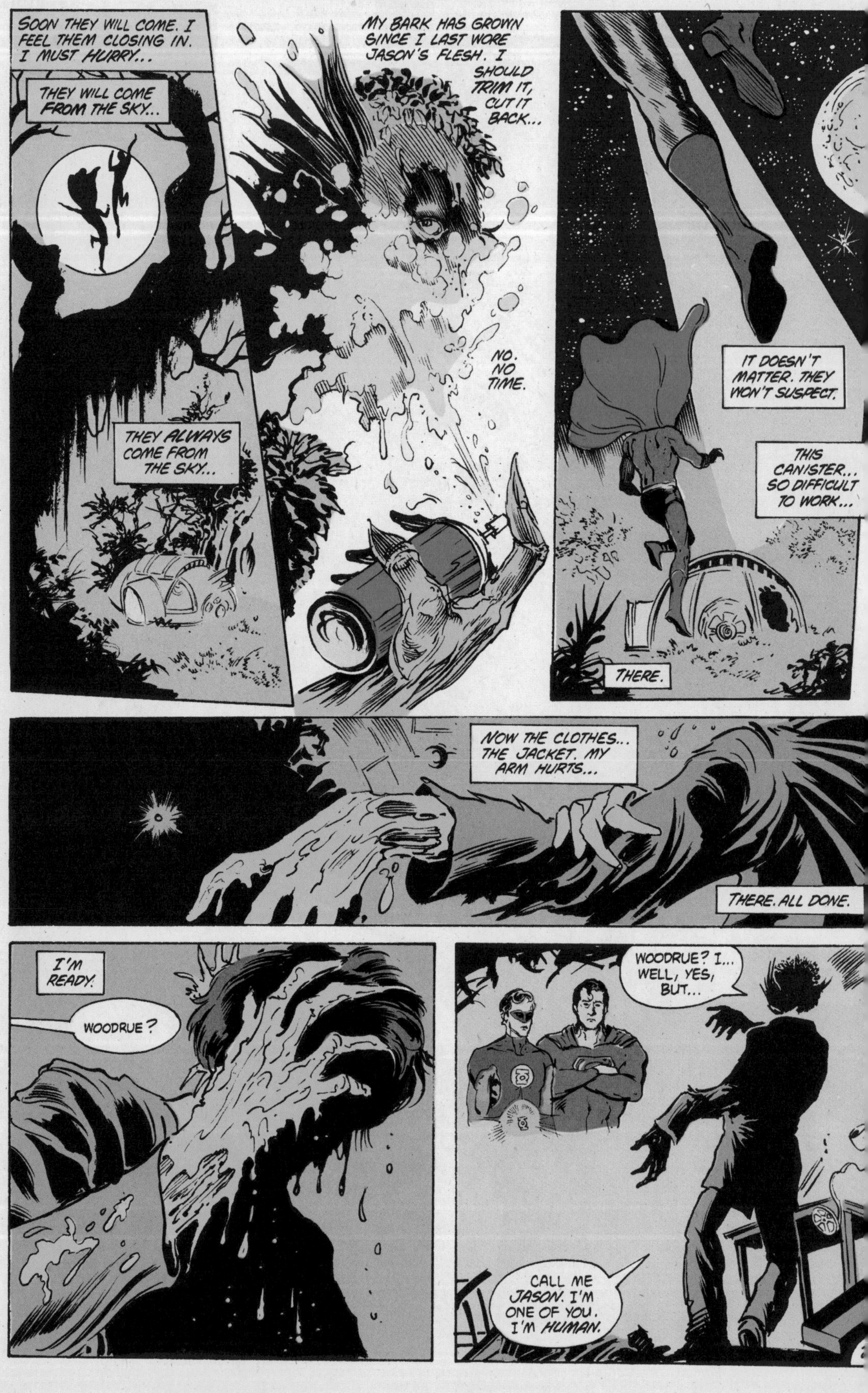
SOON THEY WILL COME. I FEEL THEM CLOSING IN. I MUST HURRY...
THEY WILL COME FROM THE SKY...
THEY ALWAYS COME FROM THE SKY...
MY BARK HAS GROWN SINCE I LAST WORE JASON'S FLESH. I SHOULD TRIM IT, CUT IT BACK...
NO. NO TIME.
IT DOESN'T MATTER. THEY WON'T SUSPECT.
THIS CANISTER... SO DIFFICULT TO WORK...
THERE.
NOW THE CLOTHES... THE JACKET. MY ARM HURTS...
THERE. ALL DONE.
I'M READY.
WOODRUE?
WOODRUE? I... WELL, YES, BUT...
CALL ME JASON. I'M ONE OF YOU. I'M HUMAN.

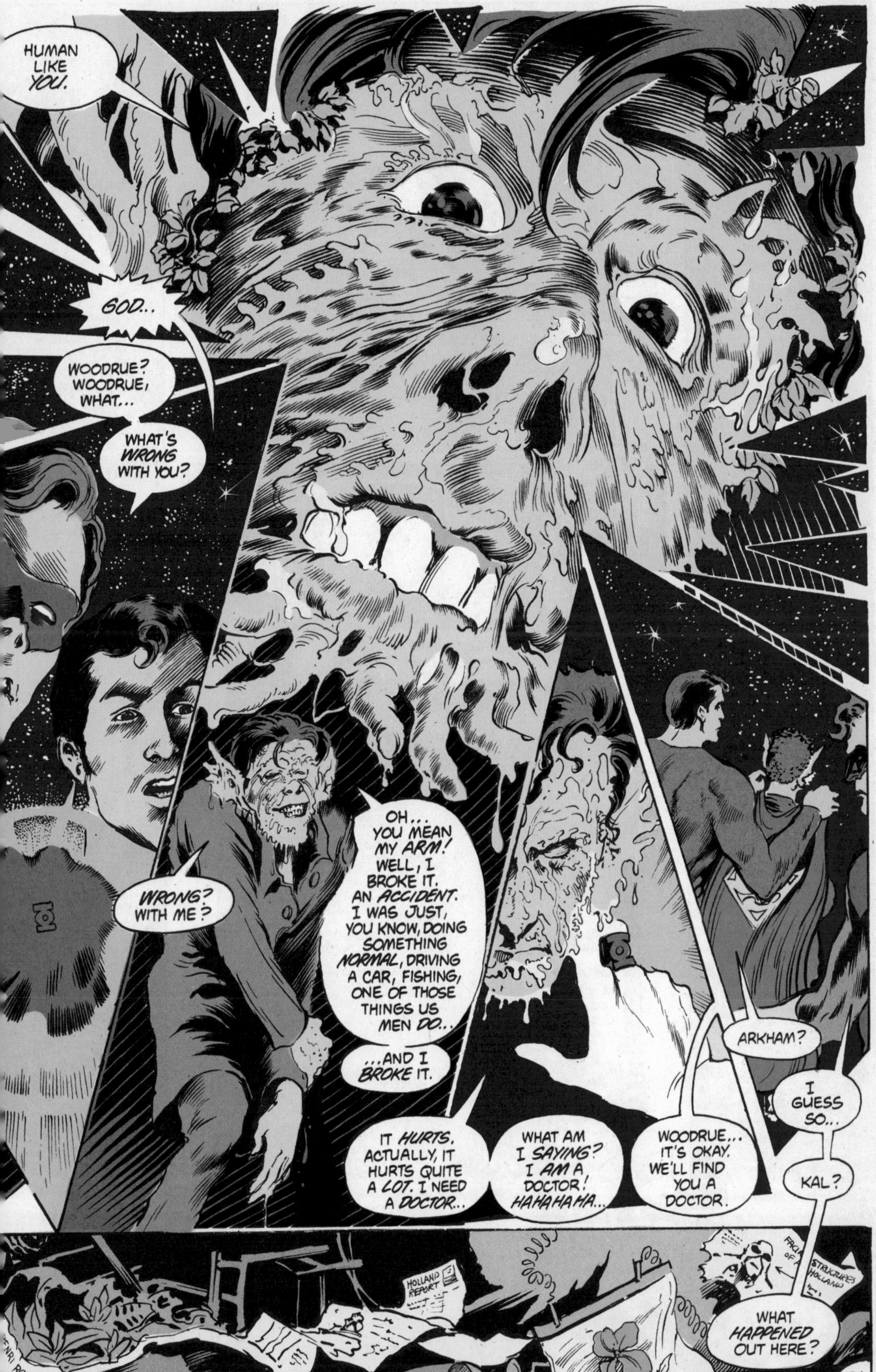
HUMAN LIKE YOU.
GOD...
WOODRUE? WOODRUE, WHAT...
WHAT'S WRONG WITH YOU?
WRONG? WITH ME?
OH... YOU MEAN MY ARM! WELL, I BROKE IT. AN ACCIDENT. I WAS JUST, YOU KNOW, DOING SOMETHING NORMAL, DRIVING A CAR, FISHING, ONE OF THOSE THINGS US MEN DO...
...AND I BROKE IT.
IT HURTS. ACTUALLY, IT HURTS QUITE A LOT. I NEED A DOCTOR...
WHAT AM I SAYING? I AM A DOCTOR! HAHAHAHA...
WOODRUE... IT'S OKAY. WE'LL FIND YOU A DOCTOR.
ARKHAM?
I GUESS SO...
KAL?
HOLLAND REPORT
FACIAL STRUCTURES OF HOLLAND
WHAT HAPPENED OUT HERE?
HENRI ROUSSEAU
21

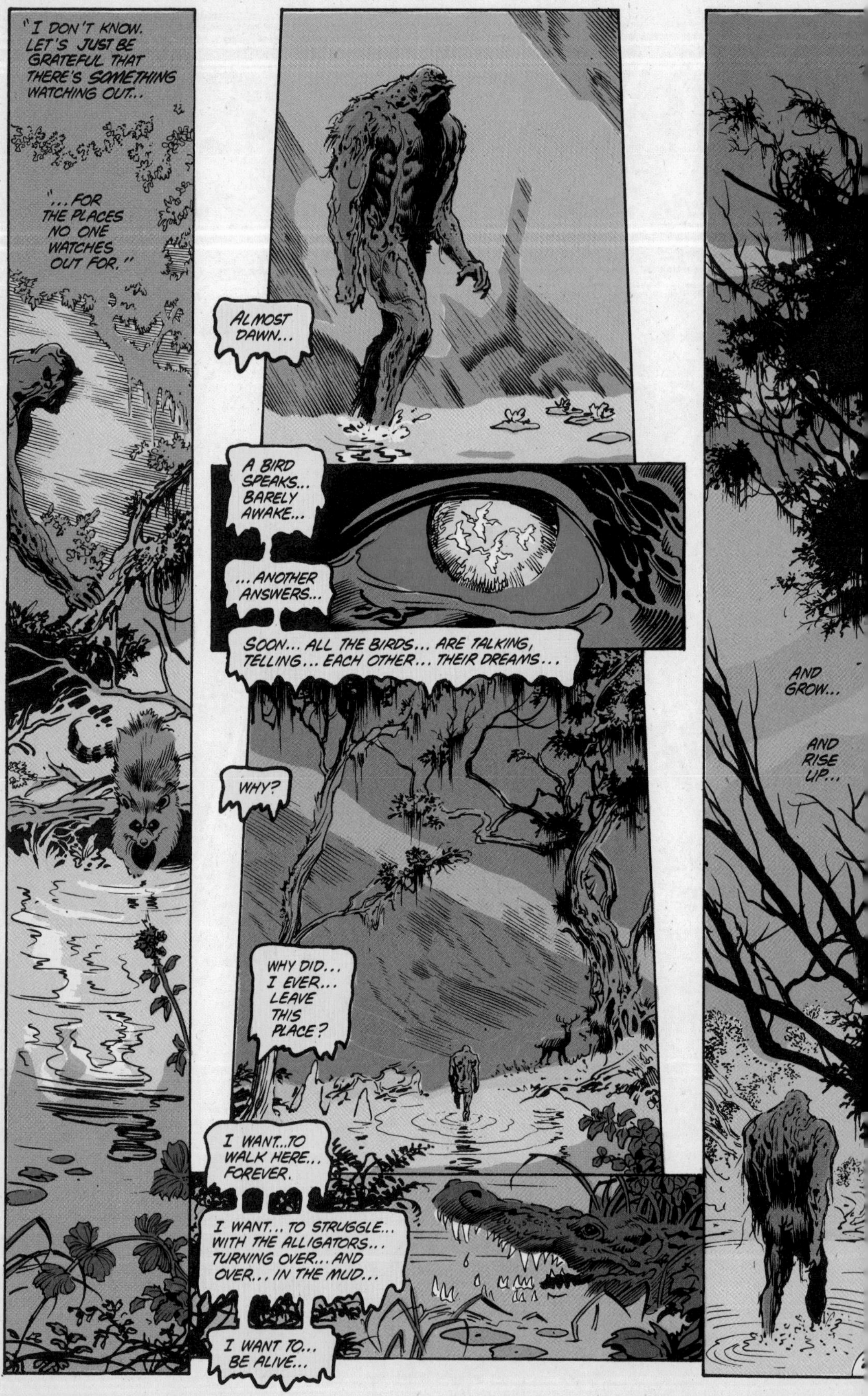
"I DON'T KNOW. LET'S JUST BE GRATEFUL THAT THERE'S SOMETHING WATCHING OUT...
"...FOR THE PLACES NO ONE WATCHES OUT FOR."
ALMOST DAWN...
A BIRD SPEAKS... BARELY AWAKE...
...ANOTHER ANSWERS...
SOON... ALL THE BIRDS... ARE TALKING, TELLING... EACH OTHER... THEIR DREAMS...
WHY?
WHY DID... I EVER... LEAVE THIS PLACE?
I WANT...TO WALK HERE... FOREVER.
I WANT... TO STRUGGLE... WITH THE ALLIGATORS... TURNING OVER... AND OVER... IN THE MUD...
I WANT TO... BE ALIVE...
AND GROW...
AND RISE UP...

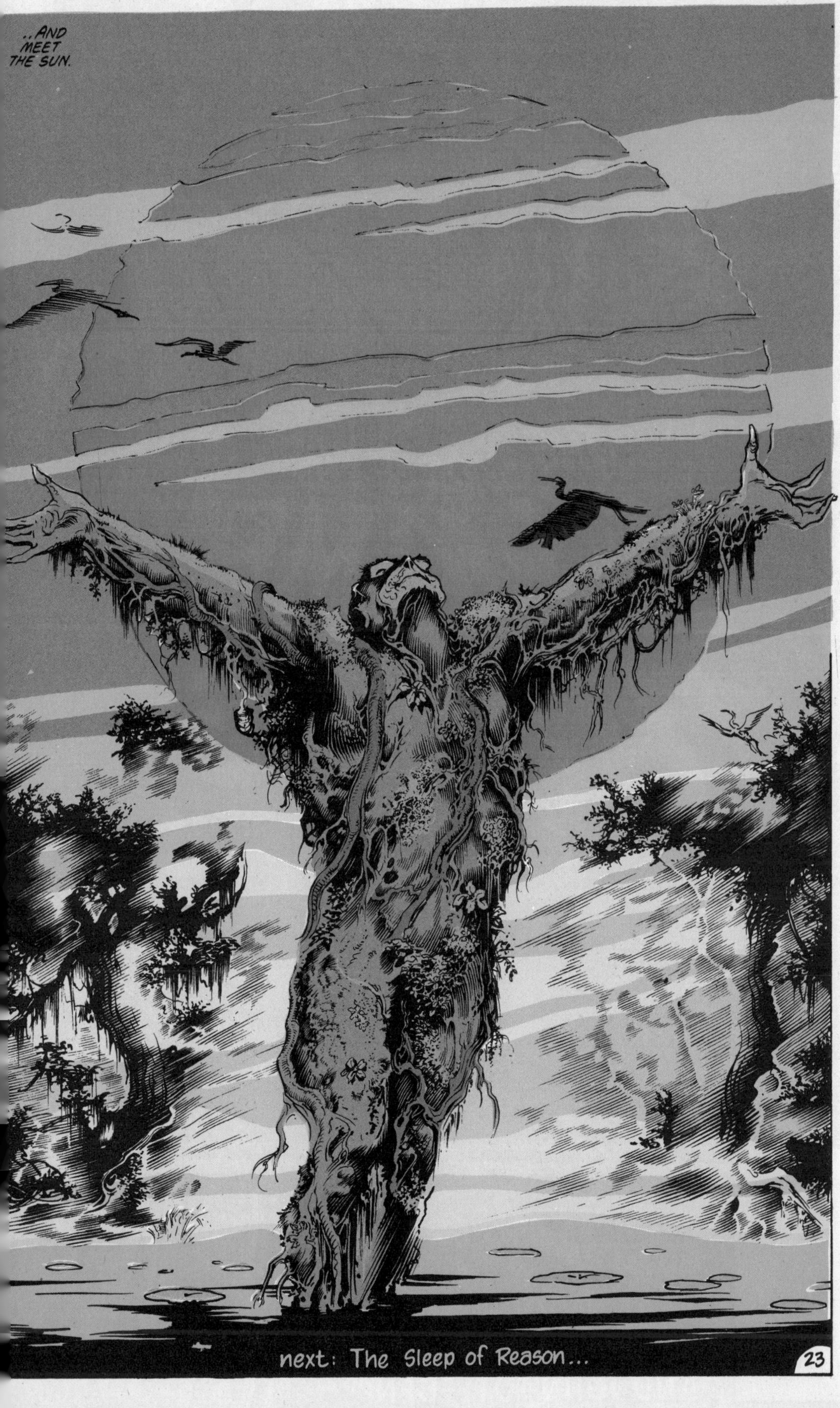
..AND MEET THE SUN.
next: The Sleep of Reason...
23

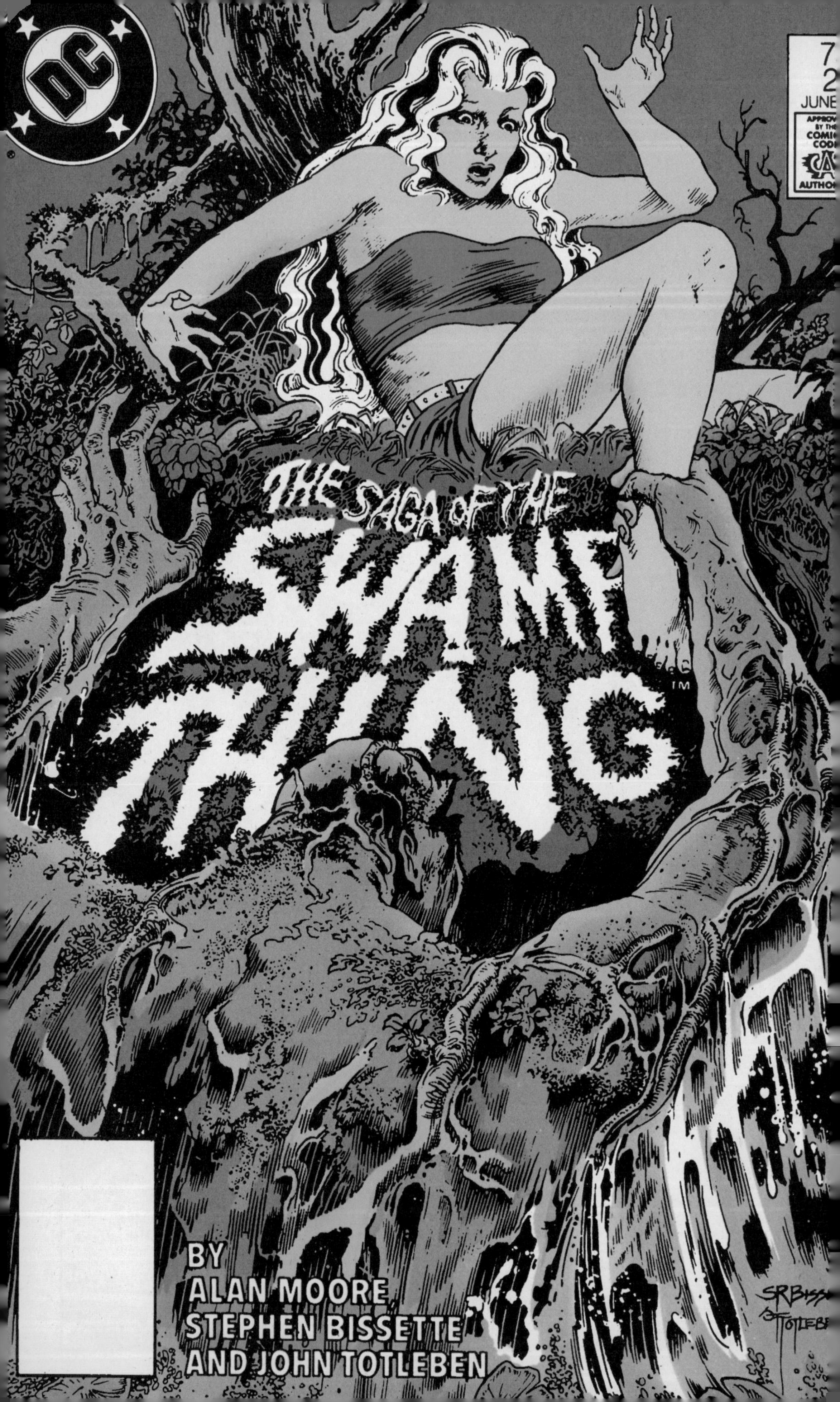
DC
JUNE
THE SAGA OF THE
SWAMP THING
BY
ALAN MOORE
STEPHEN BISSETTE
AND JOHN TOTLEBEN

...E ARRIVED AT THE ...ATON ROUGE ...US DEPOT AT ... LITTLE AFTER ...EVEN ON ...ONDAY ...ORNING...

GATE 16

BATON ROUGE

... SO ANYWAY, ...ISTER, IT'S BEEN ... GREAT PLEASURE ...ALKIN' TO YA!

...AN' LISSEN, IF ...OU EVER NEED ANY ...OFT INSULATION, ...ARRY PRICE IS ...Y NAME, THIS IS ...Y CARD...

HA.

I'M SORRY, MR. PRICE, THIS CARD WON'T BE ANY USE TO ME.

HEY, NOW LOOK, YOU NEVER KNOW...

HAROLD PRICE MGR. FOR ALL YOUR LOFT INSULATION NEEDS IN...

I KNOW.

I KNOW THAT TWELVE YEARS AGO YOU CRASHED YOUR CAR WHILE DRUNK. YOU WALKED AWAY UNHURT, YOUR WIFE'S BEEN CONFINED TO A WHEELCHAIR EVER SINCE.

CURRENTLY, YOU HAVE FIVE DIFFERENT "GIRL-FRIENDS." YOU DO NOT BOTHER TO CONCEAL THEM FROM YOUR WIFE, ALTHOUGH YOU KNOW HOW MUCH PAIN THIS CAUSES HER...

HEY! WAIT, I NEVER TOLD YOU ANY...

...AND AT 5:32 THIS EVENING YOU WILL BE IMPALED BY A SWORDFISH.

THERE IS NOTHING TO BE DONE, IT IS WRITTEN. SELENA HAS ALREADY DECIDED NOT TO BUY THE LAWN FURNITURE.

SO YOU SEE...

HAROLD PRICE LOFT INSULAT...

...YOUR CARD WON'T BE ANY USE TO ME AT ALL.

GOOD DAY.

ON HIS WAY TO HIS HOTEL, HE CALLED AT "THIRD EYE BOOKS AND PARAPHERNALIA" AND PURCHASED SOME AMBER INCENSE.

EXCUSE ME...

YHUH?

NEW SINISTER DUCKS 45 ON SALE HERE

BUY BONG! CHEAP!

COMIX

GET YOUR GRIS GRIS HERE

SALE ON TAROT DECKS

BEANO PILLS. HEY KIDS... TURN YOUR FRIENDS INTO ZOMBIES! BE THE LIFE OF THE PARTY!

ASAFOETIDA

COBRA BRAND COMPANY ASAFOETIDA

DO YOU SELL MANY OF THESE?

NAH, AT THE MOMENT, I'M DOING A LOT OF AURA GOGGLES AN' STUFF LIKE THAT, BUT OUIJA BOARDS...

I THINK I SOLD ONE SIX MONTHS AGO. YOU WANT ONE?

POSTER 607

POSTER 361

DRINK TREEFF BEER

NICE DAY FOR SOMETHIN'

CDEFGHIJKLM
PQRSTUVWXYZ
YES   NO

NO...NO, I DON'T THINK SO

AHH, BUT THIS... THIS IS GOYA, ISN'T IT?

UH, IS THAT L-402 GOYA. YEAH. I THINK SO "THE SLEEP OF REASON

POSTER 224

"...BRINGS FORTH MONSTERS." YES. HE SHOWED ME THE ORIGINAL SKETCHES, BUT I LOST TOUCH WITH HIM AND SOMEHOW NEVER GOT TO SEE THE FINISHED WORK.

A MOST APPROPRIATE PIECE, I'LL TAKE IT.

UH, RIGHT...

AT ELEVEN THIRTY-EIGHT HE GAVE THIRTEEN DOLLARS TO A PRIEST COLLECTING FOR THE MISSION FUND, AND THEN LAUGHED FOR A FULL MINUTE.

THE HOTEL WAS NOT THE BEST, BUT IT WAS THE MOST ATMOSPHERIC.

THE DEVIL CHECKED IN AT NOON.

2

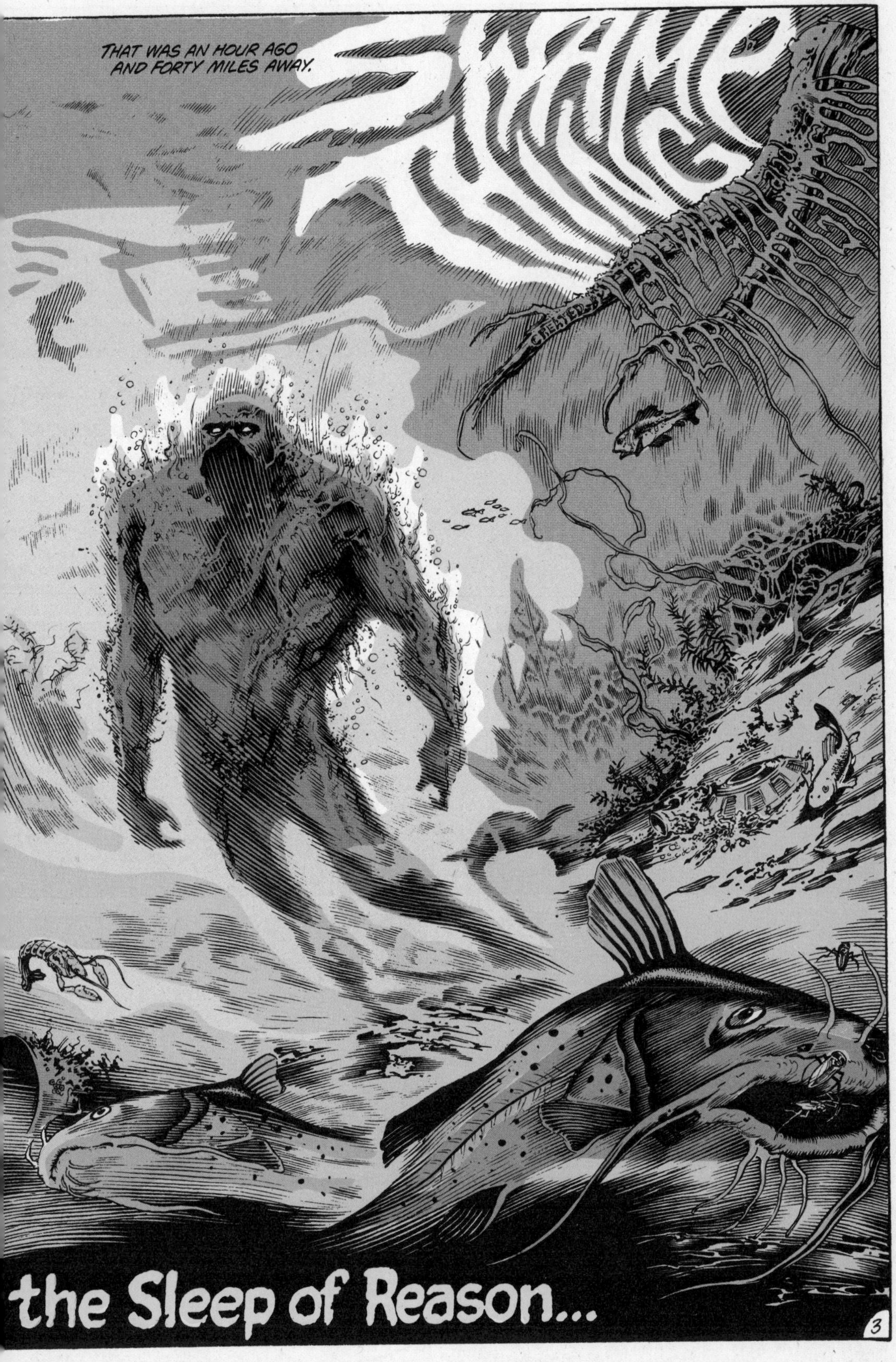
THAT WAS AN HOUR AGO AND FORTY MILES AWAY.
SWAMP THING
the Sleep of Reason...
3

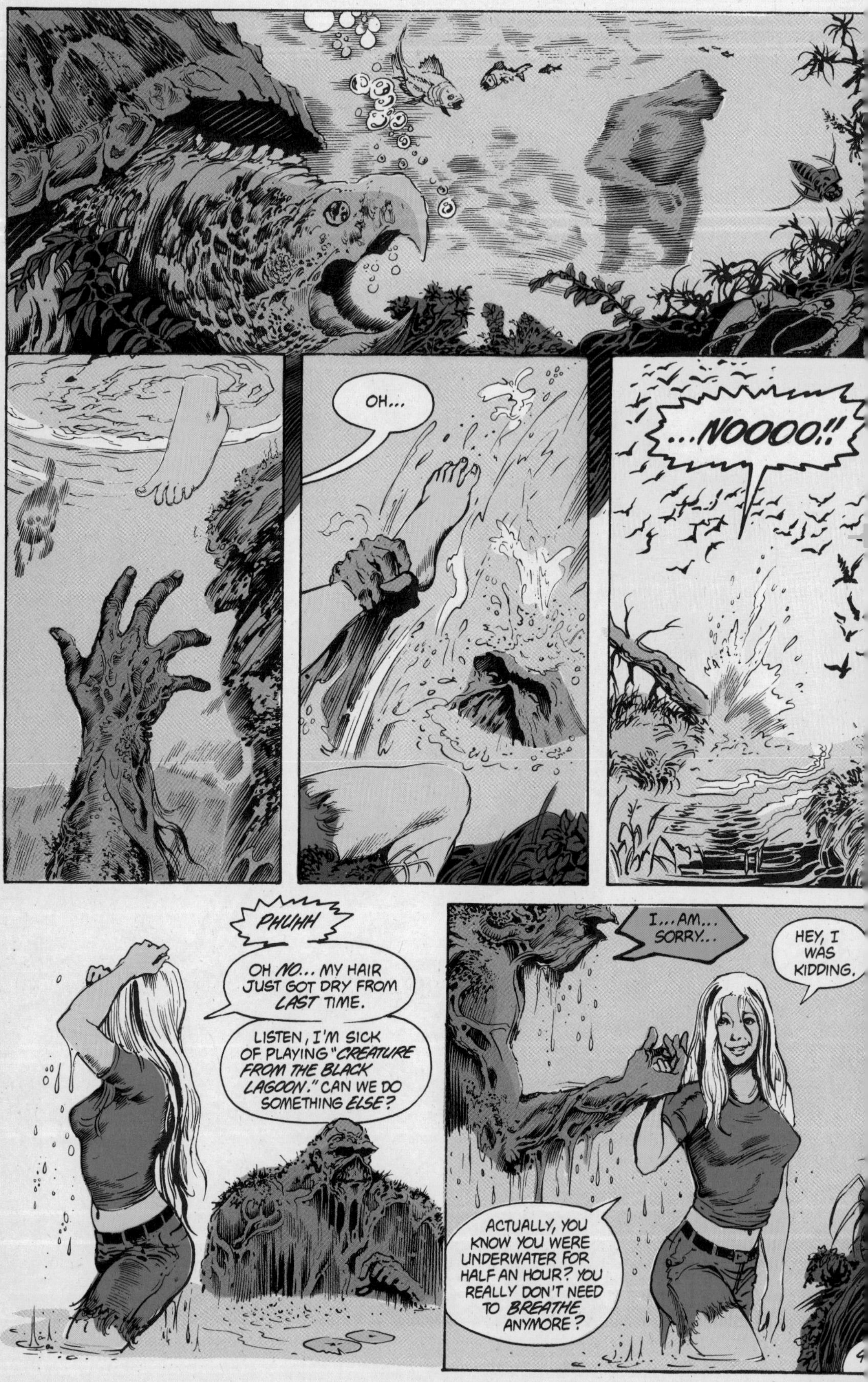
OH...
...NOOOO!!
PHUHH
OH NO... MY HAIR JUST GOT DRY FROM LAST TIME.
LISTEN, I'M SICK OF PLAYING "CREATURE FROM THE BLACK LAGOON." CAN WE DO SOMETHING ELSE?
I... AM... SORRY...
HEY, I WAS KIDDING.
ACTUALLY, YOU KNOW YOU WERE UNDERWATER FOR HALF AN HOUR? YOU REALLY DON'T NEED TO BREATHE ANYMORE?

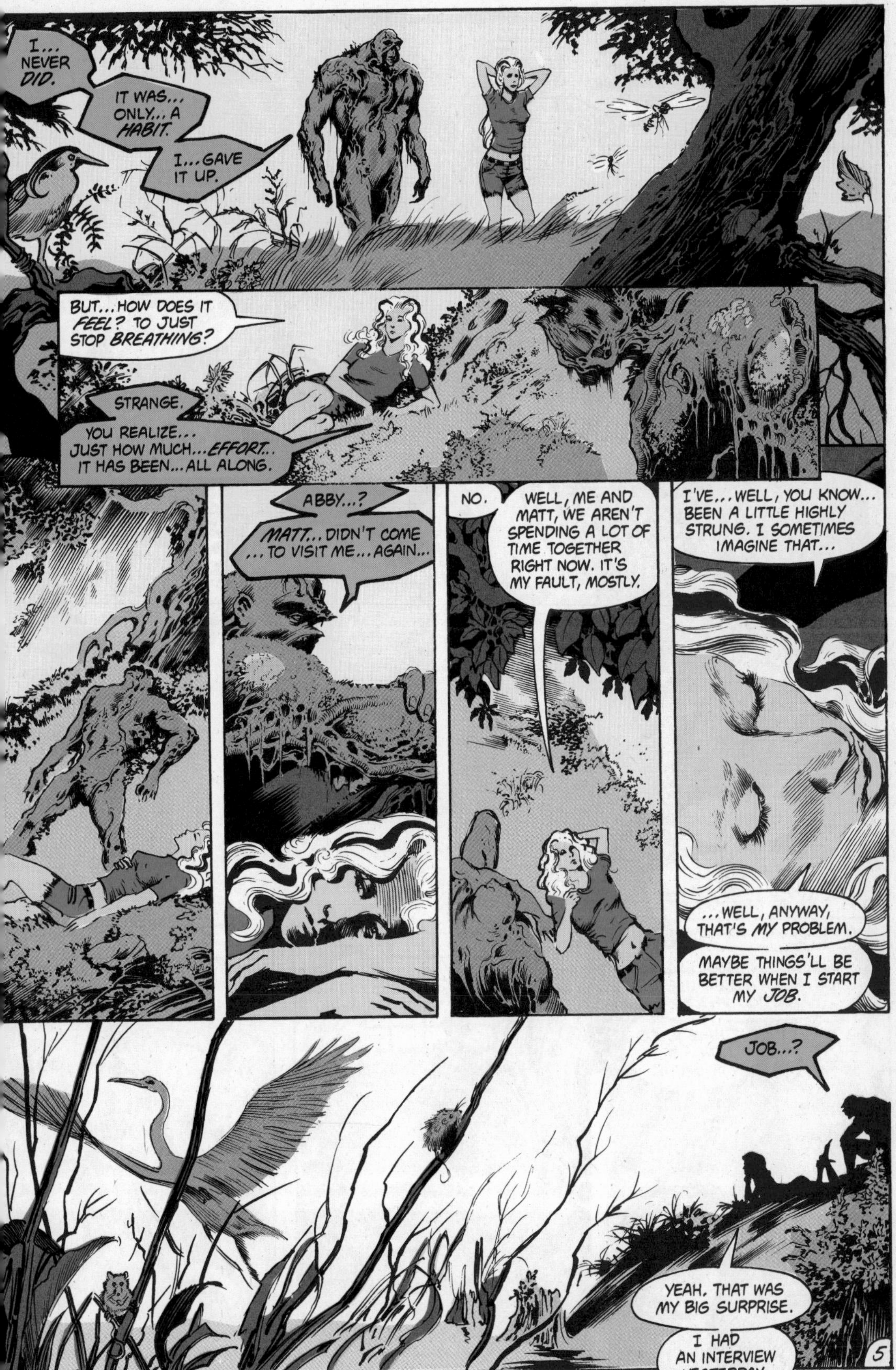
I... NEVER DID.
IT WAS... ONLY... A HABIT.
I... GAVE IT UP.
BUT... HOW DOES IT FEEL? TO JUST STOP BREATHING?
STRANGE.
YOU REALIZE... JUST HOW MUCH... EFFORT.. IT HAS BEEN... ALL ALONG.
ABBY...?
MATT... DIDN'T COME ...TO VISIT ME... AGAIN...
NO.
WELL, ME AND MATT, WE AREN'T SPENDING A LOT OF TIME TOGETHER RIGHT NOW. IT'S MY FAULT, MOSTLY.
I'VE... WELL, YOU KNOW... BEEN A LITTLE HIGHLY STRUNG. I SOMETIMES IMAGINE THAT...
...WELL, ANYWAY, THAT'S MY PROBLEM.
MAYBE THINGS'LL BE BETTER WHEN I START MY JOB.
JOB...?
YEAH. THAT WAS MY BIG SURPRISE.
I HAD AN INTERVIEW YESTERDAY...
5

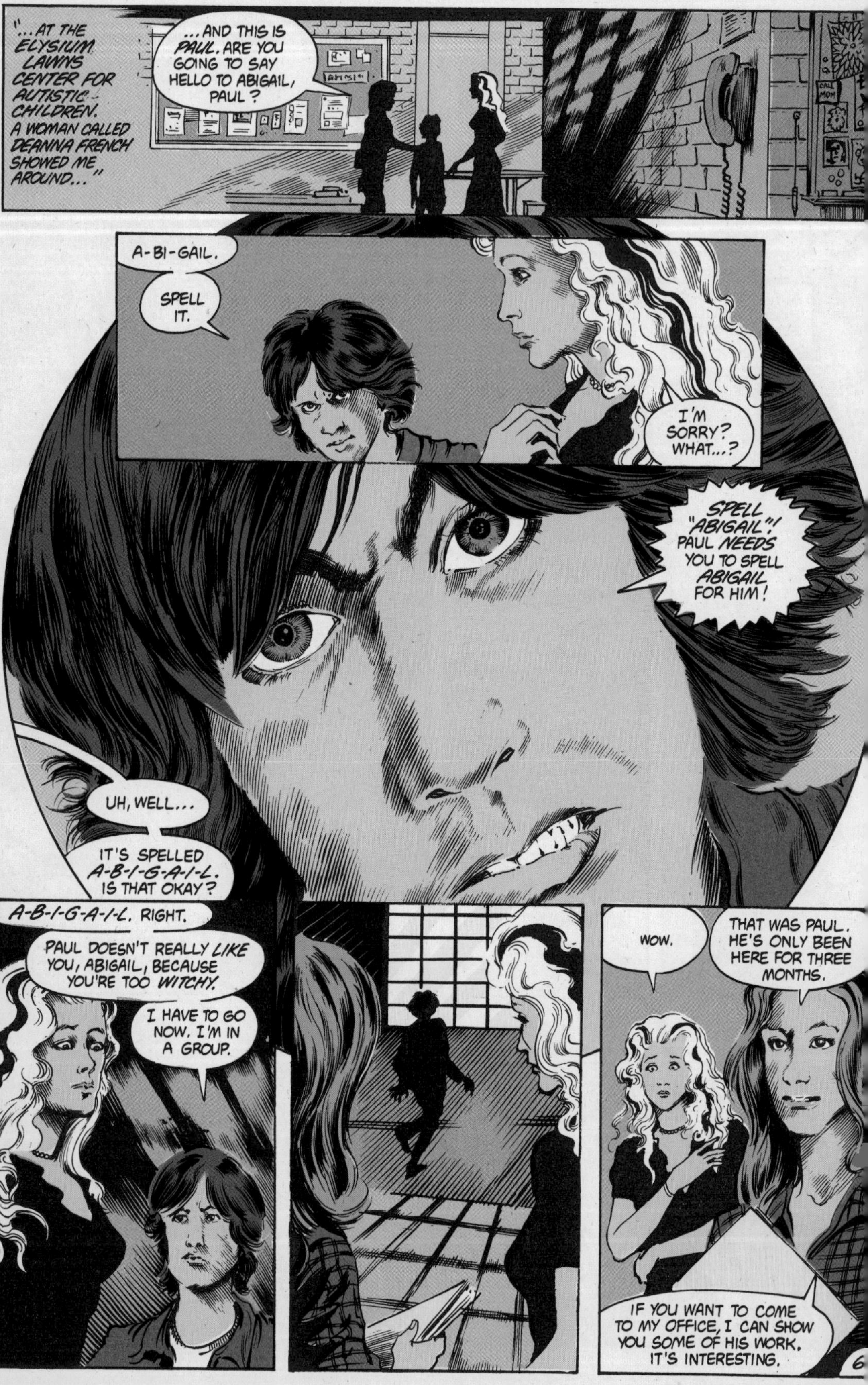
"...AT THE ELYSIUM LAWNS CENTER FOR AUTISTIC CHILDREN. A WOMAN CALLED DEANNA FRENCH SHOWED ME AROUND..."
...AND THIS IS PAUL. ARE YOU GOING TO SAY HELLO TO ABIGAIL, PAUL?
A-BI-GAIL.
SPELL IT.
I'M SORRY? WHAT...?
SPELL "ABIGAIL"! PAUL NEEDS YOU TO SPELL ABIGAIL FOR HIM!
UH, WELL...
IT'S SPELLED A-B-I-G-A-I-L. IS THAT OKAY?
A-B-I-G-A-I-L. RIGHT.
PAUL DOESN'T REALLY LIKE YOU, ABIGAIL, BECAUSE YOU'RE TOO WITCHY.
I HAVE TO GO NOW. I'M IN A GROUP.
WOW.
THAT WAS PAUL. HE'S ONLY BEEN HERE FOR THREE MONTHS.
IF YOU WANT TO COME TO MY OFFICE, I CAN SHOW YOU SOME OF HIS WORK. IT'S INTERESTING.
6

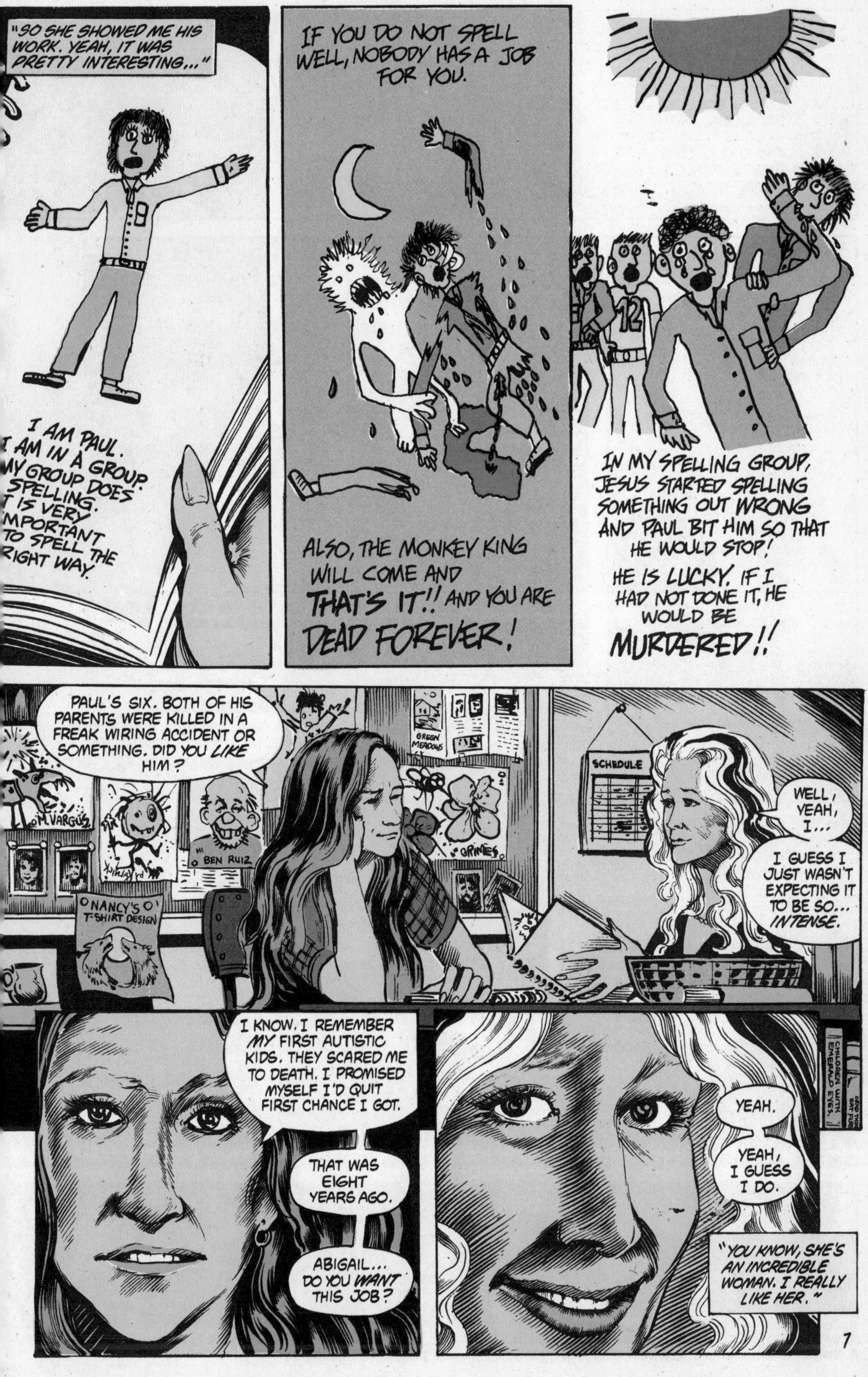
"SO SHE SHOWED ME HIS WORK. YEAH, IT WAS PRETTY INTERESTING..."
I AM PAUL. I AM IN A GROUP. MY GROUP DOES SPELLING. IT IS VERY IMPORTANT TO SPELL THE RIGHT WAY.
IF YOU DO NOT SPELL WELL, NOBODY HAS A JOB FOR YOU.
ALSO, THE MONKEY KING WILL COME AND THAT'S IT!! AND YOU ARE DEAD FOREVER!
12
IN MY SPELLING GROUP, JESUS STARTED SPELLING SOMETHING OUT WRONG AND PAUL BIT HIM SO THAT HE WOULD STOP!
HE IS LUCKY. IF I HAD NOT DONE IT, HE WOULD BE MURDERED!!
PAUL'S SIX. BOTH OF HIS PARENTS WERE KILLED IN A FREAK WIRING ACCIDENT OR SOMETHING. DID YOU LIKE HIM?
GREEN MEADOWS
M. VARGUS
BEN RUIZ
GRIMES
SCHEDULE
NANCY'S T-SHIRT DESIGN
WELL, YEAH, I...
I GUESS I JUST WASN'T EXPECTING IT TO BE SO... INTENSE.
I KNOW. I REMEMBER MY FIRST AUTISTIC KIDS. THEY SCARED ME TO DEATH. I PROMISED MYSELF I'D QUIT FIRST CHANCE I GOT.
THAT WAS EIGHT YEARS AGO.
ABIGAIL... DO YOU WANT THIS JOB?
CHILDREN WITH EMERALD EYES
YEAH.
YEAH, I GUESS I DO.
"YOU KNOW, SHE'S AN INCREDIBLE WOMAN. I REALLY LIKE HER."
7

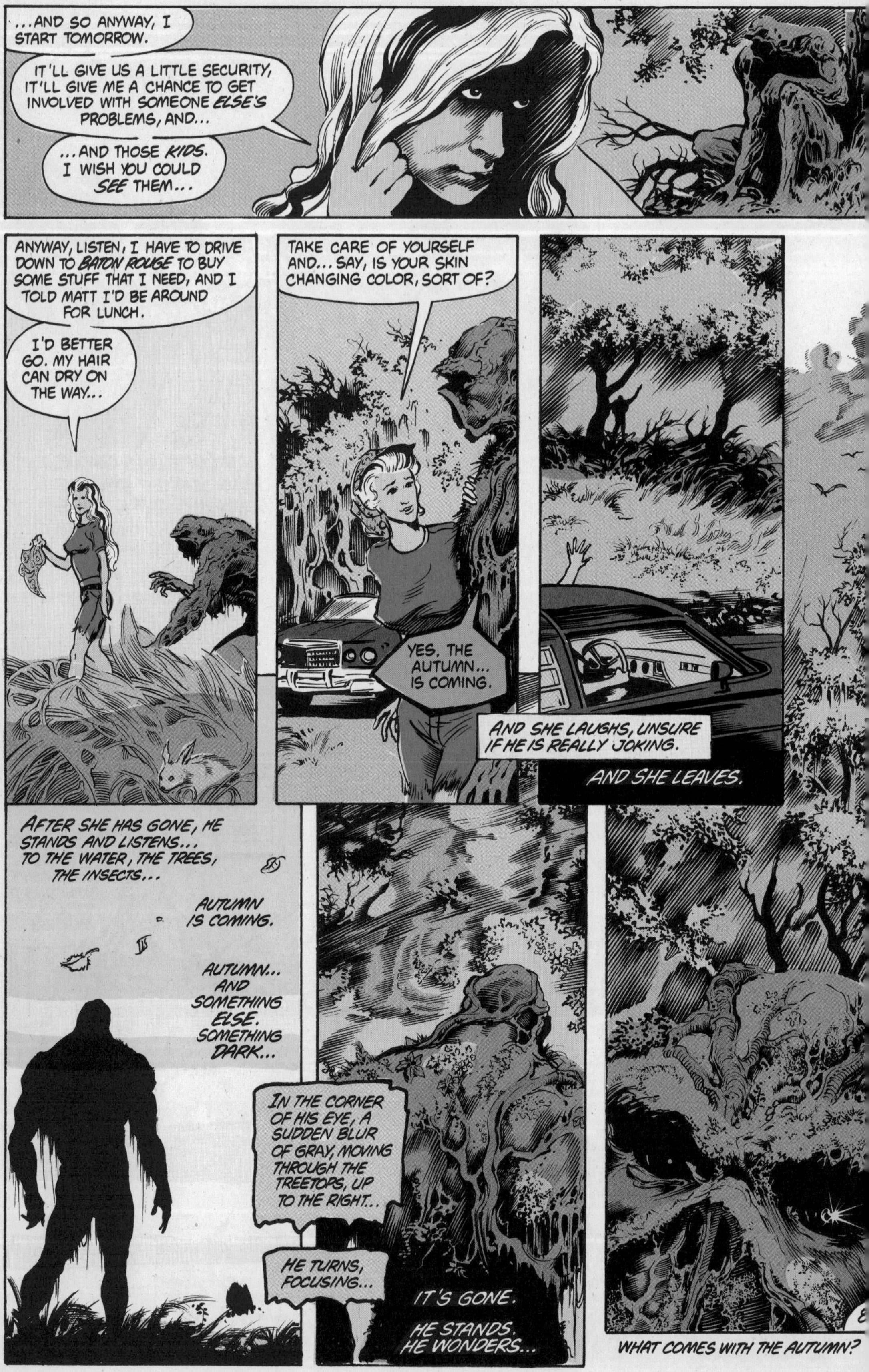
...AND SO ANYWAY, I START TOMORROW.
IT'LL GIVE US A LITTLE SECURITY, IT'LL GIVE ME A CHANCE TO GET INVOLVED WITH SOMEONE ELSE'S PROBLEMS, AND...
...AND THOSE KIDS. I WISH YOU COULD SEE THEM...
ANYWAY, LISTEN, I HAVE TO DRIVE DOWN TO BATON ROUGE TO BUY SOME STUFF THAT I NEED, AND I TOLD MATT I'D BE AROUND FOR LUNCH.
I'D BETTER GO. MY HAIR CAN DRY ON THE WAY...
TAKE CARE OF YOURSELF AND... SAY, IS YOUR SKIN CHANGING COLOR, SORT OF?
YES. THE AUTUMN... IS COMING.
AND SHE LAUGHS, UNSURE IF HE IS REALLY JOKING.
AND SHE LEAVES.
AFTER SHE HAS GONE, HE STANDS AND LISTENS... TO THE WATER, THE TREES, THE INSECTS...
AUTUMN IS COMING.
AUTUMN... AND SOMETHING ELSE. SOMETHING DARK...
IN THE CORNER OF HIS EYE, A SUDDEN BLUR OF GRAY, MOVING THROUGH THE TREETOPS, UP TO THE RIGHT...
HE TURNS, FOCUSING...
IT'S GONE.
HE STANDS. HE WONDERS...
WHAT COMES WITH THE AUTUMN?

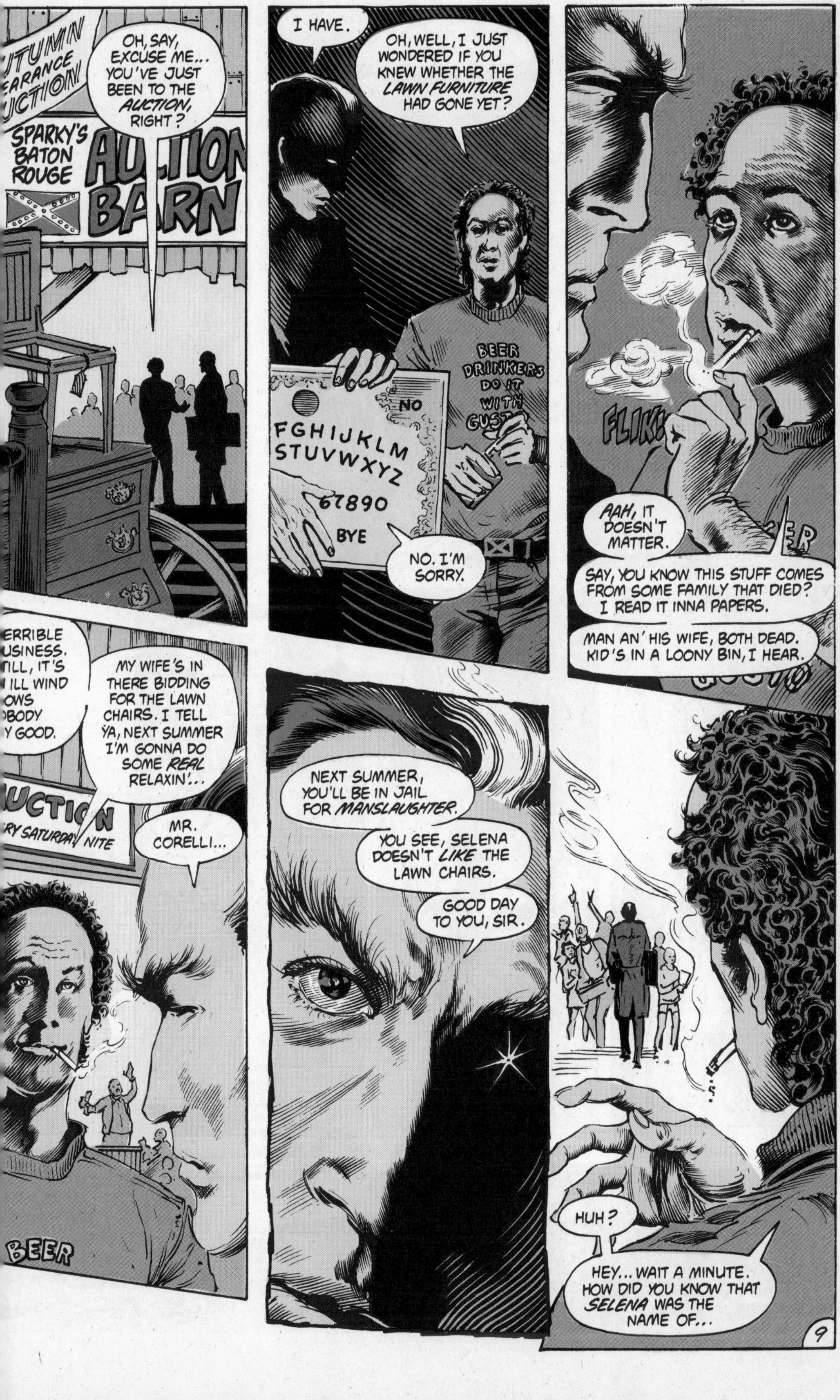
UTUMN
EARANCE
UCTION
SPARKY'S
BATON
ROUGE
AUCTION
BARN
OH, SAY, EXCUSE ME... YOU'VE JUST BEEN TO THE AUCTION, RIGHT?
I HAVE.
OH, WELL, I JUST WONDERED IF YOU KNEW WHETHER THE LAWN FURNITURE HAD GONE YET?
BEER DRINKERS DO IT WITH GUSTO
NO
FGHIJKLM
STUVWXYZ
67890
BYE
NO. I'M SORRY.
FLIK!
AAH, IT DOESN'T MATTER.
SAY, YOU KNOW THIS STUFF COMES FROM SOME FAMILY THAT DIED? I READ IT INNA PAPERS.
MAN AN' HIS WIFE, BOTH DEAD. KID'S IN A LOONY BIN, I HEAR.
ERRIBLE USINESS. TILL, IT'S N ILL WIND OWS OBODY Y GOOD.
MY WIFE'S IN THERE BIDDING FOR THE LAWN CHAIRS. I TELL YA, NEXT SUMMER I'M GONNA DO SOME REAL RELAXIN'...
UCTION
RY SATURDAY NITE
MR. CORELLI...
BEER
NEXT SUMMER, YOU'LL BE IN JAIL FOR MANSLAUGHTER.
YOU SEE, SELENA DOESN'T LIKE THE LAWN CHAIRS.
GOOD DAY TO YOU, SIR.
HUH?
HEY... WAIT A MINUTE. HOW DID YOU KNOW THAT SELENA WAS THE NAME OF...
9

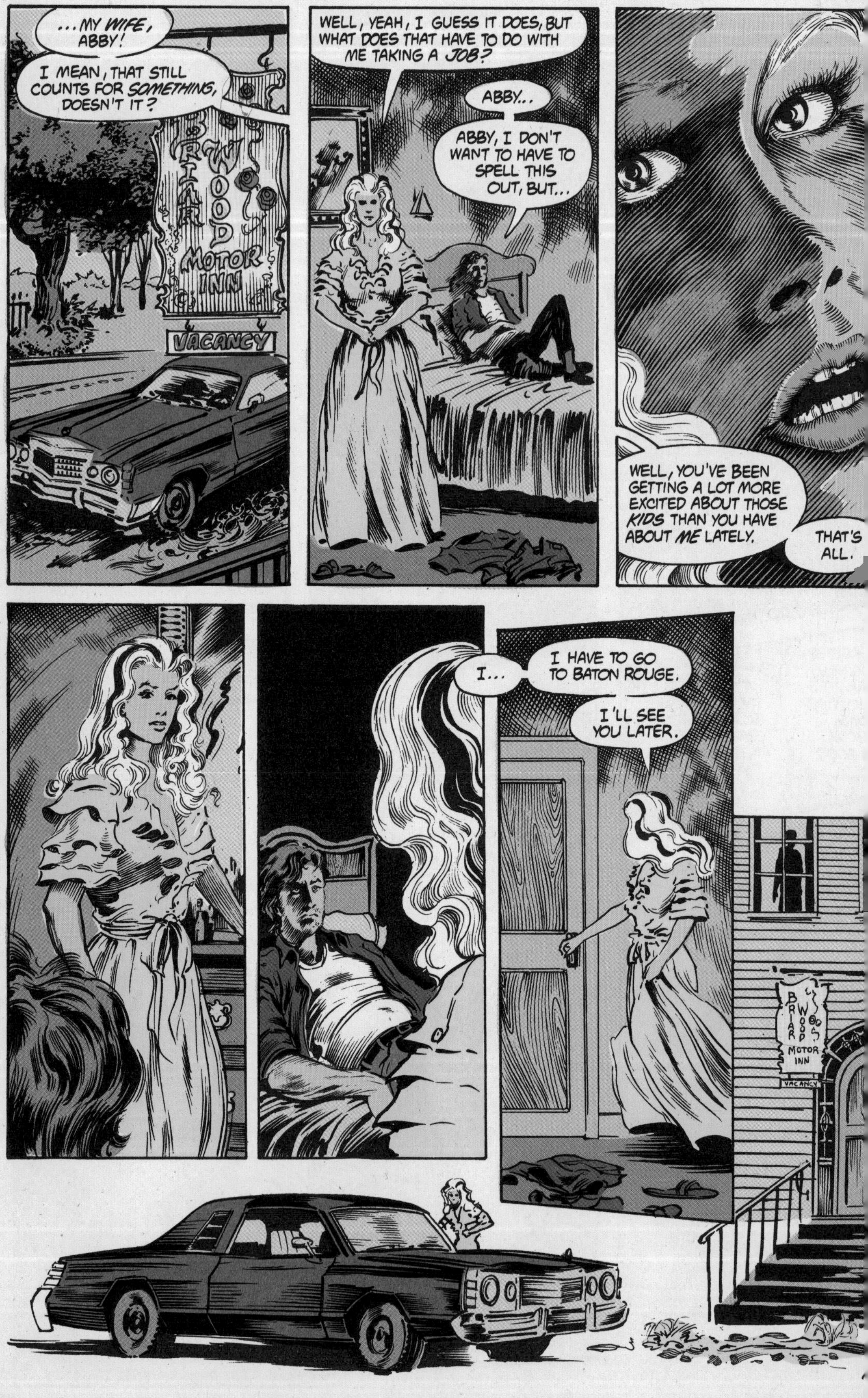
...MY *WIFE*, ABBY!
I MEAN, THAT STILL COUNTS FOR *SOMETHING*, DOESN'T IT?
BRIAR WOOD MOTOR INN
VACANCY
WELL, YEAH, I GUESS IT DOES, BUT WHAT DOES THAT HAVE TO DO WITH ME TAKING A *JOB*?
ABBY...
ABBY, I DON'T WANT TO HAVE TO SPELL THIS OUT, BUT...
WELL, YOU'VE BEEN GETTING A LOT MORE EXCITED ABOUT THOSE *KIDS* THAN YOU HAVE ABOUT *ME* LATELY.
THAT'S ALL.
I...
I HAVE TO GO TO BATON ROUGE.
I'LL SEE YOU LATER.
BRIAR WOOD MOTOR INN
VACANCY

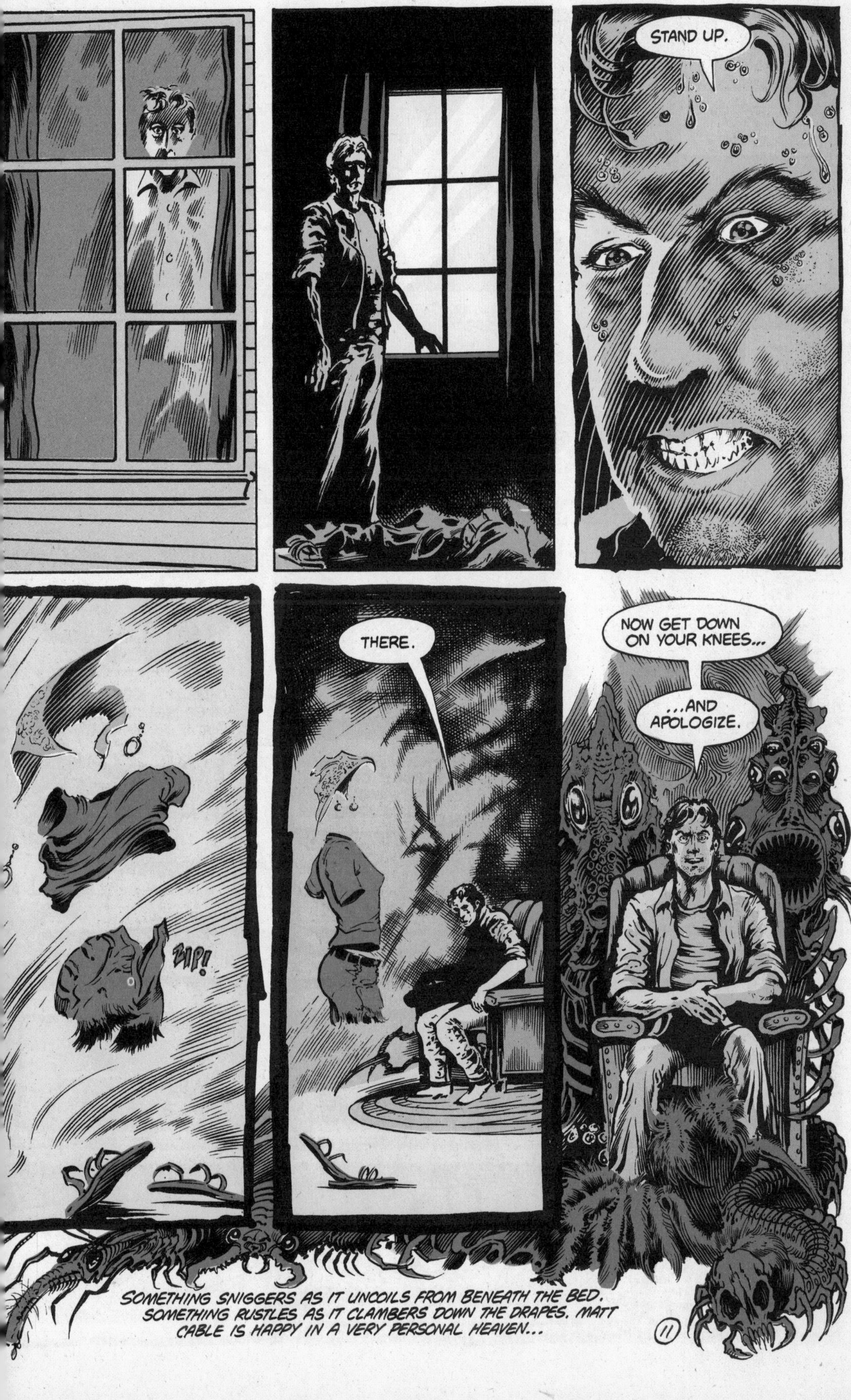
STAND UP.
ZIP!
THERE.
NOW GET DOWN ON YOUR KNEES...
...AND APOLOGIZE.
SOMETHING SNIGGERS AS IT UNCOILS FROM BENEATH THE BED. SOMETHING RUSTLES AS IT CLAMBERS DOWN THE DRAPES. MATT CABLE IS HAPPY IN A VERY PERSONAL HEAVEN...
11

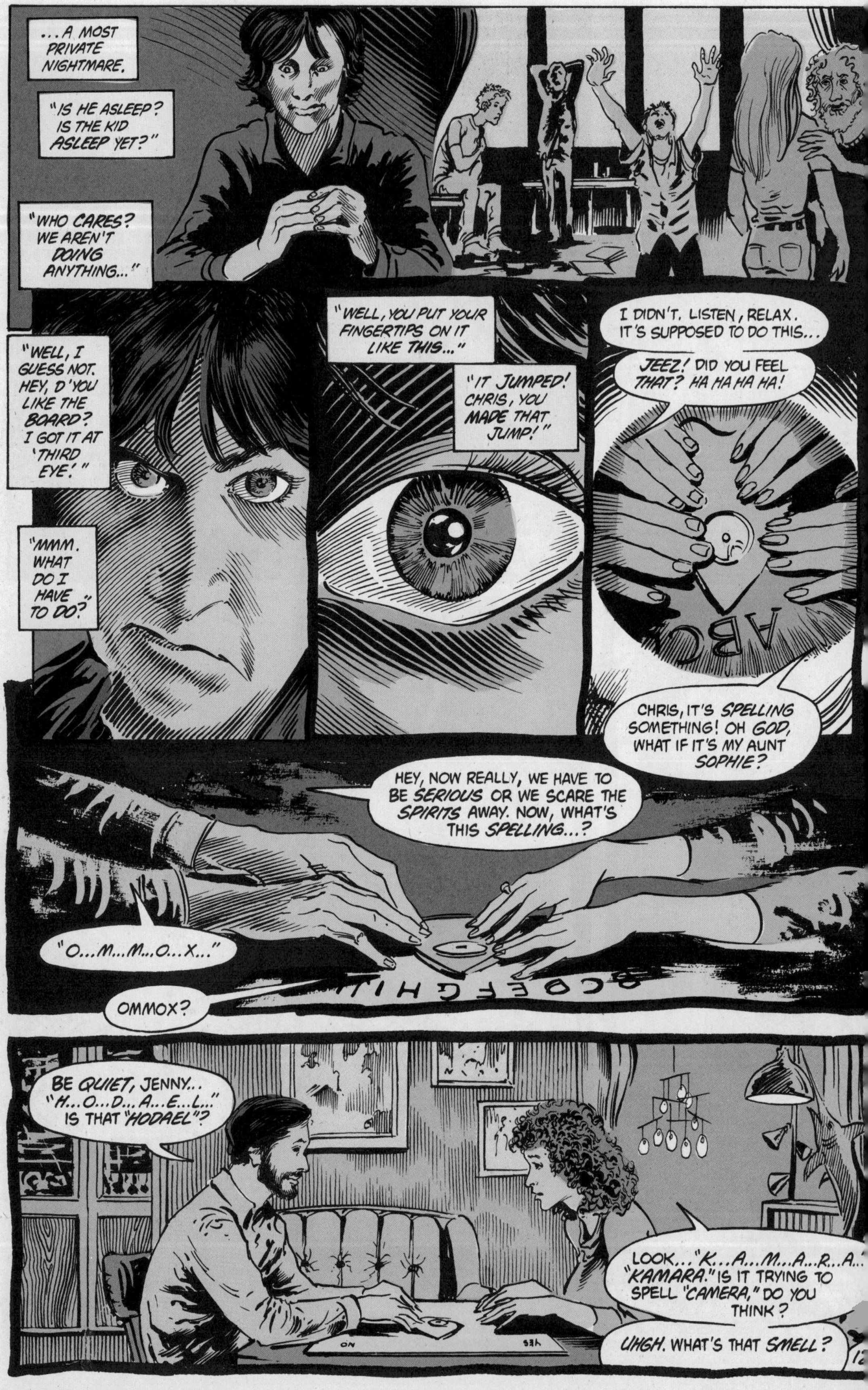
...A MOST PRIVATE NIGHTMARE.
"IS HE ASLEEP? IS THE KID ASLEEP YET?"
"WHO CARES? WE AREN'T DOING ANYTHING..."
"WELL, I GUESS NOT. HEY, D'YOU LIKE THE BOARD? I GOT IT AT 'THIRD EYE.'"
"MMM. WHAT DO I HAVE TO DO?"
"WELL, YOU PUT YOUR FINGERTIPS ON IT LIKE THIS..."
"IT JUMPED! CHRIS, YOU MADE THAT JUMP!"
I DIDN'T. LISTEN, RELAX. IT'S SUPPOSED TO DO THIS...
JEEZ! DID YOU FEEL THAT? HA HA HA HA!
ABC
CHRIS, IT'S SPELLING SOMETHING! OH GOD, WHAT IF IT'S MY AUNT SOPHIE?
HEY, NOW REALLY, WE HAVE TO BE SERIOUS OR WE SCARE THE SPIRITS AWAY. NOW, WHAT'S THIS SPELLING...?
"O...M...M...O...X..."
OMMOX?
BE QUIET, JENNY... "H...O...D...A...E...L..." IS THAT "HODAEL"?
LOOK... "K...A...M...A...R...A..." "KAMARA." IS IT TRYING TO SPELL "CAMERA," DO YOU THINK?
UHGH. WHAT'S THAT SMELL?

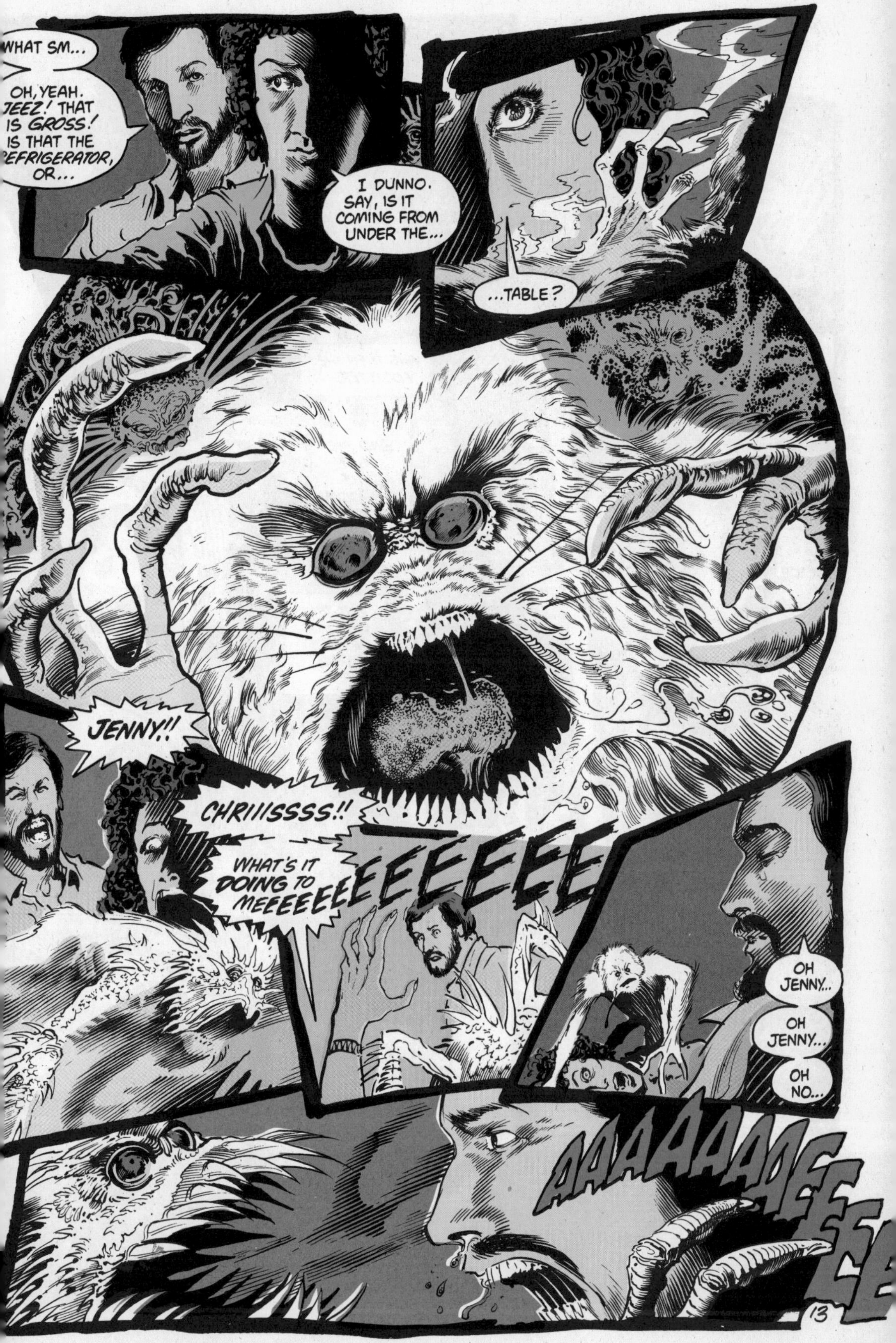
WHAT SM...
OH, YEAH. JEEZ! THAT IS GROSS! IS THAT THE REFRIGERATOR, OR...
I DUNNO. SAY, IS IT COMING FROM UNDER THE...
...TABLE?
JENNY!!
CHRIIISSSS!!
WHAT'S IT DOING TO MEEEEEEEEEEEEE
OH JENNY...
OH JENNY...
OH NO...
AAAAAAEEEEE
13

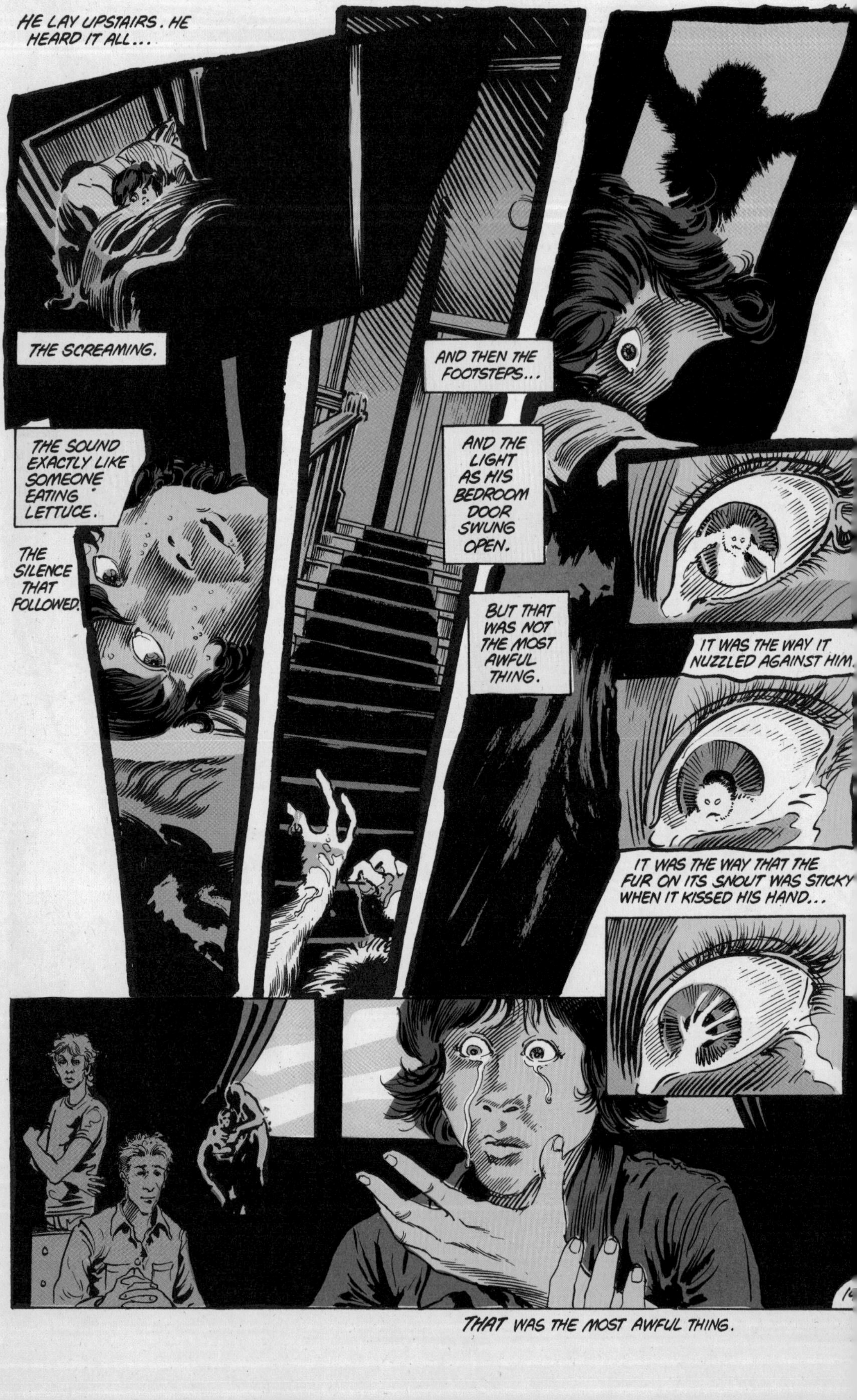
HE LAY UPSTAIRS. HE HEARD IT ALL...
THE SCREAMING.
THE SOUND EXACTLY LIKE SOMEONE EATING LETTUCE.
THE SILENCE THAT FOLLOWED.
AND THEN THE FOOTSTEPS...
AND THE LIGHT AS HIS BEDROOM DOOR SWUNG OPEN.
BUT THAT WAS NOT THE MOST AWFUL THING.
IT WAS THE WAY IT NUZZLED AGAINST HIM.
IT WAS THE WAY THAT THE FUR ON ITS SNOUT WAS STICKY WHEN IT KISSED HIS HAND...
THAT WAS THE MOST AWFUL THING.

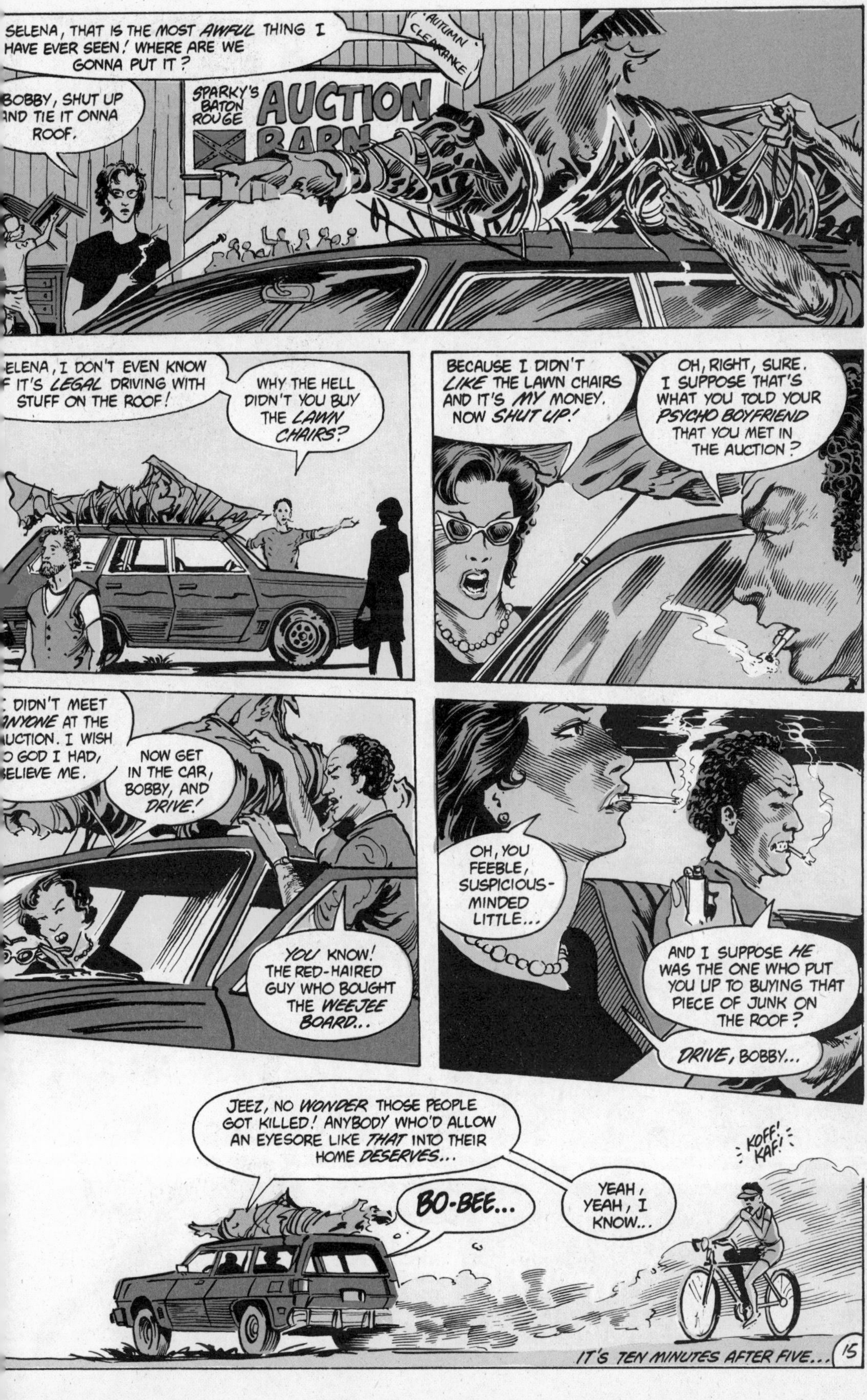
SELENA, THAT IS THE MOST AWFUL THING I HAVE EVER SEEN! WHERE ARE WE GONNA PUT IT?
AUTUMN CLEARANCE
SPARKY'S BATON ROUGE AUCTION BARN
BOBBY, SHUT UP AND TIE IT ONNA ROOF.
ELENA, I DON'T EVEN KNOW F IT'S LEGAL DRIVING WITH STUFF ON THE ROOF!
WHY THE HELL DIDN'T YOU BUY THE LAWN CHAIRS?
BECAUSE I DIDN'T LIKE THE LAWN CHAIRS AND IT'S MY MONEY. NOW SHUT UP!
OH, RIGHT, SURE. I SUPPOSE THAT'S WHAT YOU TOLD YOUR PSYCHO BOYFRIEND THAT YOU MET IN THE AUCTION?
DIDN'T MEET ANYONE AT THE AUCTION. I WISH O GOD I HAD, BELIEVE ME.
NOW GET IN THE CAR, BOBBY, AND DRIVE!
YOU KNOW! THE RED-HAIRED GUY WHO BOUGHT THE WEEJEE BOARD...
OH, YOU FEEBLE, SUSPICIOUS-MINDED LITTLE...
AND I SUPPOSE HE WAS THE ONE WHO PUT YOU UP TO BUYING THAT PIECE OF JUNK ON THE ROOF?
DRIVE, BOBBY...
JEEZ, NO WONDER THOSE PEOPLE GOT KILLED! ANYBODY WHO'D ALLOW AN EYESORE LIKE THAT INTO THEIR HOME DESERVES...
BO-BEE...
YEAH, YEAH, I KNOW...
KOFF! KAF!
IT'S TEN MINUTES AFTER FIVE...
15

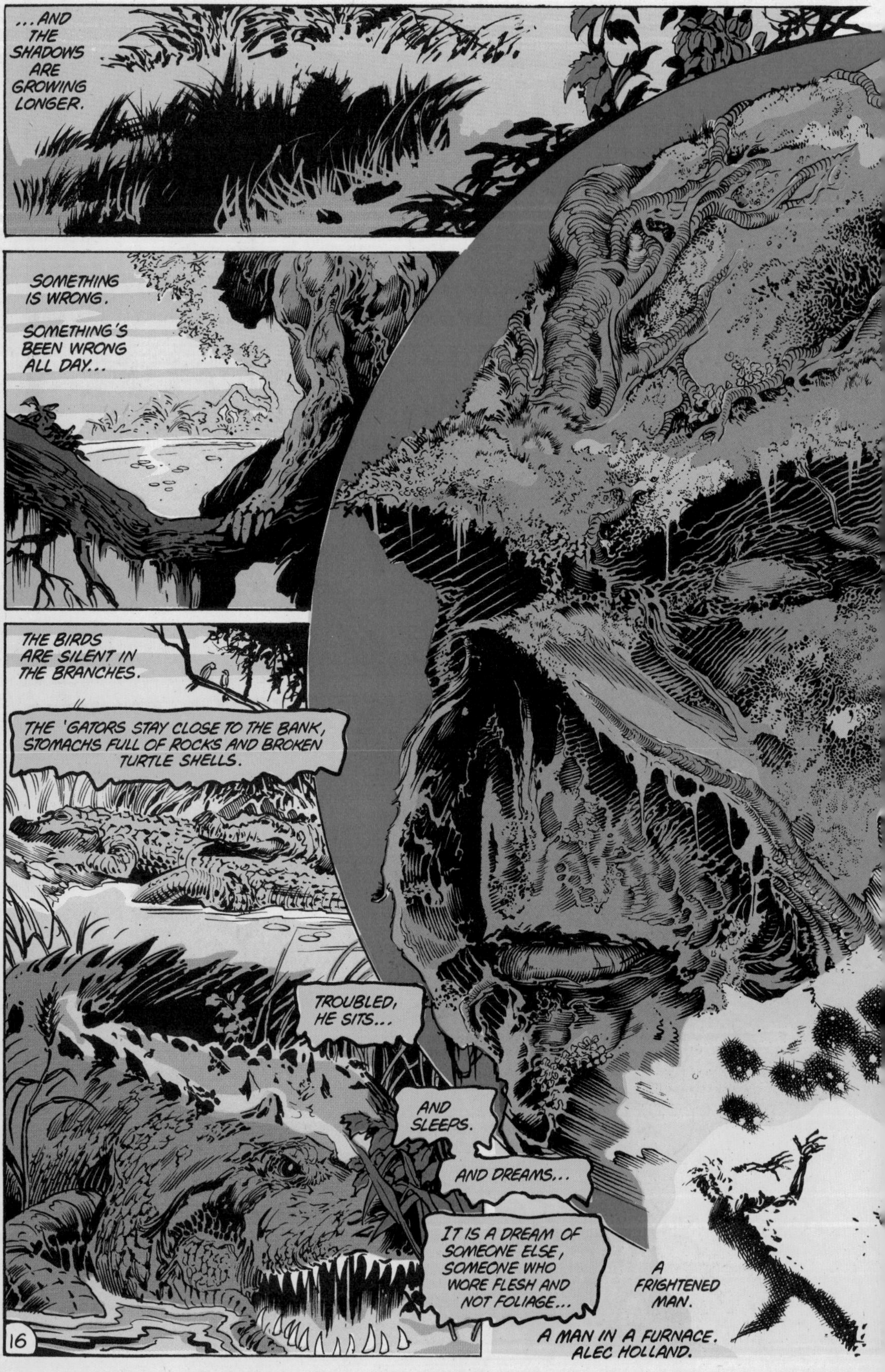
...AND THE SHADOWS ARE GROWING LONGER.
SOMETHING IS WRONG.
SOMETHING'S BEEN WRONG ALL DAY...
THE BIRDS ARE SILENT IN THE BRANCHES.
THE 'GATORS STAY CLOSE TO THE BANK, STOMACHS FULL OF ROCKS AND BROKEN TURTLE SHELLS.
TROUBLED, HE SITS...
AND SLEEPS.
AND DREAMS...
IT IS A DREAM OF SOMEONE ELSE, SOMEONE WHO WORE FLESH AND NOT FOLIAGE...
A FRIGHTENED MAN.
A MAN IN A FURNACE. ALEC HOLLAND.
16

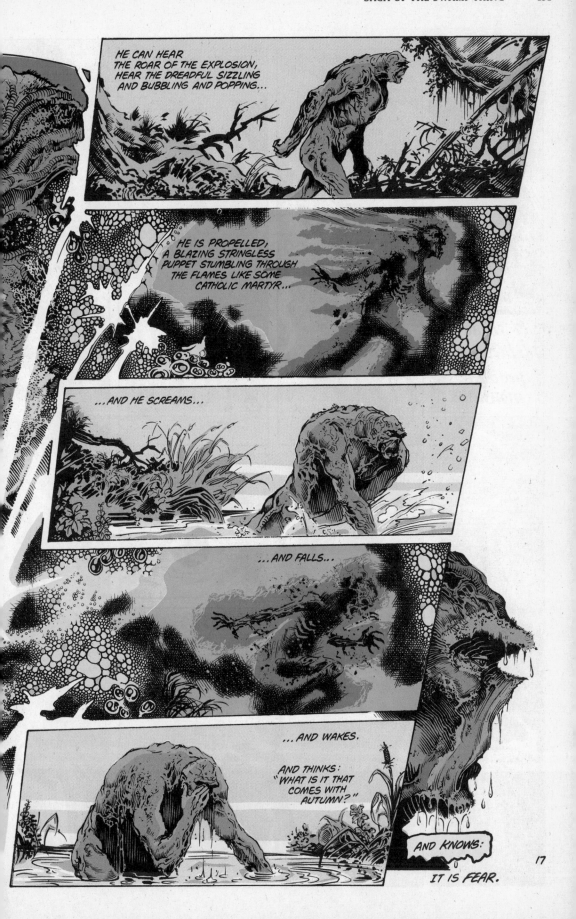

HE CAN HEAR THE ROAR OF THE EXPLOSION, HEAR THE DREADFUL SIZZLING AND BUBBLING AND POPPING...

HE IS PROPELLED, A BLAZING STRINGLESS PUPPET STUMBLING THROUGH THE FLAMES LIKE SOME CATHOLIC MARTYR...

...AND HE SCREAMS...

...AND FALLS...

...AND WAKES.

AND THINKS: "WHAT IS IT THAT COMES WITH AUTUMN?"

AND KNOWS:

IT IS FEAR.

17

IT IS FEAR THAT COMES WITH THE AUTUMN.

HE FEELS IT...

IT THRUMS BENEATH HIS THICK, POWERFUL FINGERS, AND ITS BOUQUET OF SOURED SWEAT IS NOT MASKED BY THE INCENSE.

WITHIN THE DARK POOL OF HIS MIND IMAGES UNFOLD, OPENING LIKE ANEMONES IN BRINE...

THE MAN, THE WOMAN, THE BOY AWAKE UPSTAIRS...

THE PLANCHETTE MOVING...

...ommox...

...HODAEL...

El sueño de la razon produce monstruos

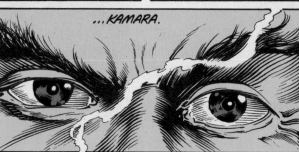

...KAMARA.

THE PENULTIMATE FRAGMENT OF THE CRYPTOGRAM TUMBLES INTO PLACE... AN INVOCATION, SPELLED OUT BY A OUIJA BOARD.

THAT WAS HOW THE DAMNED THING HAD CLAWED ITS WAY THROUGH INTO THE WORLD OF SANITY AND REASON.

THERE IS MUCH TO BE DONE.

IT IS ALREADY HALF PAST FIVE...

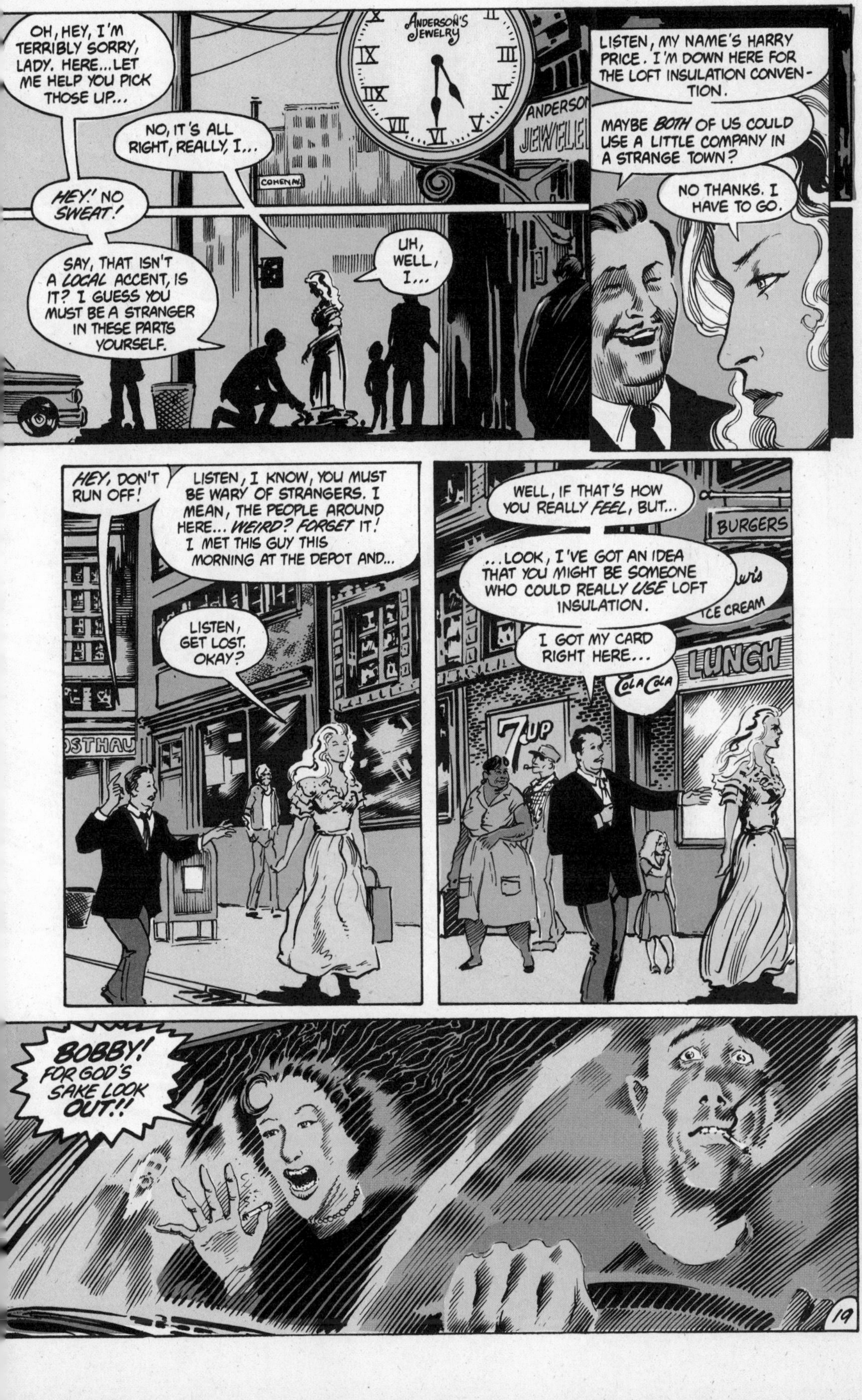

OH, HEY, I'M TERRIBLY SORRY, LADY. HERE... LET ME HELP YOU PICK THOSE UP...
NO, IT'S ALL RIGHT, REALLY, I...
ANDERSON'S JEWELRY
HEY! NO SWEAT!
SAY, THAT ISN'T A LOCAL ACCENT, IS IT? I GUESS YOU MUST BE A STRANGER IN THESE PARTS YOURSELF.
UH, WELL, I...
LISTEN, MY NAME'S HARRY PRICE. I'M DOWN HERE FOR THE LOFT INSULATION CONVEN-TION.
MAYBE BOTH OF US COULD USE A LITTLE COMPANY IN A STRANGE TOWN?
NO THANKS. I HAVE TO GO.
HEY, DON'T RUN OFF!
LISTEN, I KNOW, YOU MUST BE WARY OF STRANGERS. I MEAN, THE PEOPLE AROUND HERE... WEIRD? FORGET IT! I MET THIS GUY THIS MORNING AT THE DEPOT AND...
LISTEN, GET LOST. OKAY?
WELL, IF THAT'S HOW YOU REALLY FEEL, BUT...
...LOOK, I'VE GOT AN IDEA THAT YOU MIGHT BE SOMEONE WHO COULD REALLY USE LOFT INSULATION.
I GOT MY CARD RIGHT HERE...
BURGERS
ICE CREAM
LUNCH
7UP
BOBBY! FOR GOD'S SAKE LOOK OUT!!
19

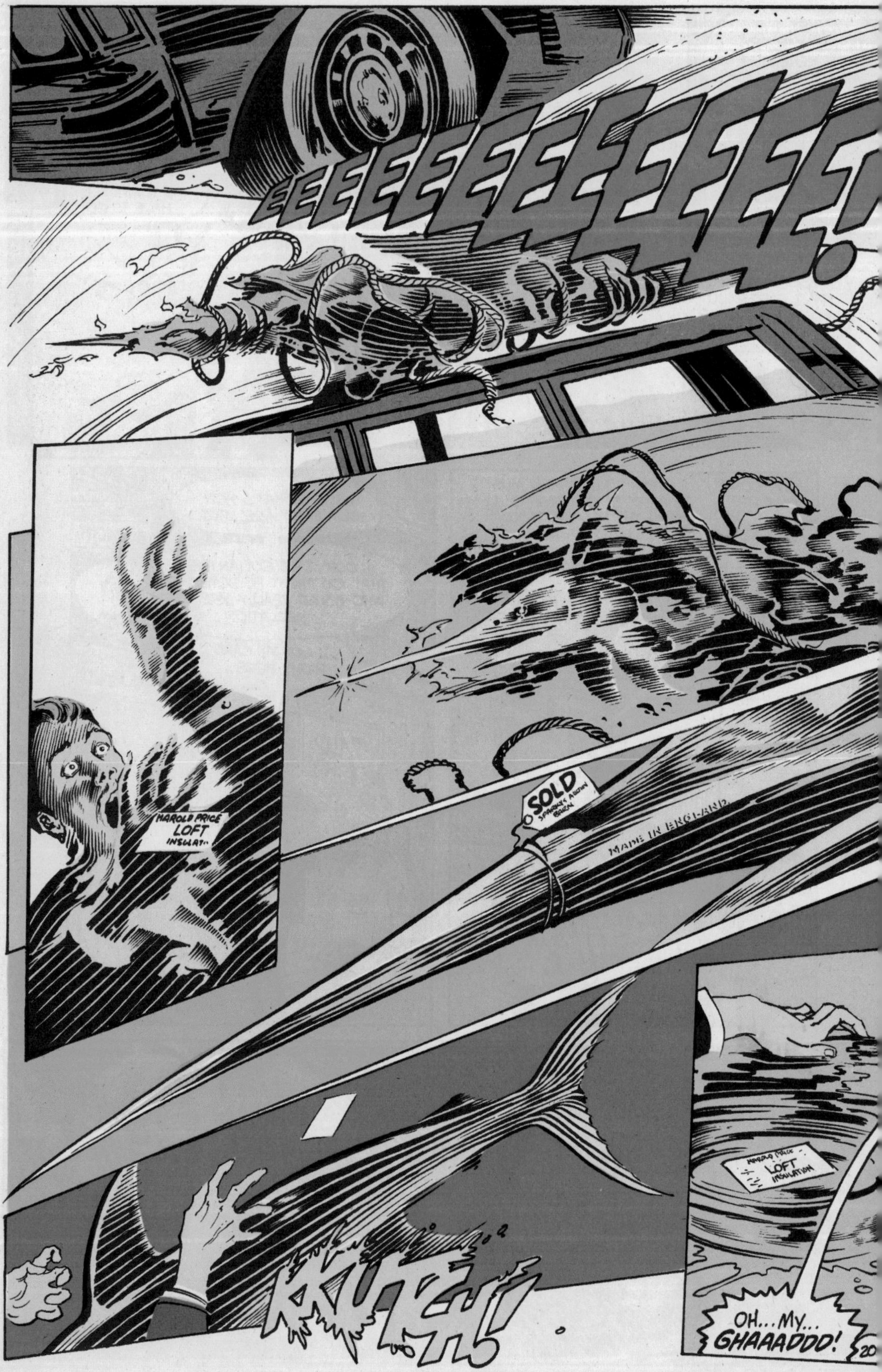
EEEEEEEEEEEE!
HAROLD PRICE
LOFT
INSULAT...
SOLD
SPARKY'S AUCTION BARN
MADE IN ENGLAND
KUTCH!
HAROLD PRICE
LOFT
INSULATION
OH... MY... GHAAADDD!
20

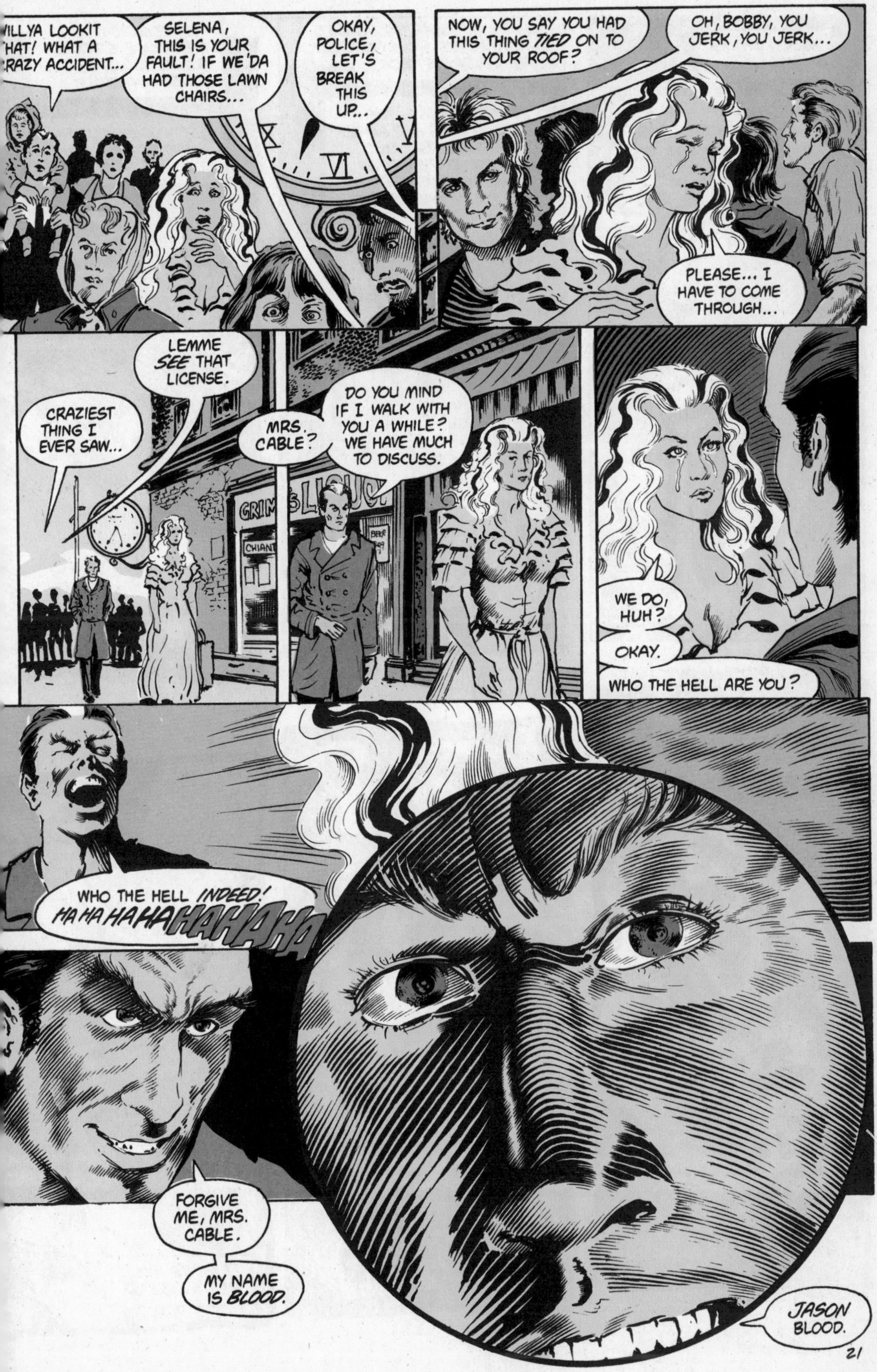

WILLYA LOOKIT THAT! WHAT A CRAZY ACCIDENT...
SELENA, THIS IS YOUR FAULT! IF WE'DA HAD THOSE LAWN CHAIRS...
OKAY, POLICE, LET'S BREAK THIS UP...
NOW, YOU SAY YOU HAD THIS THING TIED ON TO YOUR ROOF?
OH, BOBBY, YOU JERK, YOU JERK...
PLEASE... I HAVE TO COME THROUGH...
CRAZIEST THING I EVER SAW...
LEMME SEE THAT LICENSE.
MRS. CABLE?
DO YOU MIND IF I WALK WITH YOU A WHILE? WE HAVE MUCH TO DISCUSS.
GRIM'S LIQUOR
WE DO, HUH?
OKAY.
WHO THE HELL ARE YOU?
WHO THE HELL INDEED! HA HA HA HA HAHAHAHA
FORGIVE ME, MRS. CABLE.
MY NAME IS BLOOD.
JASON BLOOD.
21

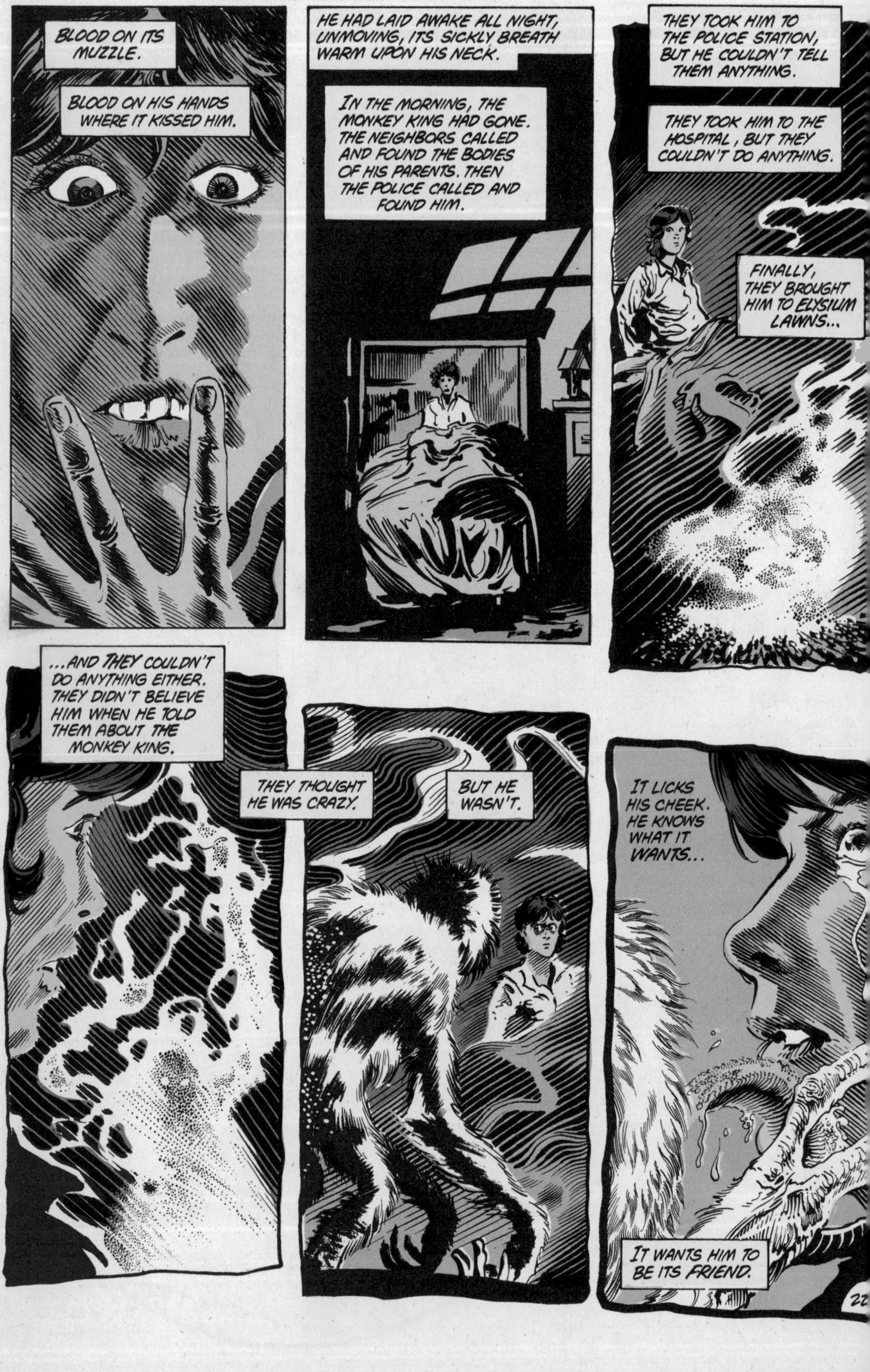
BLOOD ON ITS MUZZLE.
BLOOD ON HIS HANDS WHERE IT KISSED HIM.
HE HAD LAID AWAKE ALL NIGHT, UNMOVING, ITS SICKLY BREATH WARM UPON HIS NECK.
IN THE MORNING, THE MONKEY KING HAD GONE. THE NEIGHBORS CALLED AND FOUND THE BODIES OF HIS PARENTS. THEN THE POLICE CALLED AND FOUND HIM.
THEY TOOK HIM TO THE POLICE STATION, BUT HE COULDN'T TELL THEM ANYTHING.
THEY TOOK HIM TO THE HOSPITAL, BUT THEY COULDN'T DO ANYTHING.
FINALLY, THEY BROUGHT HIM TO ELYSIUM LAWNS...
...AND THEY COULDN'T DO ANYTHING EITHER. THEY DIDN'T BELIEVE HIM WHEN HE TOLD THEM ABOUT THE MONKEY KING.
THEY THOUGHT HE WAS CRAZY.
BUT HE WASN'T.
IT LICKS HIS CHEEK. HE KNOWS WHAT IT WANTS...
IT WANTS HIM TO BE ITS FRIEND.
22

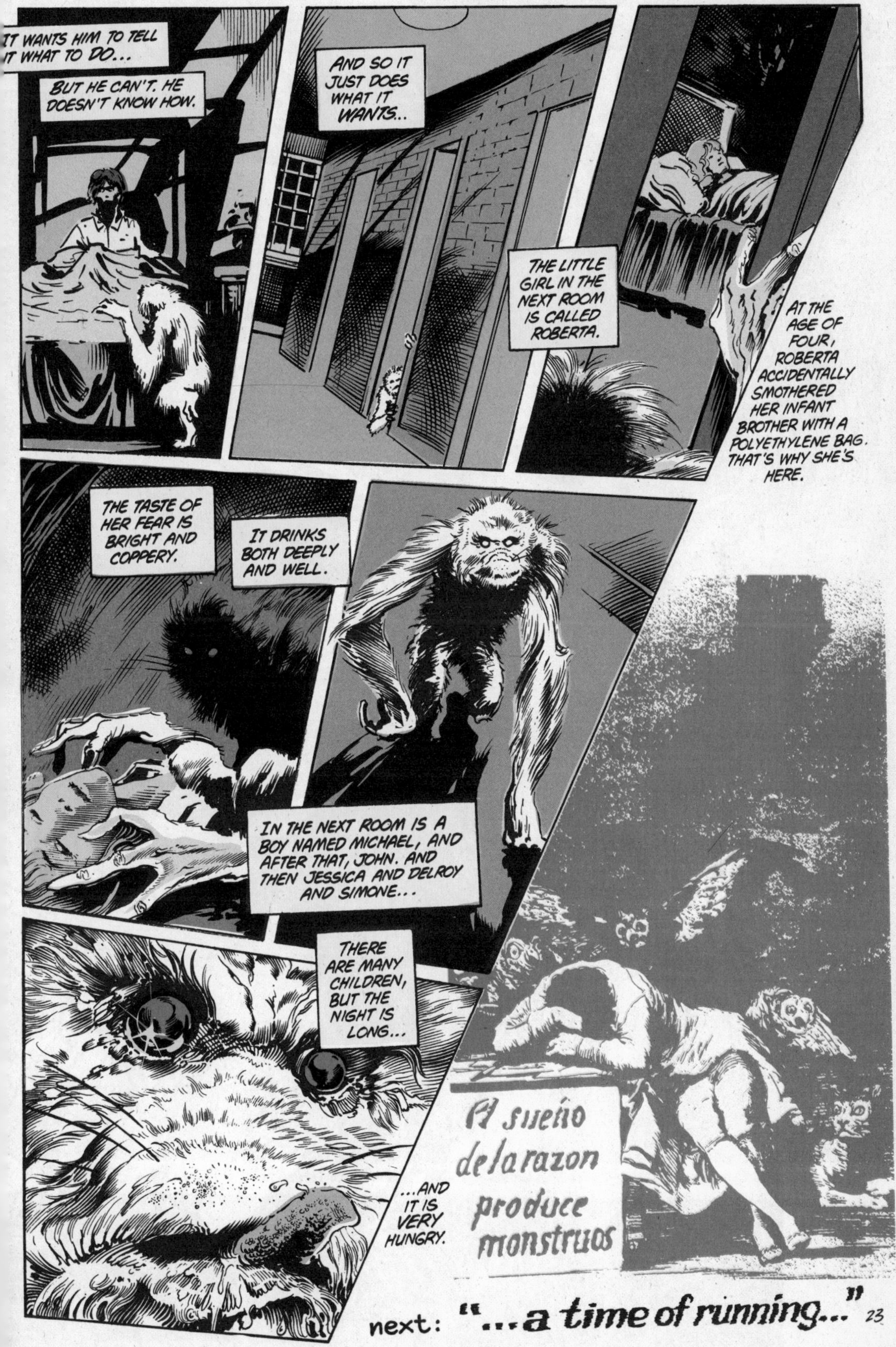
IT WANTS HIM TO TELL IT WHAT TO DO...
BUT HE CAN'T. HE DOESN'T KNOW HOW.
AND SO IT JUST DOES WHAT IT WANTS...
THE LITTLE GIRL IN THE NEXT ROOM IS CALLED ROBERTA.
AT THE AGE OF FOUR, ROBERTA ACCIDENTALLY SMOTHERED HER INFANT BROTHER WITH A POLYETHYLENE BAG. THAT'S WHY SHE'S HERE.
THE TASTE OF HER FEAR IS BRIGHT AND COPPERY.
IT DRINKS BOTH DEEPLY AND WELL.
IN THE NEXT ROOM IS A BOY NAMED MICHAEL, AND AFTER THAT, JOHN. AND THEN JESSICA AND DELROY AND SIMONE...
THERE ARE MANY CHILDREN, BUT THE NIGHT IS LONG...
...AND IT IS VERY HUNGRY.
El sueño de la razon produce monstruos
next: "...a time of running..."
23

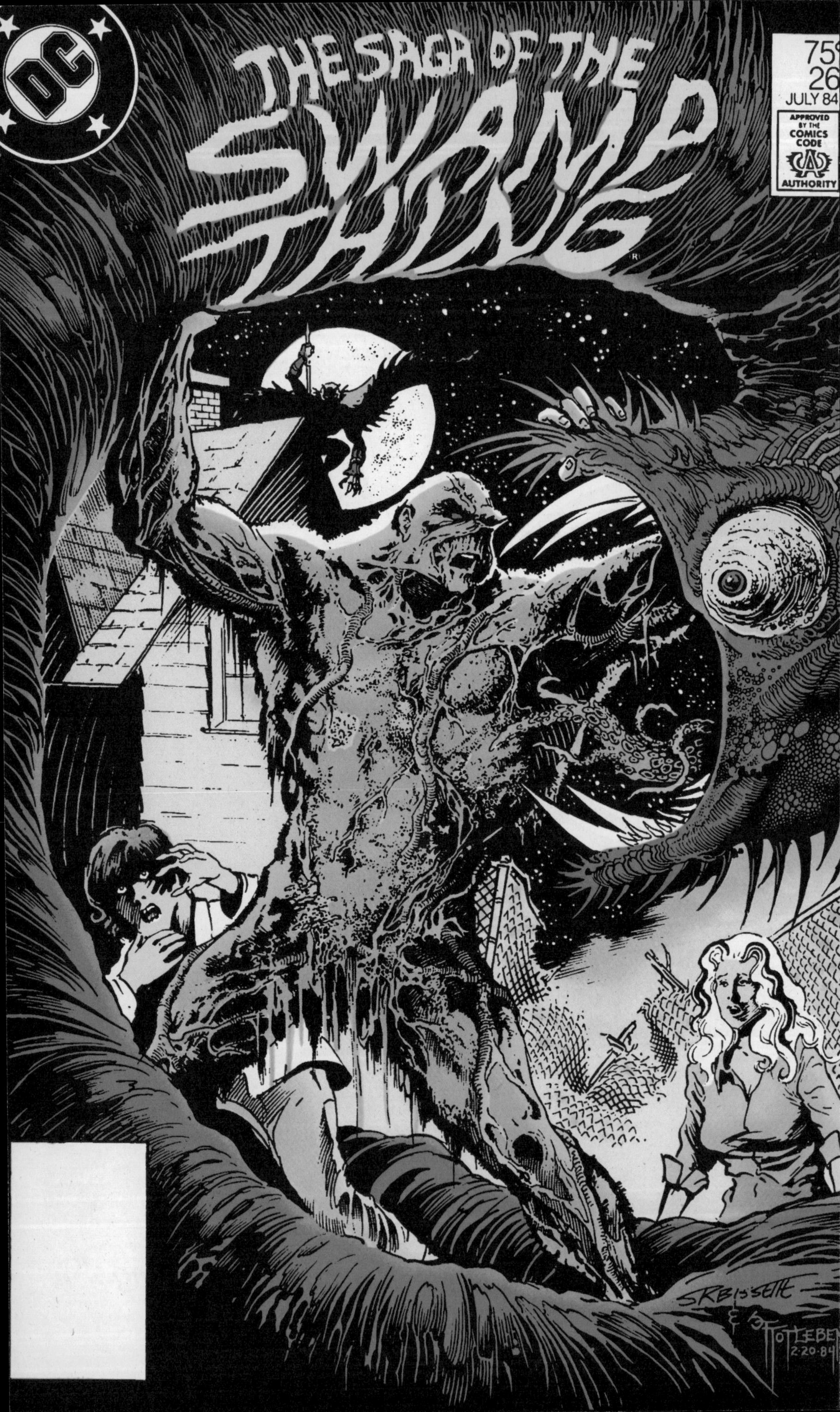

DC
THE SAGA OF THE
SWAMP THING
75¢
26
JULY 84
APPROVED BY THE COMICS CODE AUTHORITY
SRBISSETTE
& TOTLEBEN
2-20-84

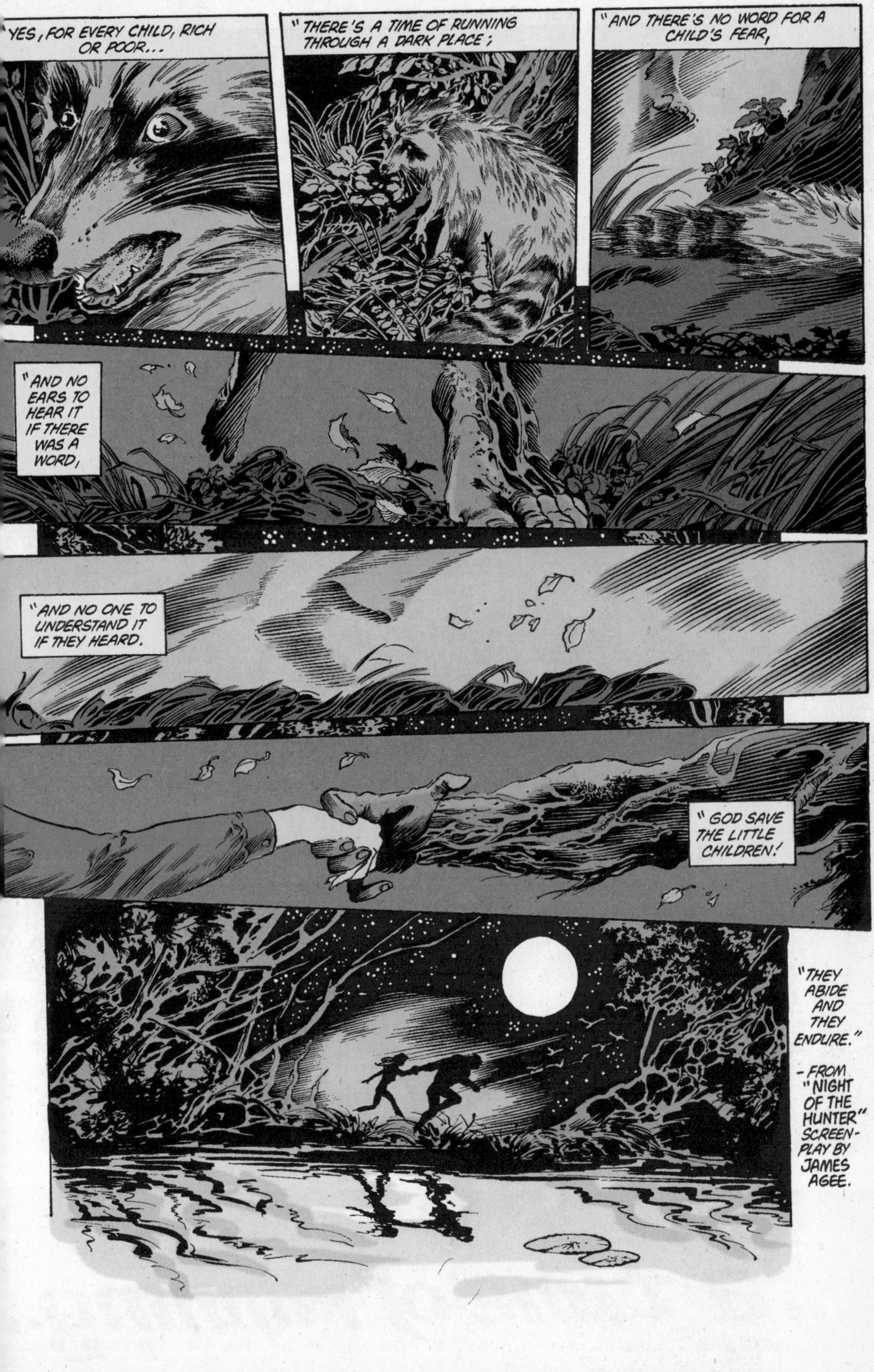
"YES, FOR EVERY CHILD, RICH OR POOR...
"THERE'S A TIME OF RUNNING THROUGH A DARK PLACE;
"AND THERE'S NO WORD FOR A CHILD'S FEAR,
"AND NO EARS TO HEAR IT IF THERE WAS A WORD,
"AND NO ONE TO UNDERSTAND IT IF THEY HEARD.
"GOD SAVE THE LITTLE CHILDREN!
"THEY ABIDE AND THEY ENDURE."
- FROM "NIGHT OF THE HUNTER" SCREEN-PLAY BY JAMES AGEE.

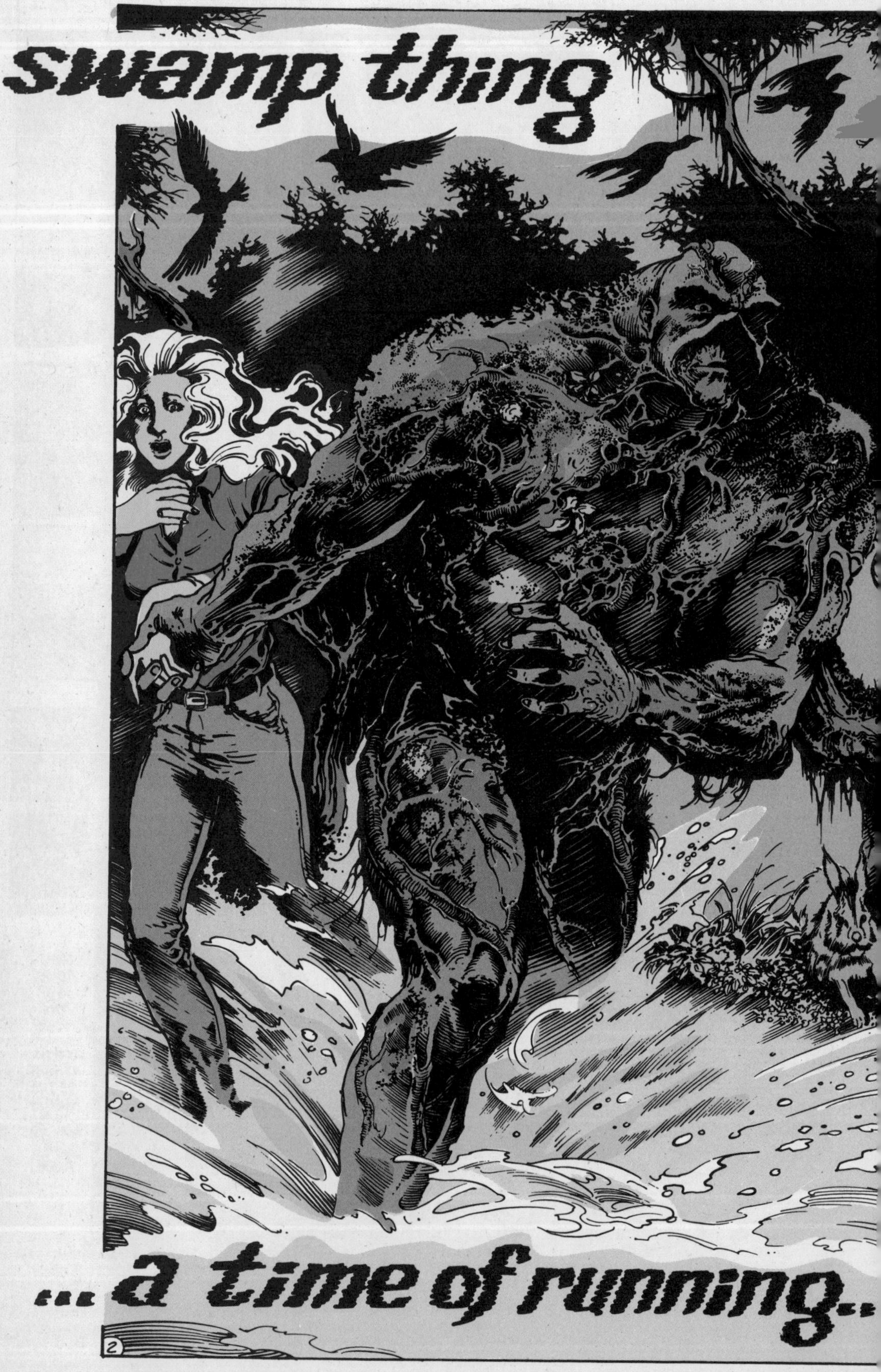
swamp thing
...a time of running...
2

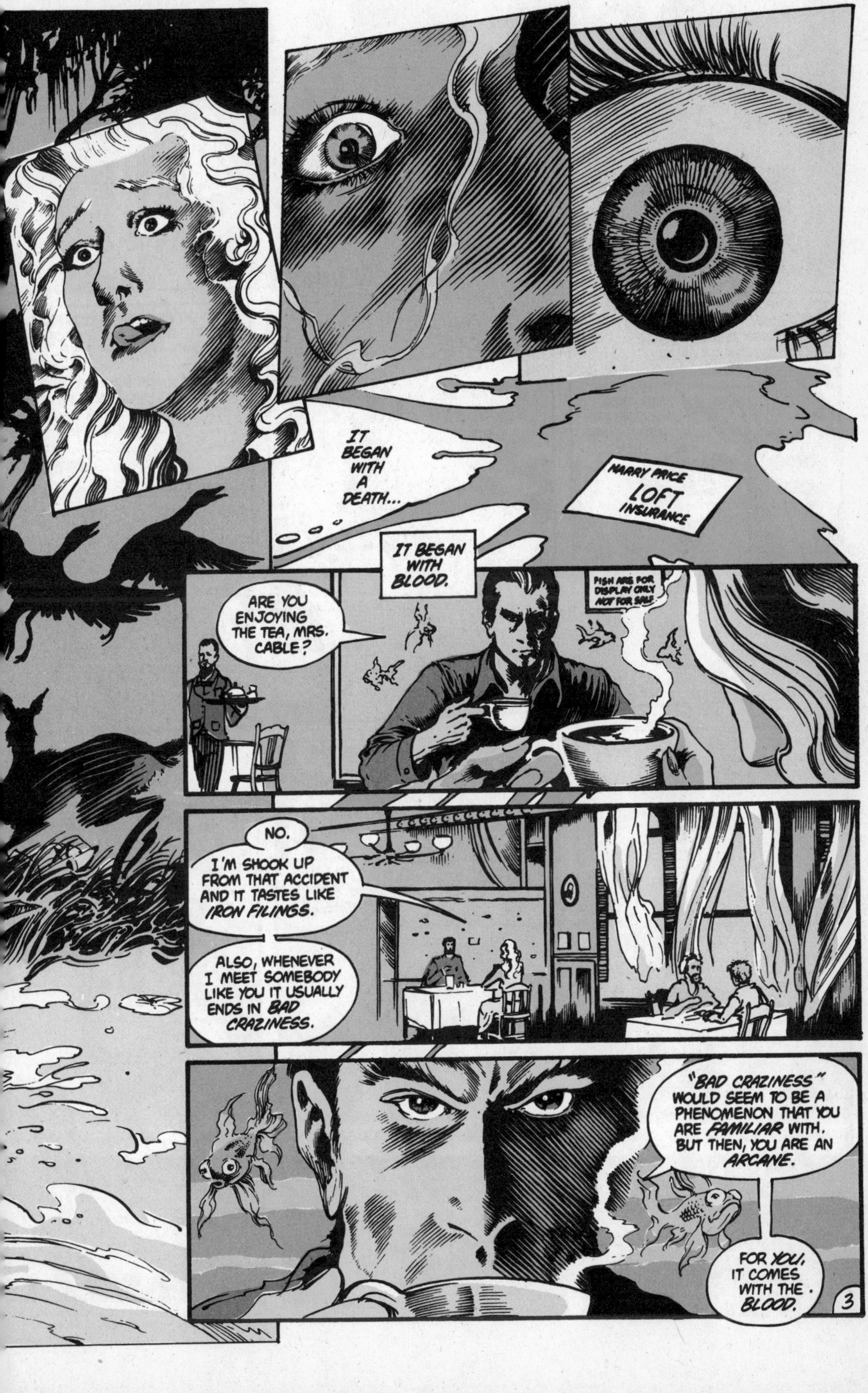
IT BEGAN WITH A DEATH...
HARRY PRICE LOFT INSURANCE
IT BEGAN WITH BLOOD.
ARE YOU ENJOYING THE TEA, MRS. CABLE?
FISH ARE FOR DISPLAY ONLY NOT FOR SALE
NO.
I'M SHOOK UP FROM THAT ACCIDENT AND IT TASTES LIKE IRON FILINGS.
ALSO, WHENEVER I MEET SOMEBODY LIKE YOU IT USUALLY ENDS IN BAD CRAZINESS.
"BAD CRAZINESS" WOULD SEEM TO BE A PHENOMENON THAT YOU ARE FAMILIAR WITH. BUT THEN, YOU ARE AN ARCANE.
FOR YOU, IT COMES WITH THE BLOOD.
3

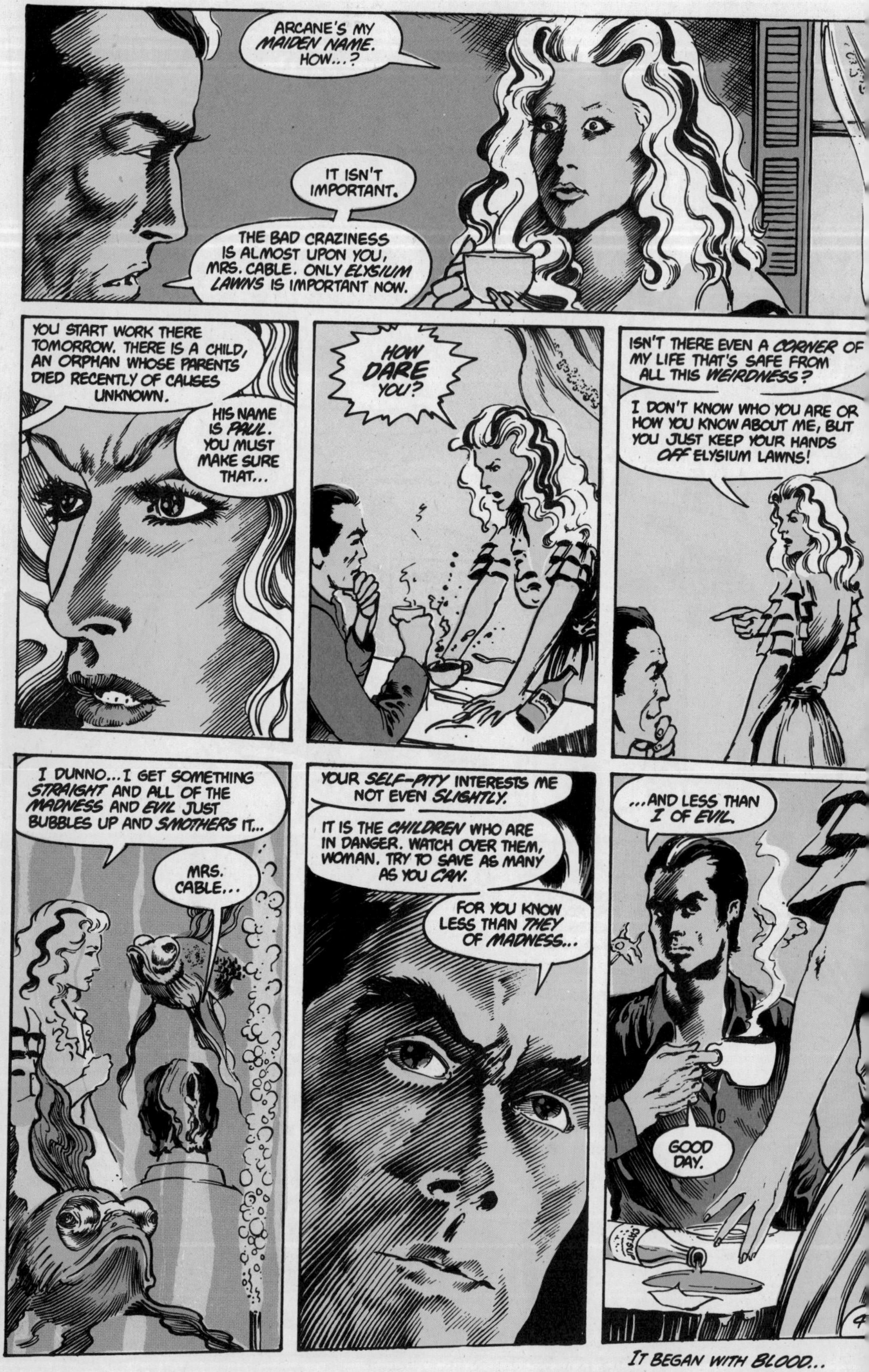
ARCANE'S MY MAIDEN NAME. HOW...?
IT ISN'T IMPORTANT.
THE BAD CRAZINESS IS ALMOST UPON YOU, MRS. CABLE. ONLY ELYSIUM LAWNS IS IMPORTANT NOW.
YOU START WORK THERE TOMORROW. THERE IS A CHILD, AN ORPHAN WHOSE PARENTS DIED RECENTLY OF CAUSES UNKNOWN.
HIS NAME IS PAUL. YOU MUST MAKE SURE THAT...
HOW DARE YOU?
ISN'T THERE EVEN A CORNER OF MY LIFE THAT'S SAFE FROM ALL THIS WEIRDNESS?
I DON'T KNOW WHO YOU ARE OR HOW YOU KNOW ABOUT ME, BUT YOU JUST KEEP YOUR HANDS OFF ELYSIUM LAWNS!
I DUNNO... I GET SOMETHING STRAIGHT AND ALL OF THE MADNESS AND EVIL JUST BUBBLES UP AND SMOTHERS IT...
MRS. CABLE...
YOUR SELF-PITY INTERESTS ME NOT EVEN SLIGHTLY.
IT IS THE CHILDREN WHO ARE IN DANGER. WATCH OVER THEM, WOMAN. TRY TO SAVE AS MANY AS YOU CAN.
FOR YOU KNOW LESS THAN THEY OF MADNESS...
...AND LESS THAN I OF EVIL.
GOOD DAY.
4

IT BEGAN WITH BLOOD...

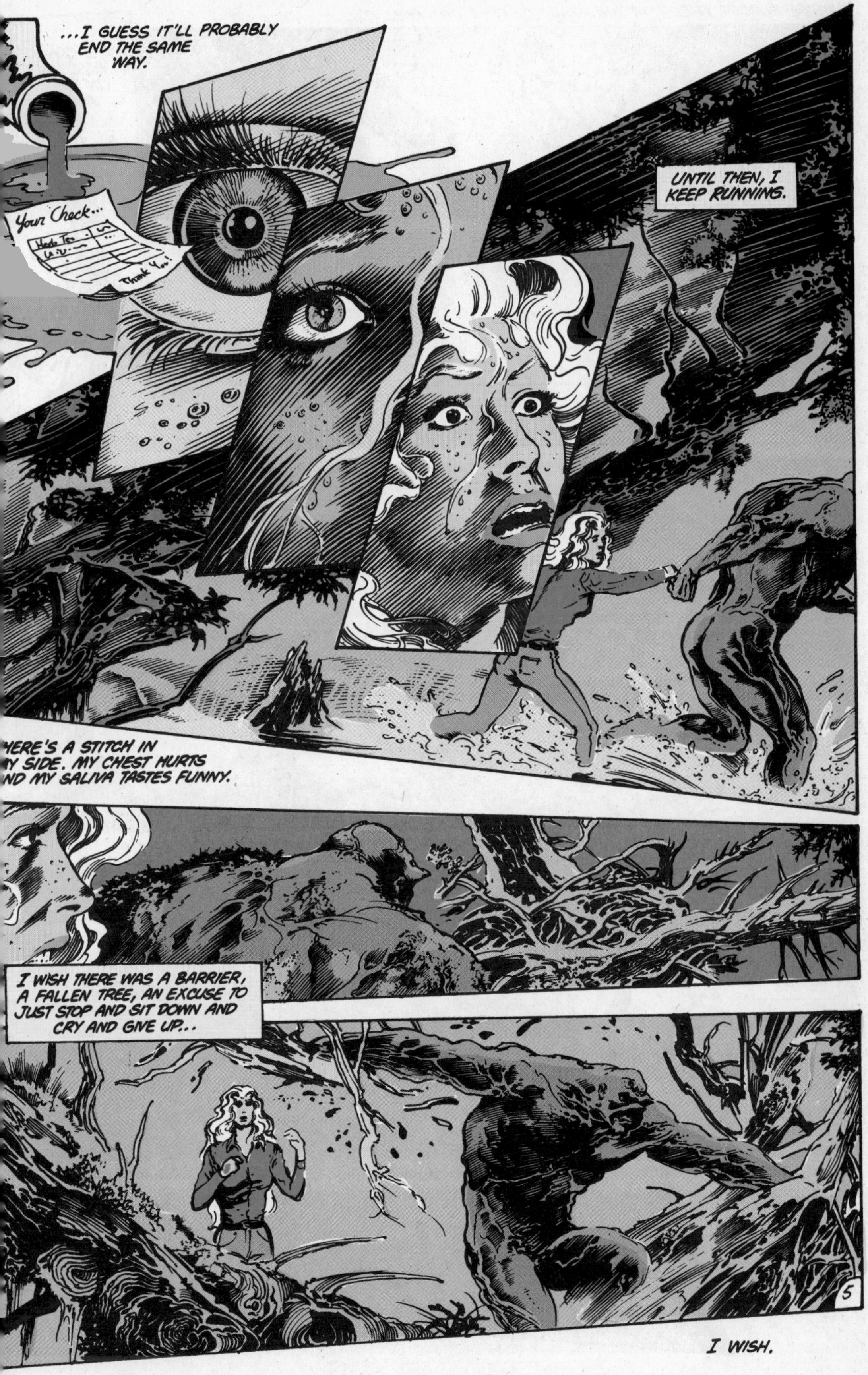
...I GUESS IT'LL PROBABLY END THE SAME WAY.
Your Check...
Thank You!
UNTIL THEN, I KEEP RUNNING.
HERE'S A STITCH IN
Y SIDE. MY CHEST HURTS
ND MY SALIVA TASTES FUNNY.
I WISH THERE WAS A BARRIER, A FALLEN TREE, AN EXCUSE TO JUST STOP AND SIT DOWN AND CRY AND GIVE UP...
5
I WISH.

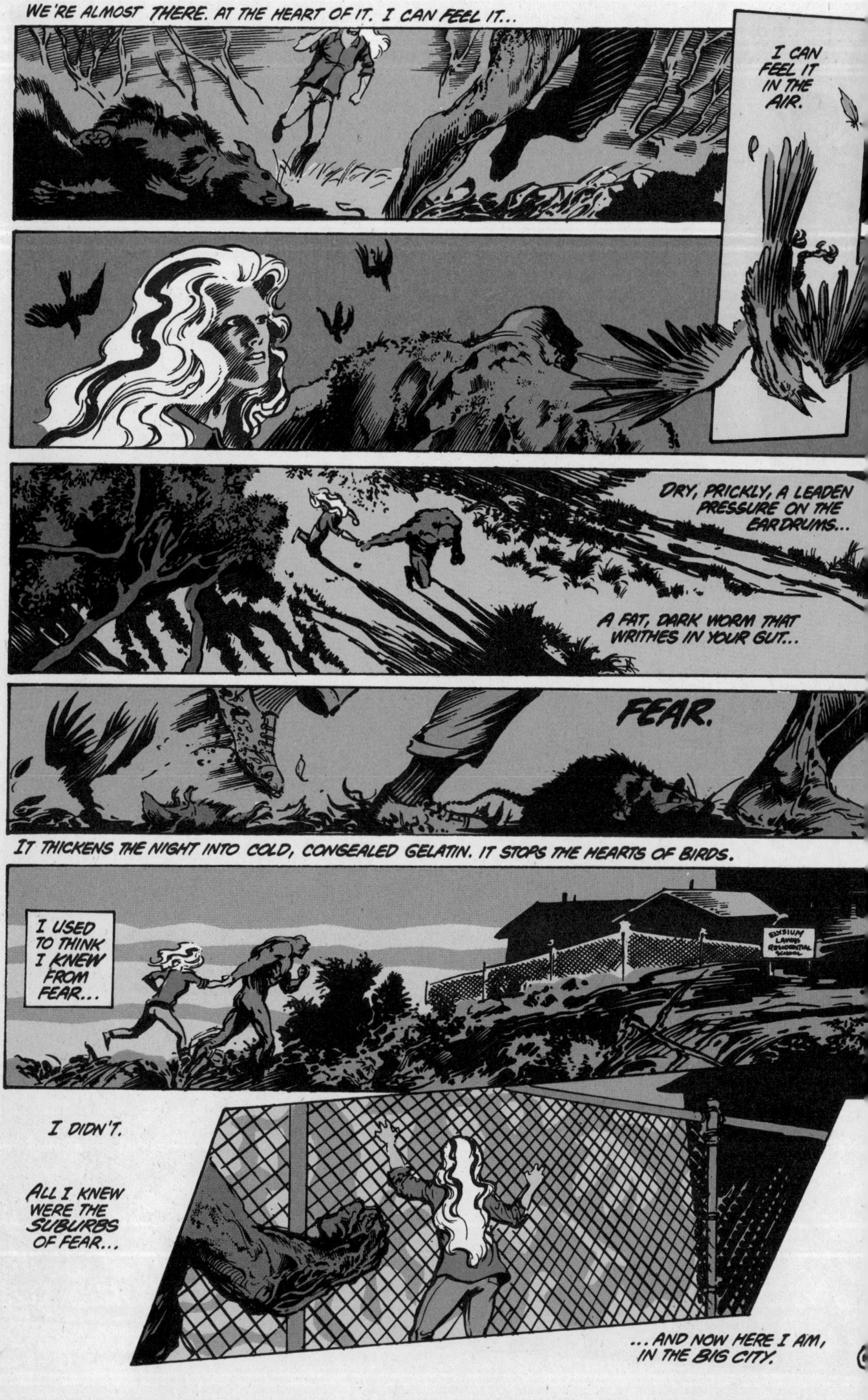
WE'RE ALMOST THERE. AT THE HEART OF IT. I CAN FEEL IT...
I CAN FEEL IT IN THE AIR.
DRY, PRICKLY, A LEADEN PRESSURE ON THE EARDRUMS...
A FAT, DARK WORM THAT WRITHES IN YOUR GUT...
FEAR.
IT THICKENS THE NIGHT INTO COLD, CONGEALED GELATIN. IT STOPS THE HEARTS OF BIRDS.
I USED TO THINK I KNEW FROM FEAR...
I DIDN'T.
ALL I KNEW WERE THE SUBURBS OF FEAR...
...AND NOW HERE I AM, IN THE BIG CITY.

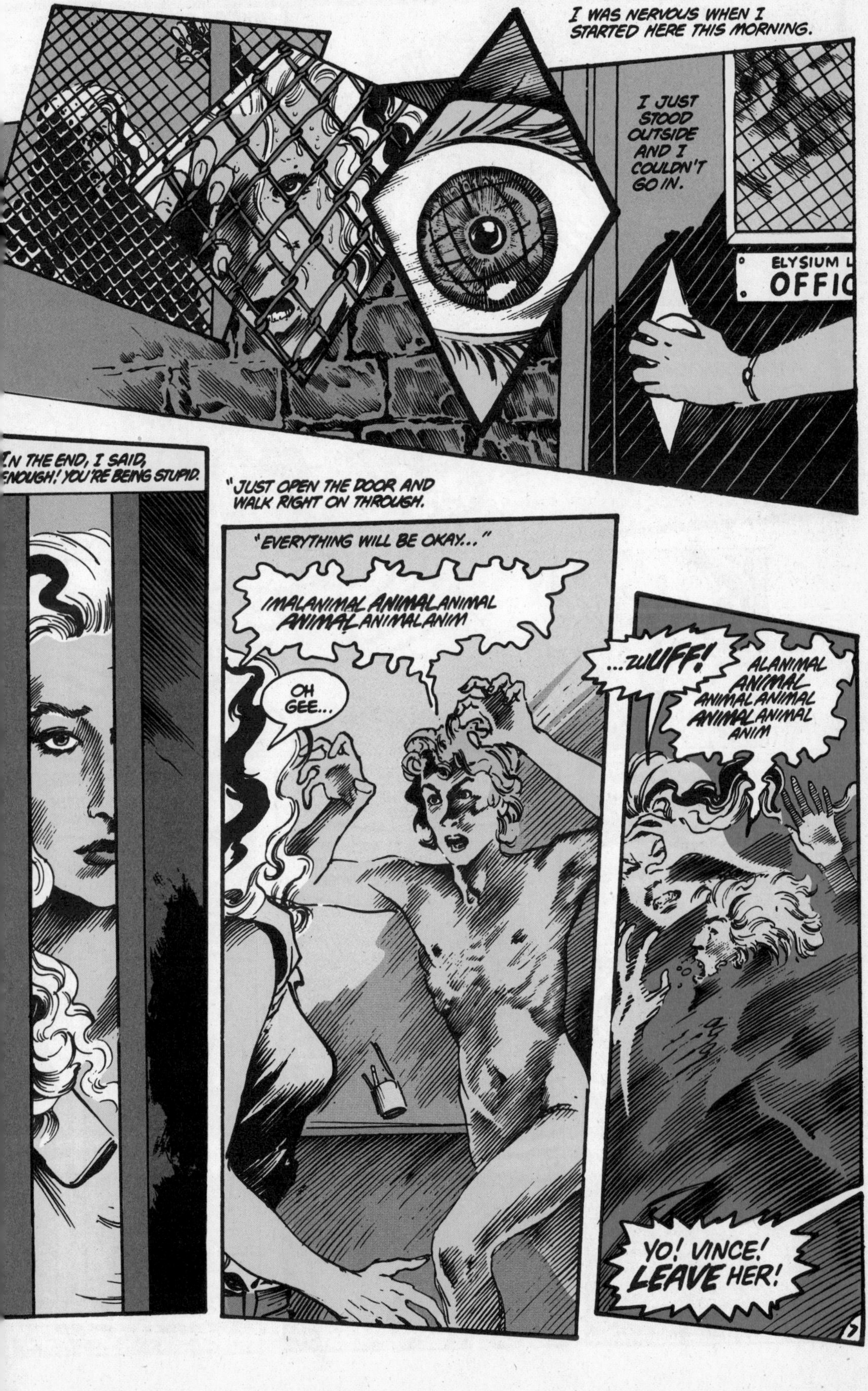
I WAS NERVOUS WHEN I STARTED HERE THIS MORNING.
I JUST STOOD OUTSIDE AND I COULDN'T GO IN.
ELYSIUM L
OFFIC
...N THE END, I SAID, ENOUGH! YOU'RE BEING STUPID.
"JUST OPEN THE DOOR AND WALK RIGHT ON THROUGH.
"EVERYTHING WILL BE OKAY..."
IMALANIMAL ANIMALANIMAL ANIMALANIMALANIM
OH GEE...
...ZZUFF!
ALANIMAL ANIMAL ANIMALANIMAL ANIMALANIMAL ANIM
YO! VINCE! LEAVE HER!
7

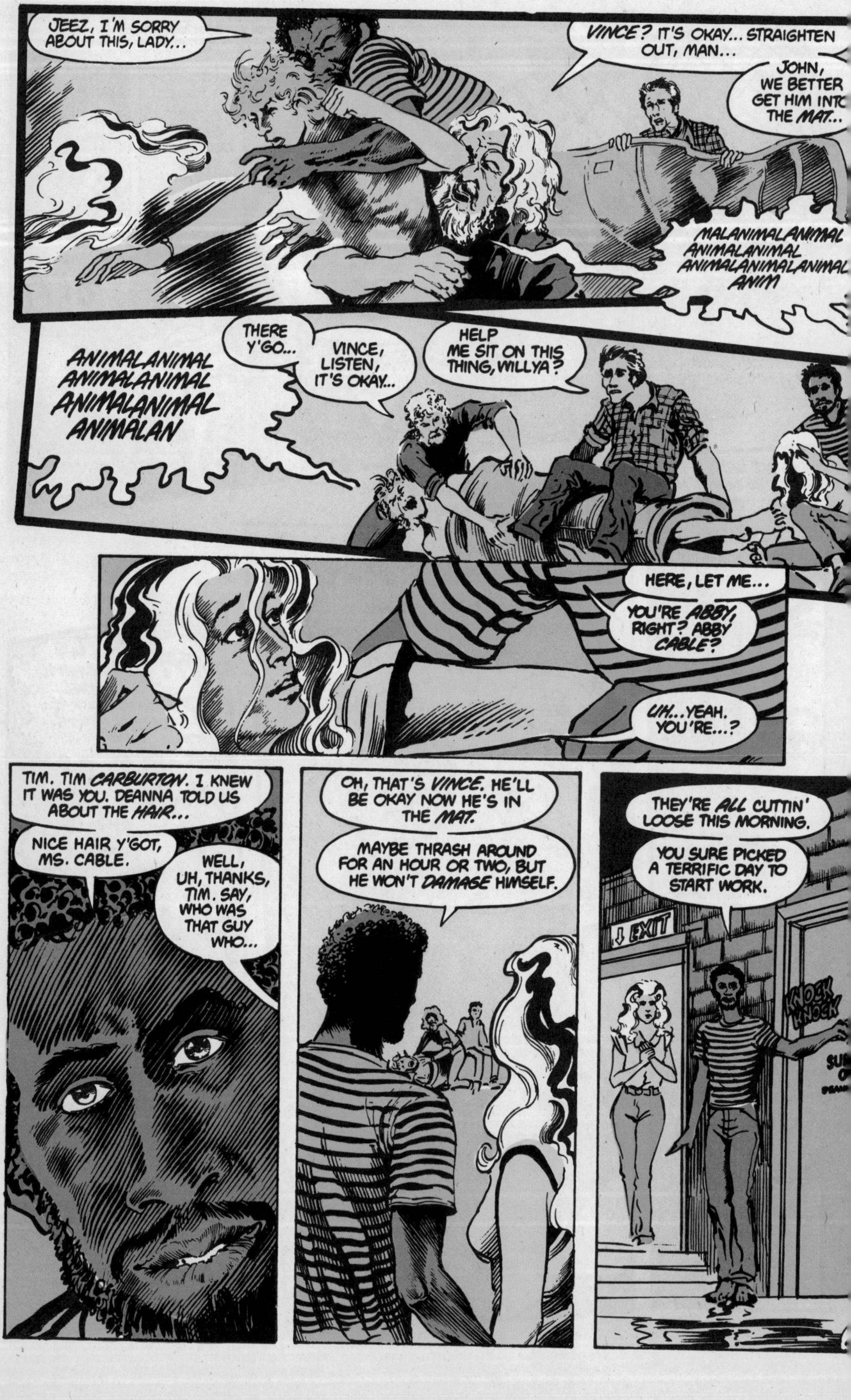
JEEZ, I'M SORRY ABOUT THIS, LADY...
VINCE? IT'S OKAY... STRAIGHTEN OUT, MAN...
JOHN, WE BETTER GET HIM INTO THE MAT...
MALANIMALANIMAL ANIMALANIMAL ANIMALANIMALANIMAL ANIM
ANIMALANIMAL ANIMALANIMAL ANIMALANIMAL ANIMALAN
THERE Y'GO...
VINCE, LISTEN, IT'S OKAY...
HELP ME SIT ON THIS THING, WILLYA?
HERE, LET ME...
YOU'RE ABBY, RIGHT? ABBY CABLE?
UH...YEAH. YOU'RE...?
TIM. TIM CARBURTON. I KNEW IT WAS YOU. DEANNA TOLD US ABOUT THE HAIR...
NICE HAIR Y'GOT, MS. CABLE.
WELL, UH, THANKS, TIM. SAY, WHO WAS THAT GUY WHO...
OH, THAT'S VINCE. HE'LL BE OKAY NOW HE'S IN THE MAT.
MAYBE THRASH AROUND FOR AN HOUR OR TWO, BUT HE WON'T DAMAGE HIMSELF.
THEY'RE ALL CUTTIN' LOOSE THIS MORNING.
YOU SURE PICKED A TERRIFIC DAY TO START WORK.
EXIT
KNOCK KNOCK

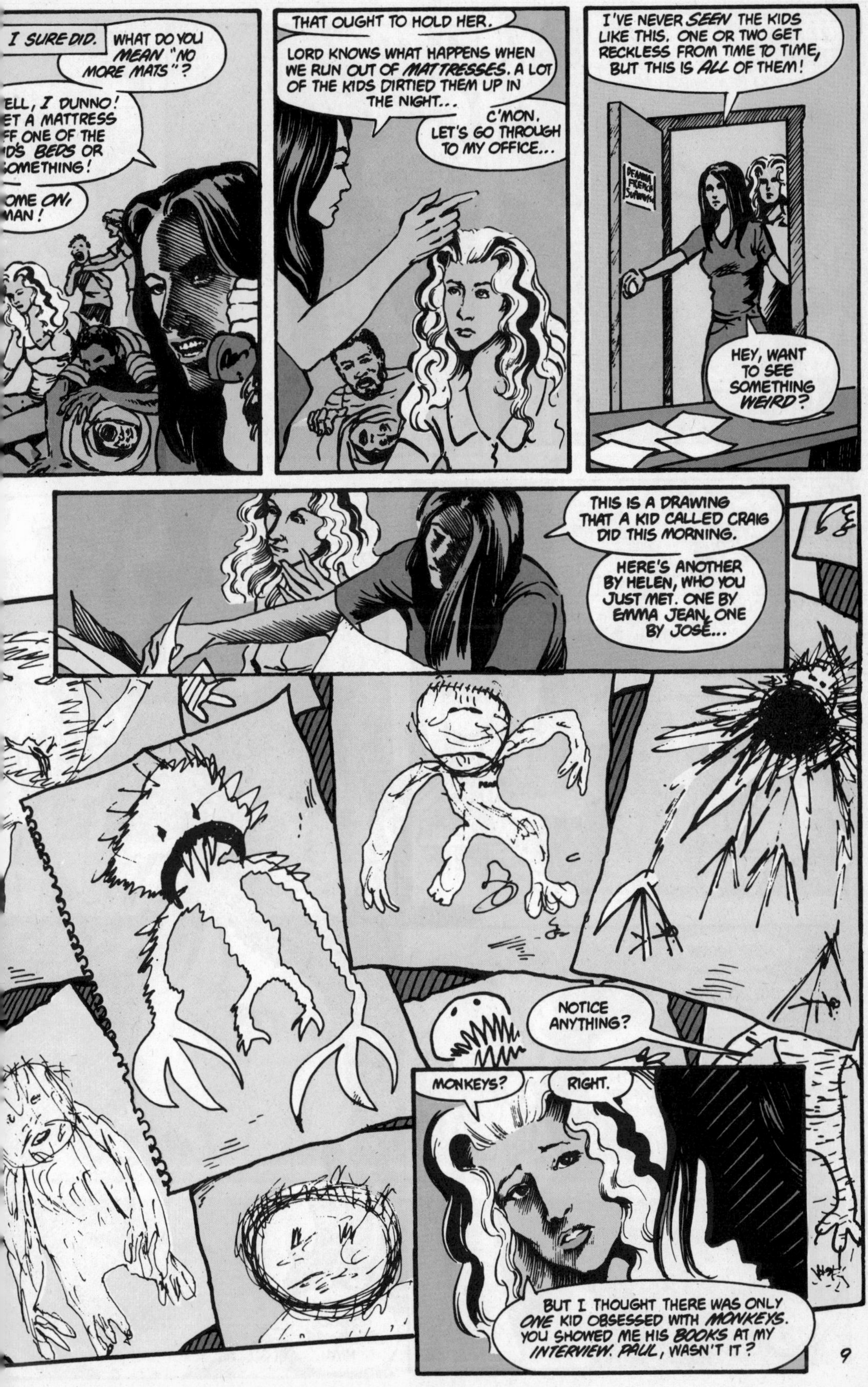
I SURE DID.
WHAT DO YOU MEAN "NO MORE MATS"?
ELL, I DUNNO! ET A MATTRESS FF ONE OF THE D'S BEDS OR OMETHING!
OME ON, MAN!
THAT OUGHT TO HOLD HER.
LORD KNOWS WHAT HAPPENS WHEN WE RUN OUT OF MATTRESSES. A LOT OF THE KIDS DIRTIED THEM UP IN THE NIGHT...
C'MON. LET'S GO THROUGH TO MY OFFICE...
I'VE NEVER SEEN THE KIDS LIKE THIS. ONE OR TWO GET RECKLESS FROM TIME TO TIME, BUT THIS IS ALL OF THEM!
HEY, WANT TO SEE SOMETHING WEIRD?
THIS IS A DRAWING THAT A KID CALLED CRAIG DID THIS MORNING.
HERE'S ANOTHER BY HELEN, WHO YOU JUST MET. ONE BY EMMA JEAN, ONE BY JOSÉ...
NOTICE ANYTHING?
MONKEYS?
RIGHT.
BUT I THOUGHT THERE WAS ONLY ONE KID OBSESSED WITH MONKEYS. YOU SHOWED ME HIS BOOKS AT MY INTERVIEW. PAUL, WASN'T IT?
9

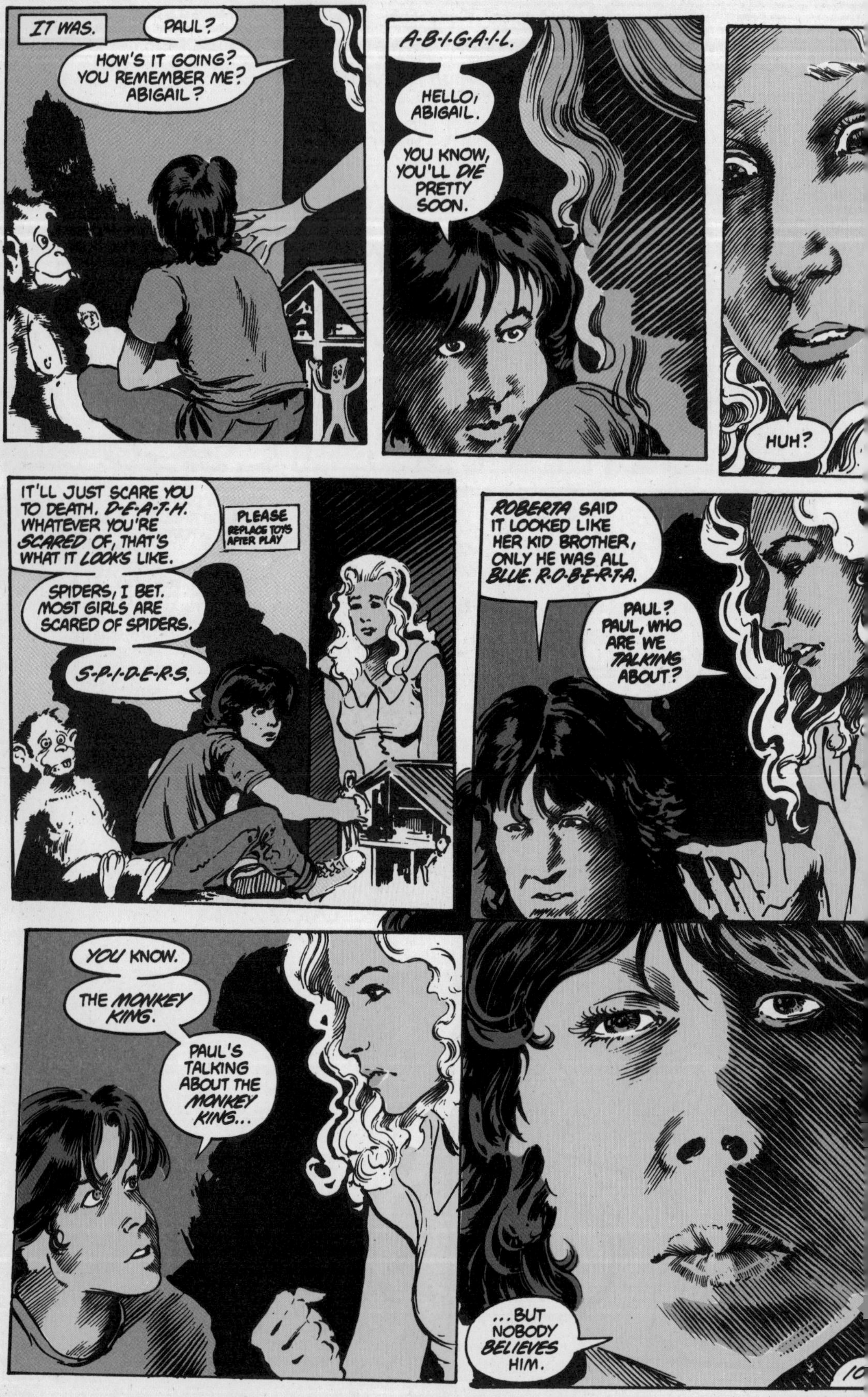
IT WAS.
PAUL?
HOW'S IT GOING? YOU REMEMBER ME? ABIGAIL?
A-B-I-G-A-I-L.
HELLO, ABIGAIL.
YOU KNOW, YOU'LL DIE PRETTY SOON.
HUH?
IT'LL JUST SCARE YOU TO DEATH. D-E-A-T-H. WHATEVER YOU'RE SCARED OF, THAT'S WHAT IT LOOKS LIKE.
PLEASE REPLACE TOYS AFTER PLAY
SPIDERS, I BET. MOST GIRLS ARE SCARED OF SPIDERS.
S-P-I-D-E-R-S.
ROBERTA SAID IT LOOKED LIKE HER KID BROTHER, ONLY HE WAS ALL BLUE. R-O-B-E-R-T-A.
PAUL? PAUL, WHO ARE WE TALKING ABOUT?
YOU KNOW.
THE MONKEY KING.
PAUL'S TALKING ABOUT THE MONKEY KING...
...BUT NOBODY BELIEVES HIM.

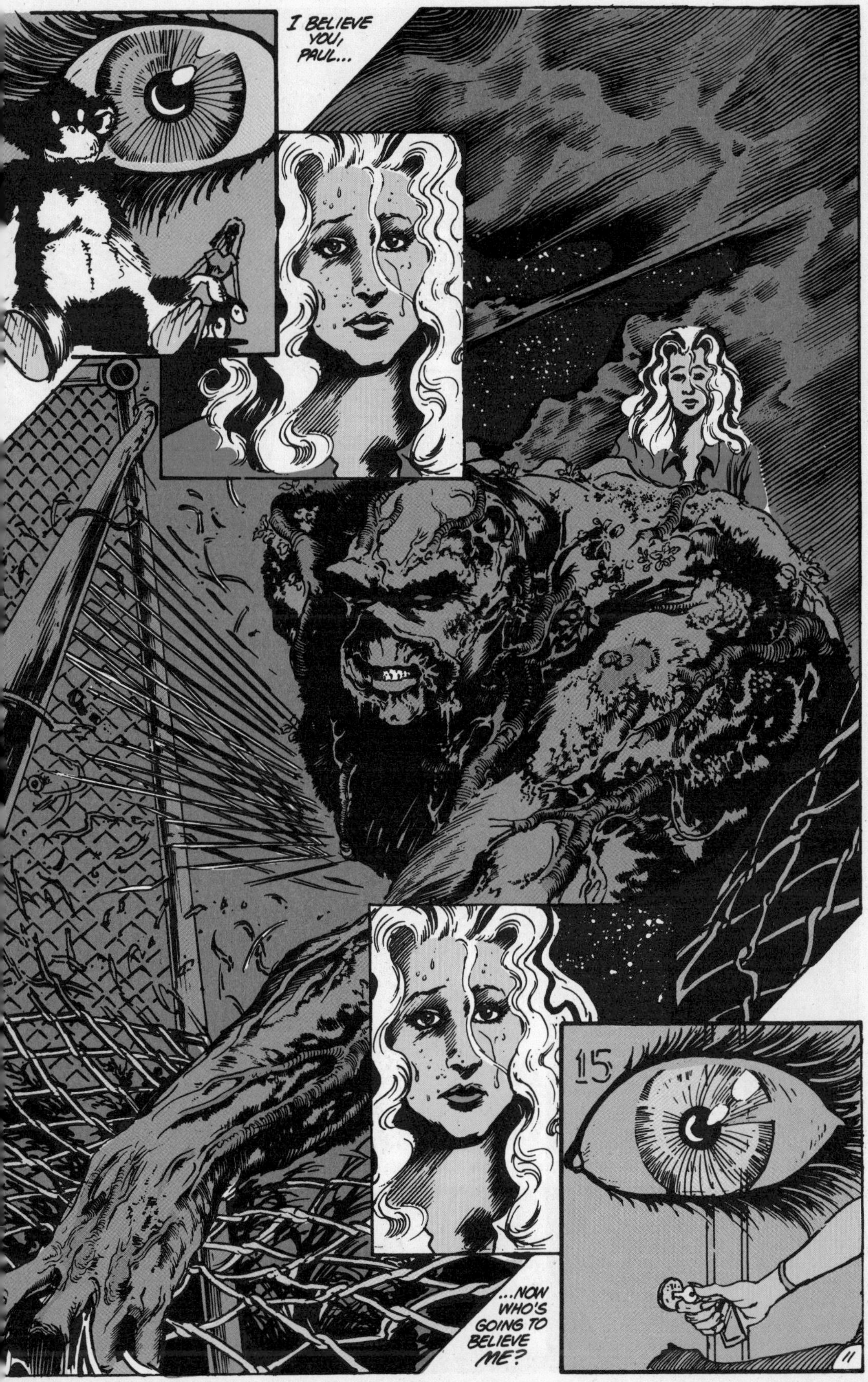
I BELIEVE YOU, PAUL...
15
...NOW WHO'S GOING TO BELIEVE ME?
11

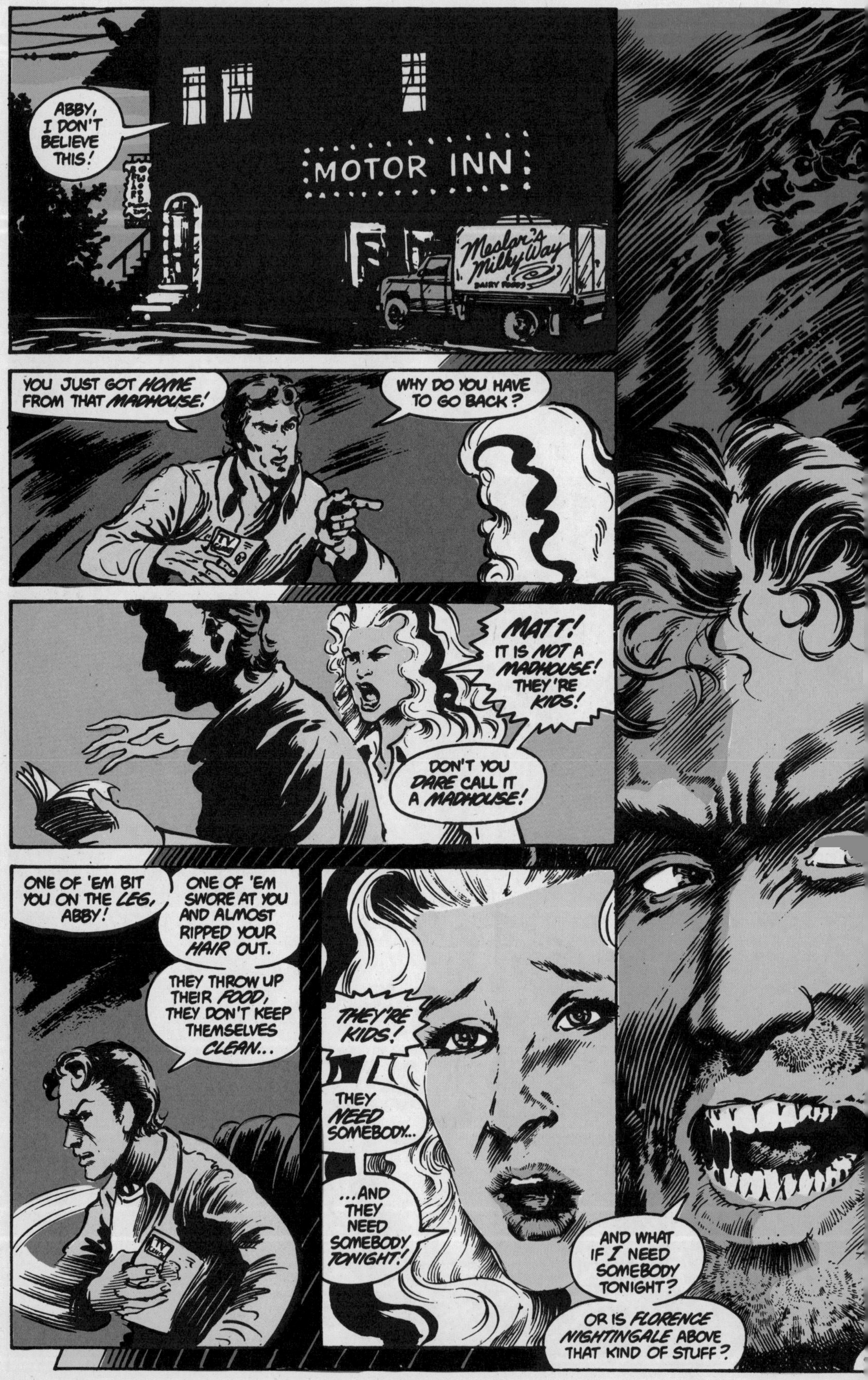
ABBY, I DON'T BELIEVE THIS!
MOTOR INN
Meslar's Milky Way
DAIRY FOODS
YOU JUST GOT HOME FROM THAT MADHOUSE!
WHY DO YOU HAVE TO GO BACK?
MATT! IT IS NOT A MADHOUSE! THEY'RE KIDS!
DON'T YOU DARE CALL IT A MADHOUSE!
ONE OF 'EM BIT YOU ON THE LEG, ABBY!
ONE OF 'EM SWORE AT YOU AND ALMOST RIPPED YOUR HAIR OUT.
THEY THROW UP THEIR FOOD, THEY DON'T KEEP THEMSELVES CLEAN...
THEY'RE KIDS!
THEY NEED SOMEBODY...
...AND THEY NEED SOMEBODY TONIGHT!
AND WHAT IF I NEED SOMEBODY TONIGHT?
OR IS FLORENCE NIGHTINGALE ABOVE THAT KIND OF STUFF?

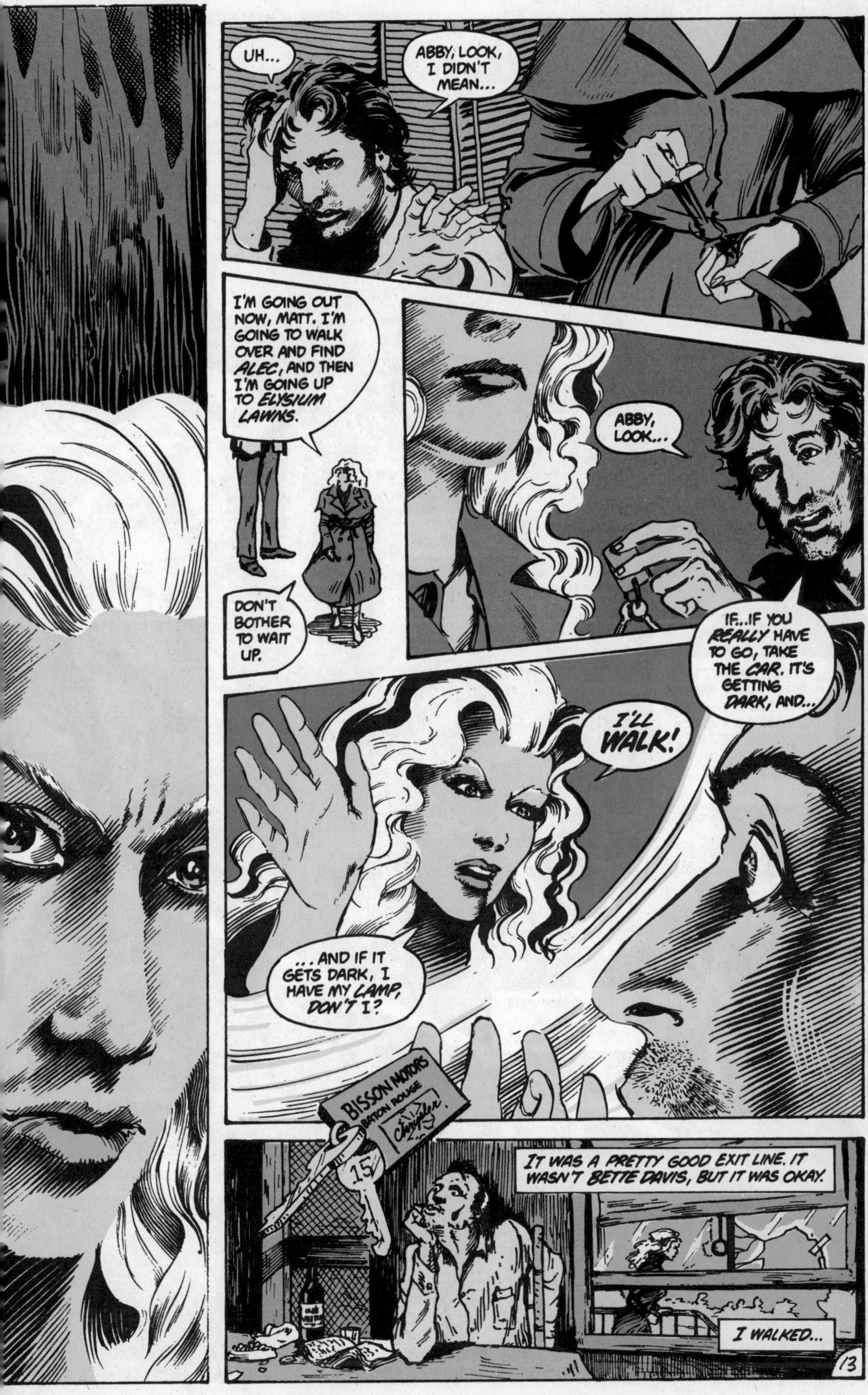
UH...
ABBY, LOOK, I DIDN'T MEAN...
I'M GOING OUT NOW, MATT. I'M GOING TO WALK OVER AND FIND ALEC, AND THEN I'M GOING UP TO ELYSIUM LAWNS.
DON'T BOTHER TO WAIT UP.
ABBY, LOOK...
IF...IF YOU REALLY HAVE TO GO, TAKE THE CAR. IT'S GETTING DARK, AND...
I'LL WALK!
...AND IF IT GETS DARK, I HAVE MY LAMP, DON'T I?
BISSON MOTORS
BATON ROUGE
Chrysler
15
IT WAS A PRETTY GOOD EXIT LINE. IT WASN'T BETTE DAVIS, BUT IT WAS OKAY.
I WALKED...
13

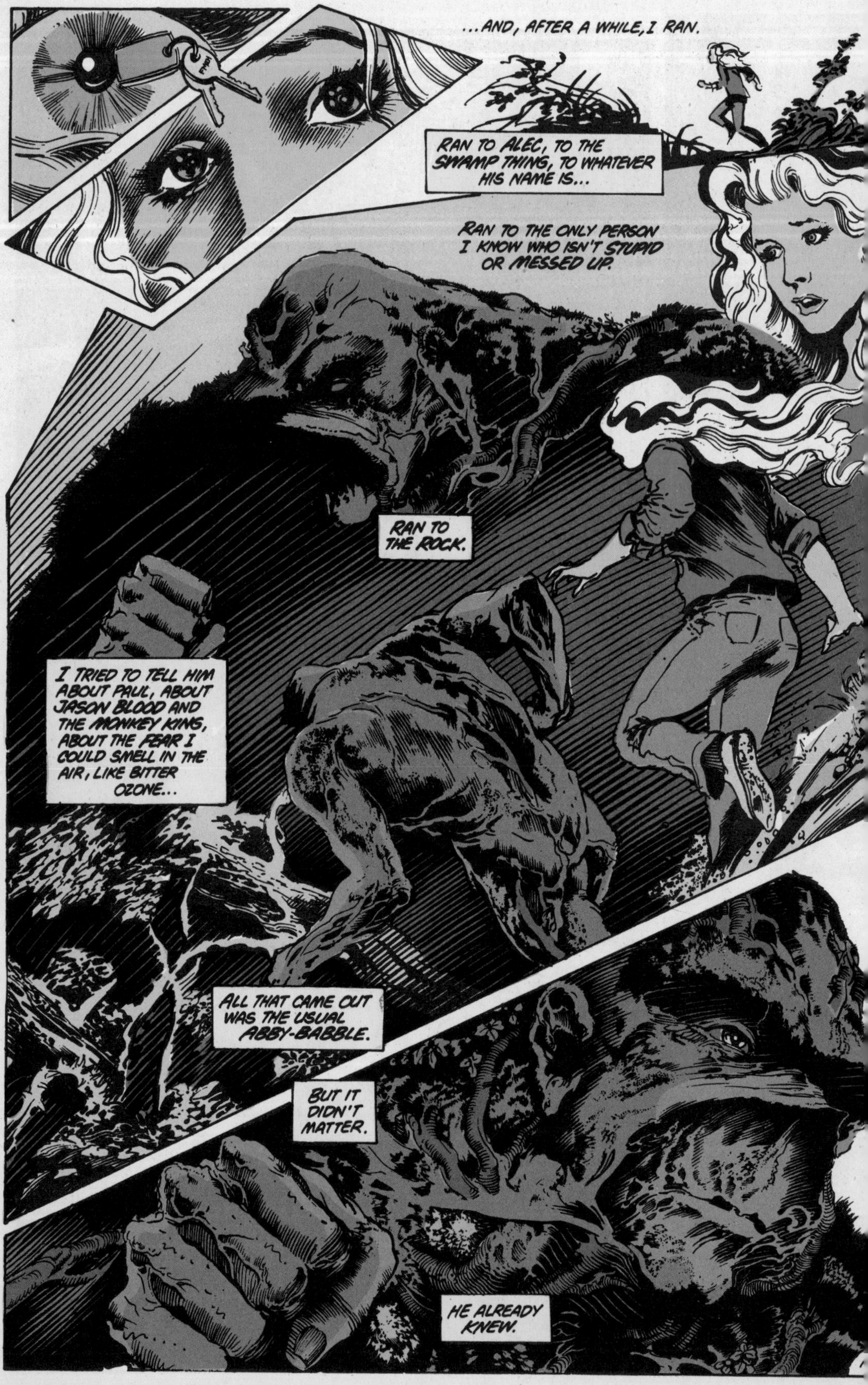
...AND, AFTER A WHILE, I RAN.
RAN TO ALEC, TO THE SWAMP THING, TO WHATEVER HIS NAME IS...
RAN TO THE ONLY PERSON I KNOW WHO ISN'T STUPID OR MESSED UP.
RAN TO THE ROCK.
I TRIED TO TELL HIM ABOUT PAUL, ABOUT JASON BLOOD AND THE MONKEY KING, ABOUT THE FEAR I COULD SMELL IN THE AIR, LIKE BITTER OZONE...
ALL THAT CAME OUT WAS THE USUAL ABBY-BABBLE.
BUT IT DIDN'T MATTER.
HE ALREADY KNEW.

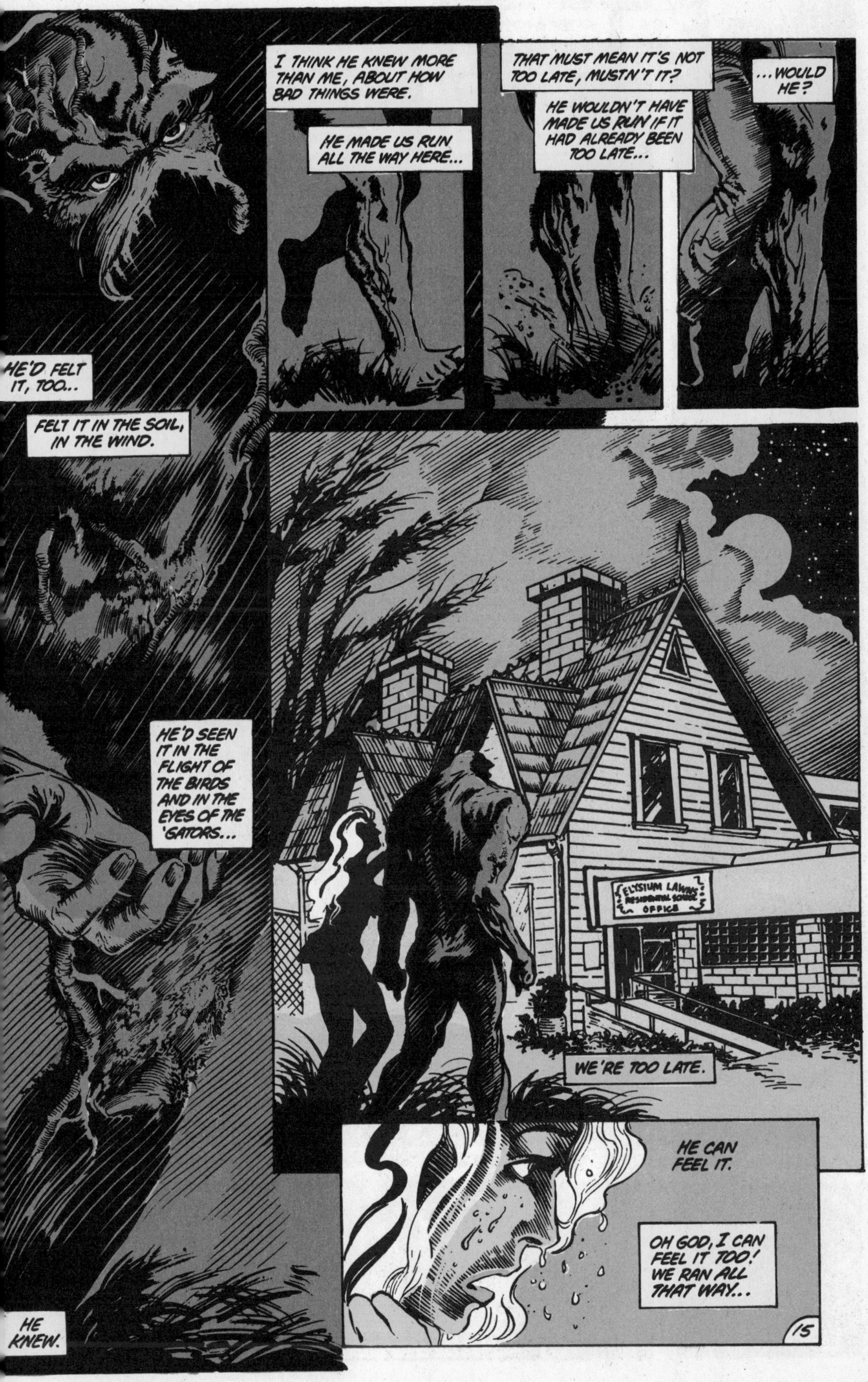
HE'D FELT IT, TOO...
FELT IT IN THE SOIL, IN THE WIND.
HE'D SEEN IT IN THE FLIGHT OF THE BIRDS AND IN THE EYES OF THE 'GATORS...
HE KNEW.
I THINK HE KNEW MORE THAN ME, ABOUT HOW BAD THINGS WERE.
HE MADE US RUN ALL THE WAY HERE...
THAT MUST MEAN IT'S NOT TOO LATE, MUSTN'T IT?
HE WOULDN'T HAVE MADE US RUN IF IT HAD ALREADY BEEN TOO LATE...
...WOULD HE?
ELYSIUM LAWNS RESIDENTIAL SCHOOL OFFICE
WE'RE TOO LATE.
HE CAN FEEL IT.
OH GOD, I CAN FEEL IT TOO! WE RAN ALL THAT WAY...
15

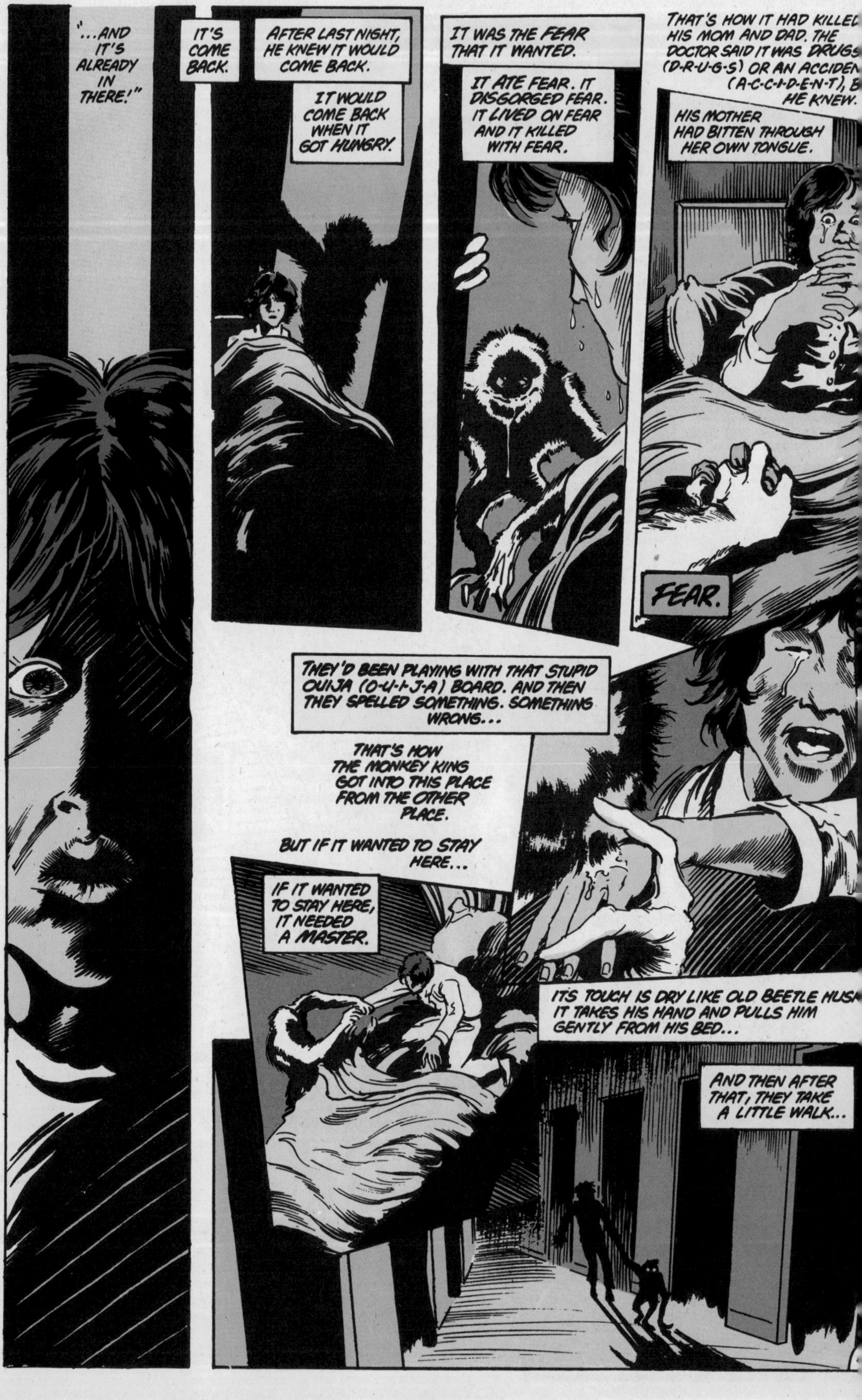
"...AND IT'S ALREADY IN THERE!"
IT'S COME BACK.
AFTER LAST NIGHT, HE KNEW IT WOULD COME BACK.
IT WOULD COME BACK WHEN IT GOT HUNGRY.
IT WAS THE FEAR THAT IT WANTED.
IT ATE FEAR. IT DISGORGED FEAR. IT LIVED ON FEAR AND IT KILLED WITH FEAR.
HIS MOTHER HAD BITTEN THROUGH HER OWN TONGUE.
FEAR.
THEY'D BEEN PLAYING WITH THAT STUPID OUIJA (O-U-I-J-A) BOARD. AND THEN THEY SPELLED SOMETHING. SOMETHING WRONG...
THAT'S HOW THE MONKEY KING GOT INTO THIS PLACE FROM THE OTHER PLACE.
BUT IF IT WANTED TO STAY HERE...
IF IT WANTED TO STAY HERE, IT NEEDED A MASTER.
AND THEN AFTER THAT, THEY TAKE A LITTLE WALK...

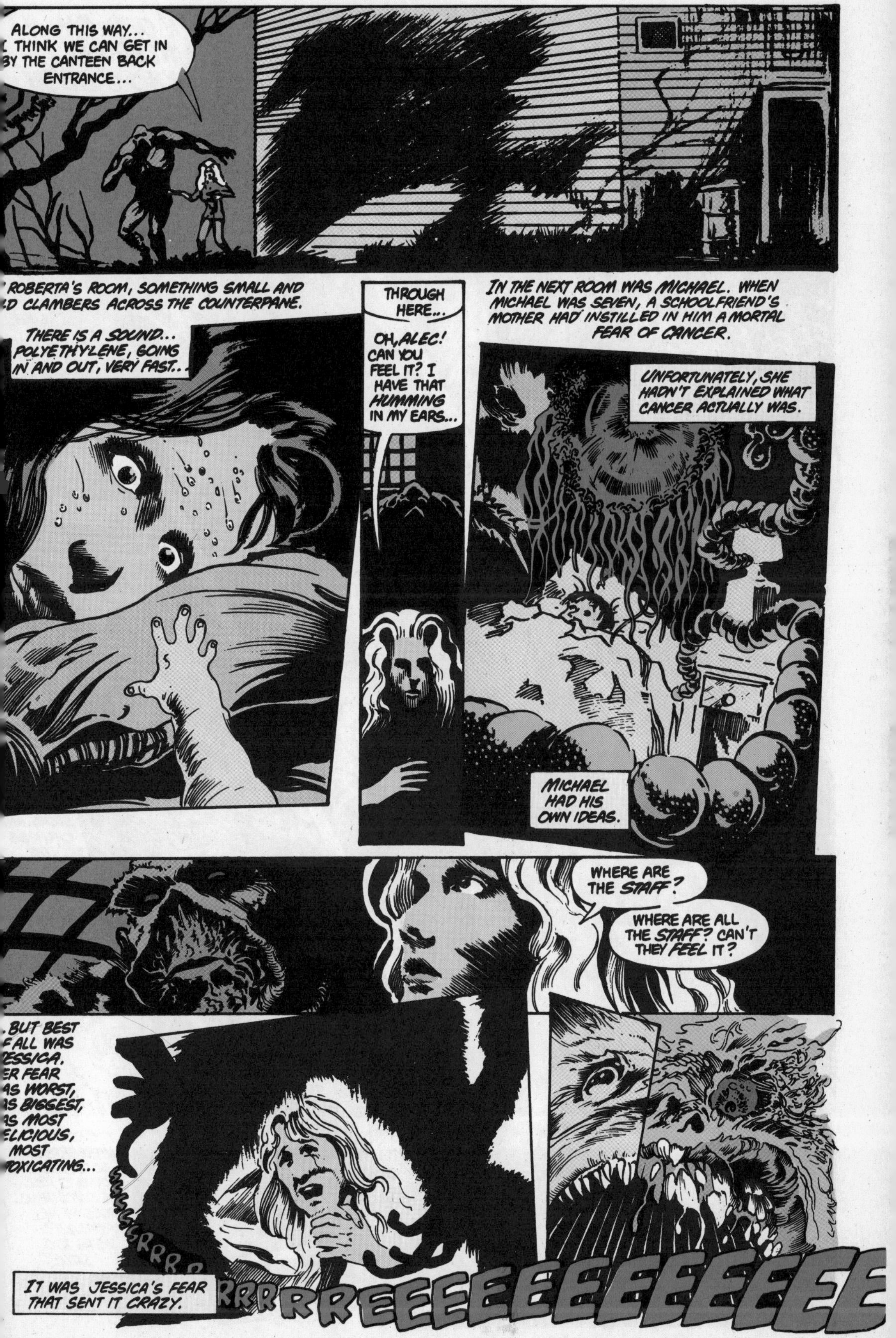
ALONG THIS WAY... I THINK WE CAN GET IN BY THE CANTEEN BACK ENTRANCE...
ROBERTA'S ROOM, SOMETHING SMALL AND D CLAMBERS ACROSS THE COUNTERPANE.
THERE IS A SOUND... POLYETHYLENE, GOING IN AND OUT, VERY FAST...
THROUGH HERE...
OH, ALEC! CAN YOU FEEL IT? I HAVE THAT HUMMING IN MY EARS...
IN THE NEXT ROOM WAS MICHAEL. WHEN MICHAEL WAS SEVEN, A SCHOOLFRIEND'S MOTHER HAD INSTILLED IN HIM A MORTAL FEAR OF CANCER.
UNFORTUNATELY, SHE HADN'T EXPLAINED WHAT CANCER ACTUALLY WAS.
MICHAEL HAD HIS OWN IDEAS.
WHERE ARE THE STAFF?
WHERE ARE ALL THE STAFF? CAN'T THEY FEEL IT?
. BUT BEST F ALL WAS ESSICA. ER FEAR AS WORST, AS BIGGEST, AS MOST ELICIOUS, MOST TOXICATING...
IT WAS JESSICA'S FEAR THAT SENT IT CRAZY.
RRRRRRREEEEEEEEEEEEEEE

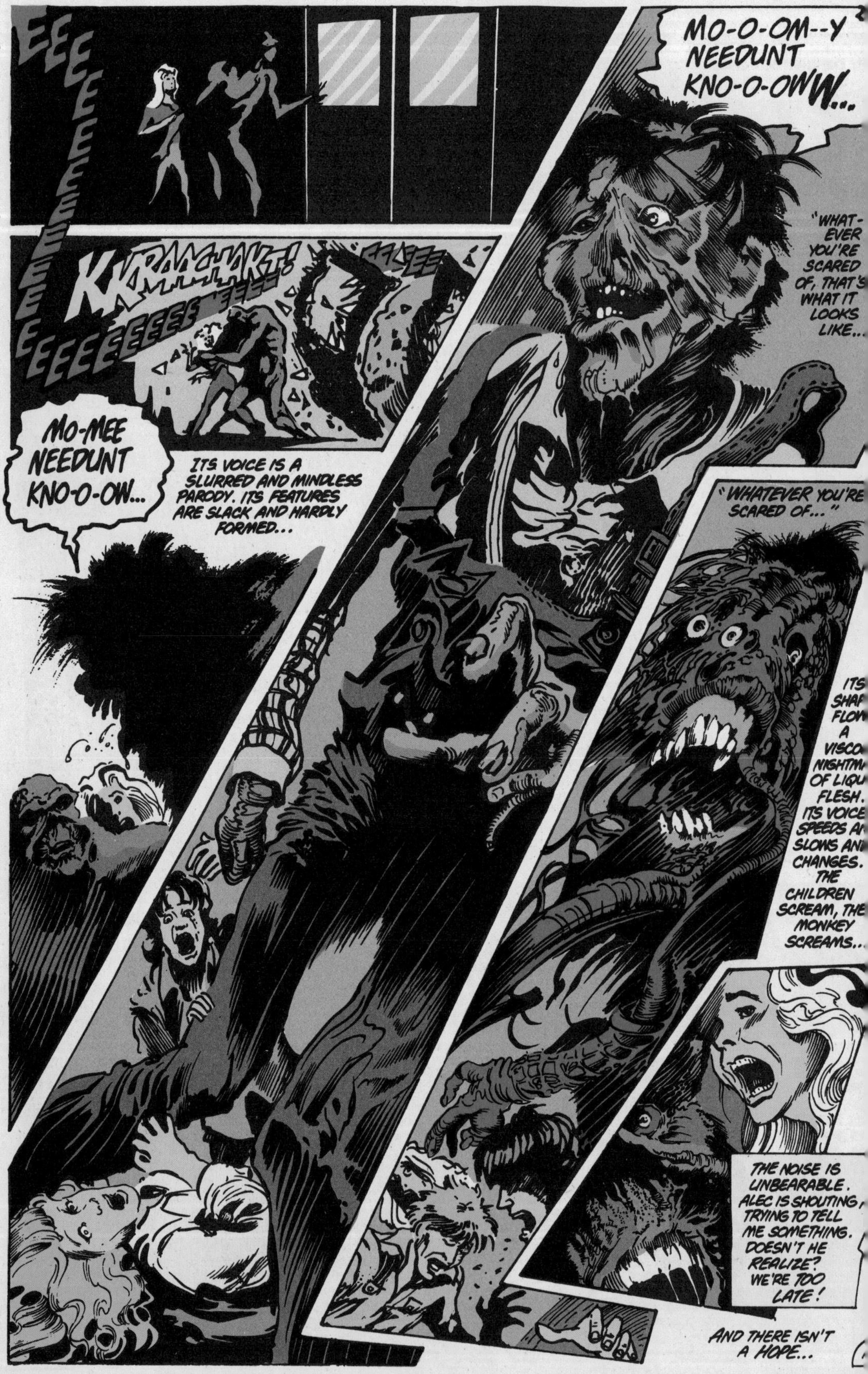
EEEEEEEEEEEEEEEEEE
KRAACHAKT!
MO-MEE NEEDUNT KNO-O-OW...
ITS VOICE IS A SLURRED AND MINDLESS PARODY. ITS FEATURES ARE SLACK AND HARDLY FORMED...
MO-O-OM--Y NEEDUNT KNO-O-OWW...
"WHAT-EVER YOU'RE SCARED OF, THAT'S WHAT IT LOOKS LIKE...
"WHATEVER YOU'RE SCARED OF..."
ITS SHAP FLOW A VISCO NIGHTM OF LIQU FLESH. ITS VOICE SPEEDS A SLOWS AN CHANGES. THE CHILDREN SCREAM, THE MONKEY SCREAMS...
THE NOISE IS UNBEARABLE. ALEC IS SHOUTING, TRYING TO TELL ME SOMETHING. DOESN'T HE REALIZE? WE'RE TOO LATE!
AND THERE ISN'T A HOPE...

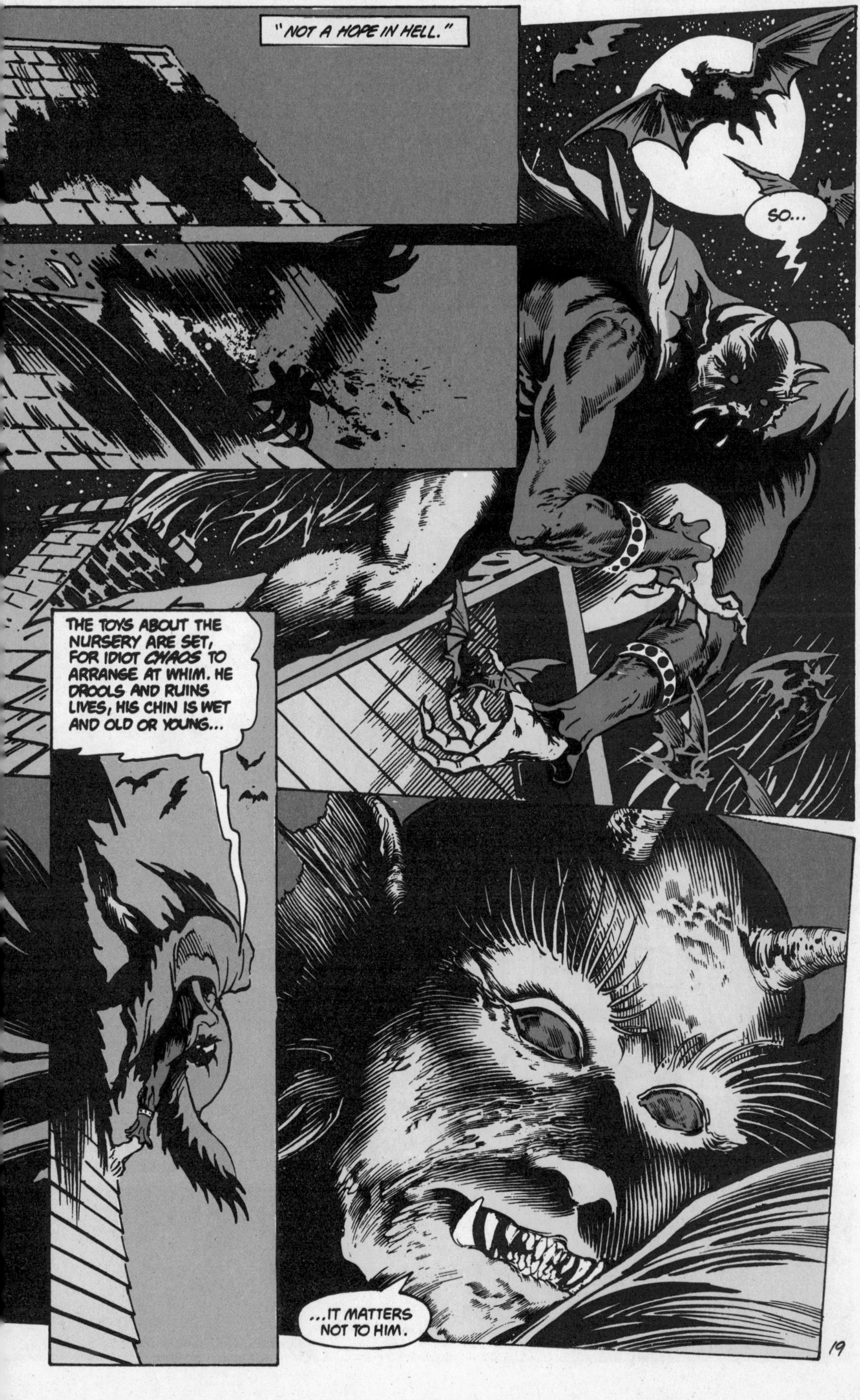
"NOT A HOPE IN HELL."
SO...
THE TOYS ABOUT THE NURSERY ARE SET, FOR IDIOT CHAOS TO ARRANGE AT WHIM. HE DROOLS AND RUINS LIVES, HIS CHIN IS WET AND OLD OR YOUNG...
...IT MATTERS NOT TO HIM.
19

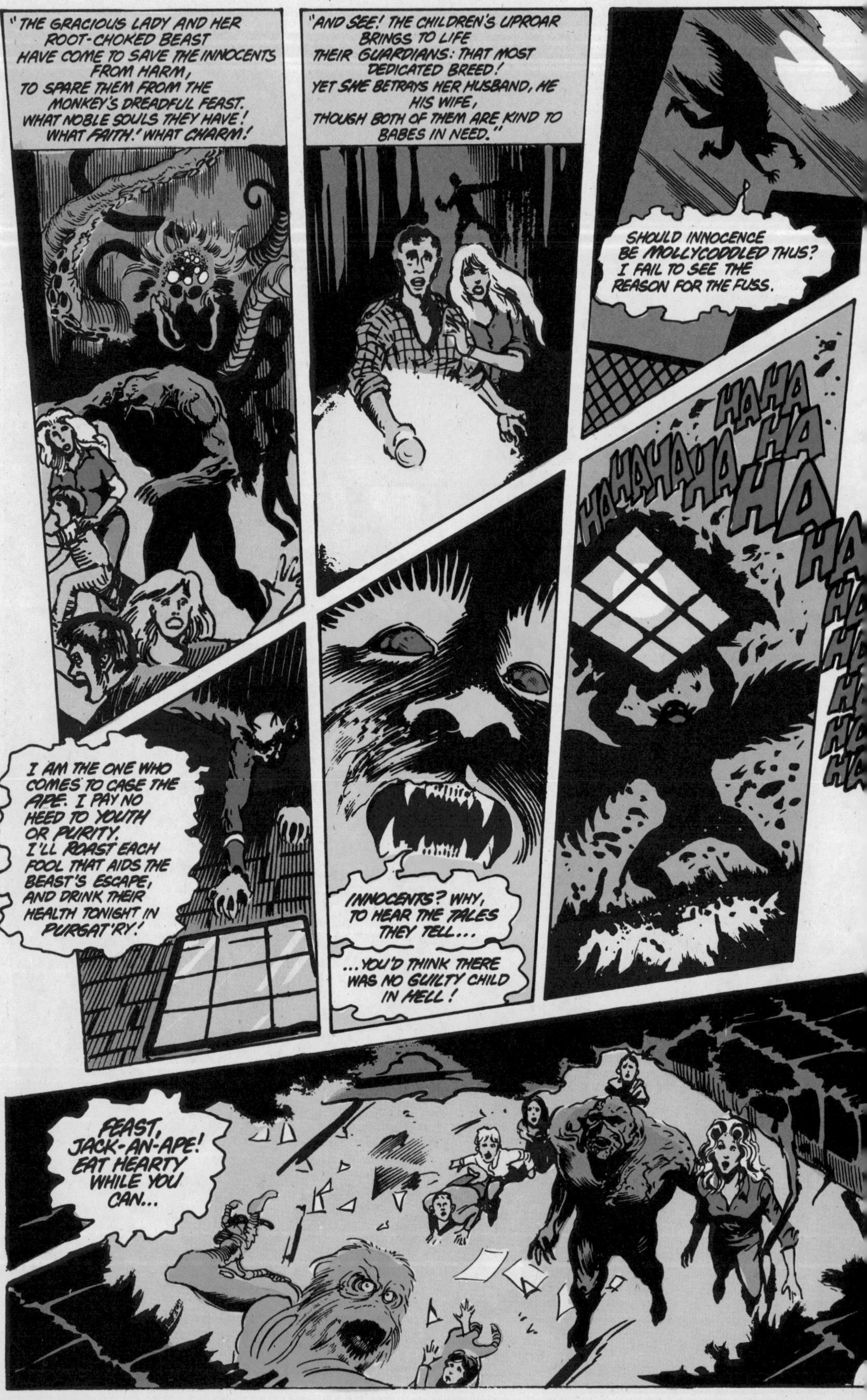
"THE GRACIOUS LADY AND HER ROOT-CHOKED BEAST HAVE COME TO SAVE THE INNOCENTS FROM HARM, TO SPARE THEM FROM THE MONKEY'S DREADFUL FEAST. WHAT NOBLE SOULS THEY HAVE! WHAT FAITH! WHAT CHARM!
"AND SEE! THE CHILDREN'S UPROAR BRINGS TO LIFE THEIR GUARDIANS: THAT MOST DEDICATED BREED! YET SHE BETRAYS HER HUSBAND, HE HIS WIFE, THOUGH BOTH OF THEM ARE KIND TO BABES IN NEED."
SHOULD INNOCENCE BE MOLLYCODDLED THUS? I FAIL TO SEE THE REASON FOR THE FUSS.
I AM THE ONE WHO COMES TO CAGE THE APE. I PAY NO HEED TO YOUTH OR PURITY. I'LL ROAST EACH FOOL THAT AIDS THE BEAST'S ESCAPE, AND DRINK THEIR HEALTH TONIGHT IN PURGAT'RY!
INNOCENTS? WHY, TO HEAR THE TALES THEY TELL...
...YOU'D THINK THERE WAS NO GUILTY CHILD IN HELL!
HAHAHAHAHAHAHAHA HAHA HA HA HA
FEAST, JACK-AN-APE! EAT HEARTY WHILE YOU CAN...

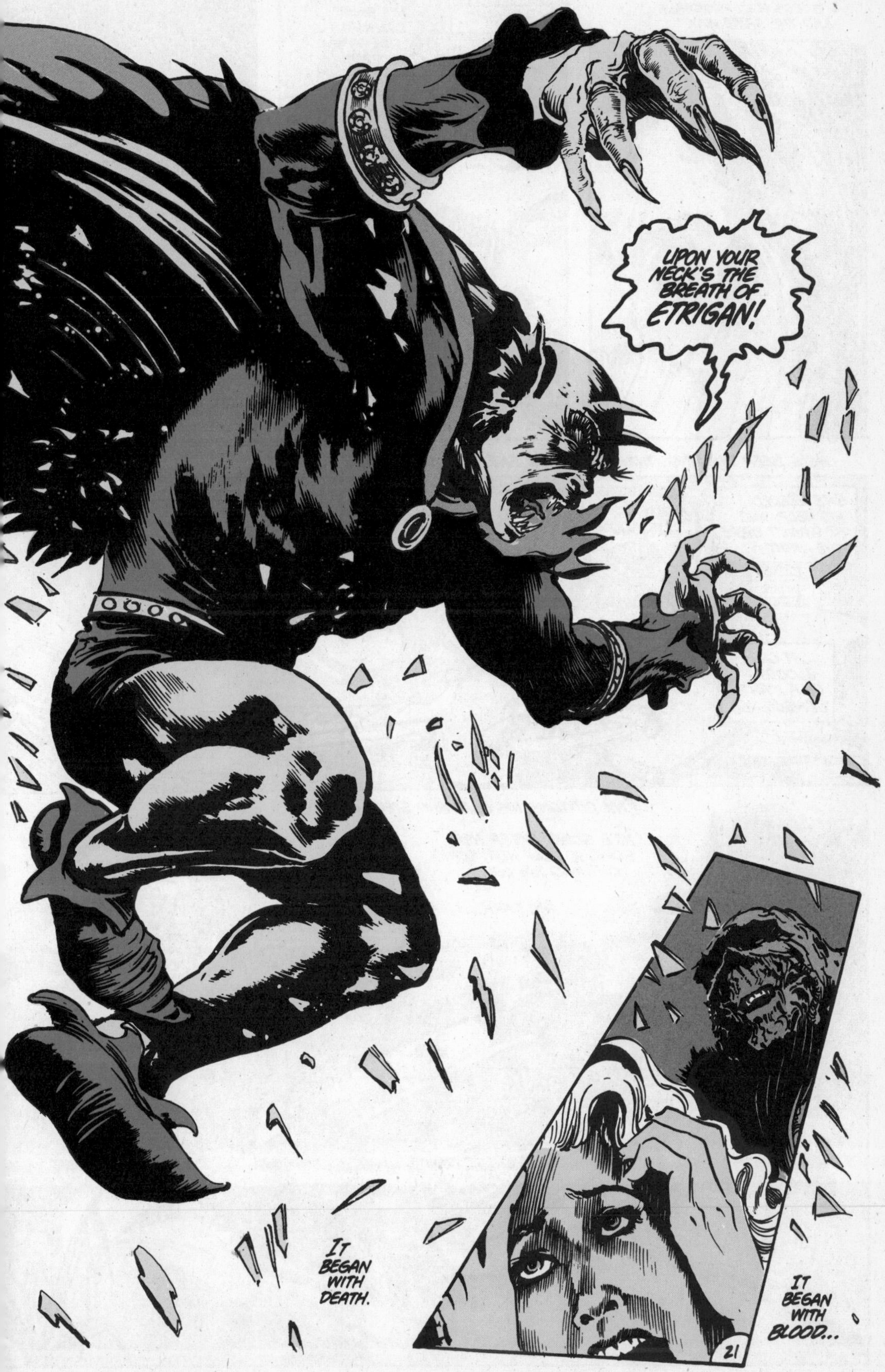
UPON YOUR NECK'S THE BREATH OF ETRIGAN!
IT BEGAN WITH DEATH.
IT BEGAN WITH BLOOD...
21

"...I GUESS IT'LL PROBABLY END THE SAME WAY."

THE NIGHT...

THE NIGHT CAN MAKE A MAN SEE HIMSELF, CAN MAKE HIM LOOK INTO HIS OWN INSIDES...

...AND THE NIGHT CAN MAKE HIM HONEST ENOUGH TO ACCEPT WHAT HE FINDS THERE.

ALL THE WEAKNESS, ALL THE SELFISHNESS, THE CLAMMY DESIRES AND THE SMALL CRUELTIES.

HE'S BEEN THINKING. THINKING SINCE SHE WALKED OUT THE DOOR...

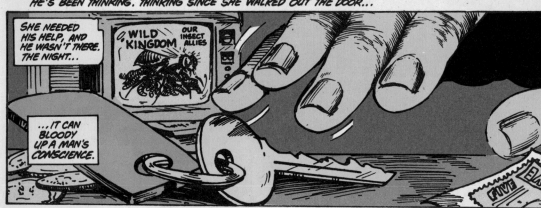

SHE NEEDED HIS HELP, AND HE WASN'T THERE. THE NIGHT...

WILD KINGDOM — OUR INSECT ALLIES

...IT CAN BLOODY UP A MAN'S CONSCIENCE.

HE BUTTONS HIS COAT AND STEPS OUTSIDE.

HE'S GOING AFTER HER, GOING TO HELP HER, GOING OUT INTO THE COLD...

...THE DARK...

...THE NIGHT.

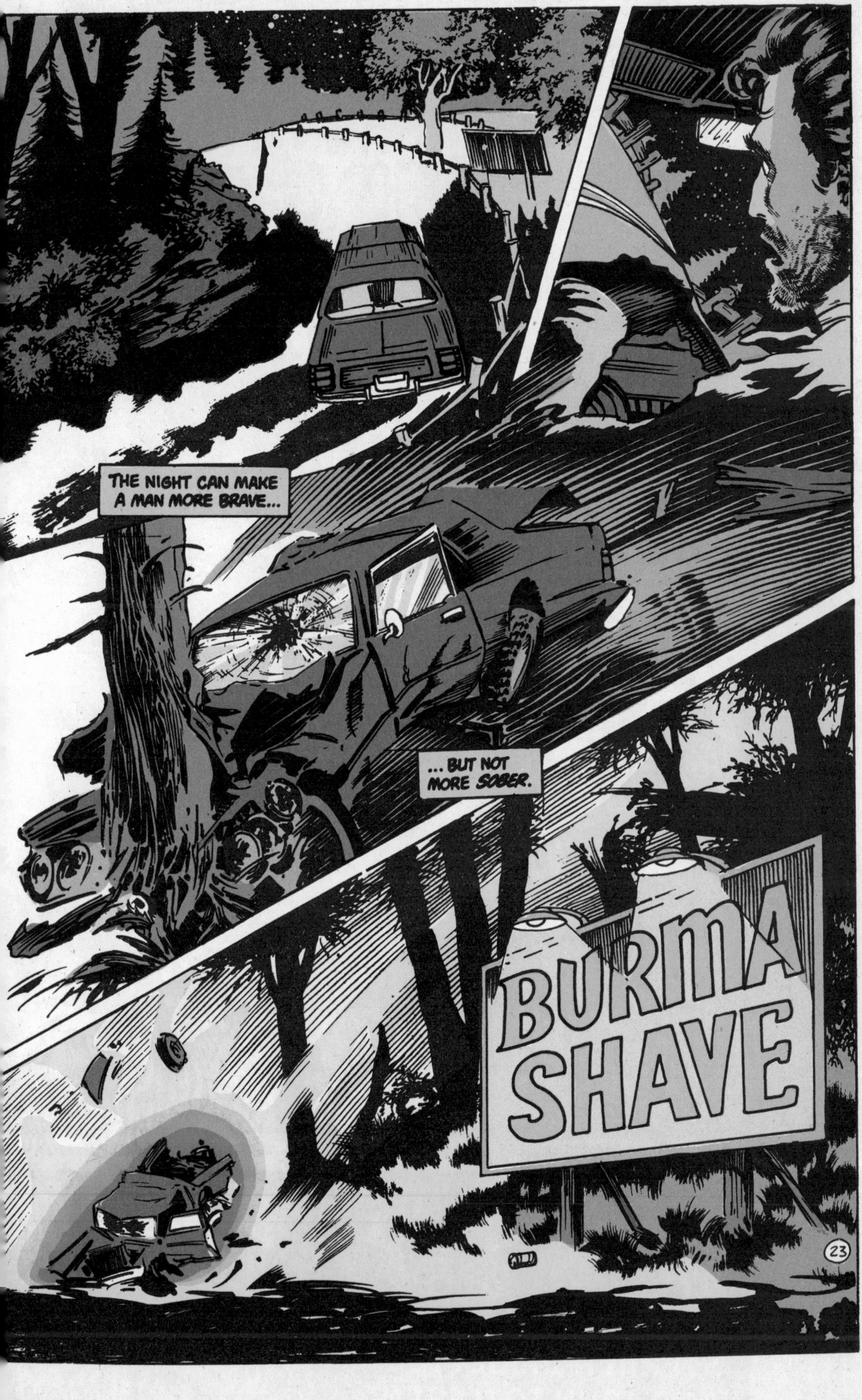
THE NIGHT CAN MAKE A MAN MORE BRAVE...
... BUT NOT MORE SOBER.
BURMA SHAVE
23

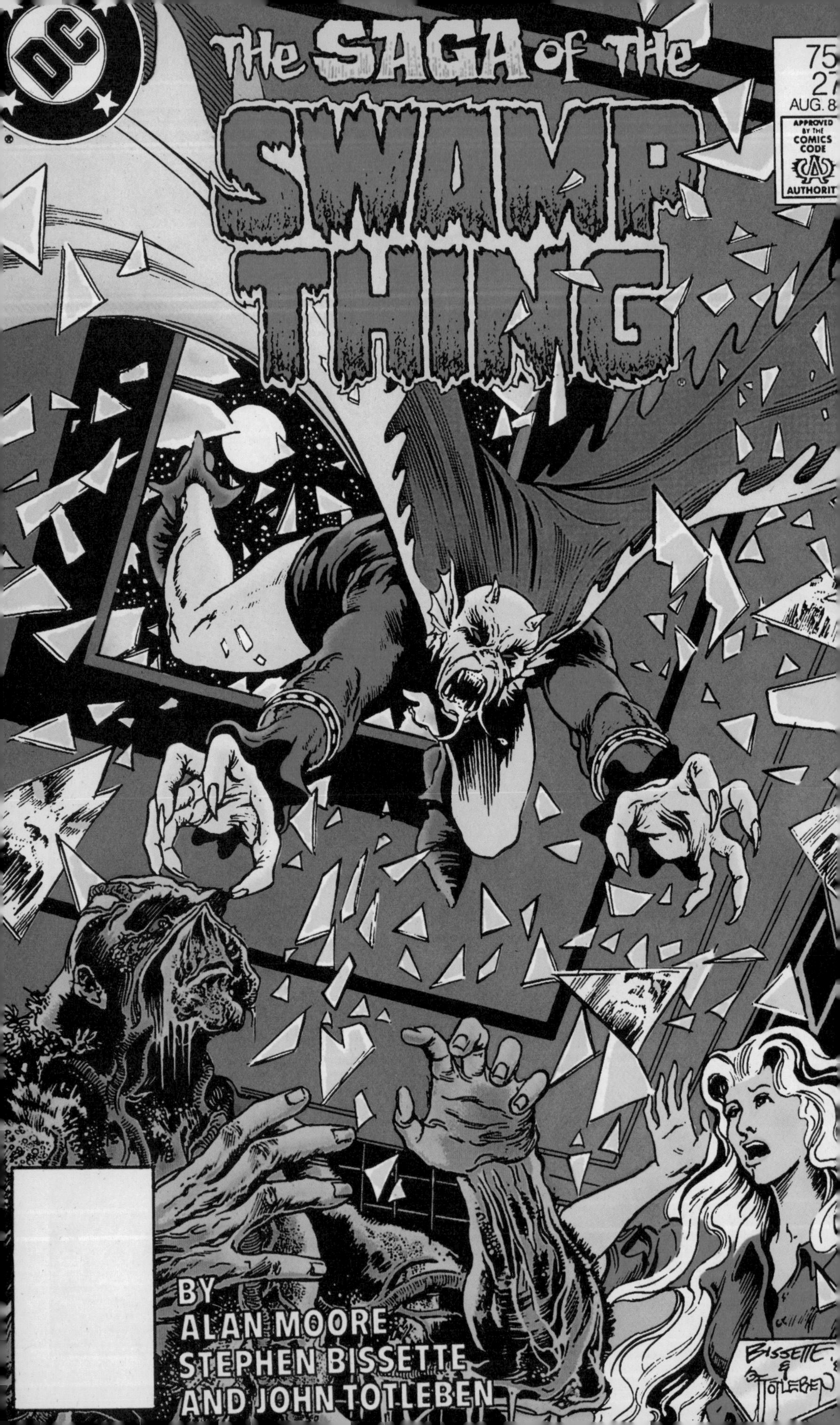
DC
The SAGA of the
SWAMP THING
75
27
AUG. 84
APPROVED BY THE COMICS CODE AUTHORITY
BY
ALAN MOORE
STEPHEN BISSETTE
AND JOHN TOTLEBEN
BISSETTE & TOTLEBEN

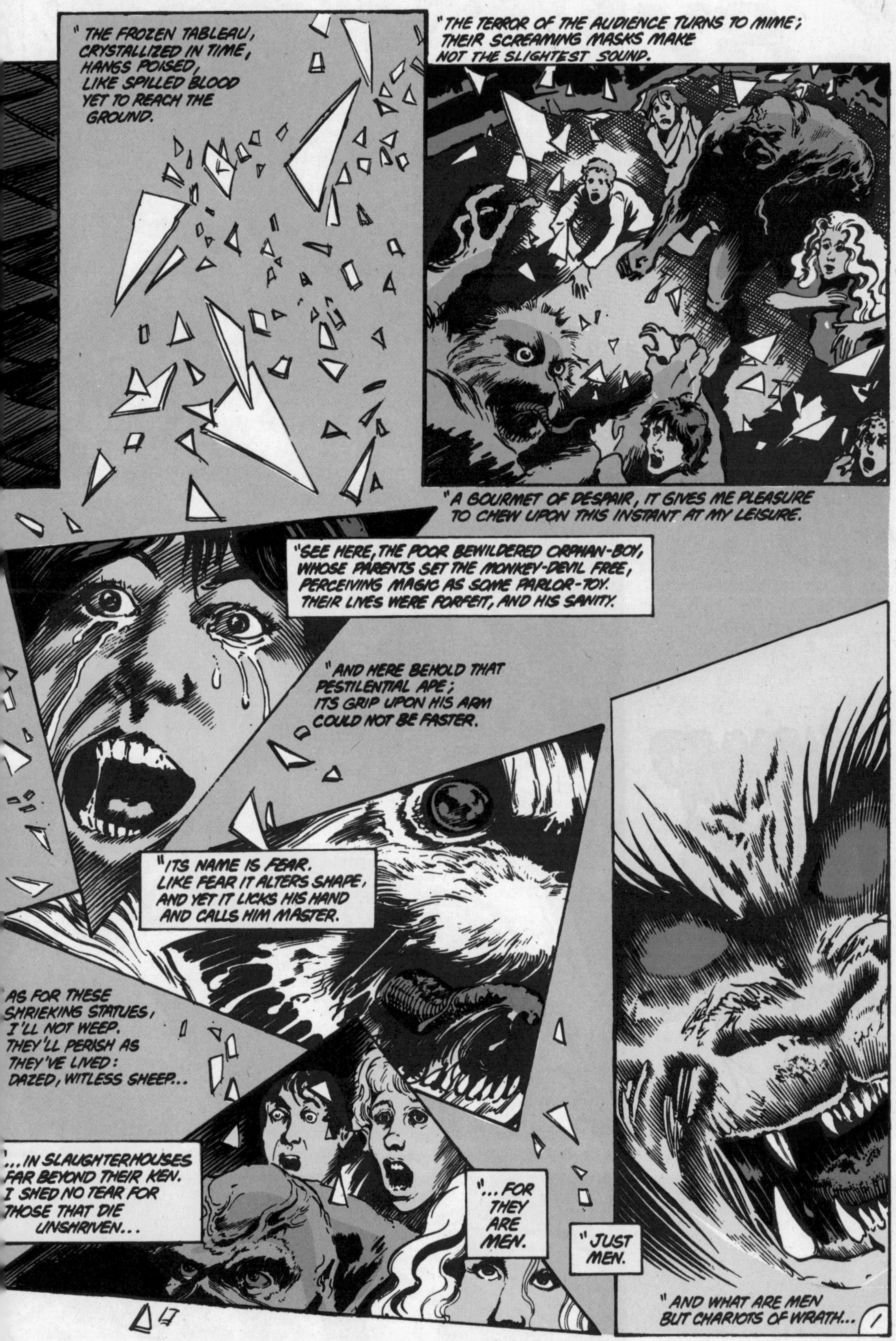
"THE FROZEN TABLEAU, CRYSTALLIZED IN TIME, HANGS POISED, LIKE SPILLED BLOOD YET TO REACH THE GROUND.
"THE TERROR OF THE AUDIENCE TURNS TO MIME; THEIR SCREAMING MASKS MAKE NOT THE SLIGHTEST SOUND.
"A GOURMET OF DESPAIR, IT GIVES ME PLEASURE TO CHEW UPON THIS INSTANT AT MY LEISURE.
"SEE HERE, THE POOR BEWILDERED ORPHAN-BOY, WHOSE PARENTS SET THE MONKEY-DEVIL FREE, PERCEIVING MAGIC AS SOME PARLOR-TOY. THEIR LIVES WERE FORFEIT, AND HIS SANITY.
"AND HERE BEHOLD THAT PESTILENTIAL APE; ITS GRIP UPON HIS ARM COULD NOT BE FASTER.
"ITS NAME IS FEAR. LIKE FEAR IT ALTERS SHAPE, AND YET IT LICKS HIS HAND AND CALLS HIM MASTER.
AS FOR THESE SHRIEKING STATUES, I'LL NOT WEEP. THEY'LL PERISH AS THEY'VE LIVED: DAZED, WITLESS SHEEP...
...IN SLAUGHTERHOUSES FAR BEYOND THEIR KEN. I SHED NO TEAR FOR THOSE THAT DIE UNSHRIVEN...
"...FOR THEY ARE MEN.
"JUST MEN.
"AND WHAT ARE MEN BUT CHARIOTS OF WRATH...
1

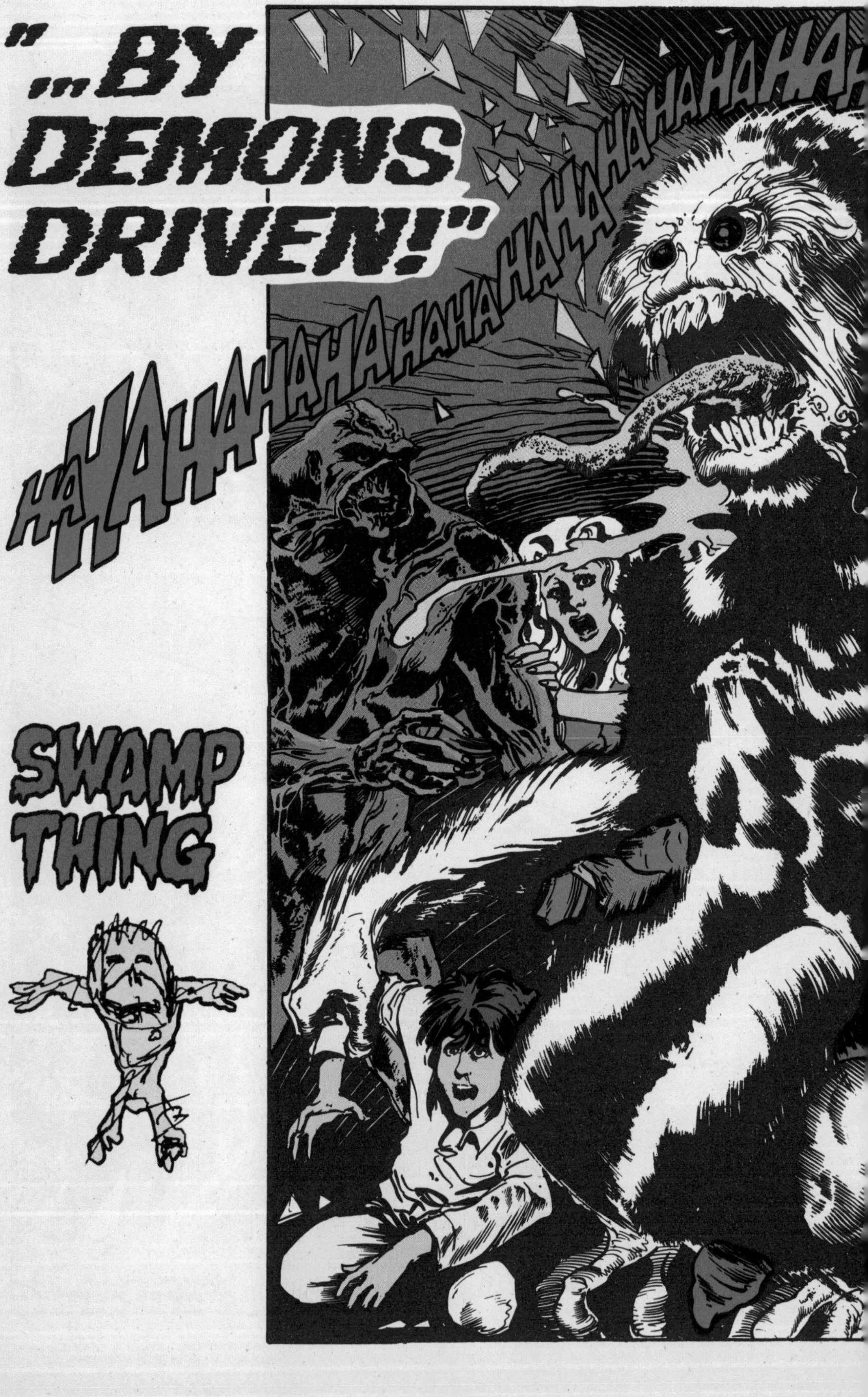
"...BY DEMONS DRIVEN!"
HAHAHAHAHAHAHAHAHAHAHAHAHAHAHAHA
SWAMP THING

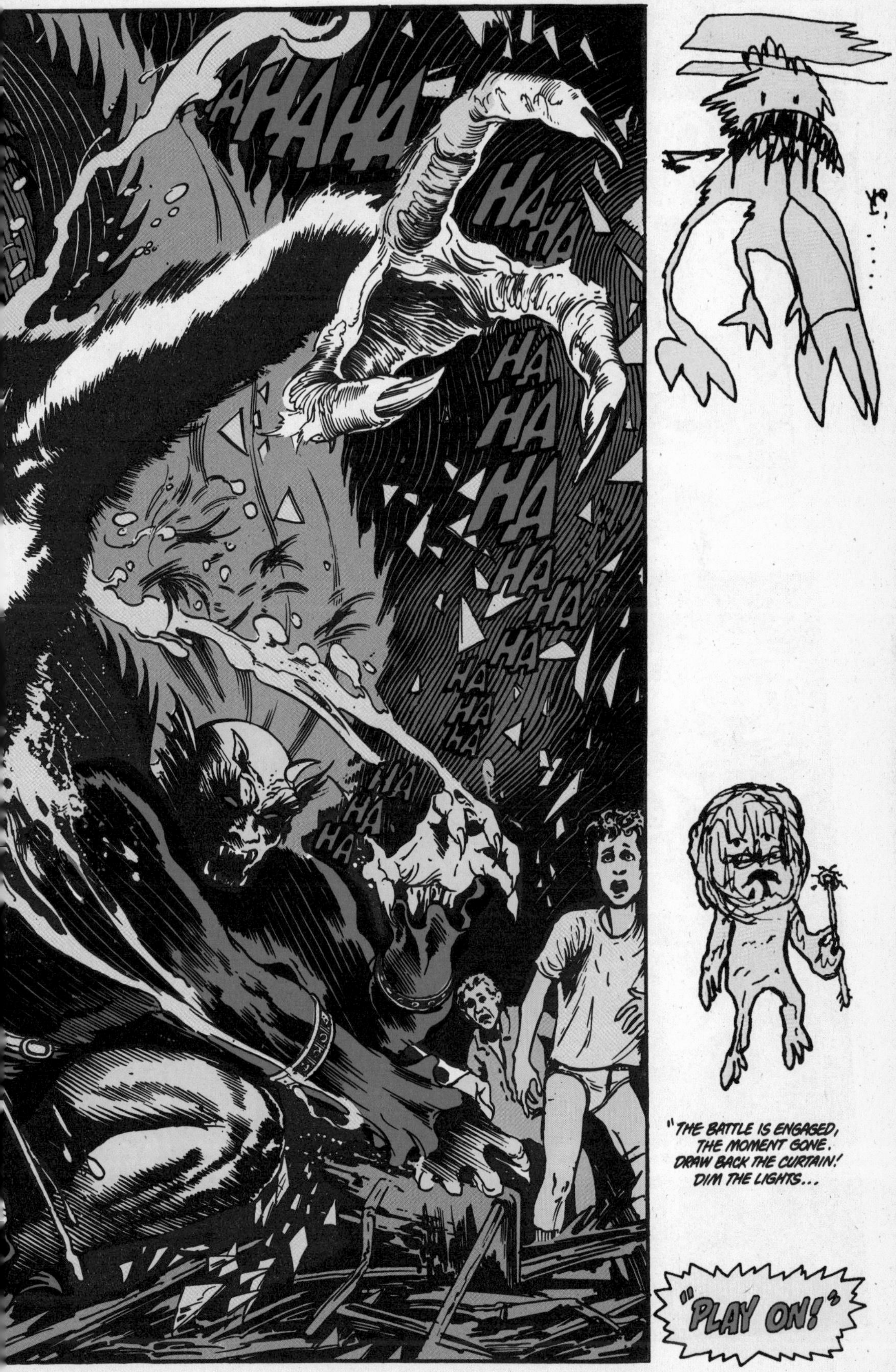
HAHAHA
HAHA
HA HA HA HA HA HA HA HA HA HA HA
HA HA HA
"THE BATTLE IS ENGAGED, THE MOMENT GONE. DRAW BACK THE CURTAIN! DIM THE LIGHTS...
"PLAY ON!"

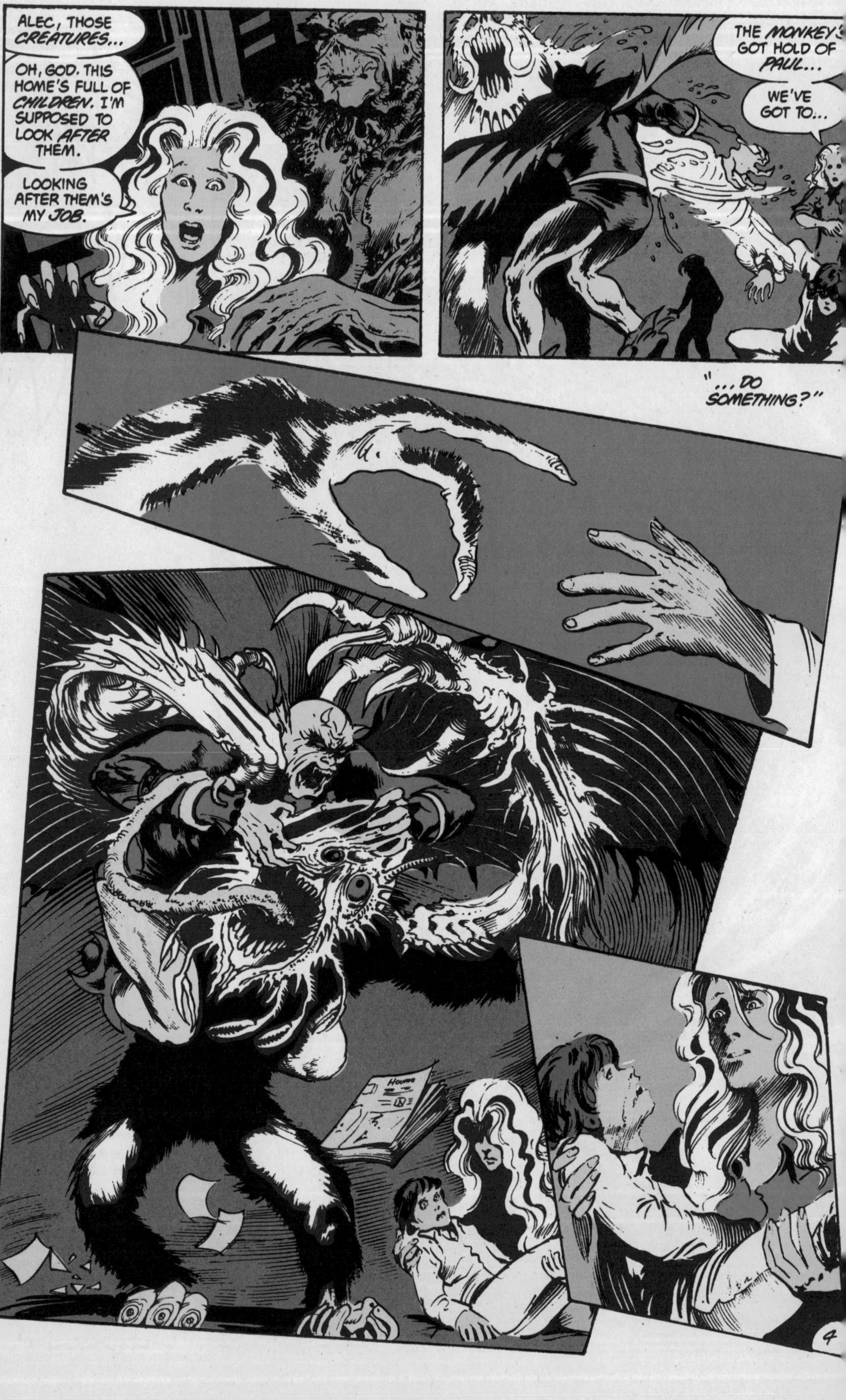
ALEC, THOSE CREATURES...
OH, GOD. THIS HOME'S FULL OF CHILDREN. I'M SUPPOSED TO LOOK AFTER THEM.
LOOKING AFTER THEM'S MY JOB.
THE MONKEY'S GOT HOLD OF PAUL...
WE'VE GOT TO...
"...DO SOMETHING?"
4

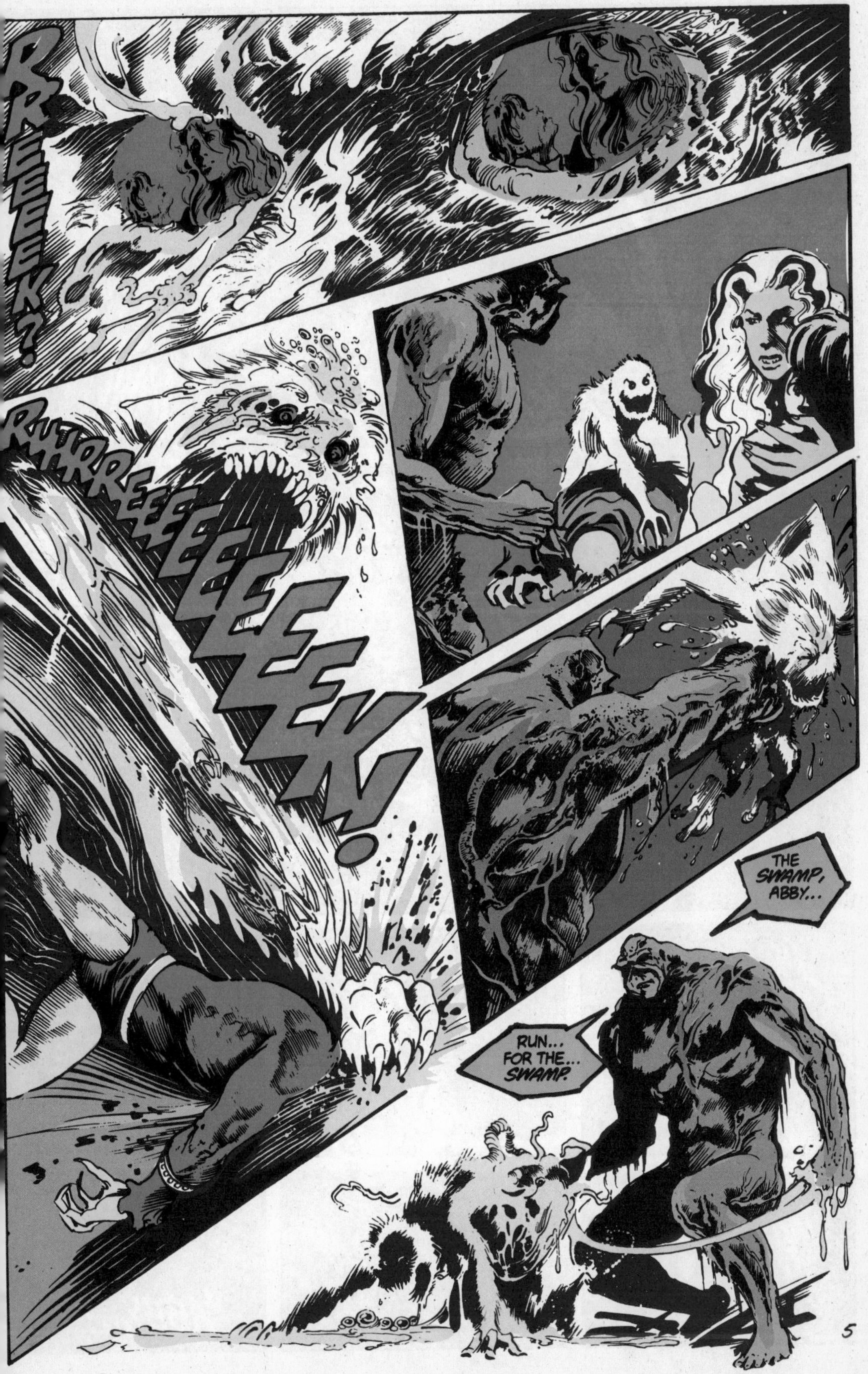
RREEEEEK?
RUHRREEEEEEEEEEEEK!
THE SWAMP, ABBY...
RUN... FOR THE... SWAMP.

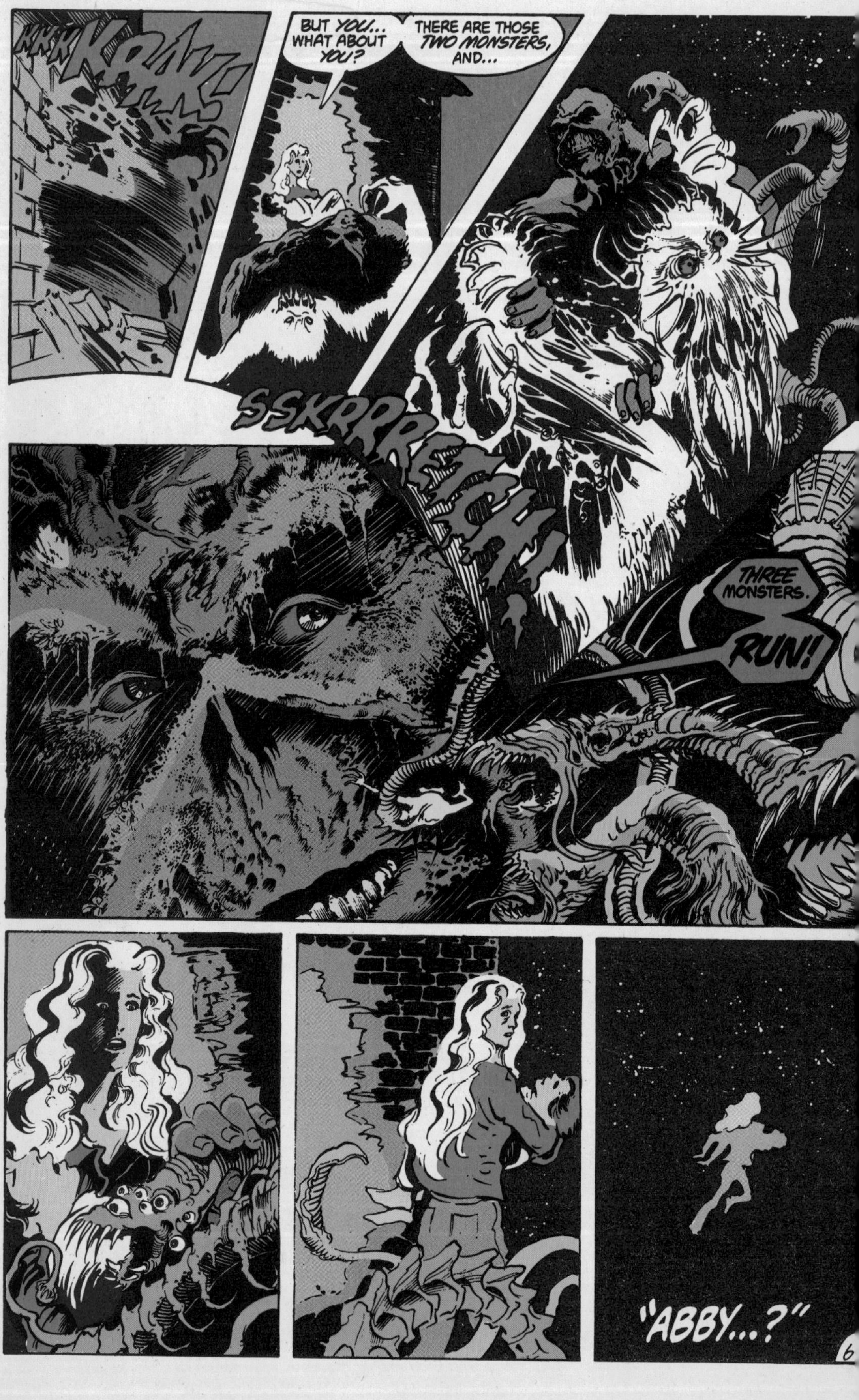
KKKKRAKK!
BUT YOU... WHAT ABOUT YOU?
THERE ARE THOSE TWO MONSTERS, AND...
SSKRRREETCH!
THREE MONSTERS.
RUN!
"ABBY...?"
6

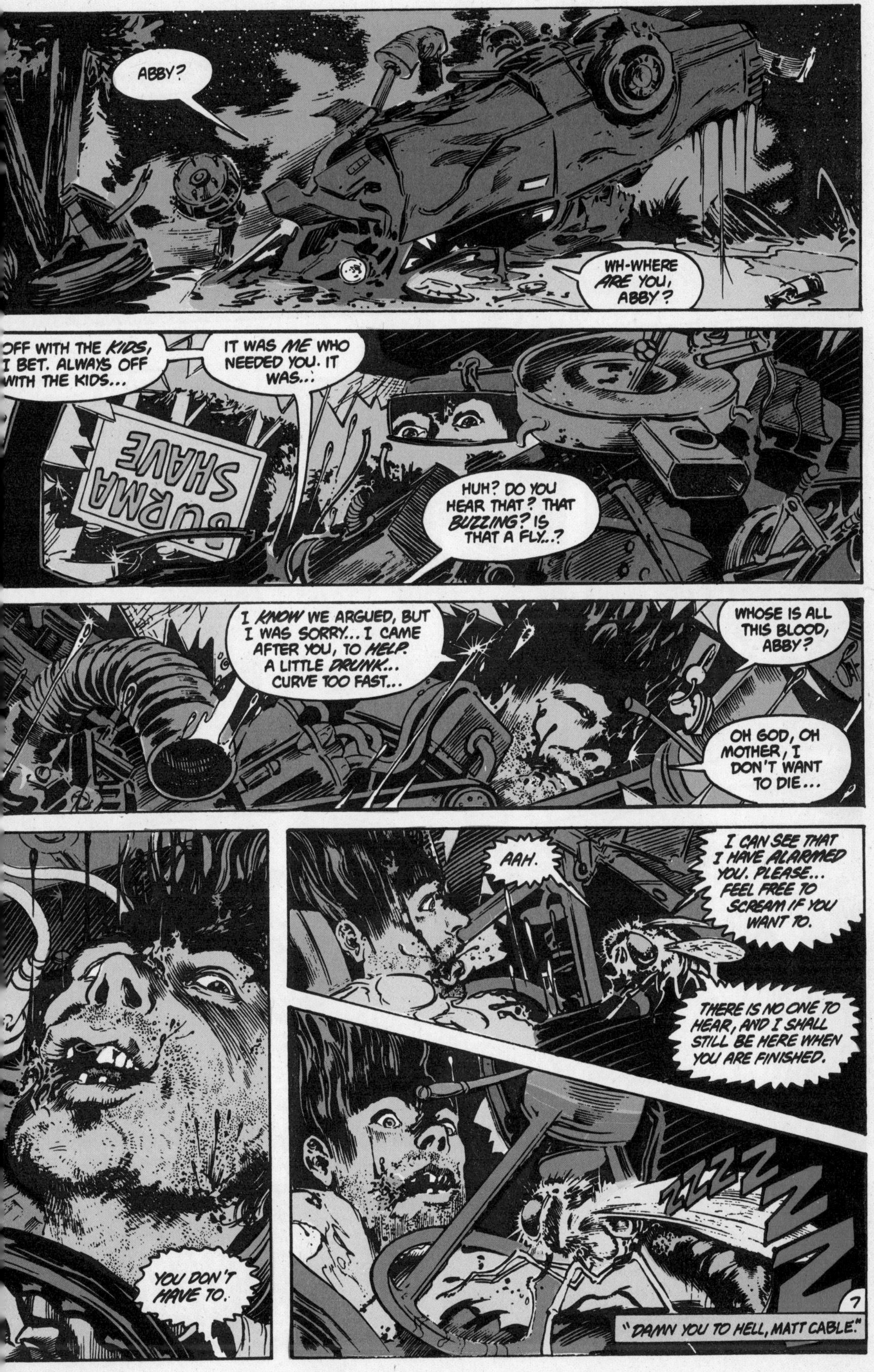
ABBY?
WH-WHERE ARE YOU, ABBY?
OFF WITH THE KIDS, I BET. ALWAYS OFF WITH THE KIDS...
IT WAS ME WHO NEEDED YOU. IT WAS...
BURMA SHAVE
HUH? DO YOU HEAR THAT? THAT BUZZING? IS THAT A FLY...?
I KNOW WE ARGUED, BUT I WAS SORRY... I CAME AFTER YOU, TO HELP. A LITTLE DRUNK... CURVE TOO FAST...
WHOSE IS ALL THIS BLOOD, ABBY?
OH GOD, OH MOTHER, I DON'T WANT TO DIE...
YOU DON'T HAVE TO.
AAH.
I CAN SEE THAT I HAVE ALARMED YOU. PLEASE... FEEL FREE TO SCREAM IF YOU WANT TO.
THERE IS NO ONE TO HEAR, AND I SHALL STILL BE HERE WHEN YOU ARE FINISHED.
ZZZZZNNN
7
"DAMN YOU TO HELL, MATT CABLE."

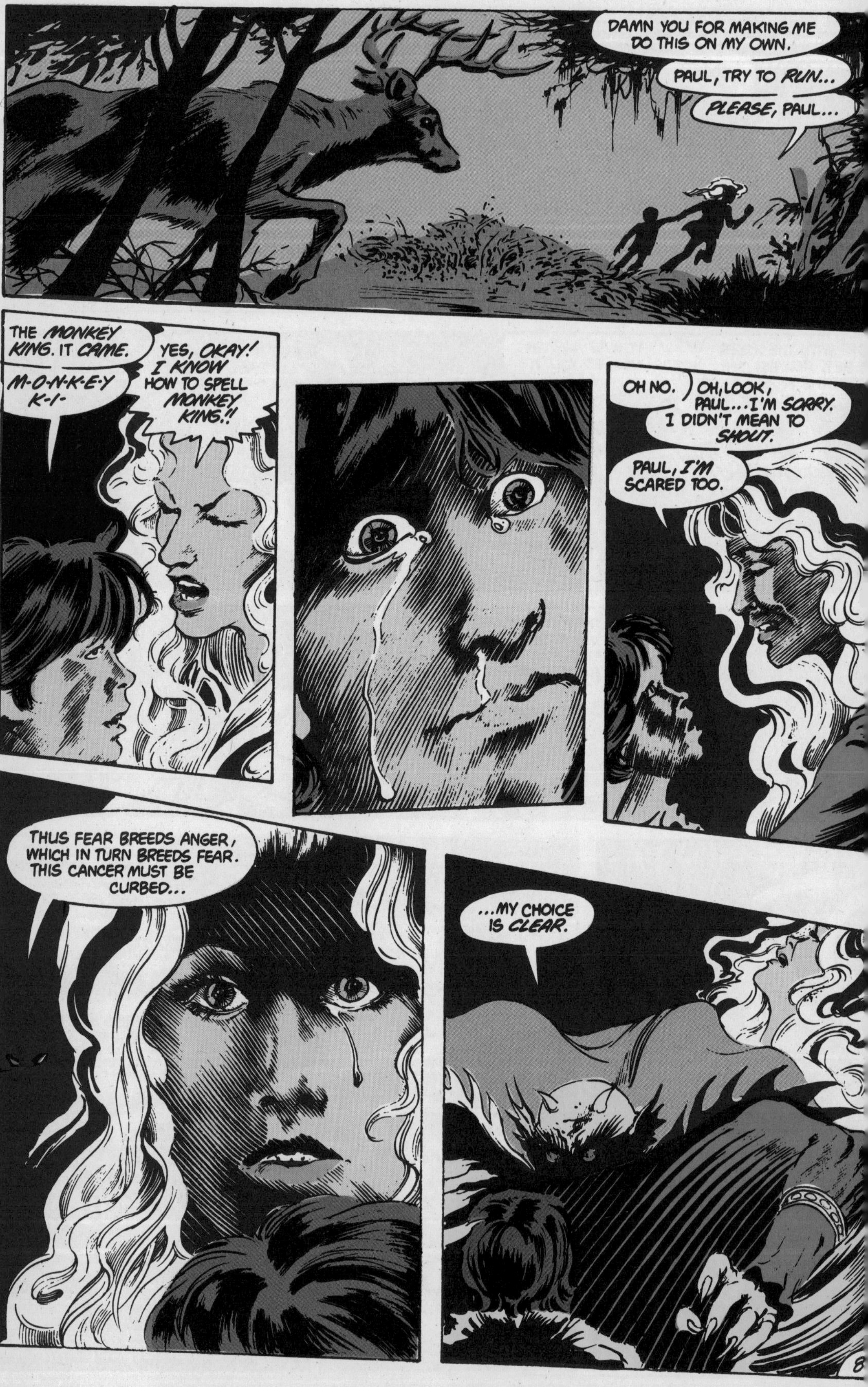
DAMN YOU FOR MAKING ME DO THIS ON MY OWN.
PAUL, TRY TO RUN...
PLEASE, PAUL...
THE MONKEY KING. IT CAME.
M-O-N-K-E-Y K-I-
YES, OKAY! I KNOW HOW TO SPELL MONKEY KING.!!
OH NO.
OH, LOOK, PAUL... I'M SORRY. I DIDN'T MEAN TO SHOUT.
PAUL, I'M SCARED TOO.
THUS FEAR BREEDS ANGER, WHICH IN TURN BREEDS FEAR. THIS CANCER MUST BE CURBED...
...MY CHOICE IS CLEAR.

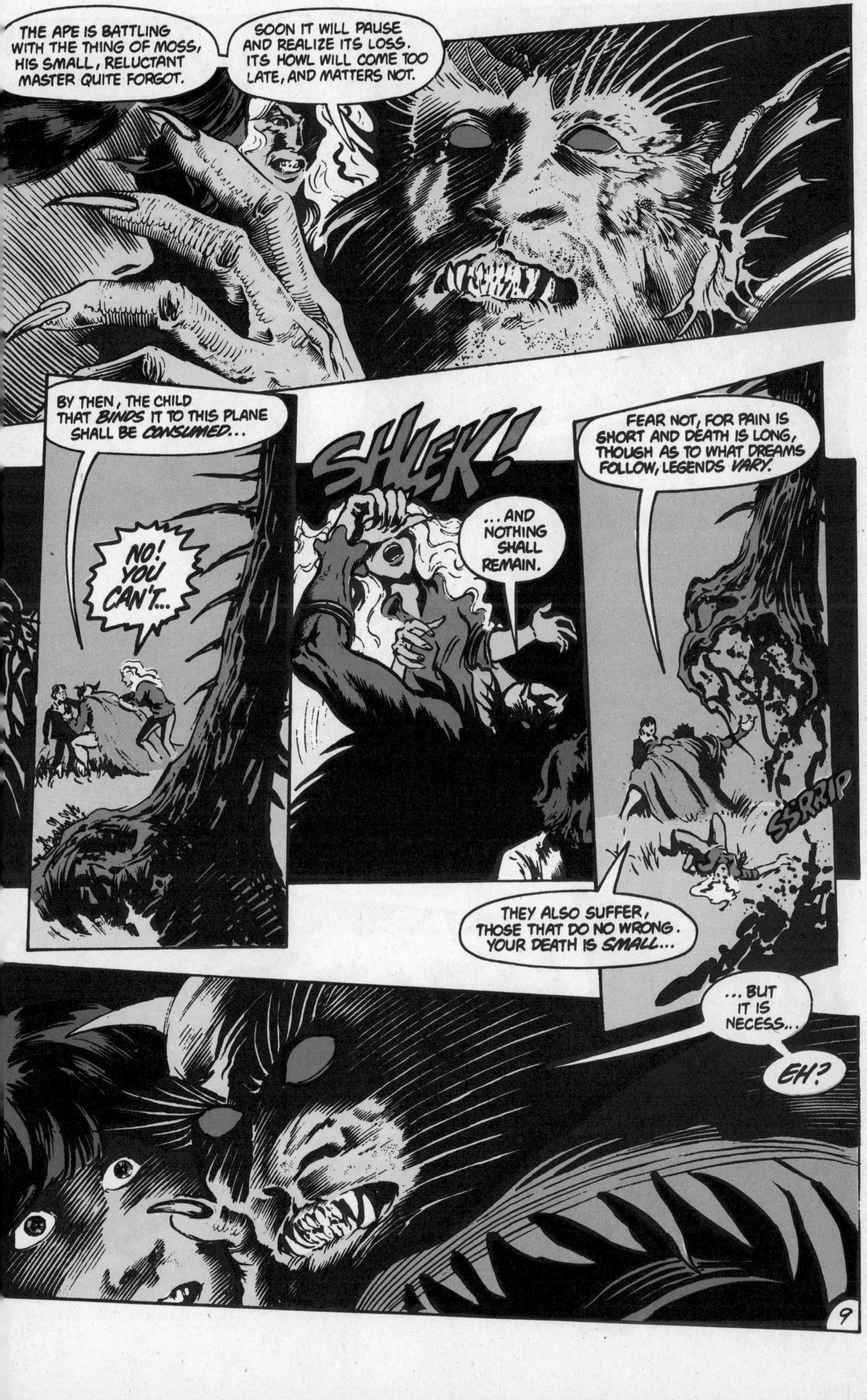
THE APE IS BATTLING WITH THE THING OF MOSS, HIS SMALL, RELUCTANT MASTER QUITE FORGOT.
SOON IT WILL PAUSE AND REALIZE ITS LOSS. ITS HOWL WILL COME TOO LATE, AND MATTERS NOT.
BY THEN, THE CHILD THAT BINDS IT TO THIS PLANE SHALL BE CONSUMED...
NO! YOU CAN'T...
SHLEK!
...AND NOTHING SHALL REMAIN.
FEAR NOT, FOR PAIN IS SHORT AND DEATH IS LONG, THOUGH AS TO WHAT DREAMS FOLLOW, LEGENDS VARY.
SSRRIP
THEY ALSO SUFFER, THOSE THAT DO NO WRONG. YOUR DEATH IS SMALL...
...BUT IT IS NECESS...
EH?
9

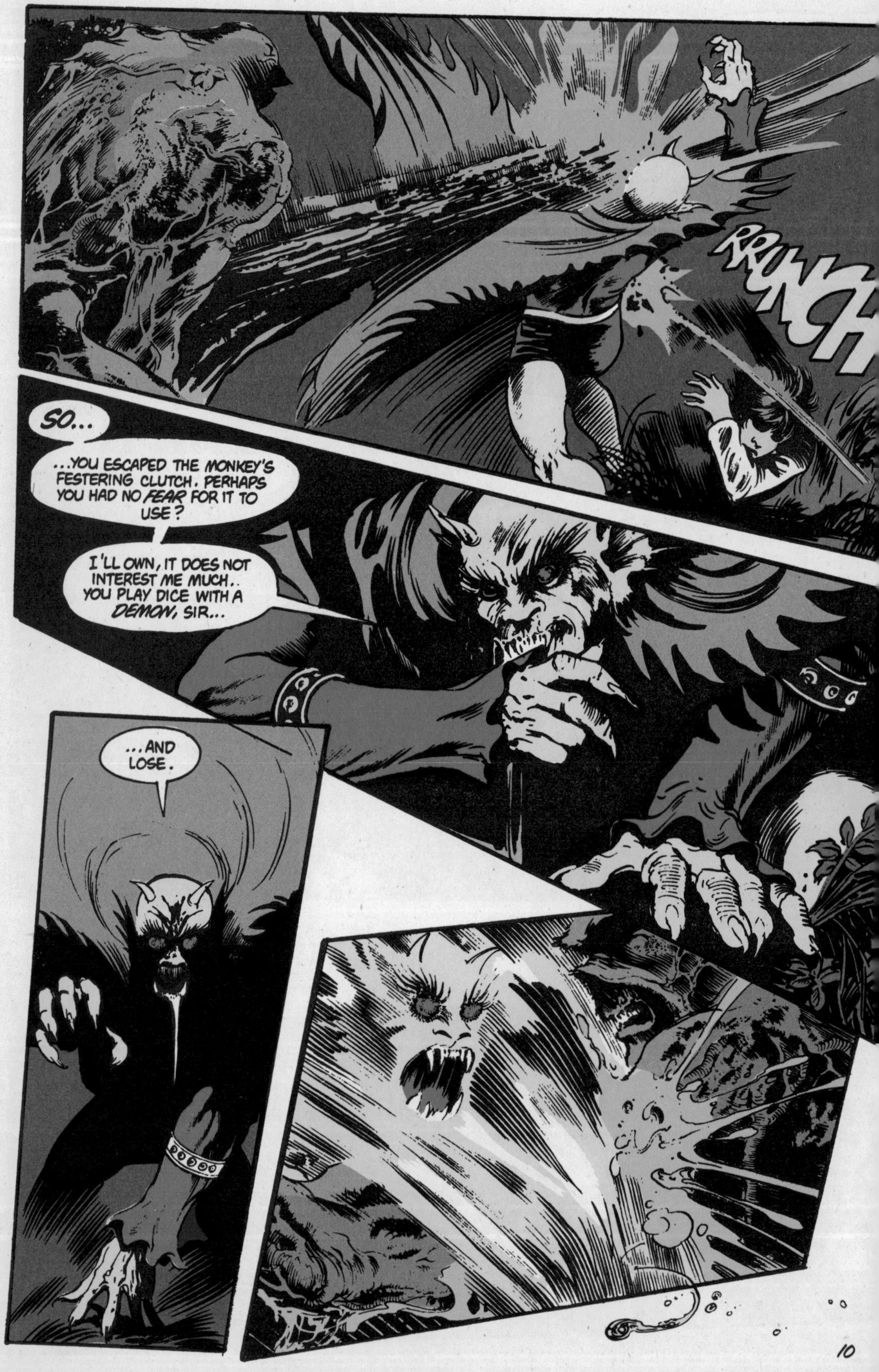
RRUNCH
SO...
...YOU ESCAPED THE MONKEY'S FESTERING CLUTCH. PERHAPS YOU HAD NO FEAR FOR IT TO USE?
I'LL OWN, IT DOES NOT INTEREST ME MUCH.. YOU PLAY DICE WITH A DEMON, SIR...
...AND LOSE.
10

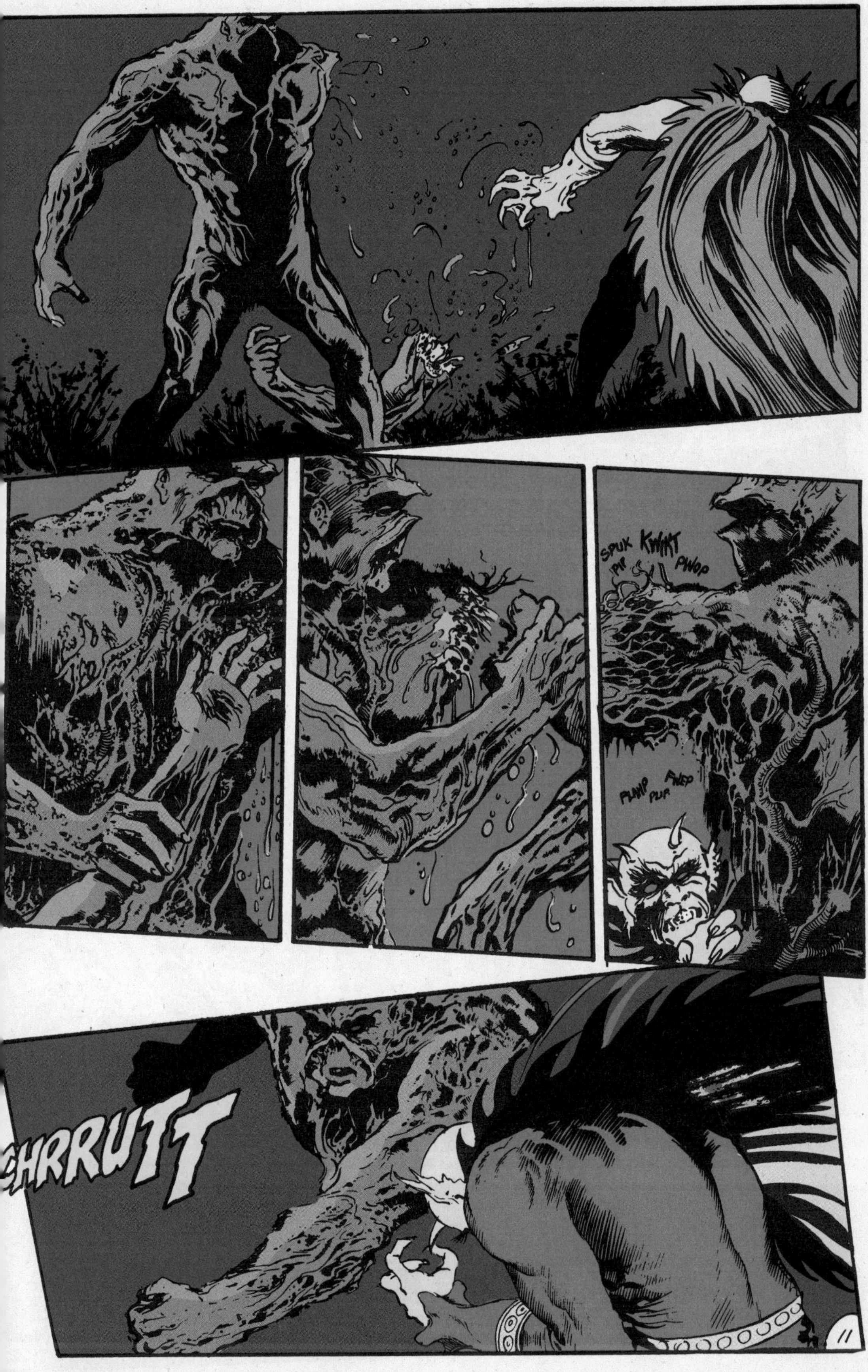
SPUK
KWIKT
PIP
PWOP
PLUMP
PLIP
FWEP
CHRRUTT
11

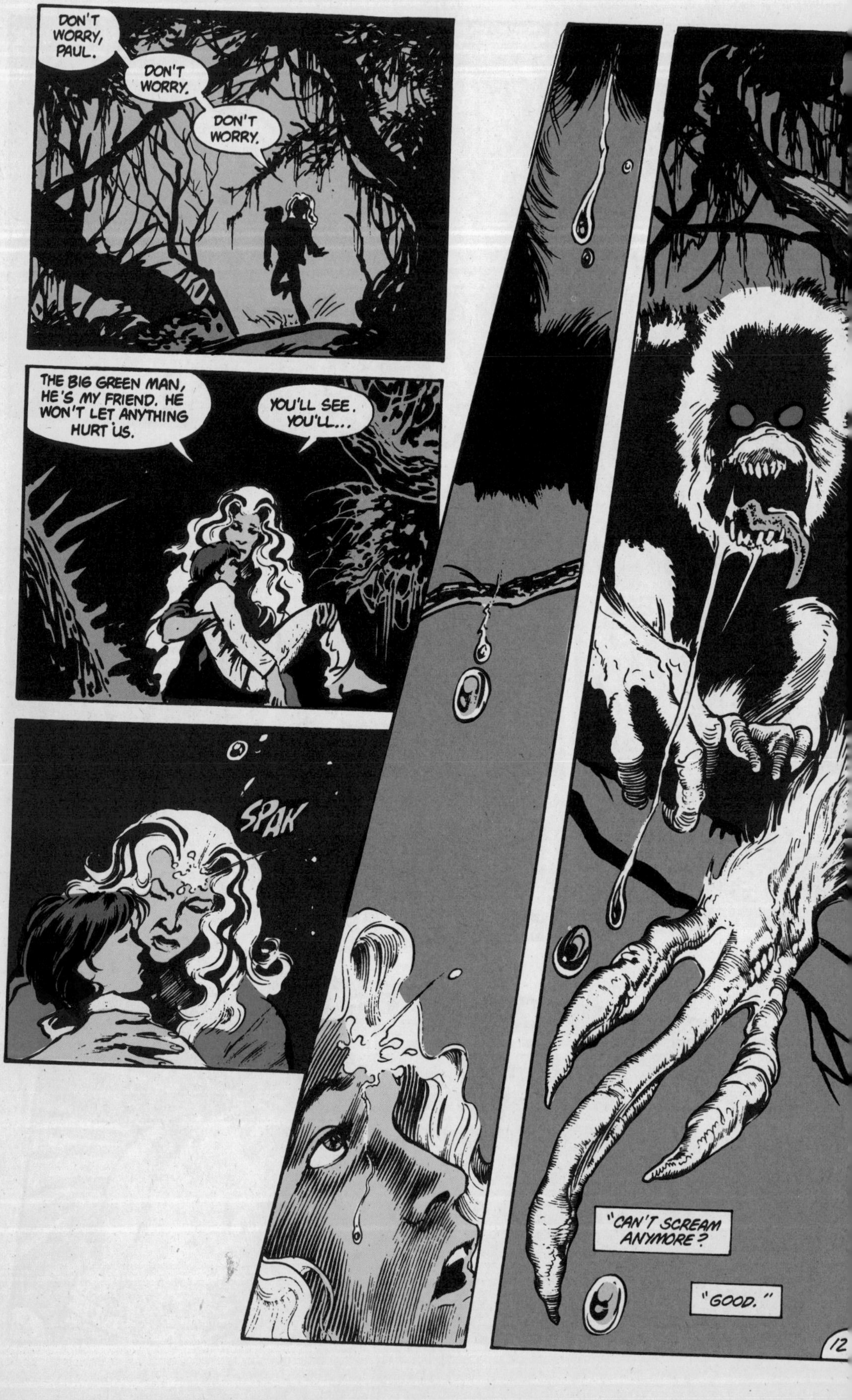
DON'T WORRY, PAUL.
DON'T WORRY.
DON'T WORRY.
THE BIG GREEN MAN, HE'S MY FRIEND. HE WON'T LET ANYTHING HURT US.
YOU'LL SEE. YOU'LL...
SPAK
"CAN'T SCREAM ANYMORE?
"GOOD."
12

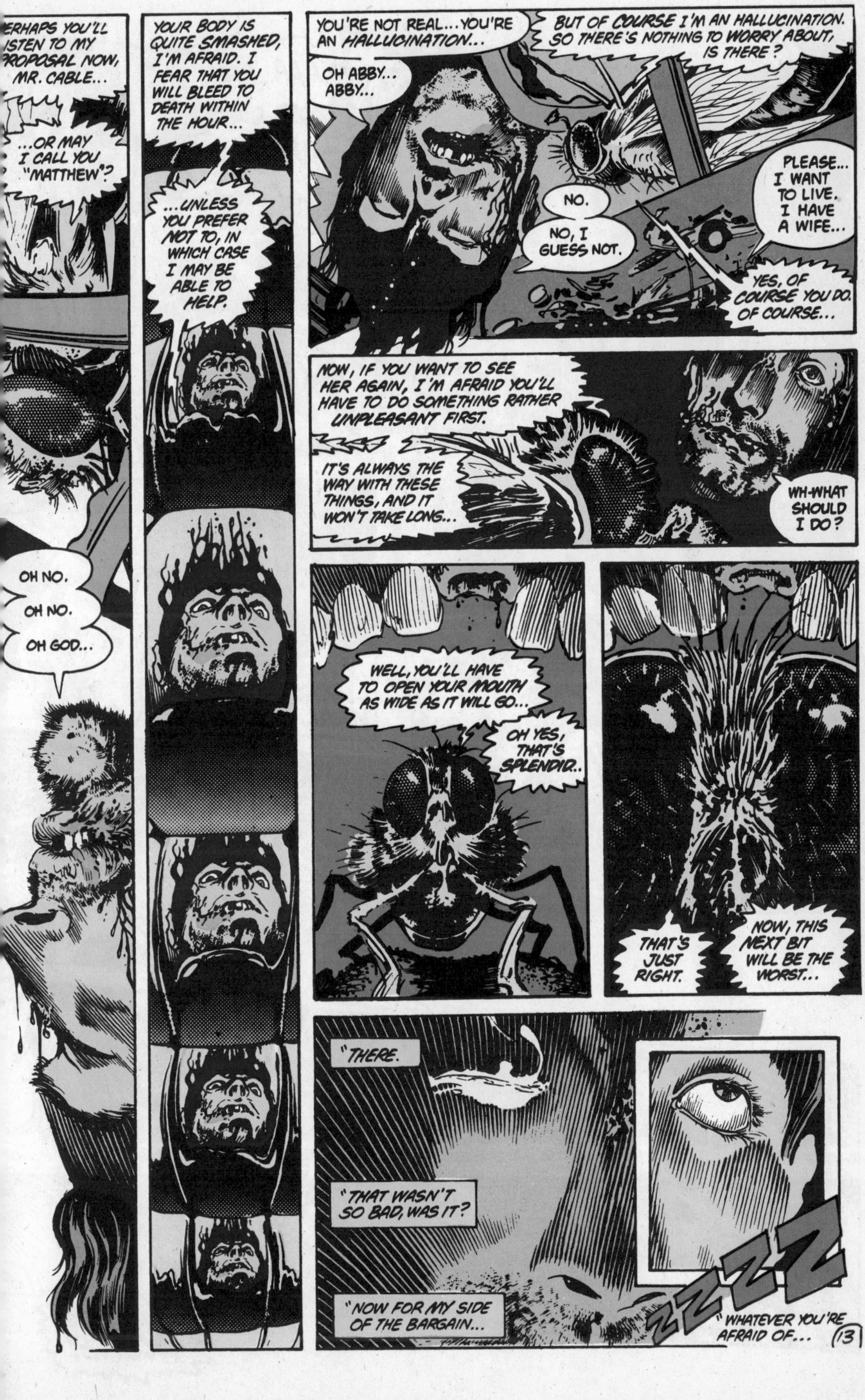
ERHAPS YOU'LL ISTEN TO MY PROPOSAL NOW, MR. CABLE...
...OR MAY I CALL YOU "MATTHEW"?
YOUR BODY IS QUITE SMASHED, I'M AFRAID. I FEAR THAT YOU WILL BLEED TO DEATH WITHIN THE HOUR...
...UNLESS YOU PREFER NOT TO, IN WHICH CASE I MAY BE ABLE TO HELP.
OH NO.
OH NO.
OH GOD...
YOU'RE NOT REAL...YOU'RE AN HALLUCINATION...
BUT OF COURSE I'M AN HALLUCINATION. SO THERE'S NOTHING TO WORRY ABOUT, IS THERE?
OH ABBY... ABBY...
NO.
NO, I GUESS NOT.
PLEASE... I WANT TO LIVE. I HAVE A WIFE...
YES, OF COURSE YOU DO. OF COURSE...
NOW, IF YOU WANT TO SEE HER AGAIN, I'M AFRAID YOU'LL HAVE TO DO SOMETHING RATHER UNPLEASANT FIRST.
IT'S ALWAYS THE WAY WITH THESE THINGS, AND IT WON'T TAKE LONG...
WH-WHAT SHOULD I DO?
WELL, YOU'LL HAVE TO OPEN YOUR MOUTH AS WIDE AS IT WILL GO...
OH YES, THAT'S SPLENDID...
THAT'S JUST RIGHT.
NOW, THIS NEXT BIT WILL BE THE WORST...
"THERE.
"THAT WASN'T SO BAD, WAS IT?
"NOW FOR MY SIDE OF THE BARGAIN...
ZZZZZ
"WHATEVER YOU'RE AFRAID OF...
13

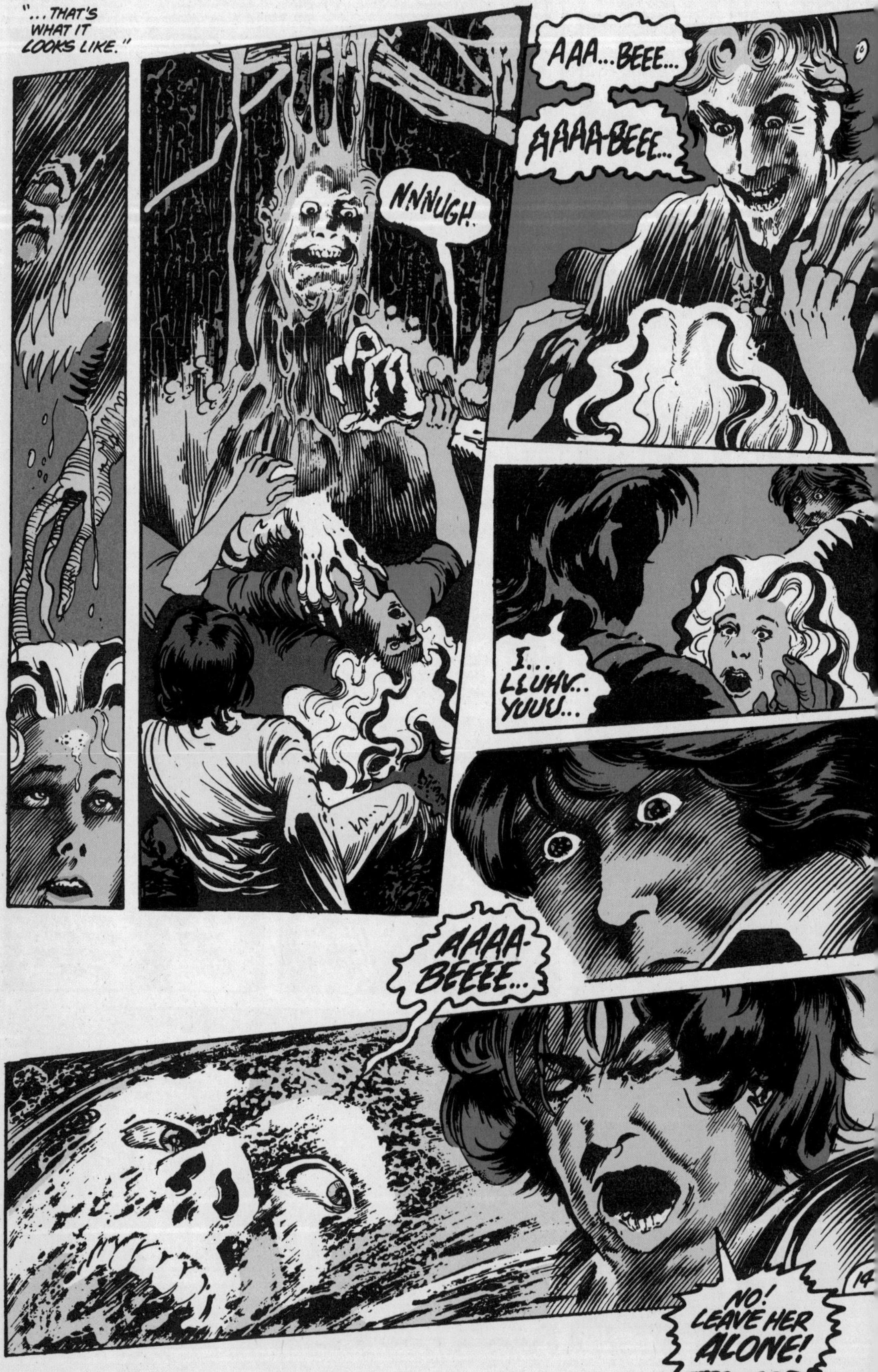
"...THAT'S WHAT IT LOOKS LIKE."
NNNUGH.
AAA...BEEE...
AAAA-BEEE...
I... LLUHV... YUUU...
AAAA-BEEEE...
NO! LEAVE HER ALONE!
14

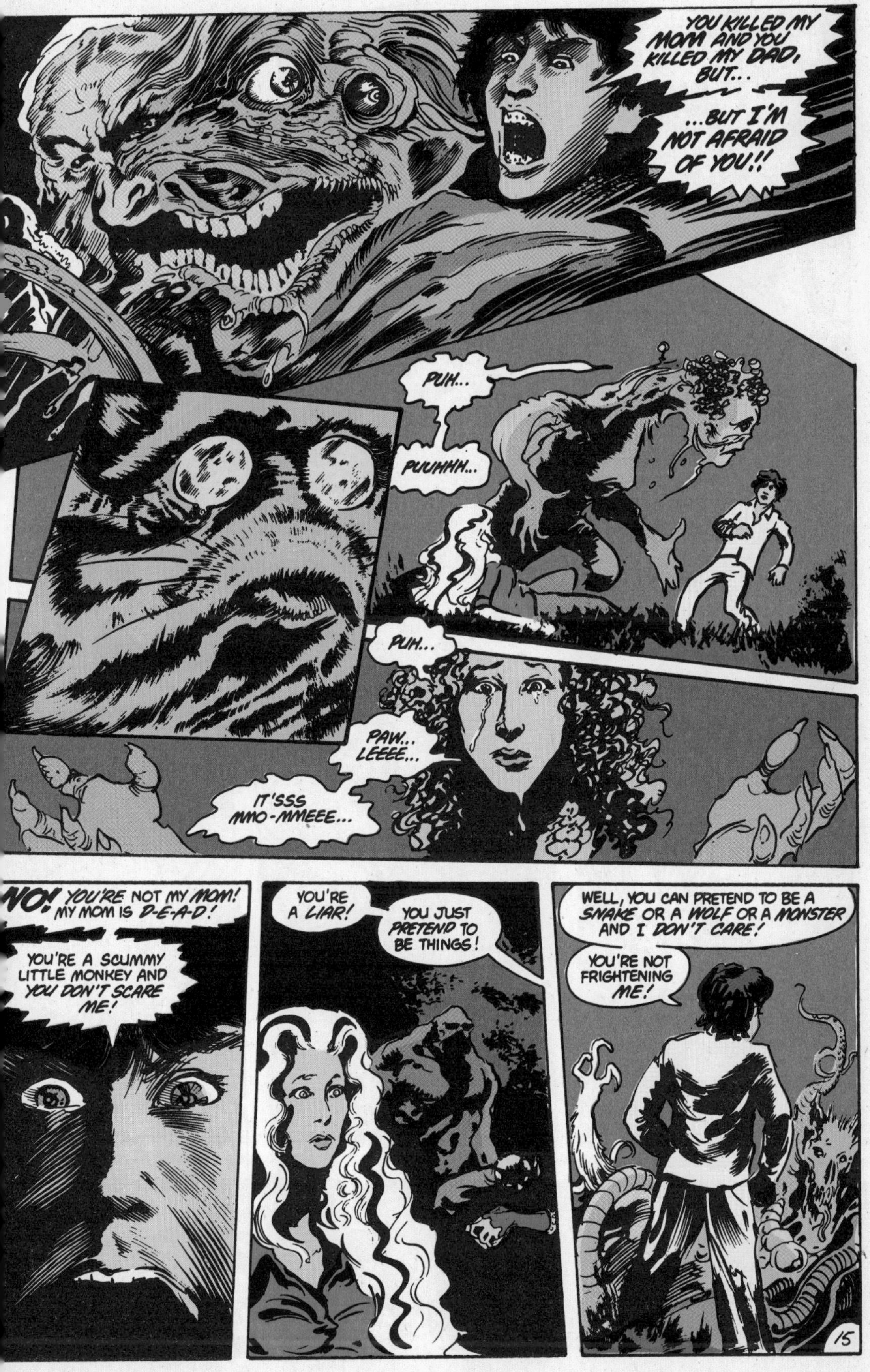
YOU KILLED MY MOM AND YOU KILLED MY DAD, BUT...
...BUT I'M NOT AFRAID OF YOU!!
PUH...
PUUHHH...
PUH...
PAW... LEEEE...
IT'SSS MMO-MMEEE...
NO! YOU'RE NOT MY MOM! MY MOM IS D-E-A-D!
YOU'RE A SCUMMY LITTLE MONKEY AND YOU DON'T SCARE ME!
YOU'RE A LIAR!
YOU JUST PRETEND TO BE THINGS!
WELL, YOU CAN PRETEND TO BE A SNAKE OR A WOLF OR A MONSTER AND I DON'T CARE!
YOU'RE NOT FRIGHTENING ME!
15

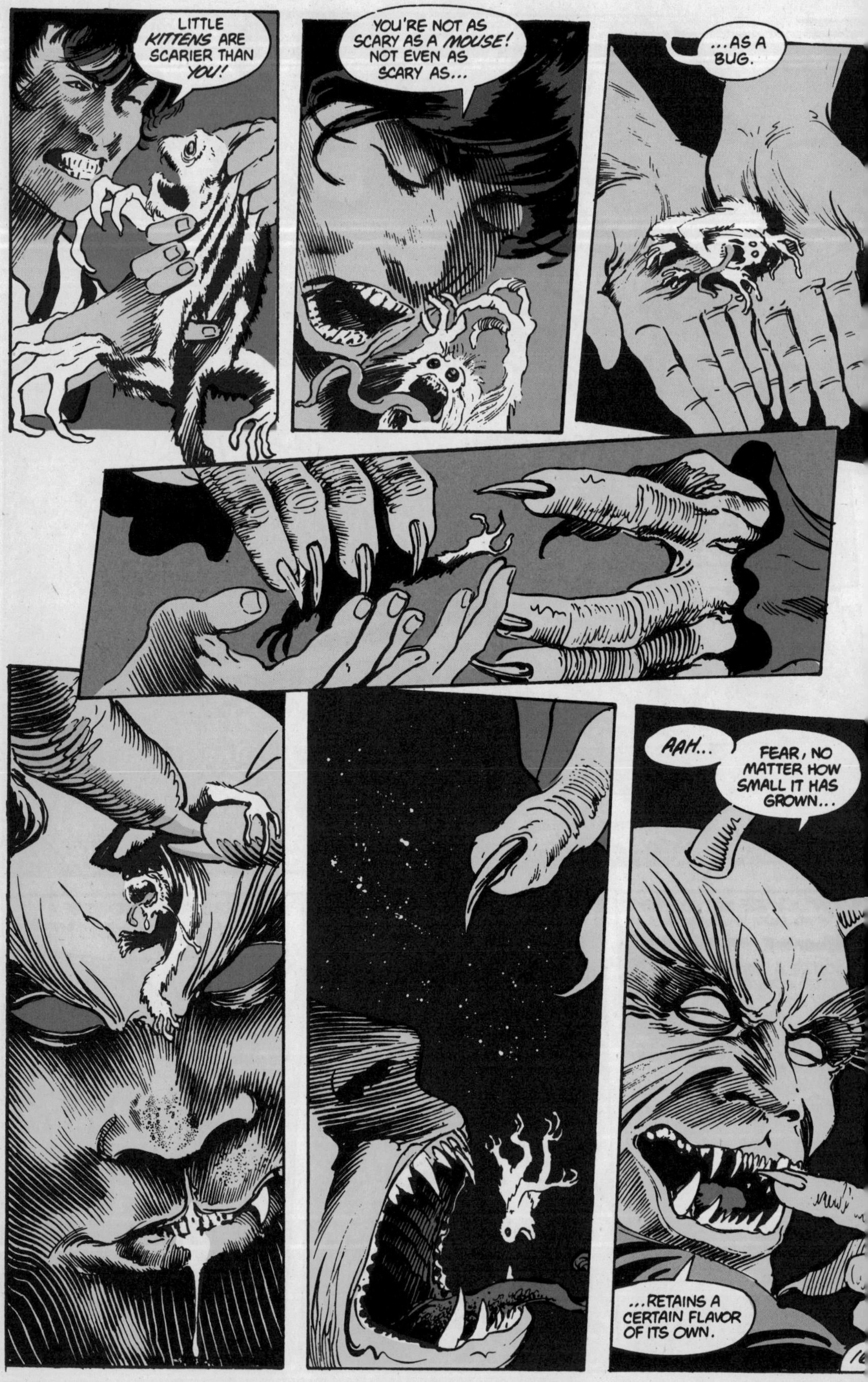
LITTLE KITTENS ARE SCARIER THAN YOU!
YOU'RE NOT AS SCARY AS A MOUSE! NOT EVEN AS SCARY AS...
...AS A BUG.
AAH...
FEAR, NO MATTER HOW SMALL IT HAS GROWN...
...RETAINS A CERTAIN FLAVOR OF ITS OWN.

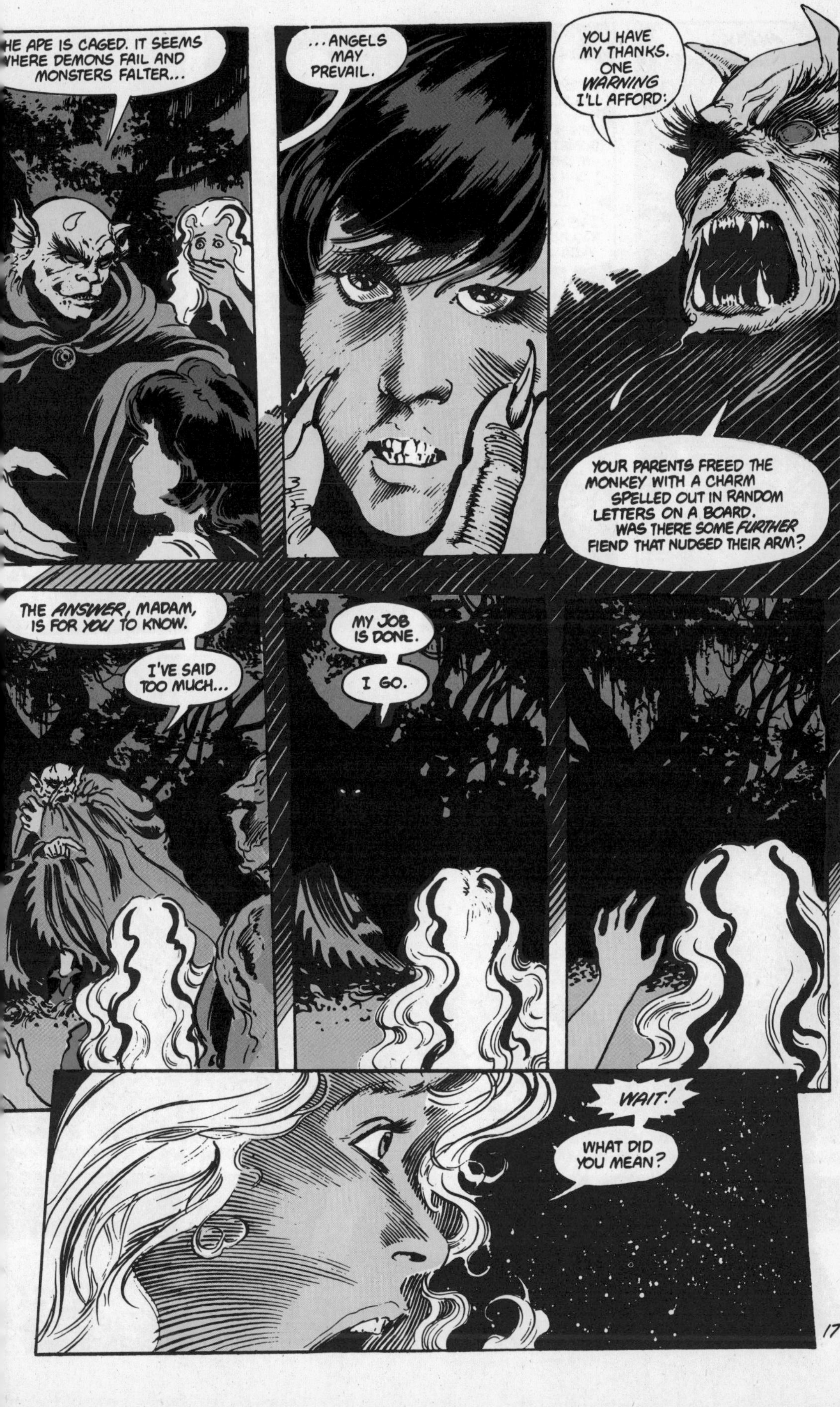
HE APE IS CAGED. IT SEEMS
WHERE DEMONS FAIL AND MONSTERS FALTER...
...ANGELS MAY PREVAIL.
YOU HAVE MY THANKS. ONE WARNING I'LL AFFORD:
YOUR PARENTS FREED THE MONKEY WITH A CHARM SPELLED OUT IN RANDOM LETTERS ON A BOARD. WAS THERE SOME FURTHER FIEND THAT NUDGED THEIR ARM?
THE ANSWER, MADAM, IS FOR YOU TO KNOW.
I'VE SAID TOO MUCH...
MY JOB IS DONE.
I GO.
WAIT!
WHAT DID YOU MEAN?
17

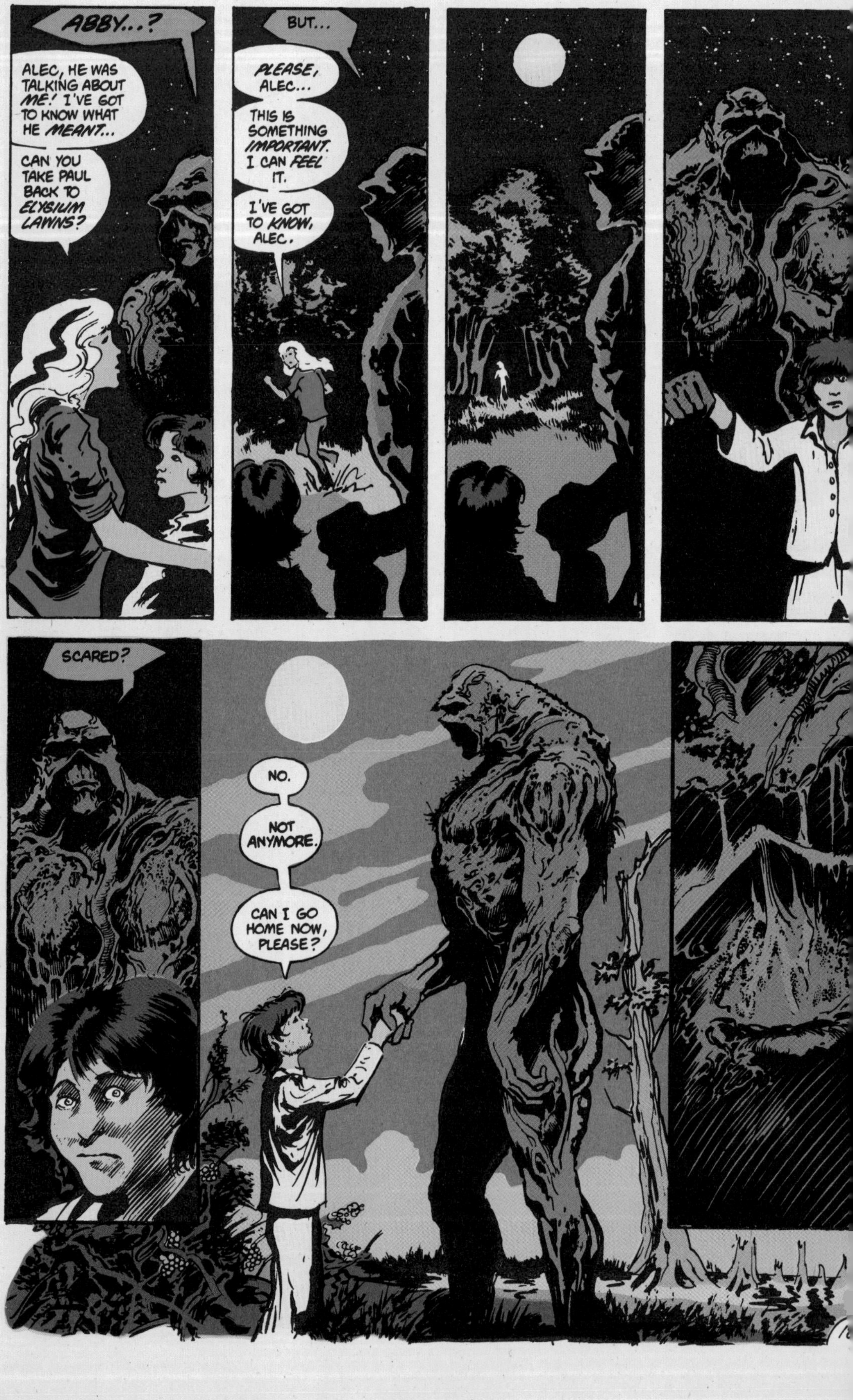
ABBY...?
ALEC, HE WAS TALKING ABOUT ME! I'VE GOT TO KNOW WHAT HE MEANT...
CAN YOU TAKE PAUL BACK TO ELYSIUM LAWNS?
BUT...
PLEASE, ALEC...
THIS IS SOMETHING IMPORTANT. I CAN FEEL IT.
I'VE GOT TO KNOW, ALEC.
SCARED?
NO.
NOT ANYMORE.
CAN I GO HOME NOW, PLEASE?

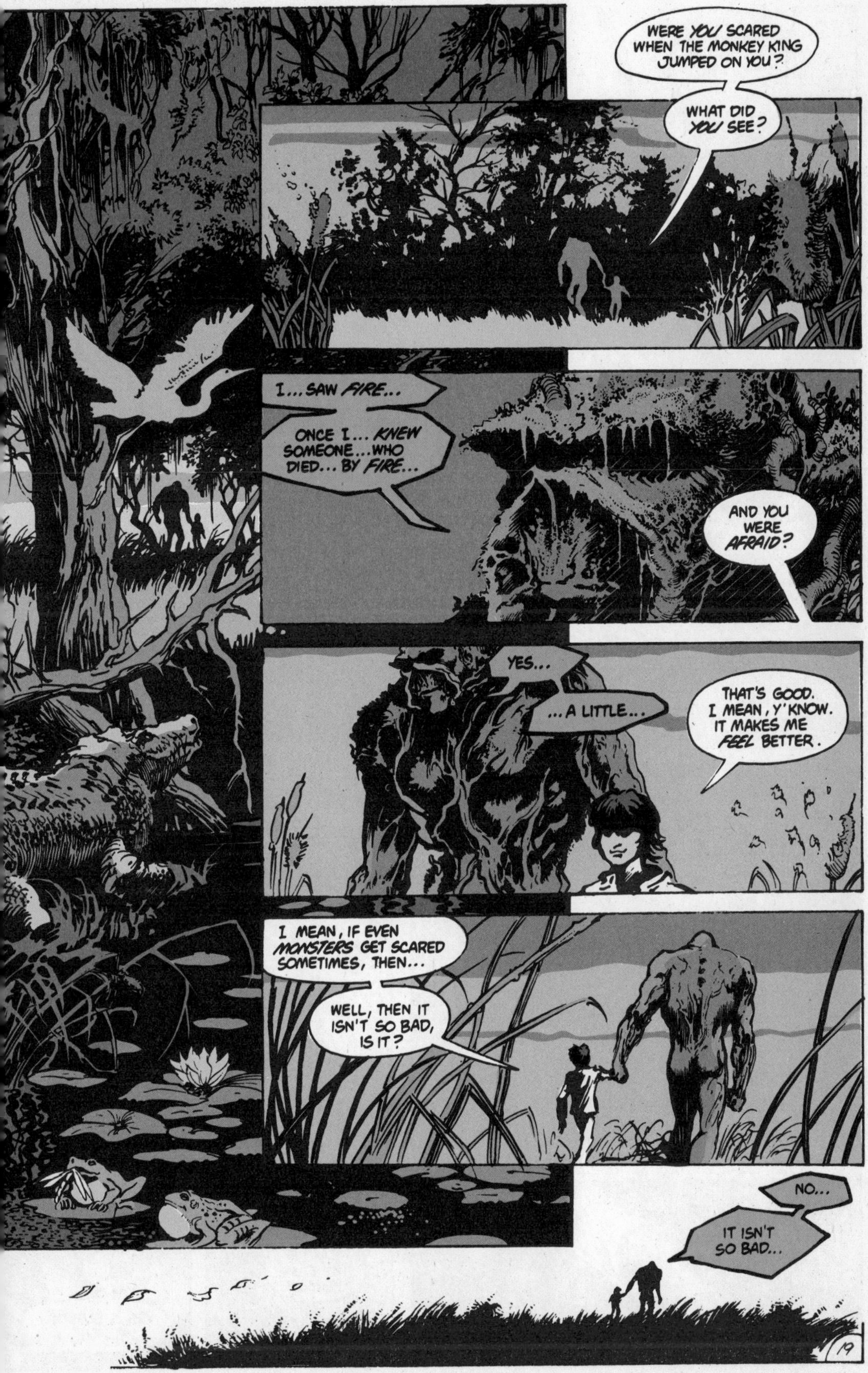
WERE YOU SCARED WHEN THE MONKEY KING JUMPED ON YOU?
WHAT DID YOU SEE?
I... SAW FIRE...
ONCE I... KNEW SOMEONE... WHO DIED... BY FIRE...
AND YOU WERE AFRAID?
YES...
...A LITTLE...
THAT'S GOOD. I MEAN, Y'KNOW. IT MAKES ME FEEL BETTER.
I MEAN, IF EVEN MONSTERS GET SCARED SOMETIMES, THEN...
WELL, THEN IT ISN'T SO BAD, IS IT?
NO...
IT ISN'T SO BAD...
19

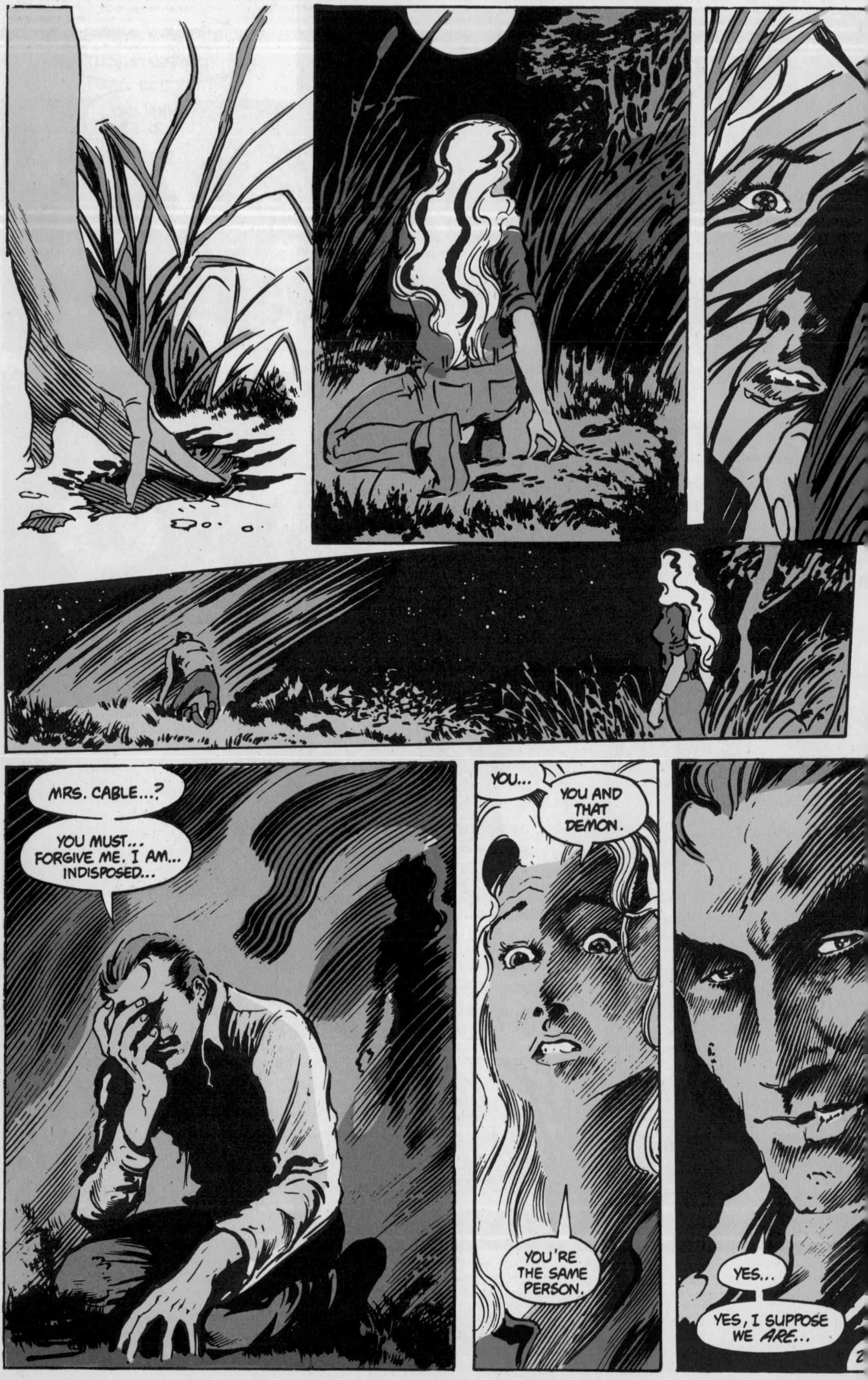
MRS. CABLE...?
YOU MUST... FORGIVE ME. I AM... INDISPOSED...
YOU...
YOU AND THAT DEMON.
YOU'RE THE SAME PERSON.
YES...
YES, I SUPPOSE WE ARE...

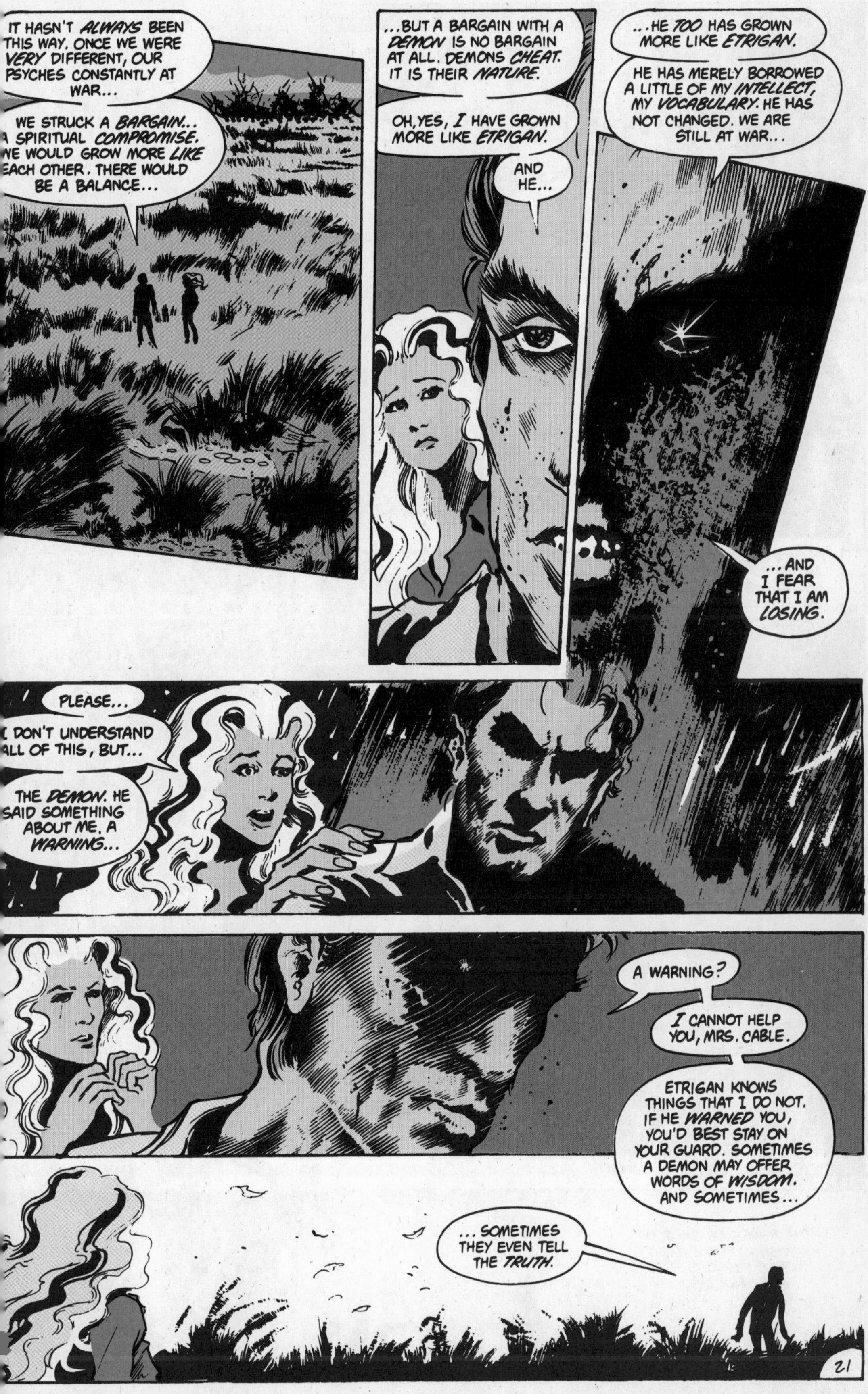
IT HASN'T ALWAYS BEEN THIS WAY. ONCE WE WERE VERY DIFFERENT, OUR PSYCHES CONSTANTLY AT WAR...
WE STRUCK A BARGAIN... A SPIRITUAL COMPROMISE. WE WOULD GROW MORE LIKE EACH OTHER. THERE WOULD BE A BALANCE...
...BUT A BARGAIN WITH A DEMON IS NO BARGAIN AT ALL. DEMONS CHEAT. IT IS THEIR NATURE.
OH, YES, I HAVE GROWN MORE LIKE ETRIGAN.
AND HE...
...HE TOO HAS GROWN MORE LIKE ETRIGAN.
HE HAS MERELY BORROWED A LITTLE OF MY INTELLECT, MY VOCABULARY. HE HAS NOT CHANGED. WE ARE STILL AT WAR...
...AND I FEAR THAT I AM LOSING.
PLEASE...
I DON'T UNDERSTAND ALL OF THIS, BUT...
THE DEMON. HE SAID SOMETHING ABOUT ME. A WARNING...
A WARNING?
I CANNOT HELP YOU, MRS. CABLE.
ETRIGAN KNOWS THINGS THAT I DO NOT. IF HE WARNED YOU, YOU'D BEST STAY ON YOUR GUARD. SOMETIMES A DEMON MAY OFFER WORDS OF WISDOM. AND SOMETIMES...
...SOMETIMES THEY EVEN TELL THE TRUTH.
21

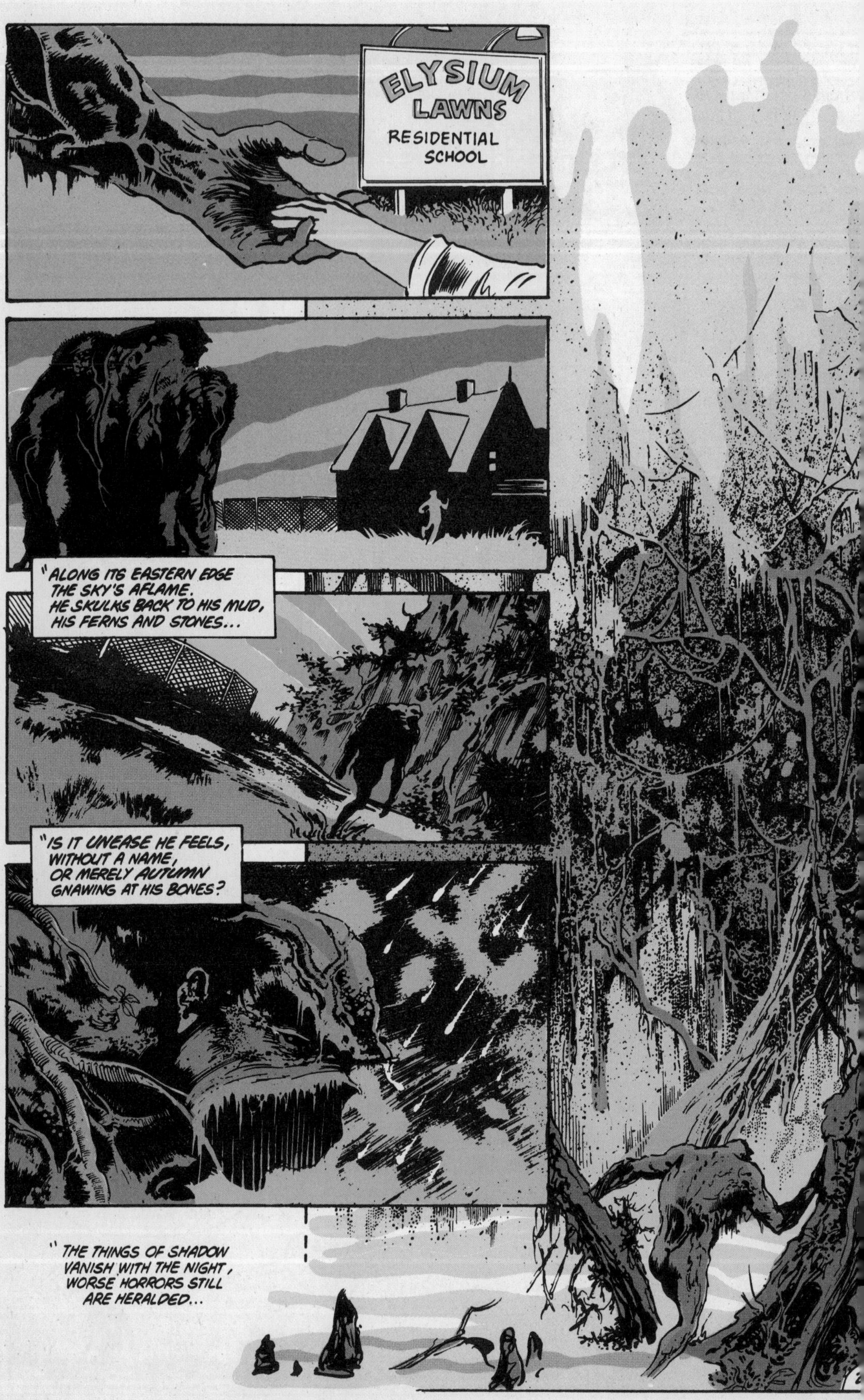
ELYSIUM
LAWNS
RESIDENTIAL
SCHOOL
"ALONG ITS EASTERN EDGE THE SKY'S AFLAME. HE SKULKS BACK TO HIS MUD, HIS FERNS AND STONES...
"IS IT UNEASE HE FEELS, WITHOUT A NAME, OR MERELY AUTUMN GNAWING AT HIS BONES?
"THE THINGS OF SHADOW VANISH WITH THE NIGHT, WORSE HORRORS STILL ARE HERALDED...

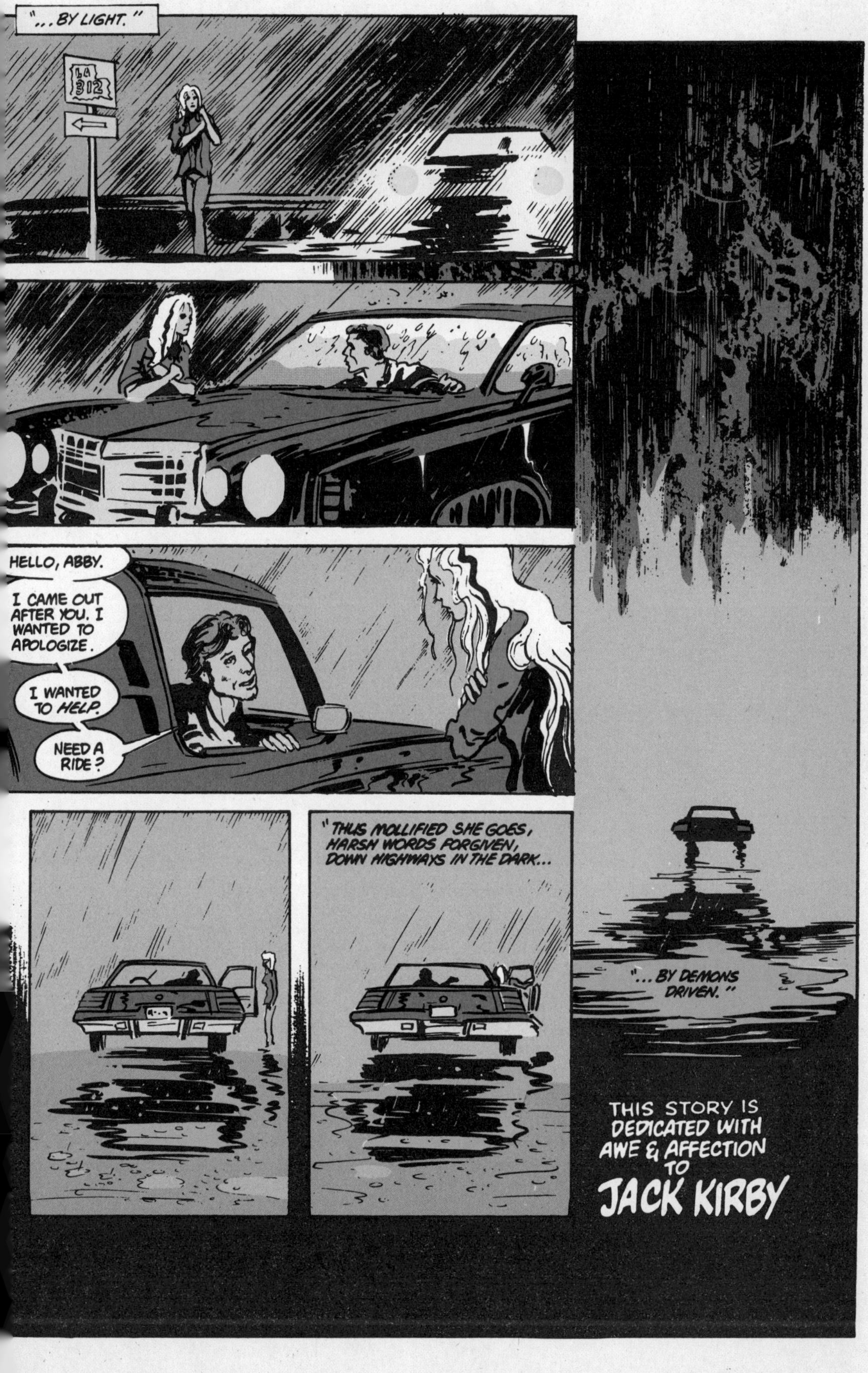
"... BY LIGHT."
LA 312
HELLO, ABBY.
I CAME OUT AFTER YOU. I WANTED TO APOLOGIZE.
I WANTED TO HELP.
NEED A RIDE?
"THUS MOLLIFIED SHE GOES, HARSH WORDS FORGIVEN, DOWN HIGHWAYS IN THE DARK...
"... BY DEMONS DRIVEN."
THIS STORY IS DEDICATED WITH AWE & AFFECTION TO JACK KIRBY

This iconic painting of Swamp Thing by artist Michael Zulli first appeared as a retail poster before becoming the cover art to the second trade paperback edition of *The Saga of the Swamp Thing*. The piece also served as the inspiration for a cold-cast porcelain statue sculpted by William Paquet and released by DC Direct in 1996.

ALAN MOORE began working as a cartoonist in 1979 with several humorous strips in *Sounds* music weekly. After a year, he turned to writing, contributing to *Doctor Who Weekly* and *2000 AD*. This was followed by *Marvelman* (published in the United States as *Miracleman*) and the political thriller *V for Vendetta*, which earned him the British Eagle Award for Best Comics Writer in 1982 and 1983. His groundbreaking run on *Swamp Thing* revolutionized comics and won him several industry awards. He is also the writer of the Hugo Award-winning *Watchmen*, a landmark series that firmly established him as the most influential writer in contemporary comics. In 1999 Moore launched his own comics imprint, America's Best Comics, through which he has created (along with many talented illustrators) *The League of Extraordinary Gentlemen*, *Promethea*, *Tom Strong*, *Tomorrow Stories*, and *Top Ten*.

Best known for his multi-award-winning tenure on *Swamp Thing*, **STEPHEN BISSETTE** also co-founded, edited, and co-published the Eisner Award-winning controversial horror anthology *Taboo*, collaborated with Alan Moore on *1963*, and wrote, drew and self-published four issues of *S.R. Bissette's Tyrant*. Bissette's film criticism, articles, and short fiction have appeared in over two dozen periodicals and book anthologies, and his original novella *Aliens: Tribes* won a Bram Stoker Award in 1993.

After a childhood in Erie, Pennsylvania spent consuming a steady diet of comics, monster magazines and monster movies, **JOHN TOTLEBEN** went to the Joe Kubert School of Cartoon and Graphic Art where he met Stephen Bissette. Together they worked on *Bizarre Adventures* followed by *Swamp Thing*, which they drew for almost three years. Totleben is best known for his illustrative work on Alan Moore's *Miracleman*. His other credits include *1963*, *Vermillion* and *The Dreaming*.

For almost 30 years, Canadian artist **DAN DAY** has been illustrating comics for young and old alike. His work has appeared in a wide variety of titles, including DC's *The Saga of the Swamp Thing*, *Batman* and *Detective Comics* and Marvel's *Captain America*, *Doctor Strange* and *Iron Man*. Day has also worked on numerous comics adaptations of characters from prose, film and television — most notably Arthur Conan Doyle's Sherlock Holmes, *A Nightmare on Elm Street*'s Freddie Krueger and the crew of *Star Trek*.

RICK VEITCH worked in the underground comics scene before attending the Joe Kubert School of Cartoon and Graphic Art. After graduating, he worked with Stephen Bissette on *Bizarre Adventures* before creating and illustrating *The One*, the innovative Epic Comics miniseries. In addition to writing and drawing an acclaimed run on *Swamp Thing*, he is the creator/cartoonist of *Brat Pack*, *Maximortal* and the dream-based *Rare Bit Fiends*, and a contributing artist on *1963*. He is also the writer and artist of the miniseries *Greyshirt: Indigo Sunset* from America's Best Comics, and the creator of the critically acclaimed graphic novel *Can't Get No* and the spectacularly satirical series *Army@Love* from Vertigo.

TOM YEATES was one of the first graduates of the Joe Kubert School of Cartoon and Graphic Art (along with classmates Rick Veitch, Stephen Bissette, and John Totleben). Influenced primarily by classic adventure illustrators like Alex Raymond and Hal Foster, Yeates has contributed artwork to a host of titles and publishers, and has served as an editor for Eclipse Comics as well as illustrating a newspaper strip revival of *Zorro* from 1999 to 2000.

TATJANA WOOD switched careers from dressmaking to comics coloring in the late 1960s and quickly established herself as one of the top colorists in the field, winning two Shazam awards in the early 1970s.

Over his long and prolific career, **JOHN COSTANZA** has lettered a huge number of comics and has won numerous awards along the way. A cartoonist in his own right, Costanza has also contributed stories and art to a variety of titles, beginning in the late 1960s and continuing right through to the new millennium.

One of the industry's most versatile and accomplished letterers **TODD KLEIN** has been lettering comics since 1977 and has won numerous Eisner and Harvey Awards for his work. A highlight of his career has been working with Neil Gaiman on nearly all the original issues of *The Sandman*, as well as *Black Orchid*, *Death: The High Cost of Living*, *Death: The Time of Your Life* and *The Books of Magic*.